From American Diplomat to Diplomatic Educator

ADST MEMOIRS AND OCCASIONAL PAPERS SERIES
Series Editors: LISA TERRY & MARGERY THOMPSON

In 2003, the Association for Diplomatic Studies and Training (ADST), a nonprofit organization founded in 1986, created the Memoirs and Occasional Papers Series to preserve firsthand accounts and other informed observations on foreign affairs for scholars, journalists, and the general public. Through its book series, its Foreign Affairs Oral History program, and its support for the training of foreign affairs personnel at the State Department's Foreign Service Institute, ADST seeks to promote understanding of American diplomacy and those who conduct it. In this latest volume of the ADST Memoirs and Occasional Papers Series, Richard Mueller's personal account as a former senior U.S. Foreign Service Officer and later as a Head of School, provides readers with an introduction to how he built bridges to international understanding through the State Department's global network of embassies and other diplomatic missions, as well as in education.

RELATED TITLES FROM ADST SERIES

For a complete list of series titles, visit <adst.org/publications>

From American Diplomat to Diplomatic Educator

Building Global Bridges to Understanding

Richard W. Mueller

Arlington Hall Press

Printed in the United States of America

ISBN 978-0-9653949-2-5 (Softcover)
ISBN 978-0-9653949-5-6 (Hardcover)
ISBN 978-0-9653949-3-2 (eBook)

Arlington Hall Press is an imprint of the Association for Diplomatic Studies and Training.

Association for Diplomatic Studies and Training
P.O. Box 41839, Arlington, VA 22204

info@adst.org
www.adst.org

Contents

Dedicated to our seven grandchildren—Jackson, Katherine, Clara, Allison, Gillian, Philip, Marilyn—in the hope they will learn about their family's heritage and, with their smarts, experience, and values, continue to take care of our Planet Earth—our Pale Blue Dot—and make it a better world for all

Acknowledgments

A word of gratitude to the many people whose support kept me at my laptop for well over three years. Their encouragement was invaluable as we endured the dangers and vicissitudes of the COVID-19 pandemic.

Let's start with family. My wife, Claire, is always my toughest critic and strongest supporter. She read every draft of the memoir and reminded me of events and people. I recall President George H.W. Bush telling us when visiting Hong Kong that Barbara Bush kept him firmly anchored to reality and truth-telling as he wrote his memoir. Claire is my truth-teller.

Our sons and daughters-in-law—Jonathan and Kimberly, Eric and Susan—were similarly always encouraging, as were our seven grandchildren in Golden, Colorado, and San Francisco, California. They would periodically ask me how I was coming along and promised to read the book. Jackson said he has already told his friends at school about the project. He plans to bring a copy to show them.

I owe a huge debt to so many professional colleagues and friends who during my diplomatic career have been supporters and mentors. You know who you are. I would note Ambassadors Nicholas Platt, Burton Levin, J. Stapleton Roy, Edwin Cronk, Parker Borg, David Passage, Richard Boucher, and Richard Teare.

I owe a similar debt to all those in the educational world who helped me learn, grow, and hopefully make a positive difference in the lives of young people. A special shout-out to Chuck Dull and Jim Handrich. Others are mentioned in the narrative. Similar to diplomats, educators are devoted to serving people. Trustees, who volunteered and collaborated with me, deserve our deep appreciation for providing leadership and ensuring good governance, the foundations for healthy institutions.

In particular, I thank William R. Rhodes, senior vice chairman of Citigroup; chairman, president, and CEO of Citibank; and chair of the North-

RICHARD W. MUELLER

field Mount Hermon Board of Trustees. He had the insight to recognize that my skills and experience in the diplomatic world could contribute to the success as head of school at NMH, at a crucial point in the school's history. His steady guidance as chair of the board kept us on track to make and execute decisions that serve the continued future excellence of an NMH education.

I would like to express particular appreciation to Lisa Terry and Susan Johnson of the Association for Diplomatic Studies and Training. Lisa has been editor and guide in the new-to-me world of book publishing as we worked to nurture this memoir to life.

List of Acronyms

ARVN – Army of the Republic of Vietnam
BDC – Berlin Document Center
BGEN – Brigadier General
CAIS – Chinese American International School in San Francisco
COD – Carrier Onboard Delivery
CORDS – Civil Operations for Revolutionary Development Support
CCP – Chinese Communist Party
CIA – Central Intelligence Agency
DSB – Diplomatic Services Bureau
DVT – Deep vein thrombosis
EARCOS – East Asia Regional Council of Schools
ESA – Eight Schools Association
FBI – Federal Bureau of Investigation
FSI – Foreign Service Institute
FSO – Foreign Service officer
HICOG – U.S. High Commission for Germany
HKIS – Hong Kong International School
ICCS – International Commission for Control and Supervision
IPR – Intellectual property rights
LCMS – Lutheran Church Missouri Synod
MFN – Most Favored Nation
NASA – National Aeronautics and Space Administration
NATO – North Atlantic Treaty Organization
NSC – National Security Council
NMCC – National Military Command Center
NMH – Northfield Mount Hermon
PE – pulmonary embolism
PNTR – permanent normal trade relations
PLA – People's Liberation Army

PRC – People's Republic of China
PX – post exchange
SAS – Shanghai American School
STEM – Science, technology, engineering, and mathematics
SNJ – Sierra Nevada Journeys
S/S – Executive Secretariat
S/S-O – Executive Secretariat, Operations Center
S/S-S – Executive Secretariat, Office of the Secretary of State
UAW – United Auto Workers
USAID – United States Agency for International Development
UNESCO – United Nations Educational, Scientific, and Cultural Organization
USLO – U.S. Liaison Office/officer

Preface

O ur family has been blessed in so many ways. This memoir de- scribes lives well-lived and in service to rearing a loving family and contributing to a better world.

The narrative focuses first on my diplomatic career as an American Foreign Service Officer (FSO) of thirty-two years who rose in the service to a senior level, with a plethora of experiences and adventures. Sec- ondly, it explores my serendipitous service as an educator over fifteen years as head of school of three different schools in Massachusetts, Hong Kong, and Shanghai. It weaves in personal family experiences, which were of much importance to my wife Claire and me.

The narrative is designed to provide family members and good friends some insights into our professional and personal lives. It includes frank opinions about foreign and domestic policies as well as U.S. statecraft approaches to national security. It provides specific insights and advice on the conduct of diplomacy and how best to educate the next generation. It describes selected historical events of interest. It will tell you more about how the U.S. Foreign Service and international schools function from an insider's perspective. And it will leave for grandchildren more insight into their families' heritage and history. It is designed neither as a historian's history—though it does include the considered views of an engaged and knowledgeable "practitioner" of diplomacy—nor as a full history, nor as a psycholog- ical tract delving into individual or family lives.

A particular hope is that readers will appreciate the many adventures life can bring, and how through them, with deliberation, one can make a positive difference in a world always in need of more "tender loving care." To be more specific, America and the world need better education for young people and better political leaders who are honest, who believe in service and public service, and who put the public interest ahead of their own. Perhaps it will provide insights into career paths of interest to young people.

Claire has read this draft more than once, adding her thoughts and memories and correcting my recollections. We've been on this adventure together for nearly half a century. I appreciate all she has done for and meant to the family and to me.

Claire has written her own memoir and printed it in book form using the Storyworth memoir approach of answering questions the writer wants to answer. It is personal and family oriented. Our young grandchildren love reading about themselves. She graciously allowed me to make suggestions and add additional relevant thoughts on family history. Between our two volumes, much will be known by our descendants about the Mueller and McCormick families and about the world and its many fascinating cultures and histories. And hopefully they will find compelling examples of how to lead lives of service to make the world a better one.

Here are three thoughts for posterity:

Words matter! Words carry far more weight and import than most people appreciate. Writing and speaking with just the right words can make a huge and positive difference. Words can uplift or cause anguish. Words can clarify or confuse. Words can wound or cause joy. Words put together well can serve to educate and persuade. Pay attention to your words and use the ones which carry your precise meaning. Well-written descriptions, essays, arguments show an educated and active mind and one capable of good observation, insight, and love of others. Well-developed literacy skills in all their dimensions are the foundation for human development and advancement.

Be kind! We hear that admonition a lot these days. Do enough people practice kindness and compassion? Simply put, no. Kindness doesn't indicate weakness or wishy washiness. It doesn't mean you are disguising ulterior motives. Instead, it means that kind words to a friend or stranger can be comforting at a time of distress. A kind word can signify "welcome." A kind smile can mean you recognize the other person is human also. Scientific evidence says a smile can make you feel better yourself. I love to say "good morning" or "hello" unexpectedly while passing someone on the sidewalk or in a store or on the sidelines of one of the girls' soccer games. The surprised reactions combined with a smile in return are priceless.

A gift for you: If you take away just one thought from this memoir, I hope it will be that you do have the gift of leadership in setting your own personal course in life, learning wherever you can, seizing opportunities whenever

possible and, as you do so, use that gift to help make you, your family, your friends, and the world better than they were before!
Enjoy the adventures and journeys that lie ahead!

Richard W. Mueller
Claire Mueller—Co-pilot
Golden, Colorado—2023

Introduction

March 2020

The novel coronavirus, COVID-19, is upon us in Golden, Colorado, and across the United States and around the world.

Claire and I have reached the grand experienced age of seventy-six years. It's time I wrote some words about lives blessed and well-lived as we contemplate the many years behind us and the many ahead. We refuse to concede we can't find ways to shelter in place and otherwise stay safe enough to escape the ravages of this pandemic.

So many friends have told us over the years that we have lived such "interesting" lives and have been part of so many satisfying professional and personal endeavors from diplomacy to education. Separately, Claire has begun to write extensively about her life and careers for Storyworth, so I will focus more on Richard Mueller and what we did together.

My life is divided by BC—*Before Claire*—and AC—*After Claire.*

I choose to begin with After Claire and a few personal and family observations in the beginning years of our lives together. These have been as important to me as my professional accomplishments in diplomacy and education. I will then focus the story by looking backwards at family origins and growing-up years and then by chronicling our professional and personal lives around the world through the countries of Vietnam, China, Hong Kong, Asia; several assignments at the Department of State in Washington, DC; and finally at three schools: Northfield Mount Hermon (NMH) School in Massachusetts, Hong Kong International School (HKIS), and Shanghai American School (SAS).

Claire and I found each other in 1973 when we were both twenty-nine and working as American Foreign Service diplomats in the office of Henry A. Kissinger, legendary secretary of state who now has just celebrated his one hundredth birthday.

Claire had just returned to the Foreign Service after assignments to the American Embassy in Paris and American Embassy in Singapore. I had just returned from a seven-month temporary duty assignment at the American Embassy in Saigon, Republic of Vietnam, stationed in the Vietnamese Central Highlands in Kon Tum. It was a fascinating assignment observing and reporting on the ceasefire right after the signing of the Paris Peace Accords in January 1973. I had just been awarded the Department of State Director General's award for reporting, which recognized the best foreign service analysis and reporting that year. Embassy Saigon, the secretary of state, the National Security Council (NSC) staff, and the White House all closely observed the events during my seventh months in Kon Tum, Vietnam, because they reflected some of the hopeful expectations of Kissinger and President Richard M. Nixon (ceasefire, exchange of prisoners, local lines of demarcation, and local accommodations).

Claire and I worked together in the Department of State's Executive Secretariat (part of Kissinger's office) for the next year and a half, which included staffing a visit to Mexico City by Kissinger in early 1974 and then a five-week Kissinger "shuttle" mission to the Middle East in April–June 1974, which produced the historic Israeli-Syrian disengagement agreement.

While we were working together, we were also dating. We thought we were discreet, but it turned out our colleagues were on to us, with many a wink and nod. Two of our colleagues with a playful streak conspired for us to travel with Kissinger on the five-week Middle East trip.

We both loved what we did, worked long hours, and felt we were contributing to the success of U.S. foreign policy. But our work styles were different and led to some clashes of will. At one point on our trip with Kissinger, in our temporary office of the King David Hotel in Jerusalem, I jokingly told her I might throw her out the window of the hotel if she wasn't more restrained in telling me how to do my job. Claire tells that anecdote frequently!

A six-week trip across the United States in my trusty Volvo in June 1974 gave both of us time to cool off and slow down and think of our futures.

A highlight of the trip was meeting many Americans concerned about the economic slowdown at the time and their futures. Most had only a hazy understanding of Henry Kissinger as secretary of state and U.S. foreign policy. It was fascinating being able to use my experience as a political and economic observer and analyst to understand my own country and people. The country's strengths and challenges came through in so many of my interactions with my fellow Americans that summer.

Among other things, I learned that Americans can be talkative and curious once you engage them. I loved the early morning patrons in small town cafes. After I broke the ice to start a conversation, they seldom hesitated to talk about themselves, their communities, and opinions. One man in Ohio in the construction business was deeply concerned about the economic downturn and pressed me on how "Washington" and "Kissinger" could possibly make a difference to him. In Montana, while lining up for a firefighters' July 4 pancake breakfast, a young woman with two young children described with some emotion how difficult life could be in a small community.

An important insight I never forgot: American foreign policy is successful only if understood and supported by Americans. Seems obvious. But too many politicians and leaders fail for ignoring that truism.

On March 15, 1975, Claire and I were married at our home in Falls Church, Virginia, by Pastor Otto Schuetze, the Lutheran pastor of my growing up years in Bethesda, Maryland. We still smile at the memory of the Kennedy Center where we treated our small wedding party to that evening's performance of *The Constant Wife* by Somerset Maugham and starring Ingrid Bergman in person. A fitting show for a newly married couple!

By the summer of 1975, I was finished with my first year of Chinese language training at the Foreign Service Institute (FSI) in Arlington, Virginia. It was a tough year of learning, particularly because of the tones in the Chinese language. Fortunately, I had previously learned Vietnamese, another tonal language, in 1968–1969, also at FSI. Once my ears had caught on, the Vietnamese flowed more easily during two assignments to the American Embassy in Saigon.

The second year of learning Chinese was to be at FSI's Chinese language school in Taichung, Taiwan. Claire and I drove across the country in our trusty Volvo, visiting my sister Linda and her husband Bill in Loveland, Colorado, and then my cousin Stephen Mueller in Portland, Oregon. We embarked on the SS Mariposa in San Francisco for a several-day crossing to Hawaii, a short rest break, and then on to Taiwan.

Nine months of study in Taiwan was hard work. Learning Chinese was like learning three different languages. One was learning to speak. Another was learning to read, made much more difficult because written characters did not show how they were pronounced. And the third was learning to write the characters. One can learn to speak and read, but if you don't endlessly practice writing the characters you can forget them quickly.

Taiwan also offered new experiences and adventures for a newly married couple. We learned so much in addition to the language about Chinese and Asian cultures and peoples. Our colleagues were friendly and supportive as we traveled around the island, practicing our Chinese, climbing Yu Shan (Mount Morrison) with Chinese climbers, and learning about the country. Of course, we tried every regional cuisine. I could pontificate on how a country's culinary histories—and China had innumerable ones—can give great insights into other peoples. Still, Claire let me know how much the garlic-infused dinners did not endear me to her when I came home!

We laughed at how problematic cross-cultural communication could be and how a person often is mistaken in what they think they hear or see. One story described two American language students who stopped to chat in Chinese with a couple Chinese farmers and to ask for directions. Assuming the foreigners to be speaking English, the farmers indicated they didn't understand and couldn't help, but one of them commented on how well the foreigners spoke Chinese!

Often we experienced how little most people—Americans and people in Taiwan—knew about the infamous *da lu* (the mainland). The civil war between the Chinese Communists and the Kuomintang led to a "bamboo curtain" between the two in 1949. We were all proverbial frogs at the bottom of the well seeing only a portion of the sky. The school did provide some daily language training for Claire, who was on "leave without pay," which gave her a better focus for our time in Taiwan before heading to Beijing in June 1976.

Our time in China and meeting Chinese people—whom we for years officially called CHICOMs (Chinese Communists) or Red Chinese—was the experience of a lifetime. A personal highlight was the birth of our son, Jonathan Richard Mueller, on August 10, 1976, an auspicious Dragon Boy according to Chinese culture.

What was it like living in China during those years of 1976–1978, formative years in modern Chinese political history? What was it like to be there when Chinese Chairman Mao Zedong died, and we watched—mesmerized—from the Beijing Hotel as a million Chinese gathered in Tiananmen Square and on Chang An Avenue in front of us? What was the significance of the arrest of the leftist "Gang of Four," including Mao's widow?

What was it like as China began to loosen up travel and implement its ambitious plan of "reform and opening up?"

How did we feel surrounded by numerous Chinese people in Tiananmen Square watching our young blond, blue-eyed Jonathan reach out to a young Chinese girl offering his rub-a-dub toy in exchange for her apple? She smiled shyly back at him. My camera captured and memorialized that connection across civilizations.

Read my answers to these and other questions about China in coming chapters. Before the story of AC—*After Claire* continues, a look back at BC—*Before Claire* will introduce you further to Richard Walter Mueller, helping to propel this memoir forward before it turns "back to the future."

Chapter One

Roots and Joining the Foreign Service

Y ou don't know who you are until you know from whence you came.

Whoever first said something like that is on the mark. I've already introduced you briefly to important events in my life: *meeting Claire*, working for Henry Kissinger, and serving in Vietnam and China. At this point let's look back to some of my growing up years that helped make me who I am before we return "back to the future."

Germany

The Mueller family is from Coburg in southern Germany. We trace our roots back hundreds of years. It was Martin Luther country, a man and an area that fought the existing establishment, namely the Catholic Church and the various monarchies that ruled everyday life. The resulting historical changes—breaking the power of the establishment; rise of civil society and a broader access to education, a move from Latin to German and other local languages making the Bible and other works more accessible; expansion of religious approaches and practices—helped to change the world forever. Fascinating history worth pondering.

Our ancestors came to the United States in the second half of the nineteenth century and brought with them business skills, a willingness to work hard, and a belief in good education. My father has written at length about many of them in his own ten-volume memoir. Shortly after the Civil War, one ancestor moved to Wilmington, North Carolina to start a hardware store. Can you imagine a German immigrant in those fraught post-war years? He fled back to the North. My father's parents, Carl Stephen Mueller and Johanna Kaiser (Nana or Nea), lived in Berlin, Connecticut, and had four children: Marjorie, Walter (my father), Robert, and Elizabeth (Betty).

The Maacks, on my mother's side, were from Hamburg and Schleswig-Holstein in northern Germany. As with the Muellers, the Maacks trace their family back hundreds of years. They immigrated to the United States in the late nineteenth and early twentieth centuries. My maternal grandfather Carl Heinrich Maack died in New York City in 1918 during the deadly Spanish flu pandemic. He rode a bus home and several days later was gone, leaving his wife Christine and three young children: Martha, Eleanor (my mother), and Walter. "Oma" was determined to rear her children well and fortunately had help from her brother, a Lutheran pastor.

Now that I'm writing in the middle of the 2020–2021 COVID-19 pandemic, having had a less severe case of the disease in December (along with Claire), I find myself every day thinking about Grandfather Carl and his life and death. For me, his grandson, to have similarly suffered from a dangerous virus, engenders a strange feeling of empathy and deep sadness not to have known him.

What do I have to thank these ancestors for, other than life which began on December 1, 1944, in Walter Reed Hospital in Washington, DC (because my father was a U.S. Army corporal during World War II)?

A huge thank you to Mother and Dad and the Muellers and Maacks for instilling:

—*A love of learning*, especially about the world and its peoples. I loved nothing more than reading every afternoon after school: Landmark and Signature books about the U.S. space program and the U.S. Navy in World War II, or the *Evening Star* about distant conflicts in Southeast Asia. A wonderful gift might be a biographical or geographical dictionary to put on my shelf. From non-fiction, I learned about history, the world's peoples, and the realities taught by science. My horizons continued to expand. From fiction, I learned so much about people and relationships and what a good story might look like. A favorite from those early high school years was William Dean Howells, one of the realist novelists of the nineteenth century.

—*The importance of learning.* What better way is there to improve society than providing good education for *everyone?* Bringing women, people less well-off, and marginalized groups fully into society and providing equal opportunity to everyone is the route to a much more successful and humane society. We talk a lot these days about teaching collaboration. Imagine how much better all kinds of outcomes might be if far more people worked together or played together today no matter their skin color or other background. Both the Maacks and Muellers ensured my parents' generation received excellent educations that helped prepare them for professional lives and those of their children.

—*A willingness to work hard, responsibly, and with initiative,* whether in school or later in professional life. At Longfellow School, I recall working very hard on academic assignments with lots of homework and projects. Writing themes and other papers came thick and fast. Teachers provided feedback, then another assignment. It was the only way to learn to write well, even if at times painful. When living in Bethesda in about 1958, I wanted a pet rabbit. I wrote to the Department of Agriculture, which sent me plans for rabbit hutches and care of rabbits. I found the wood, nails, tools and built the outdoor cage myself. My parents then let me bring "Frisky" (aka Harvey) home. I often worked at babysitting for families in the neighborhood and was able to pay my parents for the Olympia typewriter my father brought home from Italy. Even more satisfying than the money was being able to watch television while babysitting. My parents had not bought a TV, so watching my favorite *Gunsmoke* while babysitting was almost better than the money. At home, I happily read everything.

At the Northfield Mount Hermon School laundry, which was part of the educational work program for all students, I worked eight hours a week sorting students' dirty laundry (without doubt a humbling experience), washing and ironing, and then running back and forth to stuff clean clothes into student's lockers. Mr. and Mrs. Green of Greenfield were strict but kind taskmasters who invited us to Sunday dinner periodically. My next year I was chosen as a student librarian, a satisfying job given my love of books. My experience at the laundry running to stuff clothes in lockers prepared me for running to stuff books back on shelves.

Not surprisingly, all of my many "hard" jobs prepared me well for Secretary Kissinger's voracious demands at the State Department, for pursuing American and Vietnamese "truths" at the American Embassy in Saigon, leading a large consulate general in Hong Kong as consul general, and then for 24/7 leadership of three different international schools.

—An appreciation for Christianity and other religions. Dad had attended and loved the relatively spare liturgy of his Congregational Church in Berlin, Connecticut. Mother was reared Lutheran, with a Lutheran pastor great uncle, and a Lutheran Pastor uncle. We attended Christ Lutheran Church in Bethesda, Maryland, where I made my confirmation with Pastor Otto Schuetze. I know I absorbed many of his teachings about life. Years later, he married my sister and her husband, and then Claire and me.

I loved many of Martin Luther's theological ideas and the Christian idea of redemption, forgiveness, and second chances. That fundamental belief helped guide my approach to parenting as well as student discipline at my three schools, namely, that we were there to help students *learn.* Often good learning comes from mistakes or screwing up. The idea of "one strike and you're out" always struck me as wrong and ineffective, even detrimental to good learning. I also began to learn about other religions around the world and the ways differing peoples absorbed religious and spiritual beliefs into their lives.

Christ Lutheran Church in Bethesda was part of the American Lutheran Church, which over the years became what today is the Evangelical Lutheran Church in America, the largest and most progressive Lutheran church in the United States. Without doubt my Lutheran background helped move me over the years to a more progressive view of society and the world.

—One does not lie, cheat, or steal. The military academies in their honor codes add to those words *"nor do they tolerate those that do."* As I think back to my upbringing and subsequent life, there was a clear expectation that these moral demands were to be woven into life's fabric. I believe the first lie I told was at Sunday School in Frankfurt, at about the age of six, when they were creating classes by age. I added a few months to my age so I could be with my friends. It's amazing to me that I remember that lie, but it's indicative of the family values that were repeatedly instilled with insistence. God and I alone knew I had told a lie!

I don't want to mount a high horse today. We are all human and all cut corners or make mistakes from time to time. Still, to this day I find it deeply offensive to encounter people lying, cheating, and stealing—particularly leaders to whom we look for moral leadership. It's just as offensive to see others accepting such actions as just part of life.

We visited the Air Force Academy in Colorado Springs a while back and observed the honor code and oath inscribed in bold letters on a wall overlooking the Academy:

"We will not lie, steal, or cheat, nor tolerate among us anyone who does. Furthermore, I resolve to do my duty and to live honorably, so help me God." We need to demand that all our political, economic, business, and other leaders live up to that standard.

—A sense of what a stable life and family life can be. This was a huge positive as so many families in the following years experienced instability, divorce, difficult finances, or lack of job opportunity. Dad had a stable career position in the State Department and a follow-on tenure as dean of the College of Arts and Letters at the University of Alaska. My sister Linda and I were never hungry and never missed attending good schools. Mother was always there for us, even as Dad often worked long hours or traveled abroad. She always said her new career after college (Barnard) and teaching at an elementary school in New Jersey was as a mother and wife; she never complained to us about not returning to education. We were the beneficiaries of her experience and love. I remember her as kind, to us and others. She and my father kept us close to the extended Mueller and Maack families with frequent get-togethers, the result being our understanding of the strengths of extended families and networks. She was close to her mother, who I believe was a strong source of support for her and us.

My Father's Foreign Service Career in Germany and Elsewhere

Dad was a PhD Cornell University instructor in linguistics and Germanic languages when he was drafted into the U.S. Army in 1942. The war raged in both Europe and the Pacific. With his background, he was assigned to the Office of Strategic Services (OSS), the forerunner to the Central Intelligence Agency (CIA)—preparing for postwar government in Germany. He had reached the rank of corporal by the time the war ended in 1945 and was demobilized quickly. He joined the Foreign Service/State Department the same year. (He joined as a diplomat and not as an intelligence officer "under cover.")

My mother did what so many professional women did in those days. She left her teaching position in New Jersey to follow her husband in support of his career and to take care of the family. She did that wonderfully successfully her entire life. Mother and Dad were a great "team."

Linda Christine Mueller, my only sibling, was born on February 2, 1948, in Washington, DC, at Columbia Women's Hospital. We lived in Kensington, Maryland. I recall Dad bringing home one of the earliest television sets—small, and of course, black and white. Today, we would be called "early adopters." I still have clear memories of watching the *Howdy Doody Show,* with Clarabell the Clown as one of the stars. Her horn would go "Beep, Beep." Perhaps "Clarabell" was foreshadowing of my marrying "Claire" and having a granddaughter, "Clara!"

In February 1950, we pulled up stakes in Washington, DC, and boarded a Military Air Transport Service Douglas DC-6 in Massachusetts for our flight to Frankfurt, Germany. Dad was assigned to the U.S. High Commission for Germany (HICOG) where he worked to build the postwar German government. To this day the German government reflects in many ways what the United States required the Germans to include in their constitution and laws. For example, Dad always pointed out that—as with the U.S. education system—the educational curriculum was made the purview not of the central government but of the individual states. A future central leader would be blocked from imposing a nationwide education curriculum as Adolf Hitler had done.

I have so many memories of our years in Germany, 1950–1956. Most are very positive, including the trips the four of us took all over Europe—to France, Switzerland, Austria, Netherlands, Belgium, Italy, Scandinavia, and more. The most negative memories, sadly, from each of the three cities we lived in (Frankfurt, Bonn, and Berlin) were the blocks of bombed out remains of commercial, factory, and residential areas. I was too young to understand very much, but old enough to appreciate that war had destroyed so much and killed so many. I can see those scenes clearly as I sit here and write.

I believe many of my views about war and peace and the emotions engendered are rooted in those early years in Germany. It's one thing to declare war, launch the bombers, open the bomb bay doors, arm the weapons, and launch the bombs to wreak their damage. It's entirely different to see that damage firsthand, learning over time the meaning of war. My two assignments to Vietnam included repeated recollections of the destruction and violence I witnessed years before.

We lived for two years in Bad Homburg, next door to Frankfurt. I remember climbing the cherry trees in the yard, taking piano lessons, and catching the bus to school under a chestnut tree in the neighborhood. I met German children to play with as we heaved chestnuts by the bushel at each other. I began to learn more German, much of which, along with college German, is still lodged in my brain somewhere. I learned the German word *Ami* (American) and phrase, "Ami go home." I did not appreciate at that age how they had been taught to dislike Americans (who had defeated Germany in war). It was an introduction to what it might feel like to be "the other."

At the time, of course, I could not have appreciated that in Bad Homburg and Berlin we lived in nice houses belonging to German families who presumably occupied them during the Hitler era and World War II. Had they perhaps been Jewish and forced out of their homes with lives ended in the horrific concentration camps? Non-Jewish children living there would have been forced to join Nazi student organizations and later the German army. Had they perished in the war in Italy, or the Soviet Union, or Poland, or at Normandy?

Or they may have perished in a naval engagement as happened to a Maack/Otten relative who served in a German U-Boat (submarine) that was lost at sea? We stayed once with his family in Hamburg that was trying to get back on their feet and revive their commercial laundry service. I remember having to make my way to the only toilet available, an outhouse at the back of the yard.

I don't believe in ghosts. But there were numerous other kinds of ghosts back then, which I now much more fully appreciate. Human history is filled with them.

When it came to school, my parents had hoped to put me into a German school for the learning experience. The principal told them he would be happy to have me attend but stressed that in postwar Germany, resources were tight and most classes had more than fifty students. He wondered whether that made sense for me. In the end, my parents enrolled me in the Department of Defense school system, which I attended for the next six years.

In 1952, in good foreign service fashion, we again pulled up stakes to move to Bonn, where the German government was settling in. We lived in Plittersdorf, an American settlement right on the Rhine River. Dad could ride his bike along the river to his office. My school—third and fourth grades—provided an education similar to that in the United States. I remember our music teacher teaching tunes such as "Turkey in the Straw" and stimulating a strong interest in music. I made a kite, kept it in the air for hours, and won the kite contest. I remember a classmate stealing his parents' cigarettes and trying to convince a couple of us, sitting in a culvert near the Rhine River, that if we learned to smoke a circus would pay us to smoke in public. What?! I smoked a cigarette in the bathroom at home; my mother's reaction is lost in the mists of time.

My school was close to the river and to a shopping area of post exchange (PX), various stores, movie theater, and Stimson Memorial Chapel where Mother and Dad were active supporters. Dad periodically gave the sermon. Mother frequently provided sandwiches and food to destitute Germans who would knock on the door asking the "rich" Americans for help.

Two years later, in 1954, we moved to Berlin, where Dad became the director of the Berlin Document Center (BDC), a part of U.S. Mission Berlin. It was created as an underground document vault by the Nazis, containing documents on a vast number of Germans, Nazis or otherwise. The United States and allies checked all appointees to the German government against available biographic information. Nazi connections? End of application. In 1992, when I took my parents back to Germany, Ambassador Bob Kimmitt (formerly undersecretary for political affairs under President George H.W. Bush and Secretary of State James Baker, with whom I had worked for three years) made arrangements for us to meet the current director and tour the facilities. Vast numbers of records continued to sit on underground shelves. They were being copied and shipped to the United States. The facility would be turned over to the German government for long-term preservation.

I remember being impressed with my father's fluency in German and ability to interact so naturally with the German staff. He loved composing poems for BDC celebrations. One of the staff told my mother that they respected Dad's perfect high German, but they could really relate to her because she spoke and made the same mistakes in grammar that Berliners did!

My memories of Berlin are the clearest of our time in Germany. They include driving through the Brandenburg Gate into East Berlin, controlled by the Soviet Union. Stalin Allee, a showcase Potemkin village-type project, was lined with impressive commercial and residential properties (with few people in sight), but just behind them lay vast acres of rubble and destruction from World War II. To this day I can see the scenes so clearly; and to this day they stop me in my tracks to ponder how humankind has treated others over the course of human history.

Berthold Brecht's play, *Mother Courage and Her Children*, which I later studied in German class at the College of William and Mary, leaves one indelibly stamped with a loathing for "man's inhumanity to man."

I feel the need to ensure clarity. Yes, the destruction I saw was caused mostly by American and allied bombs. But the bigger picture, of course, is that Adolf Hitler, Emperor Hirohito, and his generals had forced the hand of the United States. After trying to distance itself from coming conflict, the United States did what was needed to protect itself and allies by ridding the world of the scourge of these dictators. So, while I am deeply sad about all those who died, we need to be honest about what led to that destruction. To continue, to be clear, I feel differently about the American wars in Vietnam, Iraq, and Afghanistan, where we mistakenly involved ourselves and pursued unachievable goals and policies, under different circumstances, motivations, and outcomes.

Dad enjoyed driving us throughout the area in the days before the Berlin Wall went up to keep East Germans from filtering across the border into West Berlin. Several years later, when at Longfellow School, I was a finalist presenter at an Optimist Club luncheon. I wrote about the joy of East Berliners who boarded the subway in East Berlin and were able to travel right across into West Berlin and freedom. East Germany finally caught on and built the Berlin Wall, which dramatically came down decades later, signaling the beginning of the end of the Cold War.

I recall that when traveling by car between Frankfurt and Berlin through the Soviet zone (later East Germany), American military police insisted one take an extra can of gas so you wouldn't be forced to exit the highway into communist-controlled territory.

I attended fifth and sixth grades at the Department of Defense school while Linda attended first and second grades. The education was pretty good. I learned that "poetic license" was not something one applied for from the government. I learned that working in a theater show was fun and that being the quarterback of the football team at recess did not guarantee high school or college football success. I learned that jumping out the first-floor window of my classroom as a good Samaritan to retrieve a friend's pencil doesn't get one rewarded but rather sent to the principal's office. I learned that raising and lowering the American flag on school days was an honor and that working with my father to construct a room-size model railroad layout was really fun. I learned that playing the trumpet was really hard, but that I could be my parents' morning alarm clock when I would wake up early and turn up the volume on the morning Armed Forces radio broadcast playing "Bugler's Holiday." Spending periodic evenings in the Department of Defense library was fun, rich with learning, and instilled a lifelong love of libraries (witness my student librarian assignment at NMH). And of great importance—my ears were opened by early rock and roll in 1955 while ice skating and hearing for the first time Bill Haley and His Comets blast out "Rock Around the Clock Tonight."

I was active in Cub Scouts, attaining the most senior rank of Webelos. It was fun and a great learning experience. I was able to start Boy Scouts while still in Germany, but my return to the United States cut that experience short. However, at William and Mary, I picked up the baton again and served as assistant scoutmaster to the local Peninsula scout troop.

A love of baseball was born on the playing fields of our school in Berlin. Second base was where I hung out. We went to a U.S. Army-organized championship tournament in Garmisch, in southern Germany. The family accompanied us. We did not win the tournament, but we did visit the Eagle's Nest, Hitler's retreat in the mountains nearby. In those days, one could visit the bombed-out remains of the vast residential compound and imagine the *Führer* gazing through his huge living room window at the peaceful forest while the war raged around him. I still remember so clearly my standing in the midst of the remains of that same living room and looking out to the same forest through the remains of the picture window.

Our Return to the United States

In summer 1956, we returned to the United States. We were fortunate to sail back on the SS *America*. It was a multi-day adventure and so different from the trusty TWA Constellations we usually boarded when crossing the Atlantic. The low point was crossing the Irish Sea through heaving swells that caused many hours of debilitating seasickness.

After visiting relatives and spending time at the Maack family's favorite vacation spot—Silver Bay on Lake George in New York—we settled into 6012 Welborn Drive, Bethesda, Md. The area was called Wood Acres.

Longfellow School for Boys

My mother decided that an independent school would offer me more academic stimulation for my middle school years. Linda attended and did well at the respected Wood Acres elementary school near our house.

Four years at Longfellow, grades seven to ten, passed quickly. I think my mother was right: good teaching and high standards helped me continue to grow and improve. One year, I received the headmaster's award for showing the most improvement. Another year, an award for academic excellence. Mr. Cooke, my English teacher, was a hard taskmaster but profoundly supportive. He drilled down hard on my writing and told my parents I was already writing on a college level. Copious writing projects were required across the curriculum. Mr. Didsbury made history fascinating and accessible. He was also provocative. He predicted that within decades, there would be no more racial divide in the United States because there would be widespread intermarriage and thus no color line. Was he ever wrong on that one.

A deep recollection about race came one day when I joined a small group of friends at school. I heard one of them say something about withdrawing from school. He said there was a rumor that a "colored" student would be admitted. George was agitated. I asked, "What was wrong with that?" George vehemently insisted that he would not go to school with a "colored" student. I was so naive about race in America at that point that I could not grasp the import of the exchange. I said I didn't see any reason not to stay in school if a "colored" student attended. That seemed to break up our conversation.

Ever since, I have learned more and more painfully about our "original sin" of slavery beginning in 1619. Writing now in 2022, we see the deep cleavages in our society based on continued racist attitudes and the destructive impact it is having on our democracy and broader society.

Those four years in Wood Acres and at Longfellow were fairly typical of a young teenager's life in suburbia in those days: playing sports (football, soccer, baseball, tennis); making model planes and ships while listening to Washington Senators baseball and Washington's football team (now in 2022 with the new name of "The Commanders") on the radio; reading voraciously about World War II and the U.S. Navy, particularly submarines; and reading all kinds of books because we did not have a television after being early adopters in 1948. Reading the *Evening Star* introduced me to the looming war in Laos, Vietnam, and Southeast Asia.

A brief word about my intense interest in the budding U.S. space program. I was intrigued with the ever more desperate attempts to successfully launch rockets that would put an artificial satellite in orbit. Vanguard rockets, developed by the U.S. Navy, regularly toppled over and exploded. The Juno rocket that carried the Explorer 1 space satellite successfully reached orbit, but only after the shocking news that the Soviet Union had put Sputnik 1 into orbit on October 4, 1957. That galvanized the United States and led to President John F. Kennedy's direction several years later to land a human on the moon by the end of the 1960s. I regularly read and clipped all kinds of articles about our space program, including on the impact of new intercontinental ballistic missiles that would be able to deliver nuclear warheads. The Cold War intensified. (Eric will be the recipient of all those notebooks, for what they're worth.)

As tenth grade approached, my parents were conscious of Dad's upcoming transfer overseas to parts unknown. They began the search for a good boarding school. Only one really appealed to them, partly because of its Christian roots and foundation by the great American evangelist of the nineteenth century, Dwight L. Moody. He founded two schools in western Massachusetts: the first was the Northfield Seminary for Young Ladies in 1879, and then Mount Hermon School for Boys in 1881. They were strong academically and espoused values my parents supported, many of which remain pillars today. Moody located the school on opposite sides of the Connecticut River—for a reason, I'm sure.

The next winter Dad and I set out by train from Berlin, Connecticut to Northfield. We arrived in a snowstorm and spent the night at the old Northfield Inn, which hosted regular religious conferences featuring Moody and others. By the morning, I had developed a full-blown fever and illness. I rushed through an entrance exam and an interview with the admissions director. Dad made a pitch to the admissions director to cut me some slack given my illness, and then we headed for the train station. A short time later word came from Mount Hermon that I had been accepted. Joy all around. I don't recall any nervousness about leaving home.

As it turned out, Dad was assigned to the American Consulate (personal rank of consul general) in Saint John, New Brunswick, Canada. Family would only be a short flight away from Boston.

Mount Hermon School—Now Known as Northfield Mount Hermon School

Mother and Dad dropped me off in August 1960. They recall that I was not eager to have them hang around. I was ready to begin my newest adventure.

Chuck Ives was my roommate, and we were assigned to South Crossley dorm. We hit it off quickly and became fast friends for several years. I learned first-hand how important peer friendships are in the dorm and elsewhere, and how much one learns from them. As in any school, the learning outside the classroom can be as important as what one learns inside. Dorm life, sports, clubs, and dating girls at Northfield School all added up to a well-rounded educational program.

After welcoming and orientation days, we jumped right into our academics. The teachers were all excellent. I was well prepared by Longfellow, but I also learned that the bar could be even higher. The academic load was heavy and there were times I wondered whether I was up to Hermon standards. Suffice to say, I hung in and found myself quickly expanding my horizons.

The work job program (described above) was very much a part of the educational program. Some parents would offer to pay to have someone do their son's work job. When I later returned as head of school in 1998, we would pro-actively explain the virtues of the program, such as taking responsibility for learning to contribute directly to the life of the community, learning skills of organization and meeting timelines, and working with a broader range of staff who often came from very different backgrounds than classroom teachers. In so many ways, I learned from my jobs in the laundry and as a student librarian my senior year in Schauffler Library with a great mentor, Bill Morrow.

Given the compact campus, we felt we were a close-knit community, a virtue of boarding schools. We knew or recognized many of our faculty and other students. My only regret at the time was that coming as a junior, I had much less time to get to know classmates. Many friendships and routines were already well-established since freshman year.

We also had the unique privilege, not found in many other boarding schools, of communicating with and dating girls on the Northfield campus. The rules specified what sports events, movies, or special occasions couples could attend. There was an elaborate system of creating blind dates for those willing to take a chance. I dated one girl several times over two years, and we went together to the senior "Chat" at the Chateau in Northfield, built to resemble a French *château*. Years later, at Shanghai American School in 2014, I hired a deputy head of school whose mother it turned out was the girl I dated. We had not kept in touch, but when she visited Shanghai, Claire and I had a good time over dinner reminiscing about our high school days. Small world.

True to its roots, the school had required chapel both during the week and on Sunday. I loved the church music and hymns, many of which were already familiar to me. I loved watching the organist pumping out the unique sounds of the organ pipes dominating the chancel. I didn't have much of a singing voice, but that didn't hold me back. I didn't endear myself to the guys sitting within range.

Charlton L'Hommedieu was the organist and the school music teacher. He worked with Al Raymond to plan the annual Christmas Vespers and Sacred Concert, as well as the many special church occasions. Al Raymond was a beloved music teacher on both campuses. Linda similarly had great respect for him when she attended Northfield School herself. I developed a special respect for "The Man of God," as my father called Mr. L'Hommedieu. I took his music appreciation class senior year and finally learned why my father so loved his classical music. My ears and eyes were opened. I came to love Ludwig van Beethoven's nine symphonies, so much so that I took graduation money to buy records of all of them by Arturo Toscanini and the National Broadcasting Company Symphony Orchestra. They followed us around the world over all these years; I still have them all.

I loved the Christmas Vespers concerts in December and Sacred Concerts in the spring. I always felt they were among the best traditions of the schools. They continue to this day and to me are a wonderful antidote to what seems to count as "music" these days.

We had a regular procession of speakers for chapel talks. The one particularly lodged in my memory is the Reverend William Sloan Coffin. He was a noted activist who supported social justice, anti-racism, and peace. I don't recall any specifics of his talk but do remember many of us were profoundly moved by what he said. He was chaplain at Yale University at the time; later he became senior minister at Riverside Church in New York City and an internationally known activist.

I can't help foreshadowing that years later in my first year as head of school of NMH, I invited Rev. Coffin who lived just up the road to be our 1999 graduation speaker. He was the perfect person to talk to us, particularly in the wake of a serious incident at NMH which gained national attention. Stay tuned to learn more.

I adapted to the many rhythms of life at Mount Hermon. Time went by quickly but seemed to slow as the days became colder and the sun set earlier. I remember walking up the steps of Siliman Hall at 4:00 p.m. for two classes and thinking: I can't believe I have almost two years of cold weather ahead of me.

But despite the winter months, time glided along. Before I knew it, summer 1961 was at hand. I went home to Wood Acres to help with moving to Dad's new post in Saint John, New Brunswick. We sadly said goodbye to our rabbit, Frisky, who was healthy, going strong, and destined for a new home, since we couldn't take him to New Brunswick. The four of us finally piled into Dad's beloved Oldsmobile and headed north to new adventures awaiting us in Canada.

The summer passed quickly as we moved into a large house in Rothesay, outside Saint John, and met our new neighbors. There were a number of young people we spent time with. Linda enrolled in the Netherwood School, a private girls' school nearby. She was destined to have the experience I had: two years at NMH, then known as Dwight Moody's Northfield School. I believe she grew significantly there before attending Washington College. To this day, I have hundreds of letters she wrote to me about school and her personal feelings.

Senior year at Mount Hermon was a blur with academics, senior activities, and the college search process. My courses included German with Frau Henderson, biology with Mr. Baker, French with Monsieur Weber, religious studies, American history with Mr. Bailey, and English with Mr. Wise.

I have lots of recollections. Top ones include:

—Giving a presentation to the entire six hundred-student-body in Memorial Chapel. I was nervous starting off; one of my kneecaps kept jumping up and down. But I got into the rhythm, and all went well. I have long since forgotten the subject, but at lunch afterward a faculty member came over to say I had done well but he needed to correct my pronunciation of a word!

—Learning that I had been accepted into *cum laude* in recognition of excellent academic work. That felt good. I signed the book during the ceremony. The next time I saw that signature was in 1999 when, as head of school, I inducted the newest members of *cum laude* and was able to point out my signature many pages earlier from 1962. As I did periodically with students, I commented that perhaps one of the newest *cum laude* awardees would also eventually become head of school of NMH!

—Spending a great deal of time learning about Southeast Asia and helping to organize a weekend conference that covered history and U.S. interests in the area. The seeds of future conflict were already sprouting.

—Appreciating the amount of interest in a global world shown by both faculty and students. Mount Hermon had a long history of welcoming students from England, Africa, China, and elsewhere as well as an historic commitment to teaching about other cultures, peoples, and countries.

—Taking a stand on my personal politics. I read Barry Goldwater's classic *Conscience of a Conservative.* A classmate and I became enamored of his proposals for limited government, limited spending, and personal privacy. We were quite vocal in history and other classes. Our history teacher showed some annoyance at having to explain why Goldwater's approach was not right for America. Suffice to say, I went off to college still believing in Goldwater's approach. By the time Goldwater was nominated for president in 1964, I had become worried about his foreign policy inclinations, particularly in Southeast Asia. Stay tuned for my college experience with Young Republicans.

When it came time to apply to college, I decided I wanted a co-educational school. After six years of boys' school, it was time to recognize that women held up half the sky (as the Chinese saying goes) and that learning alongside women would be worthwhile. I checked with my father that he didn't hope for me to go to Wesleyan, the "family university." It was fine with him. I had to live the decision on which school to attend. The choice was between William and Mary in Virginia or Middlebury in Vermont. I narrowly chose William and Mary because I liked the educational program, the campus, and the warmer weather. It proved to be a good choice.

Finally, the last weeks of high school drew near. The final senior dance at the Chateau was historic. It was the last dance before the Chateau was torn down because of the immediate need for prohibitively expensive repairs. We danced the newest dance on the veranda, the twist, made popular by Chubby Checker. I wasn't a great dancer, but we were game. My date and I enjoyed the evening, then went our separate ways until we met again by serendipity in Shanghai in 2014.

Many Muellers and Maacks made their way to Mount Hermon for graduation day. The ceremony was simple and nice with low-key remarks by the head of school outside of Beveridge Hall.

That was my last visit to Mount Hermon until 1997, when I saw firsthand the profound changes that had taken place since 1962. Keep reading!

The College of William and Mary in Virginia 1962–1966

I arrived in Williamsburg after a summer of work at a construction company in Saint John, New Brunswick. The next four years were my final maturation years before beginning a lifetime of professional work in diplomacy and education. Looking back, I appreciate how many different experiences I had that helped me learn and grow.

Academically, I was well prepared for my freshman year at William and Mary. The faculties at Longfellow and Mount Hermon deserve credit for having taught and supported me. After my first semester of English, the department moved me up to a higher-level class. At the end of the year, I had a high grade point average.

My sophomore and junior years I took on a heavier course load, including demanding economics courses, which truly opened my eyes to new ways of understanding the world. I decided to major in economics and minor in international relations and German. In my junior year I realized I had taken on more than I should have, even though the subject matter across the board was of great interest to me. Two semesters of statistics were maddeningly close to being like alien hieroglyphics to me. Recently, I found a draft letter to my parents saying I was facing some overwhelming demands and was contemplating taking a break from college. Fortunately, I never sent it. I brainstormed with my educational counselor at school, gave up some activities, bore down, and by the end of the year was feeling more on top of things.

In my senior year, a bright light appeared at the end of the tunnel. My economics senior honors thesis was a bear—"Profit Theory in Classical Economics." I can't tell you how much time I spent in the new library, nose to the grindstone, puzzling out how early economists felt about the subject. To this day, I cannot tell you why I chose the topic, nor tell you much about it. I was awarded an "A" and kind words from Professor Sancetta. There were other rewards. I loved two courses in art history and felt I had really matured in international relations under Professor Margaret Hamilton and in German under my German professors.

My non-academic life and activities were important to me, and all were great learning experiences. Among the highlights:

—I found good friends and roommates, and we enjoyed doing things together. We would even write letters to each other during summers with real paper-and-pen letters, envelopes, and stamps—no smartphones or Facebook in that era.

—Bob Gates, who would later become CIA director and then secretary of defense, was a good friend for three years. We roomed together in my junior year (his senior year). We shared similar views on many issues and were compatible roommates. As a history major, Bob recorded many news announcements of major world events. Later, we crossed paths periodically. Once when I, as a new FSO in 1966, was visiting the CIA for briefings, I walked into the cafeteria to find Bob walking toward me. I never saw him more taken aback to see me. He was non-plussed because he was not yet publicly identified as a CIA employee (that came later—in the meantime, he was U.S. Air Force). I gathered it was okay in the end when his superiors learned I was a State Department employee with my own top secret security clearance.

On November 22, 1963, I was sitting at my desk in the dorm when the radio station broke in to say President Kennedy had been shot in Texas. He was in critical condition. I was stunned and began to think of the consequences for our politics and society. The rest was history. After he died and plans were made to have his body lie in state in the Capitol, my roommate, Jim, and I decided on the spur of the moment to take a bus to Washington to pay our respects in the Rotunda. We waited for hours and finally were allowed entry. The violence and death were just shocking to us. The direction of our country was changed in that instant.

I had joined Young Republicans on campus, still enamored of Barry Goldwater's *Conscience of a Conservative.* There weren't many of us; the Democrats were still well dug in. I was a strong supporter of civil rights and wrote regularly to Virginia Senator Robert Byrd to tell him so. He always replied, addressing me as, "My dear Mr. Mueller." I had a chance to meet the grand old Republican, Illinois Senator Everett Dirksen, thanks to my mother's cousin who worked for him. I'll never forget how he described the taxation game on Capitol Hill and who pays the bills: "Don't tax you, don't tax me, tax that fellow behind the tree."

Election time for Young Republican leaders at William and Mary rolled around. Joy, the chapter president, encouraged me to run for president; in turn I encouraged her. She finally said yes, and I consented to be vice president. All was fine until the Republican National Convention in summer 1964. Goldwater was nominated. And then my nervousness set in around his foreign policy priorities. Partly through his own words, but also Democratic messaging, Goldwater was painted as a hawk. I didn't want war in Vietnam or anywhere else. I couldn't support him any longer. I did like his phrase: "Extremism in defense of liberty is no vice. Moderation in pursuit of justice is no virtue."

In the fall of 1964, I wrote my resignation letter to Joy. Even though we were friends, I was very formal, addressing it "Dear Ms. H...." Bob Gates looked at the letter and rightly convinced me to just write "Dear Joy."

That was the end of my Republican years. Ironically, I voted for Lyndon Johnson and then found we got the war in Vietnam I was afraid Goldwater would get us into.

On a happier note, I joined Alpha Phi Omega, a service fraternity that worked to do good deeds. We demolished a building so a church could build a new one; we supported the William and Mary theater; we did service projects around town. I became president. My only regret is that it couldn't be co-ed at even a co-ed university. They have since welcomed women. One of our desires was to have a physical fraternity home, but the College was not supportive, so we explored renting a house in town. Heated meetings discussed the pros and cons. Bob Gates was an eloquent opponent of the idea. It led to a close vote—the nays won. I felt let down, but later decided it was the right decision; too much time would have been spent keeping it going. All in all, a good learning experience.

I became involved in Saint Stephen's Lutheran Church next door to the campus and was a regular church attendee. I appreciated Pastor John Beyerly's friendship.

I accepted an invitation to become an assistant scoutmaster for the local Boy Scout troop. It got me off campus and let me mentor the boys. Bob Gates was also an assistant scoutmaster. Jim Fuller, a senior official of Colonial Williamsburg, was scoutmaster and our mentor. We met parents who gave us a window on the local community. Back then there was no hint of any sexual abuse issues as we have now learned have been widespread elsewhere. It is unfathomable to me that adults could so violate their responsibility to protect and care for young people.

At the beginning of my junior year, I was hired as a paid Williamsburg Theater usher and ticket taker. I must have seen every movie of that era a dozen times. It was at the theater that I met my first real girlfriend. We dated seriously until I went off to Australia for my first Foreign Service assignment.

My best jobs were with Colonial Williamsburg. One summer I was an "interpreter" at the Wig Shop, in an eighteenth-century costume, explaining to visitors the skills of barbering and dentistry. Wigs were worn over newly shaven heads and a special tool snapped bad teeth from one's jaw. During the next year I worked on Sundays at the Apothecary Shop, dispensing information about eighteenth-century medicine. And in my final summer of 1966, I worked outside the windmill, "interpreting" the process of grinding corn and wheat and its importance in the economy. It was a wonderful job. But anyone who asked me about working there received my same reply: "I enjoy it, but it's a real grind!"

The best part of summer jobs was taking part in the Colonial Militia. We assembled and with our rifles marched to the armory. There we demonstrated loading and firing our weapons: remove powder from knapsack; tear off end paper with teeth; pour powder into rifle pan; cock; aim high; and fire! Lots of loud explosions, but happily, no musket balls were ever loaded.

I came to love Colonial Williamsburg and its eighteenth-century buildings and gardens. Just walking the streets and visiting the gardens open to the public was calming, like a three-dimensional painting of nature at its best. The grounds of William and Mary were highly walkable and similarly appealing. Some of my happiest times were walking and talking in the many gardens with my girlfriend. Periodically, I thought it might be nice to live in the area or perhaps retire there. My strong interest in photography, which sprouted in Europe—and Italy in particular—was nourished at Colonial Williamsburg where I walked in all seasons to enjoy its beauty.

But as the calendar marked off the days in 1965 and 1966, the increasing tempo of the war in Vietnam became more and more a focus on campus. A couple friends who were in Reserve Officers' Training Corps (ROTC) talked grimly about the high percentage of deaths among second and first lieutenants in the field. One of the military services brought a fighter jet to campus to display in front of the student center. It was the wrong thing to do. Every day, bands of students circled it in protest.

It was the beginning of significant divisions on campus between those protesting America's involvement and those supporting it.

I clearly recall the chills I felt in summer 1965 listening to President Lyndon B. Johnson's announcement that he was sending many additional troops to Vietnam and concurrently significantly increasing the monthly draft. Listening to Johnson's address, I said to the girl I was dating that that was the single most alarming and sobering announcement. I had never really thought about joining the military, but now the very real prospect of being drafted for the war was starkly in front of me.

In the coming months we all contemplated our futures and how they would be changed with the increasing conflict. One friend burned his draft card in front of the Williamsburg Theater even as we wrestled him to the ground. Other friends made plans to apply to graduate school thinking they might earn a deferment. Some signed up for the National Guard thinking the Guard would not be called up. Some preemptively joined another branch of service to avoid the infantry. Some headed to Canada.

In the end, I recognized there was a high likelihood I could be drafted, but the best approach would be to just pursue my top interests and hope for the best.

I will note that during my senior year, I became a protester of a different kind. When the university announced a much earlier closing of Swem Library, we organized a large group to stage a "sit in" in the entrance. We sat for some time. The dean finally was roused and came to talk with us. We were only asking for a later closing time, so we had more time to study. He promised to review the decision and in fact did reverse it shortly thereafter. It wasn't life or death, but it was important to us academically.

As the year went on, word spread that there would be no commencement speaker. We thought that was a mark of disrespect to us soon-to-be graduates. I wrote up a petition, got a bunch of seniors to sign it, and one morning stopped by President Davis Young Paschal's office. When I described what we had for him, his assistant invited me in to make our case directly to him. He said he understood and was sympathetic. Lo and behold, we soon received an announcement that the secretary of the treasury would be our commencement speaker.

Two small victories for student activism showing that concerted action by a determined group could be successful! I wish the anti-war protests had become more successful much earlier.

I scored high in the Graduate Records Exams and was accepted at the University of Pennsylvania and the University of Virginia for graduate work in international relations.

I also passed the Foreign Service written and oral exams, a major step toward my life's work in diplomacy!

In the summer of 1965, Dad finished up his tour in Saint John and moved to Knox College in Illinois as diplomat-in-residence for a year. He enjoyed the assignment immensely, joining his love of academic life with his professional diplomatic career. The next year Mother and Dad moved to Washington, DC, and Dad's new assignment as dean of area and country studies at the Foreign Service Institute of the State Department.

Graduation was a dilemma for the family. Linda and I were graduating on the same day, she from Northfield School and headed to Washington College in Maryland, and I from William and Mary. Mother went to Linda's graduation, Dad to mine, and then we all met up for some good celebrating.

Life Gets Serious: Why Join the Foreign Service?

What drew me to the Foreign Service? First and foremost, I grew up in a foreign service family, so I had some appreciation for international relations and the wide range of cultures and histories around the world. When we lived in Bethesda, Maryland I recall being intrigued with stories in *The Evening Star* about the conflict in Southeast Asia, especially in Laos, that later grew into the Vietnam War. My education at Northfield Mount Hermon and William and Mary built on that interest. I was also aware of the regular diplomatic transfers among different overseas posts and the United States. In my younger years, I periodically thought fondly of my Uncle Walt's family rooted in one home in New Jersey, never having to change schools every two years.

By the time I reached my junior year at William and Mary diplomacy seemed like an attractive profession and life. I considered two tracks: graduate study at either the University of Pennsylvania or the University of Virginia or the Foreign Service.

In my senior year in December 1965, I took the Foreign Service written exam in Richmond, Virginia. Usually only about 20 percent of applicants passed. To my surprise, I did pass and was invited to take the oral exam in Washington in the spring. I expected it to be a three-hour grilling, but it turned out to feel more like a three-hour conversation about U.S. history, economics, international relations, art, music, and topics of the day.

In those days, I recall about one in five who passed the written test passed the oral exam. I did not get my hopes up.

The examining panel of three Foreign Service officers asked me a wide variety of questions to ascertain the diversity and depth of my learning. They also observed my approach to engaging in conversation and exchanging thoughts. Bottom line: they were looking for candidates who could engage thoughtfully in representing the United States abroad and in analyzing and reporting on other countries' economic and political developments. Since I was only twenty-one, I believe they were also gauging my potential for growth and maturity.

They asked me about unique American architecture. My answer started with Native American teepees. They asked about music. I said I loved Beethoven's nine symphonies; I learned later they were skeptical until I described the symphonies in more detail (thanks, Mr. L'Hommedieu, my music teacher at NMH). On the subject of American literature, I referred in one of my answers to *The Jungle* by Upton Sinclair. They asked me a question beginning, "When you read the book..." I interrupted, "Actually, I haven't read it, just read about it!" They laughed.

After the interview, they asked me to wait outside while they deliberated. Shortly after, they called me in, informed me I had passed, and offered congratulations. I was now eligible to undergo background, security, and medical tests and await a call to join.

I then faced the question: join the Foreign Service or pursue graduate school? I had been accepted at both the University of Virginia and the University of Pennsylvania, leaning toward the latter. In the end, after conversation with my parents and others, I opted for the Foreign Service and accepted an entering class for August 1966. A good decision it turned out.

My Selective Service draft board reclassified me as 1-A for the next year, meaning I was fully eligible to be drafted. They did not ask me to report right away. In subsequent years, I remained 1-A, fully expecting to be called. The State Department would not ask draft boards for deferments. I did write the board when I was headed for Vietnamese language training and then on assignment to the embassy. I described that I was serving the nation as a FSO diplomat in Vietnam, working with the U.S. military.

I sometimes pondered how different my future would have been if called up. I have no doubt I would have "done my duty" as my father had many decades before in World War II. I can't imagine I would have fled to Canada as others did. A stint in the U.S. Army would have made a different person of me, with very different experiences. I periodically wondered how I would react as a first lieutenant ordered to lead a squad up a mountain in the face of withering enemy fire. I'm sure I would have obeyed orders as thousands of other young men did, many of whom never returned home.

Life Becomes More Serious—A Diplomatic Education and Service in Canberra

I entered the Foreign Service in August 1966 as a young and eager recruit for a lifetime of diplomacy. I didn't know it then, but thirty-two wonderful and varied years lay ahead—of building bridges; solving problems; negotiating agreements; meeting and working for secretaries of state; and continually learning new skills and absorbing new knowledge.

Nor could I ever have imagined becoming head of school/superintendent of three independent and international schools, Northfield Mount Hermon School in Massachusetts, Hong Kong International School, and Shanghai American School. Yes, all my diplomatic experience went a long way in the world of education, as I was told by the chairman of the board of trustees.

As the sixty-some other new FSOs gathered to join the Service, I had the honor and fun of witnessing my father do the formal swearing in of our class! It was a thrill for both of us. Subsequently, the "A-100" course for new diplomats for six weeks introduced us to the Foreign Service. Then, several months in German language training to build on my high school and college German got me off language probation.

I suspected I would be assigned to a German-speaking post, but no; at the final gathering, they announced I would be assigned to the embassy in Canberra. As I walked to the front of the room, I kept asking myself, "Where's Canberra? Where's Canberra?" Ah, yes, I had asked for an assignment to Australia!

In January 1967, I was off, saying goodbye to family and winter weather. Two days in Honolulu hooked me for life on the tropics and warm weather. Two days in Tahiti and the island of Bora Bora? Heaven. I thought about jumping ship and staying. Two days in Auckland, New Zealand to see a new country. Finally, Canberra.

I was a junior officer on the bottom rung of the career ladder. Colleagues at the embassy were warmly welcoming. Big Ed Clark from Texas, United States Ambassador to Australia; Ed Cronk, deputy chief of mission; Cronk's wife, Dorothy; their daughter, Maryed, whom we have stayed in touch with ever since; many others. The young Australian people I met were equally welcoming. I liked to tease them about their Australian accents. They delighted in reminding me that in Australia it was I who stood out with an American accent.

As part of my training, I rotated first through general services. An important lesson came when asked to survey the embassy to see what we needed to spend our year-end money on. I reported back to the chief administrative officer that we didn't need year end funds because "Kansas funds," provided earlier for a visit by the president, had taken care of everything, including deferred maintenance. We could give money back to the State Department. The administrative counselor exploded: "Richard, in the State Department you never, never, ever turn funds back. If you do, they will cut your budget the next year!" I never forgot. So true. Do the right thing and you pay the penalty.

I also served as the one consular officer at the embassy. Most services were provided by the consulate general in Sydney. I issued diplomatic visas, helped wayward American citizens, and was also the go-between for the State Department and the Australian Foreign Ministry on the unique extradition of an Australian citizen to the United States.

The follow-on stints were in the economic and political sections. The goal was to learn about Australian developments, talk to knowledgeable people, and write analyses for Washington. The officers staffing those sections were generous in their time and support as I learned about the Foreign Service.

Suffice to say, Australia was in transition away from its historic "White Australia" policy, away from Britain and closer to the United States, and its economy was moving into higher gear. Closer relations with the United States were symbolized by the annual Coral Sea celebrations, commemorating the World War II Battle of Coral Sea where the United States stopped the southern Japanese advance toward Australia.

There were many noteworthy points of my eighteen months in Canberra:

—The drowning of Australian Prime Minister Harold Holt and President Johnson's subsequent visit to Canberra for the memorial service in December 1967. Since Holt's body was never found, there were later outlandish rumors that he had defected to Communist China and had been picked up by a People's Republic of China (PRC) submarine. I helped with arrangements and even rode down the elevator with President Johnson. He was not in a talkative mood. He shook hands with me later at the airport before departure. This was shortly before he announced he would not run for re-election and would work for a peace agreement with Vietnam. After leaving Canberra he flew home via Vietnam to see the troops.

—A Christmas visit to Norfolk Island after Johnson lifted off and "wheels up" was announced. The island was beautiful with its Norfolk pines and eerie with its bloody history of transportation of hardened criminals from Britain.

—A two-month stint in Melbourne to help the consulate and Department of Commerce mount an American trade show.

—Regular visits to Sydney, the mountains, and beaches with friends. A flight to Tasmania for a couple of days in the embassy defense attaché's C-47.

—Becoming friends with Colonel Alex Butterfield, the representative of the commander-in-chief, Pacific representation, who later gained fame for revealing the White House taping system that helped lead to Nixon's impeachment.

—Periodic demonstrations outside the embassy protesting the Vietnam War. I still was something of a believer that our involvement was right. In my role as writer and editor of the embassy newsletter, I once wrote an "editorial" suggesting we should be openly supportive of the war effort. I was quietly told it was a subject better avoided. My views changed radically as I later served in Vietnam. Riots and demonstrations in the United States were the backdrop throughout my time in Canberra, demonstrating the wrenching strains in our country.

—Chinese cuisine served at the ambassador's residence. A Hong Kong Chinese couple served as chefs. The ambassador was delighted to point out to everyone that I didn't know how to use chopsticks. No matter; I had lots of practice over the next decades. An interesting fact I learned later about Jackie Chan, the martial arts actor: he lived with his parents while they worked for the American ambassador in Canberra at the time I was there!

—And the highest point of many: a multi-week trip through the outback with embassy colleague, Clyde Taylor: Adelaide, Coober Pedy (opal-mining), Alice Springs, climbing Ayers Rock (Uluru), visit to a cattle station, east coast of the Great Barrier Reef, Townsville, Lightning Ridge (New South Wales) (opals again). It was an epic trip. To this day, Clyde kids me about wanting to stop every few yards to photograph yet another seemingly unique gum (eucalyptus) tree.

Shortly after our return from the outback, a personnel memo arrived for me. I was assigned to the American Embassy, Saigon, Republic of Vietnam via one year of full-time language training at the Foreign Service Institute beginning summer 1968.

Many FSO's were being assigned to Vietnam those days. The war was raging, both on the battlefield and in our country. I did not have a family, so I was a prime candidate. I was intrigued. I knew there would be danger. It was daunting in many ways, but I was eager to serve in a new part of the world where the Foreign Service needed me.

A friend at the embassy, with dark humor, told me he would visit the State Department to observe my name on the memorial wall of those who died in service to their country. With great good fortune, during two assignments to Vietnam, I avoided the honor of the wall.

I returned home via American Samoa to visit another tropical Pacific island. Many years later, with Secretary of State George Shultz, we visited the other half of Samoa, Western Samoa. Back in the United States, we did much reuniting with family and friends that summer before I made my way to the Vietnam Training Center of the FSI in Arlington, Virginia in August 1968 for my next big adventure.

Life Gets Even More Serious: Vietnamese Language Training and America's War in Vietnam

I thought I had some idea what I was in for as I entered the halls of the Vietnam Training Center in August 1968. But I really didn't. In reality, Vietnamese was much harder than the German I had studied for years. It was a tonal language. It really mattered whether one pronounced correctly a rising, falling, flat, or wavy tone. My classmates and teachers laughed whenever my eyebrows went up attempting a word with a rising tone! Classroom study was six hours a day with Vietnamese native language teachers overseen by a "scientific linguist." The role of the teachers was to drill, drill, drill, forcing our minds to learn words, then phrases, then sentences, then conversation. Think of it as akin to wearing new ruts or pathways in our minds, as our linguist described it.

I struggled for a while getting my ears and tongue in sync. I was warned that if I did not make sufficient progress by December, I would be shipped to Vietnam after Christmas. Maybe that was the boost my brain needed to help me reach the top of the class.

November 1968 saw the election of Richard Nixon. I was not a fan. In fact, just the opposite. He worked to block peace negotiations with North Vietnam by telling South Vietnam not to agree with Johnson's efforts. They would get a better deal from Nixon. Despicable. Johnson should have called him out publicly. There was no secret plan for peace. Half of the U.S. casualties came on his watch and untold numbers of Vietnamese were killed and wounded. "Vietnamization" would be the new policy, but was it a strategy to end the war? Hardly.

Bottom line was that South Vietnam had to pull itself together, fight corruption, and hold off the North. A "decent interval" was our message to Hanoi: let us get out and then wait a little while to take over, if you can. The United States would not return.

Do I detect the shades of Vietnam in the current Trump plan to withdraw from Afghanistan and Iraq?

Back to the Vietnam Training Center

Wednesday afternoons were devoted to "area studies," lectures, readings, simulations to teach us about Vietnam and Asia. I loved all the learning about a new part of the world and would forever after count myself an "Asia Hand" and "China Hand."

Dad was, serendipitously, dean of Area and Country Studies at FSI during that time. He fed me lots of good articles and books and had his own good insights into the war and foreign policy. I lived with Mother and Dad for some months before finding an apartment with friends. It was good bonding as an adult with my parents and being able to discuss current issues.

The bonding experience of studying so intensively with other students led to lifelong friendships, such as that with Gage McAfee, who would tell people he thought he knew more about me than my parents. Why? Because every day we would discuss and answer questions about our backgrounds, growing up years, and views of the world, of course all in Vietnamese!

July 24, 1969, was a shining moment for humankind and the United States: live coverage of the successful landing on the moon by Apollo 11 and Neil Armstrong's first steps on the surface. Colleagues from the Vietnam Training Center and I watched the landing live. We were enthralled. It was truly an historic achievement, and we knew it at the time. I had been a huge fan of the U.S. rocket program in the 1950s and 1960s, watching Vanguard rockets exploding on the launch pad and then seeing Sputnik traveling across the night sky. I have given all my scrapbooks to Eric, our "rocket scientist."

I've discovered over the years only one real downside to the stupendous feat of going to the moon, namely, it set far too high the standard for future human accomplishment. How many times have you heard, when government tried to solve problems, "Well, if we can send a man to the moon, surely, we should be able to . . . (fill in the blank).

"Graduation" from the Vietnam Training Center came shortly after that summer of 1969. We received pep talks from speakers about the war effort and our vital role in either the embassy or Civil Operations for Revolutionary Development Support (CORDS). I always liked the edginess of the use of "revolutionary." In fact, it was too edgy for the U.S. government and later was changed to "rural."

My assignment was to have been to the CORDS program to serve somewhere in a rural area of Vietnam, advising the Vietnamese civilian and military authorities. Could a twenty-five-year-old really provide added value? Perhaps by channeling economic goods, money, and airstrikes as needed?

"In Country"—Vietnam 1969–1971

My Pan Am flight went into a steep dive in August 1969 as it approached Saigon in an accepted maneuver to reduce exposure to any hostile gunfire or rockets. Safely on the ground, I exhaled and turned my thoughts to my next adventure—a serious and potentially consequential one.

I might have expected deserted streets, fearful people hurrying along. In fact, the streets were crowded, and the sidewalks filled with people. Restaurants and stores were everywhere. Superficially, one might have thought things were reasonably "normal." Not the case, of course.

There was a great deal of commercial activity. I soon learned the countrywide Tet (lunar new year) Offensive by the North Vietnamese and Viet Cong the previous year had cost them dearly in lost cadres and troops. The succeeding months were arguably more quiet and more secure.

My quarters were a small, one-story French villa I shared with another embassy officer. In turn, we also shared it with a hardworking team of geckos who generally stayed high up on the walls and diligently decimated mosquitos and other flying bugs—my first real encounter with the tropics. The house was comfortable and secluded, down a long driveway from the busy avenue. We paid the Vietnamese couple who lived in and took care of all the cooking and upkeep. We made grocery runs periodically to the PX for food. All things considered, not a bad setup for a war zone.

Instead of an assignment with CORDS outside of Saigon, I had been assigned to the embassy's political section as assistant labor attaché. My job, along with the labor attaché, Cliff Finch, was to get to know the union leaders and workers in the country. Many of them exerted considerable political power and quite a few had ties to the "enemy." We wanted to understand them and hopefully keep them supportive of U.S. interests.

I met regularly with labor people to discuss developments in Vietnam and what people in their sectors of society were experiencing. They expressed many concerns about security; jobs and income; and the pressures of war. I was able to express U.S. policy and how our president intended to continue supporting Vietnam. We would supply resources even as U.S. troops slowly withdrew. We wanted South Vietnam to remain independent, develop, and be able to protect itself from the North.

Once, I was deputized by the embassy to help mediate a dispute between workers and a big American contractor, RMK-BRJ. One could feel the tension as the Vietnamese gamely strove to stand up to a huge company. We did make progress, and I recall shifting into Vietnamese to interpret the company's offers and to make some promises about future policies. I hope the company kept them.

I often attended dinners where the Vietnamese politely remarked on how well I spoke Vietnamese and was able to use chopsticks. Thanks, Ambassador Clarke!

I traveled to other cities where the labor movement was active, such as Danang and Hue in the north. Doing so also gave me a chance to observe daily life and other goings-on around the country. I was increasingly learning more deeply about the history and culture of Vietnam. For example, there was an interesting sculpture museum in Danang of the Champa empire which existed for hundreds of years in central Vietnam.

In Hue, the traditional capital and seat of the emperor offered insights into a wide range of Vietnam's unique history.

I often thought about how fortunate I was to be able to meet and understand in greater depth the Vietnamese people and their rich history and culture. How deeply sad, to this day, that millions of Americans, including those who fought and died in the trenches and in the mountains, knew only of war and killing. Not surprisingly, the enemy was demonized with derogatory and racist terms which live on at times in the twenty-first century. They are gut-wrenching today even as I sit and write so many years later.

I was also fortunate in making friends with Vietnamese young people who had studied in the United States and had returned home. They were happy to share their thoughts and those of their families on society and the war. They had no desire to be taken over by the North, but also had reservations about the South Vietnamese government, mostly around corruption and incompetence. I also had interesting insights into the tensions between extended families who insisted grown children live with them and the children who had lived independently in the United States and wanted more autonomy in Vietnam—an ongoing dilemma.

When the embassy decided my efforts would be better applied to understanding students and the media, I was transferred to the political section's internal unit down the hall. The skills I was developing working with labor unions were now applied to meeting and working with student organizations—also politically connected—and to the Vietnamese media world.

Getting to know students and leaders of student movements was a challenge and a joy. Much closer in age to college students than many in the embassy, I found students eager to connect and understand U.S. intentions. There were also those who were skeptical and standoffish. As with the labor unions, we needed to understand the political landscape and trends in society.

I became friends with one student leader, Doan Van Toai, who was eager to introduce me to others. He would periodically give me a rundown on how he saw the landscape of shifting student opinions. Periodically he would gather friends and we would drive to Vung Tau, a beachside resort for the afternoon. It was business, but it also could be fun.

One notable success I recall drew praise from our leaders. Many students had launched a big demonstration and sit-down strike in the middle of the city. It continued without much understanding of what they wanted. I took the initiative and went to the site and asked for the reputed leader whom I believed I had once met. There was skepticism and resistance. What was this American up to? But the leader called together some of his colleagues, and we had a good conversation about student demands and aims. This included government recognition of student organizations and financial support for students. When I returned to the embassy, I was able to provide a better understanding of the strike and the wider political implications.

My other assignment was the Vietnamese media. Following it was a chore. There were numerous publications, most supported with funds from one organization or another. They all had their biases and would spin the news according to their opinions. They ranged from supporters of South Vietnamese President Nguyen Van Thieu to fronts for pro-North sentiments. Every organization seemed to have its own rag. Most were not particularly influential.

Aside from trying to get to know more about the important people behind different publications, I also wrote a weekly summary of stories and news making the rounds. It was a dreary exercise that I began on Sunday afternoon and completed on Monday. The embassy leadership finally agreed to end the weekly summary (which had been written as such for years) and aim for twice a month instead. Most of us felt it was still pretty useless.

My colleagues in the political section were all competent and congenial FSOs. They were all supportive of each other. We socialized together periodically. The more senior ones, such as Martin Herz, had made a name for themselves in other parts of the world. They were now adapting their worldviews to a totally new situation they felt was of importance to the United States in stemming the spread of worldwide communism. Sometimes, their previous experience was applicable to Vietnam in wartime. Other times, it was not.

I was among the younger officers and one who had invested a year in language and cultural training. Many of us were far more skeptical of how we were going about trying to win hearts and minds and the war. Our superiors tended to be tolerant of our views, but we were periodically reminded we were following the national security directions of the president and secretary of state.

One evening U.S. Ambassador to South Vietnam Ellsworth Bunker, one of the grand old men of the State Department, invited a number of us younger officers to dinner at his home. Most of the details of the conversations are lost in the mists of memory. He listened to those of us who expressed our concerns about the American approach and suggestions for change. Corruption was high on the list, as was indiscriminate bombing, Agent Orange, and Rome plows, all of which turned even more Vietnamese against us. He acknowledged our concerns and expressed the administration's view of the need to contain the Communist march south from China, through North Vietnam, to the South.

Little could I have imagined that Ambassador Bunker and I, along with Claire, three years later in 1974, would be on the same five-week Kissinger Middle East Israeli-Syrian disengagement shuttle mission. One morning on that trip, Claire delivered to Bunker's hotel room the overnight classified messages from Washington. She still laughs at being met at the door by our most distinguished and buttoned-up diplomat in his shorty pajamas, rubbing the sleep from his eyes.

A few other reflections on service in Vietnam:

Regarding security—we recognized that we were potential targets if the Viet Cong decided to attack Americans on the street or in cars. The roads outside Saigon were now mostly paved and thus less susceptible to buried mines, but still they often passed through areas dominated by the VC. Helicopters were vulnerable to gunfire. The embassy had been attacked during the Tet Offensive and the defensive walls breached. I was issued a Colt .45 pistol, which I carried when traveling but seldom took it out, let alone used it.

Still, while mindful of the many dangers, most of us did not dwell on our vulnerabilities and focused on our jobs.

Colleagues and I were not averse to fun outings. A favorite was a Sunday visit to Tay Ninh Province to visit the Cao Dai Church. The religion is a blend of religions and local Tay Ninh beliefs. Victor Hugo, Sun Yat-sen, and Jesus Christ were considered saints. The church itself was beautiful and colorfully painted. It welcomed visitors to observe from the balconies. The associated vegetarian restaurant was among the best we ever found. We were aware that danger lurked as we made the trip. The road passed by Nui Ba Den, Black Virgin Mountain, which had been the scene of pitched battles. One took place the year before when on May 13, 1968, the Viet Cong attacked and killed twenty-one American soldiers manning facilities on the summit. Sobering.

Overall, the security situation seemed good enough that I proposed to invite my sister, Linda, to visit. She was graduating from Washington College in 1970, and a visit to Saigon and then Bangkok would be a great graduation present. She was enthusiastic and our parents gave their approval. She enjoyed Saigon and then went on to Bangkok to visit and stay with a foreign service friend. The time in Thailand went so well that she ended up staying for a year, finding a job, and meeting her future husband, Bill Boudra, who was in the Peace Corps. That was a consequential trip for her, both in the learning about the world and in meeting Bill!

"In Country"—Southeast Asia Travel (and Elsewhere)

Travel in the region was one highlight of my assignment to Vietnam. Visiting other countries was a relief from the pressures of daily work in Vietnam. I came to love Southeast Asia's wonderfully diverse peoples, histories, and cultures. It was a photographer's paradise.

I made it to Thailand several times visiting not only vibrant Bangkok but both the north and south. Friends there were always welcoming.

I also made it to Laos and wonderfully peaceful Luang Prabang during war. It is now a United Nations Educational, Scientific, and Cultural Organization (UNESCO) World Heritage site. The Buddhist temple on the hill in town at sunset was special. One of my favorite photos was of three monks watching the sunset from the top of the hill. I recalled in the 1950s being fascinated with the war in Laos and the Pathet Lao insurgents. Such a different and unique part of the world. That was before the Indochinese war shifted big time to Vietnam but still continued throughout Southeast Asia.

I was in Burma for a week to visit Rangoon, Mandalay, and Pagan. Two-plus days in Pagan, an ancient capital, were exhilarating. The Ananda temple, with its blinding white paint, was a favorite. Serendipitously, I met up with a National Geographic writer, Bill Garrett, and tagged along as the government opened one temple after another. My photographic passions were stimulated as never before. The March 1971 issue of *National Geographic* contains the article and pictures from that Garrett visit.

Mandalay was a sleepy, interesting town. Signs of British colonialism were everywhere. Curious school children who had seen few foreigners followed me much of the day. I kept thinking of the Rudyard Kipling poem expressing his longing for the East, "On the Road to Mandalay." An excerpt:

*If you've heard the East a-callin', you won't never need naught
else.
No! you won't need nothin' else,
But them spicy garlic smells,
An' the sunshine an' the palm-trees an' the tinkly temple-bells;
On the road to Mandalay, where the flying fishes play and
The dawn comes up like thunder outer China 'crost the bay.*

I love the last line with the image of a thunderous dawn, which also conjures up a mysterious civilization just beyond the water and the mountains. Several years later we came face-to-face with that new (to us) land.

As with Angkor in Cambodia, and Pagan in Burma, ancient civilizations had created magnificent cities and temples/buildings. And yet how many of us ever really learn about them today? A real defect of current society is that too many of us are so self-centered or ethnocentric when it comes to "today" that we do not appreciate others' achievements. And what should it say to us that great civilizations and societies always have had finite lifespans? How long will ours be? And the critical question: how can we successfully grapple with our current challenges in order to extend that lifespan?

Singapore was often a stop, with its efficiency, carpark food stalls, multiethnic society, and magnificent Raffles Hotel. I lingered over breakfast and lunch every day imagining English writer Somerset Maugham still writing in the garden. And the Singapore slings invented there still flowed freely.

Malaysia held lots of appeal. I was particularly taken with Malacca. When I visited it still had the feel of a quiet, sedate town with lots of history. The obvious confluence of Malay, Indian, British, and other peoples was clearly visible and attractive.

Bali in Indonesia was and remains my favorite. In 1970, there were few foreign visitors. The people were wonderfully friendly; and the arts and culture of dance, music, painting, and carving were mesmerizing. Several of my favorite paintings and carvings are from Bali. My favorite dance was Ketjak and its pulsing rhythms. Renting a motorbike allowed me to traverse the island—highlands and coast. The various temples were exceptional. My favorite spot was just off the coast, Tanah Lot.

I loved the small villages and towns of Bali, which offered a particularly soothing respite from the war and Saigon city living.

Another visit to Indonesia with a friend was by train from Jakarta to Jogjakarta to visit the Borobudur (Buddhist) and Prambanan (Hindu) temples/monuments and the vibrant *batik* textile industry. We had an eye-opening view of the people and countryside as we traveled from Jogjakarta to Bali by local bus.

My final days in Vietnam allowed me to take a few days off and, with a couple friends, visit Nepal. I had always wanted to see the Himalayas. I love mountains and the distant views one has after an arduous climb. Time only allowed a visit to Katmandu and the immediate environs; still, it was a memorable visit walking the interesting streets of the city (lots of garlic and cannabis!). We rented a car with driver and drove several hours to the Nepalese border with China. The road was dicey; it was under construction by Chinese workers, with steep and frightening drop-offs to the river below. Reaching the border, we got out to look across into China. The next thing we knew the Chinese guards were yelling and gesturing at us. Our driver hustled us back into the car and explained that the Chinese were nervous about seldom-seen foreigners and wanted us to leave. Not the warm welcome China traditionally extends to visitors.

We made it back to the Yak and Yeti Hotel in Katmandu, safely navigating the boulders and construction bulldozers. In Katmandu, we found a store selling Chinese ping pong balls and paddles. Entranced with the April 1971 visit of U.S. ping pong players to China, the first official delegation since 1949, we bought several boxes, breaking the U.S. trade embargo but providing among the earliest increases in trade between two deeply estranged countries.

From Nepal, it was back to Saigon for farewells and then time to take on Washington, DC, and the Department of State.

Little did I imagine that twenty-seven years later, the Mueller family would visit Tibet and the Mount Everest base camp just on the other side of the highest mountain in the world.

"In Country"—The Vietnam War from the American Perspective: A Deadly Endeavor and Strategic Failure; My Views on Vietnam and the United States

Over the years I read everything I could on Vietnam and the United States, both before and after I served there. I talked with everyone I could find—people who knew the country intimately and those who knew it from a distance.

My views gradually shifted. In high school I had read avidly about Indochina and growing U.S. involvement. In college I was mildly agnostic on U.S. strategies. In summer 1965, I was alarmed when President Johnson announced a huge increase in the U.S. troop presence. The war and the draft came closer. Dark humor on campus was that if one became an officer, the highest rate of death and wounding was among first and second lieutenants who led platoons on the front lines.

At the embassy in Canberra, as mentioned earlier, although appalled at the scale of the violence and death, I was hopeful there might be some reasonable outcome. I was mindful of the Cold War imperative of confronting the Soviet Union (and China) and Communism. The Cold War was an existential challenge for the United States.

In Saigon, as I became more deeply immersed in the conflict, my perspective changed. While keeping my views "in channels" and not contemplating resigning, I could see that our involvement truly was mired in quicksand. We were accomplishing neither what we wanted nor what the establishment claimed the progress to be. The price Americans, Vietnamese, and others were paying was horrendous. And yet there was no easy way out.

Nixon scared me. He was dark in his views of the world and dangerously capable of escalating military actions. Operation Lam Son across the Vietnamese border into Laos in February 1971 was designed to block the "Ho Chi Minh" trail, down which North Vietnam sent huge numbers of troops and equipment into the South. The operation widened the war and did not achieve its objective. Later, the so-called "Christmas bombing" of Hanoi on December 18, 1972, involving 129 fully loaded B-52s was to show the North Vietnamese they could not win and needed to return to the Paris peace talks. They did come back. But in the end, they did win.

After the Paris Peace Accords were signed in January 1973, many of us thought the real goal was a reduction in military activity for a "decent interval" before the inevitable North Vietnamese takeover of the South. Several dozen FSOs who spoke Vietnamese and served in country were mobilized for a seven-month tour to observe and report on implementation of the agreements.

Nothing I saw or heard in-country during those months of 1973 as I served a temporary assignment in the Vietnam highlands of Kon Tum changed my mind about the folly of our endeavor. It has pained me for years to see what our involvement has wrought. We did the honorable thing by taking in a million Indochinese refugees. In the years after 1975 we gradually recovered, as did Vietnam. Both countries suffered beyond measure. Our relationship now is gradually warming as China's increasing pressure on Vietnam in the South China Sea recalls its centuries-long colonial control of Vietnam. The Vietnamese to this day have no real love for China.

Here are some of the reasons I became a critic of the U.S. involvement in Indochina:

—Using large unit military operations and large-scale, often indiscriminate bombing; B-52 bombing runs during Operation Arc Light were often heard in the environs of Saigon; the bombing and big unit operations created millions of sympathizers for the North and the Viet Cong.

—Believing that winning hearts and minds was fine, but that the better approach was, "Grab 'em by the balls and their hearts and minds will follow." Wrong. While the squeamish might cringe at the language, it was a factual mantra of proponents of striking hard.

—Believing that American knowledge and efforts could replace Vietnamese efforts to build a new society, economy, and democratic government. They could not. South Vietnamese leaders needed to be the ones to inspire their people to believe in their future and to do the necessary building.

—Creating the Phoenix program to identify, capture, and often kill supposed Vietnamese supporters of the Viet Cong. Often it seemed out of control.

—Tolerating widespread corruption that weakened every institution and unit.

—Believing that having won World War II, we could win in Vietnam because we had endless resources to pour in, starting with people and endless casualties.

—Misreading history and not appreciating the huge antagonisms the Vietnamese still held against the Chinese for hundreds of years of colonialism. North Vietnam had no desire to again be dominated by China; they took Chinese aid out of necessity. Ho Chi Minh after World War II might have made a peace with the United States, but we supported the French return to their beloved colony and arguably lost an opportunity to create at least a semi-stable relationship with a united Vietnam.

—Allowing U.S. politics and anti-Communist fever in Washington to be the most important driver of decisions on Vietnam. Presidents Eisenhower, Kennedy, Johnson, and Nixon all wanted to avoid being tagged with "Who lost Vietnam?" Memories of "Who lost China?" were fresh. Our politics drove us deeper and deeper into the horrendous quagmire.

A great many South Vietnamese had no desire to be "reunited" with the North. They understood the Communist system was authoritarian and top-down. They would lose a lot. I do not blame them. Still, corruption, bad leadership, and the weight of history were just too much.

The United States believed it had good intentions when it escalated its involvement, even though they were built on the Johnson administration's dissembling about North Vietnamese attacks on U.S. Navy ships in the Gulf of Tonkin. We were spending endless resources and blood, to no avail. Could we have done things differently? Possibly. Would they have worked? Unlikely, even with the best intentions and will in the world.

One insight of utmost importance I learned in Vietnam: other countries and societies *must* ultimately be the builders of their own societies based on their own histories and values. Often, the United States can help in a careful, supportive role. But we cannot take the lead and try to guide others in ways that do not work for them.

Did we learn that lesson in our invasion of Iraq in 2003? In our embrace of Afghanistan since 2001? Simply put, the answer is "No." Hubris, grandiosity, and domestic politics led us into those quagmires and supported open-ended involvement. Our country has been left weaker, more indebted, more skeptical, and more cynical. And in the eyes of our friends around the world, it helped to tarnish the values and democratic institutions that we love and can be so appealing to others. It has also soured the American people about our involvement in other countries, and in 2016 helped to open the door to potentially dangerous presidential decisions as Trump took office.

An engaged, cooperative United States can and should work with others for a better world. Guns and money alone will seldom take us where we need to go. Creative foreign policies, supportive allies on the ground and around the world, and solid "staying power" with the right—and often modest—objectives are much more likely to be the way to go. I believe many in the United States and abroad still welcome such a role. Let our light shine from our city on a hill! But going it alone or only in the way we see things will not be successful.

The State Department's Seventh Floor—The Secretary of State's Executive Secretariat, Operations Center, and Secretariat Staff 1971–1973

"Back in the world" was quite a change of scene from Vietnam to Nepal to Washington, DC, and then the top floor of the Department of State. The "seventh floor" housed the top officials of the Department and was often seen as the epicenter of power. The Executive Secretariat served the secretary of state and other officials for two important functions: one was supporting decision making and a robust information flow and the other was to serve the critical coordination function within the State Department and, importantly, throughout the government.

How did I manage to be selected for an assignment on the seventh floor? I believe it was partly because I took the initiative one Saturday in Saigon to manage a potentially explosive confrontation between a crowd of Vietnamese and our Marine security guard.

As I exited the building, I heard yelling and the sound of a vehicle crash. It turned out that a Vietnamese woman on a motorcycle had fallen off and was screaming at the Marine at the entrance for having caused the accident. While the Marine said he had in no way interfered with her, a crowd grew quickly and began yelling at and threatening the Marine. I went over to talk with her (in Vietnamese) and the Marine and then told the crowd we would take the lady to see a doctor and help with her motorcycle.

Fortunately, the crowd began to melt away as we entered the embassy compound and headed for the health unit. I explained to the doctor on duty what had happened and asked him to examine the woman for any injuries. The lady consented to the exam. Thank goodness her injuries were superficial. She was feeling better and admitted she had lost control of her bike before she even saw the Marine. I was able to get an embassy vehicle and driver to take her home.

I subsequently wrote up a detailed memo on what had happened and received a commendation from Ambassador Bunker for having taken the initiative to deal with a situation of potential injury and subsequent threat to a Marine and the embassy.

When the State Department later asked for ambassadorial recom-mendations for officers to serve in the Executive Secretariat, Ambassador Bunker and his staff recommended me for my initiative and leadership.

Now the stakes for me were even higher in the Operations Center. (S/S-O in State Department-lingo: S = secretary of state and meaning we were part of his office; S/S = the Executive Secretariat; and O = the Operations Center.)

The Operations Center, "Op Center," was staffed 24/7 by a senior watch officer and a deputy, an editor who summarized important incoming information, and representatives from the military and intelligence communities. We monitored worldwide developments and provided alerts and situation reports to the Secretary, assisted top State Department officials, helped American citizens, coordinated with government agencies, managed crisis task forces set up on the seventh floor, and generally served as the eyes and ears of the secretary.

I served for seven months in the Op Center. It was hell on one's personal life, but fascinating and adrenaline-filled. Often when someone couldn't solve an urgent problem, they turned to the Op Center. The most poignant moment I recall was when a telegram came in from Embassy Beirut reporting the death in an automobile accident of the president of the American University. I was stunned. What a coincidence. His daughter was the girlfriend I dated for almost three years while at William and Mary.

At an entirely different level, a most consequential moment came when we were notified that Henry Kissinger, national security advisor who was on a visit to Pakistan, was indisposed and would rest for a day or two. Then, secretly, he flew to Beijing for discussions July 9–11, 1971. Those talks led to the historic agreement that President Nixon would visit China in February 1972. The news was a bombshell in the United States. We had been in confrontational, enemy mode with China for decades.

For several months I was detailed to the Pentagon to be the State Department representative to the National Military Command Center. It was another fascinating set of insights about one of the military's primary command or operations centers. State had several dozen people assigned to our Ops Center; the National Military Command Center (NMCC) had many hundreds assigned to theirs.

One memorable night on duty was watching Air Force One land in Beijing live with all my military colleagues on February 21, 1972. It was snowing lightly, and many workers were out sweeping the snow with brooms.

We were all transfixed as the First Lady and President Nixon walked down the stairs to set foot on "enemy" soil. I was startled when a full colonel in the NMCC yelled out, "What do we do if they grab him?" (That is word for word what he said.) My reaction? What?? That would not happen. What would they do with him? Hold him for ransom? Were they prepared for armed confrontation? None of that would make any sense. They have much bigger goals with the United States than grabbing a president, like countering the heavy Soviet Union pressure on China. But the colonel was not persuaded: But what do we do *if* the ChiComs (common terminology for Chinese Communists) do hold him for ransom?!

Much of my remaining time at the NMCC was focused on North Vietnam's Easter offense, extending from spring, to summer, to fall. The North threw much of its regular army and military hardware at the South, attacking from the north across the DMZ and from the west and south. They took land and destroyed entire Army of the Republic of Vietnam (ARVN) units. Heavy, continued bombing by the United States and ARVN pushback ultimately stopped the offensive and kept the North out of the city of Kon Tum in II Corps (Military Region II). Both sides took huge losses. John Paul Vann directed much of the ARVN pushback. Sadly, he was killed in a helicopter crash just south of Kon Tum on June 9, 1972. He and the entire Vietnam War are immortalized in Neil Sheehan's magnificent history, *A Bright Shining Lie: John Paul Vann and America in Vietnam.* One of my favorite books of all-time. Sheehan is also an alumnus of Northfield Mount Hermon School.

Little could I imagine that only months after Kon Tum was successfully defended and John Paul Vann was killed that I would be in the Vietnamese Central Highlands in Kon Tum myself, reporting on current military and civilian developments.

During my assignment to the NMCC, I participated in one fascinating—and chilling—"doomsday exercise" designed to prepare for nuclear war. We flew by helicopter from the Department of Defense to Andrews Air Force Base outside of Washington and boarded an Air Force plane waiting at the end of the runway ready for immediate take off. The plane was designed to carry the president and senior officials out of the area and, while airborne, direct military responses. I "played" the secretary of state. A colonel "played" the president. The scenario envisaged escalating military responses. In response to Soviet attacks, the colonel as president ordered a strike on Moscow. He then proposed a strike on another country to take it out of the conflict. He asked my opinion.

I argued—persuasively, I thought—to not broaden the conflict at that stage. It was not the answer he wanted. The script obviously called for the testing of systems countering other countries. The "president" overruled his "secretary of state" and ordered the strike.

After our day-long "war," we landed back at Andrews, and I headed home. With still-vivid memories of the destruction of World War II in Germany in the 1950s and my recent service in war-torn Vietnam, I was deeply unsettled by the day's vast destruction, even though for national security reasons, directed by us from our airborne command post.

I headed back to the State Department at the end of my NMCC duty and moved to the sister office of the Operations Center: the Staff Secretariat, Office of the Secretary of State (S/S-S). I was fortunate to be chosen by Ambassador Nick Platt for what was called the "line." (State Department lore suggests the name came from the fact that the offices were lined up along the corridor opposite the secretary's office.) It was a great job for learning up-close how the State Department operated and how foreign policy is made.

Ambassador Nick Platt, almost more than anyone else in the Foreign Service, was a great mentor and friend. He had become a China hand and served early on at the U.S. Liaison Office (USLO) in Beijing in the early 1970s. He later encouraged me to go for the two-year Chinese language training program. He and his wife, Sheila, supported us while in Beijing and in Yokosuka awaiting Jonathan's birth. Stay tuned for other important times his support and friendship influenced my career.

The Secretariat Staff was a coordinating, tasking, and reviewing office. We would work with bureaus to prepare position and background papers for the secretary and other officials, work with the bureaus, and then review them for relevancy and accuracy. We were responsible for ensuring relevant offices had opportunities to voice their views and not let other bureaus do end-runs around each other. Everything was designed to get the best information and policy options to the secretary of state.

The other major responsibility was to prepare and staff the secretary's trips overseas. The staff of our office carried a significant responsibility to work with the bureaus, the White House, and other agencies on policy focuses and itineraries for the trip and coordinate all the people and material. Advance teams would go out ahead, set up office in the relevant embassies, and serve the organizing and coordinating function. One team of an officer, an administrative assistant, and one of the two deputy executive secretaries always traveled on the secretary's plane to ensure good staffing and coordination. This requirement for good staffing became a major focus, since most secretaries after Secretary of State William Rogers began to do ever more and longer trips.

I loved the camaraderie in the office and how new tasks and assignments would pop up with no notice. My first big trip was to New York City in September 1972 for the United Nations General Assembly. Traditionally, the secretary of state would spend many days meeting with dozens of foreign leaders and hosting lunches and dinners. The preparations began in the summer and were extensive: for every meeting we needed background papers, policy issues, and talking points—all coordinated and "cleared" by relevant bureaus and often the NSC staff. But the effort was generally well worthwhile since the secretary was able to efficiently engage in many wide-ranging diplomatic issues. Secretary Shultz later called those his "dental office" meetings, where the revolving door gave him a chance to meet many visiting foreign ministers and presidents.

That fall the word came down that progress was being made in the Paris Peace talks. Kissinger had been negotiating for months and felt he was getting close. Then the State Department did something creative. It tapped several dozen officers who spoke Vietnamese and had experience in-country to prepare to return to Vietnam for temporary duty. We would fan out around the country to observe and report on the ceasefire and implementation of the provisions of the accords. We would be on our way in November or December. Many issues still needed to be addressed to ensure the viability and success of the program. Parker Borg (who was working for the director general of the State Department and was responsible for the program) and I spent the waiting time arguing for more clarity on the objectives and administrative mechanics of this new program.

Some officers, with or without families, pushed to be excused from the assignment. I was fine with the assignment since I was still single, and the seven months would be an interesting challenge. Besides, the secretary felt his office needed to show it was supportive by letting one of his officers participate.

I accompanied Secretary Kissinger on a quick trip to Belgium in December for a North Atlantic Treaty Organization (NATO) ministerial meeting. Then back to Washington to await the outcome of the peace negotiations.

The North Vietnamese then pulled back from the negotiations, angering Nixon, who ordered the B-52 "Christmas bombing" around Hanoi.

Many Americans protested. Kissinger and the Vietnamese returned to the negotiating table in January 1973 and the deal was done on January 27, 1973.

I was on a plane immediately thereafter headed back to Vietnam, a year and a half after finishing my first assignment. It was with a sense of anticipation and even excitement about contributing to a major foreign policy initiative and putting an end to America's *other* "long national nightmare," President Gerald Ford's apt description of Nixon's illegalities and forced departure from the presidency.

Time Out for Seven Months Service in Vietnam, Again—1973

I landed in Saigon and soon was struck that superficially, it did not seem to have changed much in my year and a half absence. But it became clear that the heavy 1972 North Vietnamese military attacks—the so-called Easter offensive, which also tried to take Kon Tum City where I was headed—combined with the signing of the Paris accords were weighing on everyone. While hopeful for peace, among the Vietnamese I knew there was a general disbelief that the North would ever give up its reunification efforts via military and/or political means.

After briefings at the embassy, I flew up to the new consulate general in Nha Trang on the coast established to oversee II Corps and the Central Highlands, headed by Consul General Jim Engle. Consulates general were also created in I, III, and IV Corps. I reported to the consul general, who in turn reported to the ambassador in Saigon.

Jim, I, and others heading to their respective provinces discussed our mission and expectations, namely, to seek out information about ongoing developments and trends, particularly related to implementation of the Paris accords. A focus on military and political activity was a priority. It was the traditional role of the Foreign Service even in such a unique setting: acquire information, analyze it, connect the dots necessary for understanding, and report to the State Department. Our reports would inform not only the State Department but also the White House as to the course of a critical national security issue.

I knew it would be a challenge but felt I was up to it. In retrospect, there were three phases of activity in the province during my months there: for the first weeks, fighting continued between the two sides positioning for the future; for the next months, there was a ceasefire and a variety of interaction between both forces; and in my last weeks, both sides went back to skirmishing and fighting.

I set about meeting as many Vietnamese as possible who might have insights into the current and developing situation. An important relationship was with Brigadier General (BGEN) Tran Van Cam, commanding officer of the 23rd ARVN Division headquartered in Kon Tum. The last of his American military advisors had left and only one United States Agency for International Development (USAID) officer and I were stationed in Kon Tum. It was clear Cam saw me as his only direct link to the U.S. government. He invited me to join his twice daily operational briefings, which reviewed military and other developments. My reports of military activity in the Central Highlands, including as seen by him and his staff, turned out to be an important and only real source of information available to the United States.

BGEN Cam regularly shared with me his insights. At one point he asked me to come over and excitedly showed me a letter he had received from one of his North Vietnamese counterparts to the west. It proposed talks about such things as a ceasefire, lines of demarcation separating forces, and exchange of prisoners. He let me keep it overnight so I could translate it and then send the text the next day to the consulate general and embassy. The letter drew considerable attention in Washington. (Here's a great example of the importance of language training.)

Around the same time word spread that Viet Cong and North Vietnamese forces had appeared to the west of a river close to Kon Tum City. They obviously wanted to send a message that they controlled that territory.

I decided to drive out, with a Vietnamese colleague and interpreter, to see what was happening. We walked up to the edge of the stream and, sure enough, troops and equipment were camped on the other side, no more than perhaps twenty yards away. Suddenly, a Vietnamese voice from the other side called out to my colleague to ask who I was and what I was doing there. My colleague said I was an American diplomat interested in developments in Kon Tum. I decided to enter the conversation in Vietnamese and explained that the American and North Vietnamese governments had signed agreements in Paris agreeing to a ceasefire and then other measures leading to peace. I was there to see how those agreements were being implemented and to further encourage them. My interlocutor acknowledged my task and made it clear his colleagues were in control of that area and of course were in favor of a ceasefire.

My report of the encounter and subsequent dispatches, I learned, caused quite a stir in Saigon and in Washington. For the State Department, Henry Kissinger, and the White House it could be a sign that some aspects of the peace accords were being implemented. A small sign perhaps, but still potentially positive.

In the following days, we continued to learn of discussions between the two sides. BGEN Cam kept me informed of his exchanges with the other side. Lines of demarcation were discussed, some prisoners were exchanged, and the ceasefire held. It was an unexpected scene, but the question remained: would it continue, or would longstanding suspicions harden and undermine the tentative moves at de-escalation?

I also stayed in touch with a wide variety of people, such as the province chief, government officials, businesspeople, and the Montagnard community in the area. Dom D'Antonio, the USAID representative, was extremely helpful since he knew the area. We were the only American officials in the province. Informal lunches and dinners were good opportunities to ask questions and gather insights. The Montagnards, so-called by the French, were natives of the area; many had served with the U.S. military. Sadly, many Vietnamese looked down on them. They knew Kon Tum and the Central Highlands well. Their gatherings were always fun and marked by generous quantities of liquor drunk through a straw from a large ceramic pot. Roasted dog meat was a staple of such occasions.

My daily routine was to write in the evening and early morning, in longhand, and then head to the airport for the periodic flight of an Air America C-47 that dropped off supplies and took back mail. No typewriter, word processor, nor internet. Old school. The consulate general in Nha Trang would put my reports into cable form and send them to Washington and the embassy.

Periodically I would hop on the plane and spend a day in Nha Trang catching up and enjoying fresh lobster. I found Jim Engle, Parker Borg, Dick Teare, David Passage, Lange Schermerhorn, Jim Mack, Sheldon Krebs, Jim Nach, and so many other colleagues over the years extraordinarily capable and dedicated to ferreting out and analyzing information that would help the embassy and the Washington community put together a good picture of trends throughout the country.

I also periodically drove to Pleiku, just south of Kon Tum, to understand the latest from regional governmental bodies and to visit with my old friend, Parker Borg, who was reporting on regional political and military developments. The drive took me directly past the crash site of John Paul Vann's helicopter from the previous June. Vann was the leader who by all accounts spurred United States and Vietnamese forces to blunt the North Vietnamese offensive. I always slowed down to tip my hat to him. Neil Sheehan's brilliant biography of Vann, *A Bright Shining Lie: John Paul Vann and America in Vietnam,* that I mentioned earlier contains some of the most insightful commentaries on U.S. involvement in Vietnam. For compelling insights into the brutal ground war GIs faced and the resulting fog of war, one should read *Matterhorn: A Novel of the Vietnam War* by retired Marine Colonel Karl Marlantes.

Vann's crash site was a sobering reminder that helicopters could be dangerous aircraft. We lost upwards of five thousand in Vietnam over the years, both to enemy gunfire and operational problems. It's only one example of the astounding waste of resources, particularly people. But I admit to enjoying riding the old Hueys. One maneuver was teeth-rattling. I flew up to a northern outpost, Dac To, the scene of vicious fighting the previous year. Because of possible enemy units still in the area, the pilot flew directly over the outpost, sharply banked the chopper, and spiraled down like a corkscrew at breathtaking speed. It was better than any amusement park roller coaster, and it got us there in one piece.

I need to record the most gut-wrenching experience of my life. One morning I was asked to go urgently to government headquarters. The province chief told me he wanted to show me something that happened overnight. We arrived at a village and saw a crowd surrounding a small, dark object on the ground. They explained it was the body of a small child killed by an incoming North Vietnamese artillery round during the night. The body was badly burned, but one could tell it was a child. The mother was beside herself with grief and demanded that I do something.

What could I possibly do other than say repeatedly how sorry I was, which of course counted for nothing? How unjust it was. I promised I would report to higher authorities and ask that they publicize the death of an innocent child caused by an unprovoked attack by the North Vietnamese on a civilian village.

That one small child has ever since epitomized for me the millions of people—Vietnamese, North and South; Americans; Lao; Thai; Korean; Australian; and many others—killed and injured in Southeast Asia over many decades. There is much blame to be shared. Too often, children and women are the victims of revolutions and decisions of far-off leaders who neither know nor care what they have wrought.

I will never forget a poster from that era that conveyed both hope and hopelessness: *"Suppose they gave a war and nobody came?"*

Another story. One day I received an urgent message that an otherwise unidentified U.S. aircraft had made an emergency landing at the Kon Tum airstrip. When I made it to the airport, I found the American crew surrounding the plane and warning away the sizeable crowd drawn to see the unusual sight. It turned out to be a U.S. military plane that developed mechanical problems while carrying out communications activities across the border in Laos. Kon Tum was the closest airstrip to set down. Because of the classified nature of the equipment on board, the crew was understandably nervous. They were relieved to see me, an American official, who could help them.

We radioed the authorities with a situation report and then waited for a maintenance team. We put the crew up for several nights in our compound and lugged as much of the equipment as possible from the plane to safe-keeping. Finally, after making repairs, the greatly relieved crew waved farewell and headed back to their base in Thailand. They were fortunate to have found a safe haven in Kon Tum as opposed to crash-landing in the jungles or into the arms of the North Vietnamese.

Here's an insight into international diplomacy and the International Commission for Control and Supervision (ICCS) which was agreed on as part of the Paris accords. It was designed to supervise the ceasefire, help implement the accords, and monitor importation of armaments. Canada, Indonesia, Hungary, and Poland were members, two non-Communist countries and two Communist. According to official figures by the end of July, they recorded eighteen thousand ceasefire violations and seventy-six thousand Killed in Action, Wounded in Action, and Missing in Action.

So much for the negotiators in Paris who devised this ICCS fig leaf to beef up the accords and promote peace. Great idea, but I'm sure they knew it would not be enough.

In Kon Tum, we kept in touch with the ICCS team, provided information, and in turn reported what they were seeing. Did they in any way serve as a restraint on the two sides? No. The Vietnamese government tried to keep tabs on where they traveled. At one point the Canadian and Indonesian representatives had a heart: the Vietnamese policeman assigned to follow them on his motor bike kept falling behind, so they generously told him to just come ride with them wherever they went.

So much for the diplomacy in Paris. It reminds us that international organizations such as the United Nations have limited powers in their own right; they depend on member states to act in concert with them and each other.

Will the world's nations someday empower an international peace-keeping body that has military, political, and economic powers to enforce transgressions? Sadly, it seems unlikely given the existing vast range of nations, leaders, cultures, political systems (democratic and authoritarian), ideologies and personalities. Arms and weapons technologies continue to increase in numbers and sophistication, em-powering even the lowliest of tin pot dictators. In the meantime, hu-mankind is held hostage and decimated around the globe.

But I do still have a nice souvenir scrapbook of pictures put together by the Indonesian representative to the ICCS in Kon Tum as a going away gift!

As an Easter weekend road trip, Parker Borg and I decided to drive to Saigon and back. The roads were all paved and there was no security alert. We went via Qui Nhon, Nha Trang and south to Saigon, then back via Dalat and Pleiku. No untoward events along the way, just a chance to see more of the rural areas of Vietnam, Vietnamese people and water buffalos, and catch up with friends. A thought: on a trip like that today we would take satellite phones and have a heavily armed security detail that warned people away. Maybe even a helicopter hovering overhead. In 1973 there was no such thing as a mobile phone or any other way to communicate if there were problems. We were out of touch with the embassy and "alone" with the Vietnamese people. It was fully "liberating."

In my last weeks in Kon Tum in July, military action again picked up as it had around the country. The ceasefire was over. As best I understood, President Thieu became skittish at the local accommodations going on and as the other side kept probing and weakening the South's resolve. I followed the action by attending the general's twice daily operational briefings and venturing toward front lines to observe directly.

Before I left, the North Vietnamese Army began firing artillery rounds toward the South Vietnamese military base just a few yards across a small river from our compound. The explosions brought home how dangerous the security situation was. While none hit us, the closeness of the war did concentrate my attention. I had my .45 Colt pistol. It provided no comfort. I was an easy target if anyone wanted me gone.

As I prepared to bid farewell in July, I asked myself whether I had lived up to my own expectations for meeting the challenges of the assignment. I gave myself a passing grade and knew my colleagues and I contributed to a better understanding of the situation on the ground. That had been the hope of the State Department in creating the temporary program using experienced diplomats to address critical national security issues. It was one of the more creative programs designed by the State Department to meet a specific need, and it depended on having experienced, trained diplomats who knew the culture and language. It showed what the Foreign Service can do better than anyone else.

At the same time, I was deeply saddened that although there perhaps had been some progress, most of the systemic and deep-seated problems I had previously seen were still there: debilitating corruption; continuing lack of sufficient political unity and determination on the part of the South Vietnamese; and the continued push by the North Vietnamese to use main force military units—forget guerrilla warfare—to eventually re-unite the country on their terms. There was no American will left to re-engage in a large-scale defense as we had in 1972; the American people had already given their all.

There are some Americans whose later writings suggested the South was on the cusp of being able to resist successfully if only the United States had maintained our commitment a while longer. I wish it had been true. It was not.

Everyone—Vietnamese (North and South), Americans, other countries who sent troops—all paid an extraordinary price in Indochina over many years, but only North Vietnam's senior leaders—who for decades relentlessly spilled their countrymen's blood—came out a winner. Ho Chi Minh had his own reward: a city formerly known as Saigon adopted Ho's name, and he received the honor of embalming and display to the public in a mausoleum in Hanoi.

I grieved two years later in 1975 for Vietnamese acquaintances and all the Southerners who bore the brunt of the brutal North Vietnamese invasion of the South and for years after suffered the imposition of draconian policies and an authoritarian Communist system.

The end of the Republic of Vietnam, as the North Vietnamese military divisions swept south and finally into Saigon, was heartrending and deeply unsettling. Thousands fled in planes. Thousands fled in boats into the South China Sea where the U.S. Navy picked them up. Hundreds of thousands more fled in the following months and years.

The scenes of desperate escape kept coming. The United States stepped up to create resettlement programs and helped create more orderly processing of asylum requests in neighboring countries. We eventually accepted at least a million Indochinese refugees in the following years. I give our country credit for at least doing the honorable thing.

We cannot gloss over the fact that the Republic of Vietnam, supported by the United States—despite many laudable objectives—lost the war. The deep rifts created within our society haunt us still.

The final days of retreat in Vietnam were not orderly or organized. Fast forward to 2021, when the United States and other forces left Afghanistan with similar scenes of panic and desperation. Criticism of that withdrawal may have some merit, but its harshness is way over the top and unjustified. *Wake up, critics!* When you and your partners on the ground have a losing hand—and in this case a losing war strategy—and a President Trump who negotiated a flawed agreement and did not react when the Taliban kept violating it, combined with the Afghan president fleeing the country to save his skin, do not expect to turn it into a winning hand in the final days. More than one hundred thousand Afghans were airlifted out at the end, an amazing feat that deserves commendation. Am I sick over the Taliban's treatment of women and girls, ending education for them and again relegating them to a veiled and marginalized existence? Am I sick about the overall imposition of a tyrannical regime that has no desire to liberate the creativity and talents of the Afghan people? Absolutely.

But did we at least learn the right lessons in Vietnam to help guide our future foreign policy? To me the answer is clearly and frighteningly: no! In particular, we have not learned well how to use our huge pool of resources in a targeted and sensitive way to support another country or government experiencing internal rifts and instability. We can support but cannot create cohesive and stable societies and governments. And when we do try, we often become the target as a hated colonial or occupying power. Among others, witness our involvement in Iraq and Afghanistan and our intervention in Libya and the continued quagmires in all of them.

I will save for another forum my invective for those of our leaders who so ignorantly and tragically, and often for political considerations, did not understand the lessons of history. They convinced themselves they were serving a noble cause, but in the process, they sacrificed so many lives, military and civilian, and squandered so much treasure. Many of them, I believe, later personally suffered depression and deep regret for their actions. Lyndon Johnson, Director of Central Intelligence William Colby, Secretary of Defense Robert McNamara, General William West-moreland? Who else? Still, I can't help regarding many of their decisions as unfounded, even though I recognize they justified them on the basis of a broader view of our national security. They also mistakenly believed that battalions of troops and special operations forces can intervene successfully to resolve another country's internal conflicts and divisions. I have great respect for the men and women of our military and other national security organizations. I have worked with many of them over my careers. Still, the fundamental truth is that our political leaders should be far more restrained and sober-minded in how and when they call them to action.

On a personal level, in the fall of 1973, I was honored to be chosen by an independent committee to receive the State Department's coveted annual Director General's Award for Reporting. The citation recorded my ability, based on my experience and understanding of Vietnam, to seek out information on significant developments and provide analysis and insights on a real time basis to guide senior policy makers in Washington, all at the risk of my own personal safety. This was the real foreign service ideal: understanding, analyzing, and writing about other countries and providing practical and actionable information to those making our foreign policy decisions.

I was the most junior FSO to receive the award and was blown away by the number of positive and congratulatory responses I received. It also gained the attention of one of the newest employees in the secretary's office, Claire McCormick, who on March 15, 1975, became Claire McCormick Mueller. It was a match made in heaven—and in the office of the Secretary of State!

I was only a few years out of college, but I felt much older. Or at least much more experienced and maybe a bit wiser.

A coda: I have returned numerous times to Vietnam since 1973, both South and North, both as a diplomat and as an educator attending conferences at schools in Hanoi and Saigon (such as Saigon South and United Nations International School in Hanoi). I'm glad to see economic development, a bustling Saigon and south Vietnam, a mostly welcoming population for Americans and our investment and tourist dollars, and an improving official bilateral relationship. Vietnam is looking to warm its relationship with the United States as old Vietnamese-Chinese antagonisms surface. Some 80 percent of the population was born after our 1973 withdrawal, helping to explain why there is less overt hostility.

I fervently hope that the Vietnamese political system evolves in a more open and transparent way. Loosening the grip of the Communist Party and allowing more civil freedoms would help to truly unleash the potential energies and creativity of the Vietnamese people.

For so many, the "Vietnam War," "American War," and "French War" now are ancient history—except for historians who need to help us with lessons learned—as we all wrestle with new twenty-first century challenges.

For your information, anyone interested in my reporting or any reporting during this challenging period can file a Freedom of Information Act request. It should all be unclassified at this point.

The Trip Home to Washington and Then a Year with Secretary Henry Kissinger at the State Department, 1973–1974

My trip home from temporary duty in Vietnam took me to Hong Kong, Taipei, and Fairbanks, Alaska. Hong Kong was to see more of a vibrant and dynamic city and check out the usual high points of the Star Ferry, Peak Tram, Lugard Road, Kowloon, Central, and all the magnificent restaurants. Of course, it never entered my thoughts that, eventually, as a diplomat and educator, I would live there with our family three different times in the 1980s, 1990s, and 2000s.

Taipei was to visit the National Palace Museum, filled with Chinese treasures—many spirited out of China in 1948–1949. The Nationalists, on the point of defeat, fled the mainland to Taiwan to create a new capital for the Republic of China. My favorite gallery was on the top floor, decorated as if it were a traditional scholar's study for reading, writing, painting, and meditating. It had a wonderfully peaceful and intellectual feeling. I loved it and lingered for a while. I recall deciding there that I would apply for Chinese language training starting the next year.

The stop in Fairbanks was to spend time with my parents who had moved to Alaska in 1970. Dad was dean of the College of Arts and Letters at the University of Alaska after his Foreign Service career. Fortuitously, Pan Am in those days had a Tokyo-New York flight that re-fueled in Fairbanks, so I was a periodic visitor. We did some traveling around the state, and Dad and I also flew up to Fort Yukon on the Yukon River, just north of the Arctic Circle, to see a different part of the state. Over the years I visited Alaska several times and was privileged to see the beautiful, varied regions of mountains, glaciers, and forests. A national treasure.

Dad was in his element as an academic at the university in so many ways. He loved brown bag lunches with faculty members to brainstorm ideas. He was an intellectual of the highest order. I believe he picked up where he left off after his years at Cornell, focusing on the academic world and how to educate young people using his many wartime and foreign service experiences to enrich the curriculum. One of his real accomplishments was establishing a Peace Arts program. It was a cross-disciplinary academic program that dealt with issues of war and peace and how we live together successfully. Another accomplishment was embedding a deeper focus on collecting and preserving Native Alaskan languages, music, and cultures.

Dad also recognized how much the higher education academy had changed over the decades. He chafed under the pressures of bureaucratic and state politics, the push to award academic credit to students who took a remedial English course, and the pushback from faculty who wanted more time off to ride their snowmobiles.

Back to the Belly of the Beast

I returned to work in the secretary's office, the Staff Secretariat, in the middle of August 1973, just as the president announced he would appoint Henry Kissinger as secretary of state, replacing William Rogers. I was now among the most experienced "line officers" and so was asked to head up a team working with Kissinger and staff from the NSC on the transition to State.

The announcement was a jolt of energy inside the State Department. After years of watching power migrate to the White House and to Kissinger, many of us were enthused by the impending change. Could we live up to Kissinger's expectations for support of his diplomacy?

An immediate priority within the overall transition was preparation for the secretary's and president's time in New York in late September. The annual meetings of the United Nations General Assembly drew many foreign leaders. It was a golden opportunity for serious foreign policy politicking. I pulled the team together and we went into high gear with the regional and other bureaus to decide on priority issues for discussion with other leaders and produce clearly focused policy and background papers. Since Kissinger was already familiar with many issues, he made clear he wanted substantive updates without lots of specific "talking points."

We set up offices and the secretary's suite in the Waldorf Astoria and began the multi-meeting marathon days. And then suddenly on October 6, 1973, the Middle East erupted. Egypt and Syria launched massive military attacks against Israel in what came to be known as the Yom Kippur War, or the 1973 Arab-Israeli War.

We all went into crisis mode to make sure the secretary received embassy and military/intelligence/political reports he needed and kept him closely in touch with the president and many others. There are many good histories giving insights into how the war and following ceasefires played out. Suffice to say, we soon headed back to Washington where we could draw on deeper and more extensive support for the secretary.

Surely, it was an explosive start to Kissinger's tenure as secretary of state with continued crises over the coming months.

In November 1973 I accompanied the secretary on his first around the world trip, with much of it focused on peace in the Middle East in the wake of the war. We left November 5 and stopped in Morocco, Tunisia, Egypt, Saudi Arabia, Iran, Pakistan, China, Japan, and Korea.

I dropped off the China portion of the trip so he could take a smaller group to Beijing where he met with Mao Zedong and Chinese Premier Zhou Enlai.

Instead, I stopped for a few days in Saigon to see friends and take the region's temperature. Sadly, there was no discernible improvement in South Vietnam's fortunes and, if anything, continued decline in effective political and military performance. The North continued with its own unceasing efforts to destroy South Vietnamese resistance and re-unite the country.

I met up again with the traveling party in Korea and then as Kissinger headed back to the United States, I flew to Fairbanks, Alaska, for Thanksgiving with Mother and Dad. It was another opportunity to see more of the beautiful land of Alaska.

Back in the secretary's office, I heard there was a new person working in the executive secretary's office. As you know by now, it was Claire McCormick. She had already read about my Department of State Award for Reporting and the fact that I was single. She sent a note to her parents saying she was going to get to know this fellow.

It was also the beginning of the era of AC—After Claire, and I was a marked man!

In April Claire and I supported Kissinger's short visit to Mexico City after his honeymoon in Acapulco. We loved the National Museum of Anthropology. Interestingly, after this trip, the State Department launched what came to be called the Global Outlook Program (GLOP) for the Foreign Service, requiring personnel to periodically serve in geographic areas outside their areas of expertise. Kissinger professed to be unhappy that many officers did not understand his world view and what he was trying to negotiate with the Soviet Union.

I then flew south to Costa Rica for a few days to visit with friends, Jim and Sheila Mack, and to see a new part of the world. It was fun: Monte Verde Cloud Forest, Manuel Antonio National Park, volcano, a narrow-gauge railroad to the east coast to Limon where many still spoke the "King's English," and there was a Chinese-style building housing the offices of the Chinese Kuomintang.

At the end of April 1974, Claire and I were off with Kissinger to the Middle East again. It was time to resolve issues of war and peace stemming from the previous fall's war. Five weeks on the road. After visiting virtually every country in the area, we began to concentrate on Israel and Syria. Kissinger was determined to bring both countries to a durable disengagement agreement. Neither country trusted the other, so Kissinger put his own credibility and American guarantees on the line to bridge the gaps. Back and forth we flew from Jerusalem to Damascus and back again, from late April to early June.

The last week of travel Claire and I were the only S/S team left, all the others having returned home because of the seeming impossibility of reaching an agreement. It was a grinding twenty-four hours a day keeping the secretary supported and in touch with the State Department and all the other world issues needing his attention. All this took place with the backdrop of what turned out to be Nixon's final weeks as president, as the Watergate crisis reached its crescendo. Kissinger, in his memoir, lamented how a weak president was undermining negotiating positions.

Here was a typical day's schedule. After a couple overnights in Damascus with the deafening calls to prayer at 5:30 a.m., Kissinger decided he preferred to stay at the King David Hotel in Jerusalem. So we were up at "oh dark thirty" in Jerusalem for a forty-five-minute mad drive to Tel Aviv airport, a forty-five-minute flight to Damascus, a thirty-minute mad drive downtown past refugee camps, which caused security nightmares, and then hours-long meetings with Syrian President Hafez al-Assad.

Later in the day we reversed the trip to Jerusalem, where, exhausted, we began preparations for the next day's odyssey. A lighthearted moment: on May 27 we had a birthday celebration for Kissinger's fiftieth birthday.

Here is the State Department historian's record of the days in each city. It's breathtaking even with the hindsight of almost half a century.

Damascus, Syria (May 3–29, 1974)Shuttle negotiations leading to an Israeli-Syrian disengagement agreement. Kissinger was in Damascus May 3-4, 12, 14, 16-17, 18, 20, 21, 22, 23, 25, 26, 27, 28, and 29.

Jerusalem, Israel (May 4–31, 1974)Shuttle negotiations leading to an Israeli-Syrian disengagement agreement. Kissinger was in Jerusalem May 4-5, 6-7, 7-8, 8-9, 10-12, 12-14, 14-16, 17-18, 18-20, 21-22, 22-23, 23-25, 25-26, 27-28, and 29-30.

Kissinger's determination and other skills eventually prevailed on both sides to make concessions and a disengagement agreement was reached, to great acclaim. *Newsweek* decorated its cover with a picture of "Kissinger as Superman." Or "Henry the K" came to be another *sobriquet*.

Claire and I, for a while, basked in the reflected glory of having been part of the mission. Exhilarating and exhausting. But Kissinger did give us credit on page 1,072 in his memoir *Years of Upheaval*. *"The visits to each capital had by now become stylized. I would arrive by plane with my frazzled aides and the wild-eyed press contingent."* Henry Kissinger, Years of Upheaval (New York, NY: Simon & Schuster, 1982): 1,072.

The *"frazzled aides"* were us!

Later in the same volume, he wrote, *"All this time, I had as well to conduct the other business of the Department of State. Luckily it was a quiescent period . . . . Still, a calm period for a Secretary of State is a relative term. Everyday reams of cables descended on my traveling caravan requiring some sort of action. My diligent State Department staff, on the plane and in Washington kept the paper flowing in both directions. I made key decisions on a myriad of issues."*

There we were again: *"Diligent State Department staff!"*

Much later, I read the two quotes while introducing Kissinger at an Asia Society dinner in Hong Kong. I made Claire stand up to acknowledge the encomium. It drew lots of laughter, including from Kissinger.

As we flew, with the substance of the agreement in hand, Claire was typing the final text on the plane. Kissinger was hanging over her to urge her on, at which point the assistant secretary for Near Eastern Affairs said, "Mr. Secretary, she is typing as fast as it's possible!"

On the plane returning to the United States, Kissinger at one point walked down the aisle, passed the "staff," and headed directly to the traveling press to thank them for their coverage of the trip. Another one of his staff, Jerry Bremer, an old friend, stopped to tell us what a great job we had done. Claire, in her direct way, told Jerry, "You and Richard came into the Foreign Service together. You don't need to thank us. It would be nice if Kissinger stopped to say thanks."

A decade later, when serving at the consulate general in Hong Kong, Kissinger came to meet Burt Levin, the consul general. One of our colleagues, in introducing Claire, said to Kissinger that she and Richard were on the plane with him on the shuttle mission. He said, "And you're still talking to me?" Claire shot back, "Well, sir, it has been many years, and we've both mellowed!" He smiled.

Kissinger, in Brief

A few brief observations about Kissinger from my personal interactions over the years, from my S/S days in the 1970s to Hong Kong while consul general and then director of the Asia Society Hong Kong Center:

Kissinger is brilliant in many ways, an intellectual who knows his history and diplomatic practice. They often served him and the country well. He was a negotiator and problem solver who loved the high-level interaction with others to reach agreement on national security issues. Yes, he indulged in realpolitik. A hard-nosed approach designed to protect one's country in an uncertain world can be justified if based on an ethical and moral foundation.

He was rightly criticized for not sufficiently considering the economic dimensions of issues. Economic trends and forces of course play a huge role in the political sphere.

Likewise, human rights were often not a motivating factor in his decisions or worldview. His realpolitik often didn't make room for them. It would take President Jimmy Carter to make human rights a much higher priority in our foreign policy. As I have grown more experienced, now at seventy-five, I personally put a much higher importance on protecting the rights of people no matter their opinions, income levels, gender, ethnic or religious backgrounds, etc. How people are treated and taken care of, and how we do that globally, *working together,* is potentially one of the great unifying goals of humankind. It is the antidote to power for the sake of power by the narcissists and nationalists who so often strive to shape the world in their own ways—others be damned.

On China, Kissinger experienced frequent interactions with Mao Zedong, Zhou Enlai, and many others. He certainly learned a lot. I sometimes wondered how deep an understanding he had developed of China and Chinese people. China was more like a (potentially powerful) pawn on the world chessboard to him. My reading of State Department memoranda of conversations with Mao and Zhou showed both countries working to focus on uniting the United States and China against the Soviet Union. There seemed little hint that such opposition to the Soviet Union would turn out to be more tactical than strategic. Once the Soviet Union dissolved, China turned its attention not only to its own development, but to competing with the United States and then building a new alliance with Russia to counter U.S. interests.

Echoing Lord Palmerston, Kissinger said, "America has no permanent friends or enemies, only interests." The Chinese "pawn" has now grown into a far more powerful piece on the chessboard.

I hosted Kissinger for lunch on at least two occasions as consul general in Hong Kong. Just the two of us. I found that he listened more than he had in the past. He was a strong supporter of building more bridges between the United States and China. Hong Kong's future was increasingly a focus for the United States and others. I also chalked up his interest to the fact he was accompanying a private company to China and needed to be informed about Hong Kong and its pending reversion to China. But his attention span tended to be short.

When it came to Vietnam, I believe Kissinger *felt* he played out a policy approach with the bad hand he and Nixon had been dealt. Still, as I indicated above, the Nixon/Kissinger policies perpetuated the bloodshed and saw half of all American casualties come on their watch. There was far too much deception and dissembling.

Kissinger was not comfortable dealing with people he did not know. He tended to avoid them. And he wasn't a small talker, generally. It seemed there was a social-emotional deficit there. He tended to yell when frustrated, but only at people he knew, not strangers. Nancy, his wife as of March 30, 1974, was clearly a good influence. I once saw him yelling at a colleague; when he realized Nancy was nearby, he calmed down immediately. She joined the disengagement shuttle mission; we found her a welcome fellow-traveler—always friendly and polite, never demanding.

A final observation: Kissinger always had a stream of well-known visitors paying calls. Periodically, word would filter out that a particularly well-known person would be arriving—on one occasion a famous actress—and staff would take up strategic positions to catch a glimpse!

Chapter Two

Diplomacy in Beijing

Living and Working in China as a Diplomat, 1976–1978, as the Great Proletarian Cultural Revolution Gasped Its Last Breath

Simply put, those years in China were truly unique in so many ways. China was a country closed to most foreigners for so many years that it seemed we were entering another world. Studying Chinese for two full years and learning about history and culture was great preparation but the Beijing of 1976 was suffused with Communist Marxist/Leninist/Mao Zedong Thought ideology and practice.

Many Chinese traditions and practices had been deemed unacceptable, such as Confucian thought; religion; respecting parents and teachers (witness the Cultural Revolution); playing mahjong; showing interest in foreign cultures or countries; and many others. Mao Zedong was trying to create a new China.

China was just coming out of the violence and chaos of the Great Proletarian Cultural Revolution begun by Mao Zedong in 1966 to regain political power. We knew it was chaos that came on top of the Great Leap Forward, droughts, etc., but in 1976 we had no idea how bad it was in killing tens of millions and totally disrupting society. We came to understand the insights into CCP totalitarianism in Simon Ley's book, *Chinese Shadows*, and experienced its influence during our times in China over the years.

Bottom line: living and working in a city that was so removed from the rest of the world, physically and otherwise, was an enormous culture shock and required endless fortitude. That's what diplomats do to serve their country, right? At the same time there was a thrill in beginning a unique and rare adventure.

What was that adventure really like in practice?

Lend me your imagination as I describe through some of our observations of what China was like in 1976–1978.

First, what was the general atmosphere in Beijing?

Imagine:

—A slow train from Kowloon in Hong Kong to the border.

—Walking across the Lo Wu border bridge, dragging one's own luggage.

—Greeted by "Take a rest!" (the all-purpose greeting in China those days) followed by lunch and the slow train to Guangzhou (Canton), gazing at rice fields and a few communist water buffalo along the way.

—Greeted by "Take a rest" at the *Dung Fang Fan Dian*, the Dung Fang Hotel, in Guangzhou, and dinner, with the evening flight to Beijing.

—An all but deserted Beijing Capital Airport with old and minimal facilities.

—A dimly lit, deserted two-lane road from the airport to the Beijing *Fan Dian* downtown, just a short walk from Tiananmen Square.

—The entrance sign in the hotel lobby: *"Women de Peng You Bian Tian Xia"* ("We have friends all over the world.")

—Only a few cars on the streets—Hong Qi Red Flag limousines for high-ranking officials, Shanghai sedans for lower ranking officials; military-style jeeps and trucks for the military; and bicycles for everyone else.

—No vehicle headlights allowed at night—"They blind other drivers."

—Old and new drab cement block buildings, government offices, and apartment blocks.

—Huge mounds of cabbage on the sidewalks in the fall, brought from the farms by truck and dumped.

—A small group of women at night, sitting on the side of a deserted Chang An Avenue sidewalk under a streetlamp, knitting and talking.

—A small group of older men under a streetlamp, smoking—a small pleasure for many.

—Walking and bicycling through the many *hutongs* (narrow streets) where so many people lived in more traditional fashion, with few amenities.

—Numerous restrictions on where and how far you could drive—no more than a few miles from the center of the city. Police or others appeared like magic to stop you if you went astray, deliberately or not.

—A sea of cyclists on Chang An Avenue. Those traveling with the wind sailed along without exertion; those tacking into the wind pedaled with great determination. It was real people power—or pedal power.

Second, what was it like for a foreigner living in Beijing?

Imagine:

—Very few foreigners: some businesspeople, some diplomats, no tourists, only periodic "friendship" groups.

—Living inside a Chinese compound for foreigners called Chi Jia Yuan not far from the Forbidden City and Tiananmen Square. The entrance was controlled by Chinese guards. It was nice to have an elderly gentleman take you up and down in the elevator. But wait, it was an automatic elevator? He politely pushed the buttons for you! It was a form of foreigner control, and it gave him a job—and his own ups and downs every day!

—No foreign newspapers or magazines for sale; only a few Chinese publications other than *The People's Daily*, read avidly for what was said or not said between the lines. The British Broadcasting Corporation and Voice of America were important sources of news. Otherwise, we relied on mail through the diplomatic pouch.

—Crowds in Tiananmen Square, which gathered quickly around a sixteen-month-old blond, blue-eyed toddler named Jonathan Richard Mueller.

—Rearing an infant—our first, without any experience, winging it—with a baby *ahyi* (helper) who had never taken care of an infant, assigned by the full service Chinese Diplomatic Services Bureau (DSB).

—Regular shoppers at the Friendship Store—state-run stores that serve diplomats and other foreigners—for everything from food to Chinese handicrafts. Few stores in the city were open to foreigners. Only Chinese products were on sale and seasonal produce might be gone within the hour. One year word circulated that strawberries were in! We rushed to the store to find a hoped-for delicacy, but they were already sold out.

—Despite its name, the Friendship Store was not generally staffed by friendly clerks. They were bored, indifferent, with little reward for good performance, as was the case for many enterprises in China. One day I went with a friend to buy meat. Clerks kept ignoring us. Finally, we yelled: *"Mao Juxi shuo: Wei renmin fu wu!"* ("Chairman Mao said: Serve the People!") Clerks looked at us in amazement and almost horror hearing us invoke Mao's name. They jumped to serve us.

—A visit to the Great Wall with no crowds in sight and walking to the top on your own power or picnicking at the nearby Ming Tombs, a resting place for Ming emperors where we communed with history and chased Jonathan around the bushes.

—A cook provided for our home by the DSB. When asked what kind of Chinese food he cooked, he replied, "I'm sorry—I trained at the Hsin Chao Hotel and cook only Western food. We enjoyed his Chicken Kiev often!

—Attending a soccer match in the Worker's Stadium between a visiting U.S. team and a Chinese team, where the slogan was *"You yi di yi, bi sai di er."* ("Friendship First, Competition Second.")—a slogan consigned to the same dustbin of history as "Taking Class Struggle as the Key Link," or "Criticize Lin Biao, Criticize Confucius."

—Walking down Chang An Avenue one day (I still had my bushy beard), I stopped to watch two boys playing on the sidewalk. For fun I asked, *"Da huzi piaoliang ma?"* (Do you like my [black] beard?). One of the youngsters scowled back, *"Da huzi you shenma piaoliang ah!?"* (What's so attractive about a black beard?!").

Third, what was it like for a foreigner working in Beijing?

Imagine:

—The USLO on *Guang Hua Lu*, not far from the center of the city. Thirty-five staff members in a tiny office building. I had an economic position, Claire an administrative one. The chief of the liaison office lived on the compound. When we arrived, the chief was Thomas Gates, soon to be replaced by Leonard Woodcock. China loved Ambassador Woodcock. As the former head of the United Auto Workers (UAW), he was a laborer—a man of the people. The compound is still used by the United States for offices and the residence for the ambassador. Woodcock was happy to be invited to dinner, so one evening we had him over to our apartment. Jonathan played on the floor, Woodcock enjoyed his Scotch and regaled us with stories of his UAW days. A quite delightful person to work with at USLO. He married our USLO staff nurse, Sharon. They would joke that their relationship began when she had to give him his vaccine shot—in his posterior region!

—U.S.-China relations were at a low point with little forward movement on establishing formal diplomatic relations since the Nixon visit of

1972. The administration wrestled with how to develop relations with both China and the Soviet Union.

—Chinese officials scrutinizing the myriad posters and pictures we hung in honor of our two hundredth birthday—July 4, 1976—with all their references to revolution, freedom, democracy, and liberty. *Most Chinese were dumbfounded to learn the United States, too, was born of a revolution against colonialism.*

—Dinner hosted for us at the old American Legation by Vice Foreign Minister Wang Hairong and Nancy Tang Wensheng. On learning I studied Chinese in Taiwan, Vice Foreign Minister Wang lectured me about how Taiwan had impugned the honor of the Chinese people by creating export processing zones and accepting foreign investment: "The PRC would never do that." Not long after, Vice Foreign Minister Wang was out of office for her support for the leftist "Gang of Four," which also included Mao Zedong's widow.

—There were few professional contacts in the Chinese government or society. China maintained severe restrictions on any engagement. At receptions, a person might be introduced only as *fu zi ren* (a responsible person) in the Ministry of Foreign Trade. Further attempts to elicit information led only to repetition of "*fu zi ren*." Later we appreciated how subject to criticism a Chinese person could be for engaging with a foreigner.

—Any travel outside Beijing required government permission. The Chinese government made all the arrangements, with escorts everywhere. If permission was denied, the only reason given would be "*bu fangbian*" (inconvenient). Further attempts to elicit information led only to a repetition of "*bu fangbian.*"

—Despite the obstacles we managed to visit Shanghai, (then the ideological home of the Gang of Four), Nanjing, Hangzhou, Suzhou, Guilin, Shenyang, Guangzhou (twice a year for Jiao Yi Hui–Trade Fair), and of course, Hong Kong.

—Imagine visiting a factory producing at full capacity, with acres of steel pipe in storage outside but not being shipped anywhere. The manager proudly told us they were producing faithfully according to plan, but acknowledged there was little demand for the pipe. An example of the folly of central planning.

—A well-known visiting American actor, William Holden, was stabbed in Tiananmen Square by a Chinese man with a screwdriver. When inquiring two days later about the Chinese investigation, a USLO officer was told by the Ministry of Foreign Affairs, "Don't worry. He was mentally ill. We executed him yesterday." I've never forgotten this firsthand insight into the CCP's frightening treatment of its people, even if mentally ill.

—Secretary of State Cyrus Vance's visit in summer 1977 to move the relationship forward. We were invited to dinner for the first time in the Great Hall of the People on Tiananmen Square. We expected delicacies and got them. But, sadly, sea slugs disguised as "sea cucumbers" and served in the Great Hall did not taste any better to the American palette.

—Each time we went to the Great Hall, I recalled an anecdote from an earlier visit of an American sports team. A Black American athlete exclaimed to the Chinese host, "These beans are bad!" Horrified, the interpreter was at a loss for words. Fortunately, others around the table explained that the term "bad" was an American colloquialism meaning excellent. (True story about a misfire in cross-cultural communication!)

Regrettably, Vance's visit did not put any momentum into normalizing the relationship. The fight in Washington centered around those who were ready to move forward with Beijing (National Security Advisor Zbigniew Brzezinski) and those wanting to find a way to move with Moscow and Beijing at the same time (Vance). It took until later in 1978 for the administration to announce the agreement to establish diplomatic relations with the PRC on January 1, 1979.

Our Personal and Professional Lives in Beijing

I wrote earlier of our personal lives. Jonathan was at the center of our lives after we returned from Japan, where he was born at the U.S. Naval Hospital in Yokusuka. A Canadian lady took care of him during the workday. Claire went over to nurse him at lunchtime. At night, we played as we watched him grow taller and finally begin to walk. Our lives changed as he moved faster and faster.

Jonathan was our personal "toddler ambassador" to the Chinese people. Few Chinese can resist responding positively to young children, even if they are so blond and foreign. He was a magnet in Tiananmen Square, often drawing many dozens of curious people who would watch and smile.

My all-time favorite picture was of Jonathan in Tiananmen Square offering a young Chinese girl his rub-a-dub toy as she shyly smiled at him, holding her apple. A young Chinese boy watched seriously at the cross-cultural bridge-building. The picture is also my favorite metaphor for building bridges across the Pacific and around the globe.

Today, those bridges are needed more desperately than ever as both American and Chinese leaders take their countries down a dangerous path of non-cooperation and confrontation.

Welcoming Family to Beijing Was a Real World "Treat"

One Saturday morning, we received a phone call from my cousin Walt Maack and his wife, Bretta. I asked whether they had made it to Hong Kong and received our (required) invitation to visit Beijing. "No," said Walt. They were at the Beijing railway station and would appreciate a ride. Flabbergasted that they in fact had received their visa and had gotten the train north, I drove down to pick them up.

Walt and Bretta were on a round-the-world medical tour working in different countries. Staying with us for a week was a treat for all of us. They rode bikes all over Beijing, walked, slept, and ate. We took them to top cultural sites. Getting to Beijing was an accomplishment in those days, and they took full advantage.

We also welcomed my parents. After Secretary Vance left Beijing, we flew to Kuala Lumpur, Malaysia, where we all met up and introduced them to their grandchild, Jonathan. What wonderful bonding. We also visited Penang and Cameron Highlands before heading to Hong Kong, which was fast becoming one of our favorite cities.

From Hong Kong we all took the infamous train route to the border, walked across the Lo Wu Bridge, and then on to Guangzhou and Beijing. It was fun to see their first impressions of China through their eyes. In Beijing we treated them to all the top historic and cultural activities. They accompanied us to the first opening of the new Mao Zedong mausoleum in Tiananmen. After lining up in the foreigners' line, we filed slowly past the dimly lit, waxy-looking figure. Yes, it looked like Mao, but maybe the rumors were right that the Vietnamese embalmers had botched the job. Maybe there had been a creative restoration. In any case, since Mao was from rural Hunan Province, we could now say we had seen the "peasant under glass."

Mother and Dad enjoyed Beijing and their grandchild immensely. They were very proud grandparents for sure! On their way back to the world of Hong Kong, they had a chance to visit Shanghai and Hangzhou to see a bit more of the country.

Claire and I were fortunate to be able to visit numerous areas of China during that period:

—Guilin and the Li River with beautiful landscapes and where, walking along the river after dinner, we met a Chinese man who approached us and said he had studied in the United States. For some years now, through the Cultural Revolution, he carefully guarded the fact of his foreign connection; he was happy to talk with us and obviously felt much more comfortable with Chairman Mao gone. He alluded to the disruption and violence of the Cultural Revolution but would not say more.

—Shanghai, which began to come alive after the death of Mao Zedong after being thought of as the home of the leftist "Gang of Four."

—The Shanghai Bund along the river was usually deserted but still a place to imagine what the past had been like with all the foreign banks and trading houses lining the waterfront. Even though we loved getting fresh salads at the Peace Hotel, and were reasonably free to wander the streets, we often felt the dreariness of the city. It was only awaiting the openness of later years of development and bright lights resulting from Deng Xiaoping's reform and opening up. Check out the 2012 movie *Shanghai Calling.*

—Guangzhou for its twice-yearly trade fairs and history.

—Hong Kong for being Hong Kong, one of the world's most unique cities, and a great place to visit from Beijing.

In virtually all visits around China we found a sense of quiet order. Streets often weren't crowded. Sidewalks were not full of people. There was usually no feeling of hustle and bustle. The buildings all too often were dull cement gray. There was little color except in spring and fall in the public parks when the government set out potted flowers and evergreen trees. Young children often were dressed in colorful clothes. People we passed looked at us with some curiosity and did a double take seeing blond-haired Jonathan in tow. We foreigners were few and far between, even in big cities. Young female servers in restaurants loved to hold Jonathan and take him for walks.

I visited Shenyang, Liao Ning Province, in January 1977, the second foreigner allowed to travel by train through the city of Tangshan after the disastrous earthquake of July 1976. The destruction was everywhere. Ninety percent of buildings had been toppled. Huge girders of factories had been twisted into new shapes. At least a quarter million people died. It was one of the most sobering sights of my life. China had turned down all offers of aid from foreign countries. In Shenyang, I visited numerous factories and commercial establishments. The winter weather was fierce, but my heavy Chinese padded coat and trousers kept me warm.

Interestingly, the tremors in Beijing afterwards led to immediate creation of shanty housing "spaces" along the broad sidewalks, where people from the bordering apartment blocks could sleep and hang out. They were perhaps safer from a larger shock; more importantly, they served as expanded housing space, which was in such short supply.

What Did We Do at the United States Liaison Office?

Claire had an administrative position working for the administrative counselor. It was a challenging situation since Chinese regulations, restrictions, and practices were so different from traditional ways of supporting the mission. Many supplies had to be acquired abroad and either carried back from Hong Kong by USLO travelers or, with fresh vegetables from Japan, piggy-backed on a U.S. Air Force plane carrying a congressional delegation. Opportunities for getting things done creatively were everywhere. Claire enjoyed the challenges of her position and the good rapport with her boss Hal Vickers.

We faced a minor crisis when diapers for Jonathan ran low and we had to learn how to fold and use cloth ones, a real learning experience for new parents. A more serious crisis was Jonathan coming down with croup and respiratory problems. Fortunately, the USLO nurse was on hand as was a hot shower and steam. Dirty Beijing air from the Gobi Desert and soot particles from the burning of soft coal for heat were ever-present. We sealed the windows with tape to keep out the sand blown about the city, but it inevitably found its way in.

I admired the administrative officer's willingness to try new ideas and not, as so often happened elsewhere, reject them out of hand because they might take effort and creativity to try them. So it was with acquiring a lease on a summer house at the beach at Beidaihe. Our administrative officer made it happen, working with the Diplomatic Services Bureau, so periodically, we could spend a weekend out of scorching Beijing and instead gaze at the Bo Hai Gulf. We played cards with friends well into the night and enjoyed outings to Kiesling's bakery during the day, which had been started by Austrians in the 1930s. Somehow it survived the worst of the Cultural Revolution.

Chairman Mao made Beidaihe famous for yearly meetings of the top Chinese leadership to make consequential and urgent decisions. The tradition continues.

What Did I Do?

I was an economic/commercial officer in a three-person section responsible for understanding and analyzing economic developments and for supporting U.S. companies doing business in China.

On the economy, we had relatively little information to work with. Publicly available data was scarce, and we knew the Communist Party manipulated it to suit its purposes. Years later, Premier Wen Jiabao publicly admitted he did not trust Chinese statistics. We only periodically were able to meet Chinese officials, and often they would only admit to working in "foreign trade" or "economics." Interestingly, some knew of—and didn't hesitate to ask for—the periodic compilation by a U.S. Congressional committee of economic articles on China by foreign experts. If one paid attention and connected the dots, one could draw some conclusions.

Reading newspapers and party magazines, and learning to read between the lines, was an important tool for trying to understand policy directions. China-watching and reading was and is a true art form and not for the faint-of-heart. Still being new to the China reporting field, and having been pulled out of language training early in Taiwan to get to Beijing for the July Fourth reception, I was not a master of the art. It was frustrating.

Our value-added from USLO was in traveling to the provinces to visit factories and provincial governments. Those trips yielded some facts and atmospherics. For example, during our time in Beijing, tours of factories and villages around the country were usually conducted by the CCP secretary. No fee or gratuity. It was their job. Not long after, once reform and opening to the world policies were launched, I visited a factory outside Beijing. Afterward, the CCP secretary said the fee for the tour was twenty *renminbi*. I was taken aback and said I had never before been charged. With seeming embarrassment (I thought), she said that things were changing—villagers were reassessing their relationship with CCP officials and often no longer thought the CCP provided much value so were reluctant to pay her salary. The result? She needed to charge a fee for tours like ours.

It was a sign of change. There were many such signs if you knew what to look for and how to make sense of them.

Working with U.S. businesspeople was more rewarding. Still early in the relationship, Americans would come looking for possible deals. Boeing, of course, sold many aircraft and the Kellogg Company sold complete fertilizer plants. Small U.S. businesses looked to purchase consumer goods. One firm found a T-shirt manufacturer but was told the factory would only sell its own designs, not custom-ordered designs. That quickly changed as China began to open up. Another American who manufactured leather work gloves in the United States told me excitedly that a factory would make the same gloves for a quarter to a third of his U.S. costs.

The record of moving manufacturing to China is now legend. Here are two of many personal examples of the economics. A good friend, Noel Patton, whose family had manufactured fans for years in Indiana, found they were struggling to produce the quality of fans they needed, so he moved to Hong Kong and began to manufacture parts and complete fans in China. That decision lowered their costs, increased quality, and saved the company. It's still selling fans.

There's a similar story about Radio Flyer, the famous little red wagon company. We later became friends in Hong Kong with the family who owned and produced them, now in China. The brand remains popular, and the company is reportedly doing well after achieving lower costs of production in China.

The U.S. textile and garment industry experienced the same fate. After New England "stole" Britain's industry many years ago, the southern U.S. states stole it from New England (lower costs), and then the industry worked its way across the Pacific through Japan, Korea, Hong Kong, Taiwan, and finally landed in China (again, lower costs). An elaborate system of quotas slowed the transition, but continued decline was inevitable. Now, China is watching the migration of parts of the industry to Vietnam and other Southeast Asian countries such as Bangladesh. Such is the way of a globalized world.

Many other industries followed a similar path: manufacturing, electronics, shoes, toys, artificial flowers. If one paid attention, one could draw similar conclusions. We'll see how this trend of globalization fares under Trump and now under Biden and the disruptions of the pandemic.

Why Was 1976 a Watershed Year in Modern Chinese History?

It's clear that 1976 was a watershed year in modern Chinese history. We perhaps had some inkling of that as the year went by. The events of that year laid the foundation for a "new" China, putting behind it the violence and destruction of the years following the founding of the People's Republic. It promised a new era of openness to the world, greater prosperity, and personal freedoms for its citizens.

We have lived through and experienced these four decades since in Hong Kong, in China, and in the United States. What were the six events of 1976 that helped change China and the world?

—January 8, 1976, was the death of Zhou Enlai, premier since 1949 and a widely beloved and respected leader who had survived myriad political campaigns and turmoil, including the Cultural Revolution.

—April 5, 1976, was Qing Ming, the traditional day of mourning for the deceased. The "Tiananmen Incident of 1976" occurred when the government—under the influence of the Gang of Four—removed all memorial tributes to Zhou Enlai in Tiananmen Square and removed Deng Xiaoping from power.

—July 6, 1976, was the death of Marshal Zhu De, founder of the Red Army and later, leader of the People's Liberation Army (PLA). He occupied many high-ranking military and political positions. He and Mao Zedong were close allies, but he too suffered during the Cultural Revolution.

—July 26, 1976, was the Tang Shan earthquake in northern China, northeast of Beijing. There was widespread death and destruction not only in the city of Tang Shan but also for many miles away, including Beijing. When I traveled through by train, the destruction was impossible to believe, with reinforced concrete pillars twisted like pretzels. Traditional Chinese superstition suggested that the death of Chairman Mao was foreshadowed by the Tangshan earthquake.

—(On August 10, 1976, Jonathan Richard Mueller was born in Yokosuka, Japan.)

—September 9, 1976, was the death of Mao Zedong, leader of the revolution and the People's Republic of China, who died in Beijing at the age of eighty-three. Crowds marched through the streets with his picture, wearing white paper flowers. Somber music played from the ubiquitous speakers along the avenues. On the day of Mao's public memorial service, a million people marched into Tiananmen Square and filled Chang An Avenue to the east and west. We witnessed that day from a balcony of the Beijing Hotel, not being allowed outside to walk to Tiananmen Square. Never have I seen such a mass of people who remained lined up for hours, shoulder to shoulder, crying, and listening to the music and speeches broadcast by loudspeaker from each light pole. Several of my pictures of the "masses" are still iconic.

—October 6, 1976, was the arrest of the Gang of Four. October 21 saw nationwide demonstrations and denunciations. These four, including Mao's wife, Jiang Qing, were considered Mao's ideological successors with a belief in Cultural Revolution-style politics and development. The arrests opened the door to the return to power of Deng Xiaoping.

Why was 1976 so important? Why was it a turning point in modern Chinese political history?

First, it marked the end of Mao's and his supporters' approach to creating a new, revolutionary state and a new Chinese "man." Mao knew that revolutions created chaos, undermining the comfortable status quo and opening the way to new ideological strategies. He used the term, *"Geming bushi qing ke chi fan"* ("Revolution is not a dinner party"). To put it bluntly: revolution leads to death and the breaking of traditions and past practices. Taking class struggle as the key link was the mantra.

Second, it opened the door to leadership less wedded to ideology and continuous revolution and more dedicated to stability, economic growth, and becoming a world player, if still a hardline Communist regime.

Third, it began a turn to an opening to the rest of the world, even if flies came in through the open window, as Deng used to say. Candidly, I never thought of myself as a fly.

We saw and felt the changes quickly in Beijing. For example, in the next year, officials became a bit less reserved in conversation, apparently less concerned about criticism for being seen with a foreigner. Some officials cautiously admitted in conversation that they could be suddenly and severely accused if seen as close to a foreigner. The number of exchanges and delegations picked up. There were fewer responses of *bu fangbian*. The Chinese employees of USLO became just a bit more relaxed.

We Return Home

We were expecting Eric's arrival in April 1978. The State Department allowed us to shorten our tour in Beijing by a few months so he could be born in the United States. We said farewell to friends and to the country we found so fascinating, frustrating, intriguing, frightening, and just plain different. We knew we had experienced real and important world history. It turned out to be just the beginning of our decades-long relationship with China.

The highlight of our return home was a few days in Hawaii, where Jonathan got his first haircut—squirming on his father's lap as he experienced his newest adventure. We laughed as he then toddled down the beach and had his first feeling of walking in the ocean.

As we winged our way home, we could not have forecast that within months the CCP under Deng Xiaoping would meet in December 1978 at the Third Plenum and launch "reform and opening up" that would lead to China's broad political, economic, and social transformation over the coming decades.

The "opening up" also led the United States and China to an historic agreement to establish diplomatic relations on January 1, 1979. It was truly a new era.

Growing Career Maturity—Growing Family, East–West Trade, China Desk, Hong Kong Consulate General, 1979–1986

Not long after our return, we celebrated the arrival of Eric Richard Mueller on April 14, 1978. He was born in Sibley Hospital in Maryland. All of a sudden, our lives and our house at 7209 Gordons Road in Falls Church, Virginia seemed full to overflowing and infinitely more complicated with two very active young boys. Claire decided to stay at home for the next year to manage it all before returning to work.

In 1979 Claire joined the Bureau of Human Rights in the State Department, working with our friend Charlie Salmon. The bureau, headed by Patricia Derrian, had been set up under the Carter administration. It ruffled many traditional foreign policy feathers as perhaps an unwarranted intrusion into the "real" work of national security. But now, decades later, human rights have earned a respected home in the foreign policy universe.

From the Human Rights Bureau, Claire moved to the State Department's "Command Center," namely, the Executive Secretariat where we had met almost a decade earlier under Secretary Kissinger. She was there for the transition from the Carter administration to the Reagan administration. She witnessed up close the frantic minutes of the choreographed release of the American hostages from Iran thirty minutes after Ronald Reagan was sworn in as president.

Meanwhile, I did a several-month refresher economics course at the Foreign Service Institute and then joined the Office of East–West Trade in the Bureau of Economic and Business Affairs for a three-year assignment.

A coincidence: the director of the office was Bill Root, an FSO who was a good friend of my father's and our family in Germany in the 1950s. He was non-plussed upon learning of the coincidence (he still remembered me as a young boy), but said he was pleased to have me as his deputy director.

The office had a dual role:

The first was responsibility for interagency coordination on the export of dual-use technologies (civilian and military), particularly to the Soviet Union and China. These technologies were licensed by the Department of Commerce but only on the approval of State and Defense. State licensed arms and munitions separately.

The second role was responsibility for east–west trade, usually between communist and non-communist countries. An important focus was implementation of the Trade Act of 1974 with the famous Jackson-Vanik amendment that set strict standards for negotiating trade agreements and most favored nation (MFN) status with "non-market economies" (basically communist countries).

The control of dual-use exports was through a multi-country organization called the Coordinating Committee for Multilateral Export Controls (COCOM). Regular negotiations identified new technologies subject to control and reviewed applications from companies. It was a hugely complex enterprise, both for policy and technical reasons. Companies would lobby U.S. government agencies to make the case why the export of a particular technology posed no danger to the United States. Deliberations could go on for extended periods. Periodically, long negotiating sessions were held in Paris. At one point I spent several weeks in Paris representing State on the U.S. delegation.

Given the new opening to China, which wanted broader access to our technology, we were under pressure to approve exports that had been banned. The interagency negotiation process was lively and often tense. My recent assignment in Beijing was a useful backdrop for productive engagement in the myriad facets of decision-making.

Beijing has pushed continuously, to this day, for a more open U.S. and international export regime. The reality is that much dual-use technology and equipment is legitimately useful in the civilian sector, but often is too easily diverted to military use. That causes the decision-makers in the government to be cautious and reluctant while those responsible for moving U.S.-China relations forward argue for more openness. There were good arguments on both sides.

The east–west trade function focused on trade agreements and trade trends between the United States and non-market economy countries. The announcement in December 1978 that the United States and China would establish diplomatic relations on January 1, 1979, launched myriad initiatives to build more trans-Pacific bridges.

The most challenging of such initiatives was to negotiate a new trade agreement that would open more channels of trade. I served on the Washington, DC–based team that led the way. There was heavy pressure from the White House to get it done, but we needed to address the many requirements of the Trade Act of 1974. A sticky one was to obtain a legal commitment from China that it would extend intellectual property rights (IPR) protection to the same level as the United States. The only obstacle was that China had no such law. Finally, we settled on a statement that China would protect U.S. intellectual property by administrative means and would eventually strive to pass a relevant law.

Non-enforcement of IPR rights by China over the decades has been a huge frustration for American companies and often a competitive disadvantage. The U.S. government has continuously made the issue a legitimate and prominent one in our economic relationship, but progress has ranged from slow to non-existent. Aside from commercial advantage, it is now clear that China has used cyber-hacking to steal a wide variety of military and dual-use technology and equipment, including fighter aircraft design.

In the trade agreement of 1979, we were unable to extend permanent MFN treatment to China at the time. In fact, that would not come until many years later in 2000 with permanent normal trade relations (PNTR), the new name for MFN treatment. The U.S.-China Relations Act of 2000 included a clause requiring free emigration, the so-called Jackson-Vanik clause, which had been designed to force the Soviet Union to allow free emigration for Soviet Jews. But the letter of the law meant it applied to China also.

When Deng Xiaoping visited the United States early in 1979 to celebrate the new relationship, he told President Carter that freedom of emigration was not a problem. He joked by saying China had many people. How many did we want? Ten million? Canadian and British authorities have asked us to slow the number of Chinese emigrating. Too many Chinese!

Deng Xiaoping's exact words to President Carter on January 30, 1979, in a meeting in the Oval Office: *"The Jackson amendment demands that the Soviet Union allow free emigration. Would you like to import ten million Chinese?"* (Foreign Relations of the United States, 1977–1980, Vol XIII, China)

On that trip we saw a side of Deng's leadership style that was unprecedented to us. He stopped in Texas on his way to Washington and attended a real western rodeo. He allowed himself to be driven around the arena in a stagecoach wearing a large cowboy hat. China's leaders were always straitlaced and serious, we thought; this time Deng showed the flexible (and fun?) side of his personality.

The transcript of the Oval Office meeting with Carter also shows how two nations wanting to move their relationship forward could show flexibility in resolving myriad issues, whether emigration, claims and assets, the future of Taiwan, or nuclear testing. And they can do so with a degree of civility – no hot rhetoric as we experience now in 2023.

But don't be fooled. This was also the hardened Communist, anti-Japan, anti-Kuomintang politician and civil war leader. He was one of Mao's right-hand men. And he was the Deng Xiaoping who ten years later (on June 4, 1989) ordered the troops into Tiananmen square to violently clear out students, workers, and others, at the cost of many lives and much bloodshed.

Not long after his trip to the United States and securing his American flank, Deng sent the PLA into North Vietnam as "punishment" for the Vietnamese invasion of Cambodia and overthrow of China's ally, Pol Pot and the Khmer Rouge. The loser was China. The Vietnamese were battle-hardened from years of war with Americans and French; they inflicted heavy casualties on Chinese troops during the month-long war.

This 1979 conflict is yet another huge Vietnamese historical grievance against China's many centuries of colonialism in Vietnam and animosity toward Vietnamese. There remains to this day no love lost between these two peoples.

If you want to understand how to create successful foreign policy, be sure to know your history well. Too many Americans did not comprehend the many centuries of Vietnamese-Chinese conflict and animosity which continues to this day.

Another result of the opening to China was the establishment of the Joint Economic Committee, chaired by the U.S. treasury secretary on our side, and the Joint Committee on Commerce and Trade, chaired by the U.S. secretary of commerce. Each committee was designed to have regular meetings to bring together Chinese and Americans and work to build new bridges and lines of communication between the two.

Over the next several years, I participated in virtually all the annual meetings in Washington and Beijing. The committees on both sides were interagency and brought together a wide range of officials with responsibility for developing the relationship. The meetings also served to exchange information on issues of interest to both governments. It was a refreshing openness—relatively speaking—after decades of estrangement.

Joining the China Desk

In 1981 I joined the China "desk" of the State Department, the Office of China Affairs. I was deputy director for economic affairs and for Hong Kong; I had been recruited for the job because of my experience with China and most recently in east–west trade.

It was a plum assignment. U.S.-China relations were front and center in our foreign policy priorities, so there was a real buzz in the office. Implementation of the new trade agreement was a constant focus, including the annual renewal of MFN for China that ultimately became a two-decade annual struggle with Congress until 2000. To this day critics claim the United States should have continued the year-to-year renewal, despite the animosity it caused, both in China and in the U.S. business community, in the hope of retaining some leverage over China.

An issue that cut across all issues was the question of continuing sales of military equipment to Taiwan. China pressured us to end all sales; we refused. The Taiwan Relations Act required us to support Taiwan's defense needs. Ultimately an agreement was reached where we forecast that our military sales would decline over time—known as the "declining bucket." It was the fig leaf needed at the time to move the relationship forward. The bucket has long since been consigned to the dustbin of history, with military sales continuing to be a constant issue.

We also worked on a framework policy covering exports of dual use technology. Given the complexities and competing policy viewpoints, we made slow progress at best. China was still seen as antagonistic to U.S. interests in many ways, and a country whose military we did not want to strengthen to a great degree. We wanted them strong enough to deter the Soviet Union but also did not want to undermine our own security or that of allies and friends such as Japan, South Korea, Taiwan, Philippines, and others.

Of course, over the next forty years, China did find ways to modernize and expand its military through indigenous efforts, purchase of technology and equipment (including from its 2020s "friend," Russia), and IP theft.

During my time on the desk, we had frequent contact with the FBI. They were attempting to understand security risks, particularly human. They focused on Chinese-Americans, some of whom were coerced by Beijing to support China, trying to understand who could be trusted and who might be sympathetic to the "motherland." There were no easy answers and, sadly, not a few Chinese-Americans came under suspicion and often paid a price in terms of professional and personal reputation.

Since 2020 our relationship with China has been devolving to confrontational levels—not only is the FBI trying to identify security threats, but Americans are confronting Chinese and Asian "faces" in our country as though they could be threatening "foreigners." The COVID-19 pandemic has only increased the number of Chinese-Americans threatened and ostracized by their fellow Americans and blamed for the "China virus" or "Wuhan virus." President Trump doubly stoked that prejudice by calling it the "Kung Flu."

It is clear that today, the xenophobic and racist roots in our society are surprisingly alive and helping to seriously divide us as a country. The Chinese Exclusion Act of 1882 is only one of the external signs of our anti-immigrant actions over the years. Today I, as a "German-American" whose family had suffered stigma for being German over one hundred years ago, am never singled out by anyone as a foreigner because of my German name. Why? Because our "German" family eventually was welcomed as "white" and not as aliens.

How many times have we heard people of Asian or African heritage told to "go back home" even though they were born and brought up in the United States? *Shameful.*

As the Reagan administration launched its transition plan from President Carter, rumors swirled about whether a new initiative toward building up relations with Taiwan was likely. A conservative wing of the Republican Party still had good ties with Taiwan and was skeptical about the PRC. A transition team member, who is still active in intelligence and foreign policy circles, told me candidly he thought it conceivable we would see such a move.

The long-term question would be whether smart diplomacy over the years would allow Taiwan to retain its de facto autonomy and a non-official relationship with the United States and the world while avoiding aggressive Chinese attempts to undermine and take over the island.

As it was, Reagan did not reverse course on the new diplomatic relationship, and we found that the building of bridges to the PRC continued in the 1980s. U.S. businesses as well as educational, cultural, and other non-profit organizations were increasingly interested in building relationships with China and supported the new course charted by Nixon. More and more businesses were in touch with the State Department about doing business and looking for possibilities.

During my five years working on China affairs, 1978–1983, I made at least six trips to China with delegations or on my own. I was always able to add a side trip to see a different part of the country. Here are some of them.

Yunnan and Sichuan Provinces

A friend and I flew to Kunming, in Yunnan Province, to see the southwest. We visited the Stone Forest (pretty spectacular with the amazing rock formations) outside Kunming and other interesting sites before taking the train to Cheng Du. We wanted to experience a unique railway route through the mountains built by the PLA railway corps. There were hundreds of tunnels, bridges, and steep drop-offs all along. It was a once in a lifetime experience.

The train trip also allowed us to talk at some length with two older, grizzled veterans of the PLA during China's civil war. They didn't seem intimidated by two foreigners who spoke Chinese. In fact, they were curious that the new reform and opening up policies had brought us to this train trip through the mountains. One of my clear recollections is that they were incredibly knowledgeable in recalling names of so many army commanders they had served with during the war. Their sharp memories—positive and negative—of their commanders and colleagues were a reminder of the importance of *guanxi* (relationships) in Chinese society.

We saw some of Chengdu and then took a train to Leshan to see the great Leshan Buddha and Emeishan (Mount Emei). On the train, we demonstrated that even two "China hands" who could speak Chinese could go astray. As the train came to a stop, we heard the stop for "Leshan," we thought. We quickly grabbed our bags and hustled off the train as it was starting up. Close call. But lo and behold, no one was there to meet us as arranged. Upon inquiring, we learned Leshan was the *next* stop!

While waiting for our guide to drive from Leshan to pick us up, we walked into the small, very rural, town. The weekly market was underway with myriad people, animals, and assorted provisions. It was a unique opportunity to observe, without a China Travel Service "minder," a small village and its people buying and selling at their weekly gathering. At one point, a very short old man came up to us and spoke in Sichuan dialect. Of course, we didn't understand. So, he used sign language which seemed to convey a question about eating. A Mandarin speaker came over and interpreted: the man wanted to know how many cups of rice my friend ate every day—since he was so tall!

We finally made it to Leshan. The highlight was seeing the Giant Buddha statue across the river—233 feet tall, the largest and tallest stone Buddha in the world, built in the eighth century AD. It was truly a stupendous religious and cultural creation. We also visited the nearby Mount Emei, one of the great sacred mountains. We had hoped to climb to the summit through the beautiful forest filled with temples. Unfortunately, we were short of time, but we did have a chance to see and experience the foothills. Since China had not yet opened significantly to tourists, we enjoyed such travel without many other visitors.

Shanghai

An all-day train trip from Beijing to Shanghai again allowed me to observe everyday Chinese life and trade a few stories with fellow travelers. The conversations were seldom deep, but they did reveal lots of information or insights that we could connect with other experiences to understand China.

Shanghai was coming alive, little by little, after Mao Zedong's death. The so-called Bund along the river offered Puxi (west of the Huang Pu river) historical vistas of European bank and commercial buildings. And we gazed at Pudong (east of the river) at vistas of warehouses and docks. It wouldn't be many years before Pudong was built up as one of the world's most modern cities. But in the early 1980s, it was fun and instructive to wander the streets and poke our heads into small stores and restaurants. People were never unfriendly, but they were usually taken aback to see two foreigners.

Of course, it never crossed my mind that in 2013, I would be head of school at Shanghai American School, an international school of three thousand three hundred students with fully developed campuses on both the Puxi and Pudong sides of the city.

Chengde

Chengde (Jehol) was the summer home of the Qing Dynasty emperors and now an important historical center. It was a fairly short train ride north of Beijing and just right for a two-day excursion. I did a lot of walking, observing, and learning about Chinese history. Few Americans have ever heard of Cheng De. And yet for centuries, it was a center of the civilization that thought of itself as the center of the world.

Qufu

Qufu, in Shandong Province, is famous as the home of Confucius, China's most well-known philosopher and political practitioner (551 BC to 479 BC). Phil Lincoln and I visited in 1981 from Beijing by train. Upon arriving at the hotel, there was a security cordon and a familiar person whom the desk acknowledged was Hua Guofung, Mao's successor as general secretary. Hua had stayed at the hotel, which obligingly turned on the heat for him; within a short time of his departure, we found the hotel temperature close to freezing. Foreigners didn't swing the same weight as the party secretary.

We enjoyed visiting the town, particularly the Confucius Temple and Cemetery. We asked the staff about Confucius and learned that Red Guards during the Cultural Revolution had dug up what historically was considered his grave; they found nothing. That was not surprising after two and a half thousand years. But the staff did offer that Premier Zhou Enlai had been quietly proactive during the Cultural Revolution in protecting many of the valuable relics and temples. Confucius had been reviled by Mao and other "leftists" for being part of old, traditional China, which Mao had wanted to destroy. One of the recent slogans had been *"Pi Lin, Pi Kong"* ("Criticize Lin Biao, criticize Confucius.") (Lin Biao was a supporter of Mao turned adversary, who died in a plane crash over Mongolia while reportedly trying to defect to the Soviet Union.)

Tai Shan—Mount Tai

Phil Lincoln and I subsequently visited Tai Shan in eastern Shandong Province. It's one of the sacred mountains in China and arguably the most historically important. History books say there is evidence of human habitation on the mountain going back to the Neolithic period. We started climbing the many steps and made it to the summit at midday. We huffed and puffed while workers literally ran up the stairs with heavy loads. The mountain is covered with temples and historic sites. A fascinating visit.

Congressman Dingell's Delegation to China

In the spring of 1983, still on the China desk, I assisted Congressman Dingell and his staff in organizing a congressional trip to China. Dingell was the chair of the House Energy and Commerce Committee, a position he used to assert jurisdiction over many China issues. The congressman invited me to join the trip representing the State Department. It was a large delegation. The U.S.-China relationship was building rapidly, so it drew members from both sides of the aisle. Since very few had been to China, it was interesting to observe their reactions—ranging from skepticism to enthusiasm—to what they saw and heard. It was a good opportunity for me to talk with members about China, my views, and my experiences. Beijing, Xian, and Shanghai were on the itinerary. In each place we had high level meetings to profess our friendship and a desire to increase trade in both directions. We visited all the top historic and cultural sites. Shanghai was memorable to me because the mayor's dinner was among the best Chinese dinners I have ever had. Shanghai cuisine, of course.

Hong Kong—1982

In the fall of 1982, I returned home via Hong Kong. I had three objectives. One was for consultations on U.S.-China relations and how best to continue to understand China. Another was to discuss my taking the position of director of the economic section of the consulate general. The third was to visit Hong Kong International School (HKIS). All three checked out well. Burt Levin, consul general, was persuasive in describing how much they wanted my experience in a position that oversaw reporting on both China and Hong Kong. Hong Kong remained an important "China-watching" location for learning about and analyzing developments in China. The coming years would be crucial for U.S. interests in both places.

On my visit to HKIS to meet with the elementary school principal, I learned about the school we hoped to send our two young sons to. I was heartened and reassured by what I heard.

As I continue to marvel in retrospect, I had no reason to suspect that in eleven years I would become consul general in Hong Kong and in twenty-three years return as head of school of Hong Kong International School.

Chapter Three

Diplomacy in Hong Kong and with the Secretary

Hong Kong, 1983–1986 Good Family Time—Plans for Hong Kong's Future after 1997—Springboard to Senior Foreign Service Leadership

Claire, Jonathan, Eric, and I arrived in Hong Kong in the summer of 1983 and went directly to our new home in Tavistock on Tregunter Path. The boys ran from room to room and then in the kitchen met Dolly, the Filipina lady who had worked for my predecessor and agreed to stay on. Eric came running back, saying "They have homemade cookies!" I remember Claire saying, "Not *they*, *we* have cookies! *We* live here. Dolly made them."

The apartment was big—four bedrooms, old Hong Kong style with two balconies. Very livable, with more than enough room for four and good-sized quarters for Dolly. It faced the harbor and had a good view of Hong Kong's harbor, except for Estoril Court which blocked a great view.

Several months later, Li Kashing, head of Cheong Kong Hutchison and one of the richest men in the world, invited us to lunch. When he asked where we lived, Claire told him; then, in her direct way, said that unfortunately Estoril Court blocked our view. Li smiled and said, "I'm so sorry. I built Estoril Court!"

Li Kashing was a Hong Kong original, like many other people we met in our years there. He fled China as a refugee, penniless, with little formal education, and began selling (and later manufacturing) artificial flowers and toys on the streets of Hong Kong. He went from success to success, building businesses into worldwide multi-billion-dollar establishments. He maintained his publicly humble demeanor and was eager to remain in touch with Americans. He also began to build serious bridges to China and Chinese leaders in the 1980s. As part of his business success, he donated funds for many schools and universities on the mainland, Hong Kong, and the United States, making sure his name was widely known.

We got to know Li's sons. Richard struck out on his own business career. Victor became Father Li's successor in running the family conglomerate. Li Kashing to this day is still the glue that helps hold the family and businesses together as they navigate global business and Chinese politics.

There are many more such stories to be told. The Kwoks (Raymond, Walter, Thomas, Ingrid) atop a huge real estate empire, Victor and William Fung, C.H and Betty Tung (he became the first chief executive of Hong Kong in 1997), Henry and Lisa Tang (chief secretary; all four children attended HKIS), the Chengs (Edgar, Christopher, and Edward), Anna Wu and Helmut Sohmen and her three sisters, Bessie, Cissy, and Doreen, and on and on.

The summer and fall of our arrival turned out to be a watershed in Hong Kong's history. I witnessed the upheaval as Claire settled in working in the political section, I in the economic/ commercial section, and the boys safely and happily ensconced in the American-style education of Hong Kong International School.

Some Necessary Background on Hong Kong

British Prime Minister Margaret Thatcher (whom we met years later, and next to whom Claire sat an Asia Society dinner in Hong Kong) had visited Beijing in 1982 to discuss Hong Kong's future. The United Kingdom hoped China would agree to extend the New Territories ninety-nine-year lease and allow Great Britain to continue to govern Hong Kong. (Hong Kong Island and the tip of the Kowloon Peninsula had been ceded in perpetuity to Britain in 1842 and 1860.)

Predictably, Beijing firmly rejected that option for reasons of pride and sovereignty in regaining its stolen territory. As Thatcher left the Great Hall of the People in Beijing, she tripped and fell down the stairs. Superstitious Hongkongers took that as a clear sign that China would ultimately have its way with Hong Kong.

The Sino-British negotiations went nowhere in the coming months and people in Hong Kong turned pessimistic by the middle of 1983. In September of 1983, the bottom dropped out of the Hong Kong dollar. Panic set in. There was panic buying of basic food supplies. Store shelves emptied. Public confidence plunged. Desperate, the Hong Kong government, after denying it would ever do so, took the unproven theory of financial analyst John Greenwood and pegged the Hong Kong dollar to the U.S. dollar, 7.8 to 1. That peg, unexpectedly, has lasted through major international crises.

I got to know Greenwood and periodically discussed the future course of Hong Kong's economy and the Hong Kong dollar with him. He knew Hong Kong well. He admitted that his work on linking the dollar to the U.S. dollar was theoretical and was taken aback when the Hong Kong government used it in the real world, as a desperate measure. But its mechanism—not easily described—based on fluctuating interest rates turned out to work well and supported Hong Kong's continued economic growth. It even withstood determined efforts from speculators during the Asian financial crisis, when they thought they could break the link and reap billions.

The crisis of 1983 helped jumpstart Chinese-British negotiations. Britain briefly tried the idea that it could return the New Territories but retain Hong Kong Island and the Kowloon Peninsula. Such a splitting of jurisdictions was a non-starter since the entire colony was one entity that couldn't be divided; even the airport would have been in the Chinese part of Hong Kong.

Ultimately, Britain played its final card. It would consider relinquishing its sovereignty over the island and peninsula if Beijing would agree to treat the entire territory as one entity, with long-term guarantees of a high degree of autonomy and maintenance of its many features of openness and rule of law.

In December 1984, the Sino-British Joint Declaration on Hong Kong was finally announced. It was a unique document that had at least three important objectives:

—Recognition that China on July 1, 1997, would recover its long-lost territory and thereby extinguish a century and a half of humiliation by foreign countries.

—Recognition that the creation of a "one country, two systems" structure in the Chinese constitution would promise a "high degree of autonomy" for fifty years after July 1, 1997, and would maintain Hong Kong's vital energies of openness, freedoms, free trade and capitalism, and strong and trusted rule of law. These would help allow Hong Kong to continue to grow and remain stable, thus also ensuring it could support China's growing economy with investment capital and managerial expertise.

—Recognition that Macau and Taiwan would ultimately return to Chinese sovereignty under the same terms given to Hong Kong. Taiwan would be the real prize if Hong Kong's reversion was successful, and Taiwan willingly followed suit. In fact, that was a long shot and unlikely, but it fit Mao's and Deng's willingness to wait an extended period for reunification—even a hundred years, if necessary, as Chairman Mao had told Henry Kissinger.

China would take over responsibility for foreign affairs and defense. Otherwise, Hong Kong people would "rule" Hong Kong with limited direction from Beijing. That was the hope, and it depended on China's continuing willingness to be restrained in its demands on Hong Kong.

Guarantees of "one country, two systems" led to China's 1990 Basic Law for Hong Kong, which recognized the reality of deep differences between Hong Kong and the rest of China. While it didn't and couldn't satisfy everyone, it did hold some promise for the longer-term preservation of Hong Kong's way of life, stability, and prosperity.

There was both relief and anxiety in Hong Kong for the remainder of our time at the consulate general. The relief was in knowing future directions for the city; planning for both professional and personal goals could be accelerated. The anxiety was fully around the replacement of a democratic sovereign (Britain) for a communist authoritarian one, and whether Beijing would abide both by the spirit and the letter of "one country, two systems."

During my Foreign Service assignments to Hong Kong in the 1980s and again in the 1990s as consul general (1993–1996), most of us answered the never-ending question of "What's going to happen after 1997?" with something akin to, "It depends. If China continues to open up, honors its commitments, and tolerates a robust and open economy and society very different from China's, then Hong Kong's prospects are likely to be positive. But if China becomes more controlling, less tolerant of dissent or criticism, or more inward looking, then Hong Kong's prospects will be different and not as positive."

Looking back from the perspective of 2020, that prediction held considerable validity. But that story comes later.

Life and Work in Hong Kong

Our time in Hong Kong saw continued economic growth and increased investment and trade links with the very different China beyond the border. Hongkongers were adept at working in a non-market, socialist system that was trying to shed some of the shackles of restraints on individual initiative. The creation of the Shenzhen Special Economic Zone across the border was a magnet for Hong Kong and other foreign investment. One day Shenzhen—rising from a sleepy village to grow into one of the world's financial, technology, and manufacturing centers—would slowly begin to overshadow Hong Kong.

At the consulate general we were overwhelmed with visitors looking to better understand business prospects in Hong Kong and in a "rising" China. One was Secretary of State George Shultz who visited twice during our time. I was fortunate to meet him to talk particularly about economic developments. On one memorable occasion, I sat with him for lunch on the fantail of a yacht, the SS *Fairmont*. He was intensely interested in Hong Kong and its future, as well as China's developing and opening economy. He grilled me on how the Hong Kong link with the U.S. dollar was working and investment prospects in China. My previous experience working in China fortunately gave me enough experience to sketch out my observations. He was complimentary about the exchanges.

Of course, I was not a sufficient soothsayer to be able to tell him that I would be working directly for him in Washington in a few short years!

Our three years in Hong Kong, 1983–1986, also afforded numerous opportunities to travel across the border to visit a variety of areas, such as:

—Fujian Province across the Taiwan Strait from Taiwan. As we gazed from the coast to the east, we could see the islands of Quemoy and Matsu, still military garrisons of Taiwan. In the 1950s, U.S.-China tensions soared, and we came close to military confrontation over those tiny islands. It was clear as we visited the old treaty port and the mountains and rural areas of the province that historical and family ties between

Fujian and Taiwan were strong. It seemed likely that when economic and transportation ties were established, there would be a natural, closer relationship. To us visitors, it was also hard to imagine that the political differences could be overcome amicably anytime soon. That observation still held true from the vantage point of my writing in 2023.

—Hainan Island, then a part of Guangdong Province, pointing south to the South China Sea. We were royally treated to a tour of the island, including its capital, Haikou, and then the famous southern beaches and resorts of San Ya. In those days, the area drew mostly high-ranking cadres from the north to enjoy the warmer weather. Provincial officials were just wrestling with the new "reform and opening up" promulgated by Deng Xiaoping, but they were full of enthusiastic plans for new enterprises that developed their forest and fishing resources. In more recent years, they have developed a vast tourism industry that draws people from around the world. The island also holds numerous military installations, which host the ships and other military backup for domination of China's newly constructed islands for military bases in the South China Sea.

—Visits to the rapidly developing delta region of the Pearl River with Hong Kong and Guangzhou as two anchors. Guangdong and the Cantonese seized the opportunities for economic development both in the Shenzhen Economic Zone and in numerous cities along the river. Transportation corridors were being constructed for much of the cargo to be transshipped through Hong Kong. Many of the industries began as light industry for export. We visited one village that specialized in manufacturing artificial flowers. We saw the many boxes of imported materials—many from Taiwan—to construct the flowers. We counted boxes from at least ten different areas. Of particular interest was that they had an arrangement with a large American retail company. Flower bunches were labeled with the name of the company and price, and then packed into large cardboard containers for direct shipment to individual stores. All the American clerk needed to do was open the box and put the flowers on the shelf.

—A visit to Shanghai and then with Richard Boucher, a visit to Anhui Province and the famous Huang Shan—the Yellow Mountains. It was a memorable trip. We drove to the base and started our climb of thousands of steps to a high part of the mountain range. Chinese porters literally ran up past us with their bamboo poles and heavy loads. We saw the beginnings of a new gondola to take future visitors to the top. We felt good that we were doing the climb the traditional way to get the full experience.

At the top we walked along the ridges, with beautiful views in all directions. As the afternoon wore on, the mist drifted in and changed the atmosphere completely. Never had either of us seen so many "Chinese painting" views in real life. We stayed overnight in a hostel high in the mountains, enjoyed the sunrise and fresh views in the morning, and then made our way to the base camp below.

In the many succeeding years after those initial visits described above, Guangdong and many other areas have become home to China's powerhouse industries of manufacturers and financiers. Shenzhen, as a Special Economic Zone, has grown from a rural rice-producing region to a mega-city of some thirteen million people, rivaling Hong Kong in many ways. Gone are all the rice paddies, exotic "communist" water buffalos, and farmers we were mesmerized by on the train to Guangzhou in the early days of China's opening.

Back to Hong Kong

Back at the consulate general in Hong Kong, Claire was in her element, happy to be working in her career field and not having to worry about good childcare for the boys. After a year in the political section, she moved to work for the deputy consul general, Dick Williams. I continued to head the economic/commercial section, which analyzed and reported on both Hong Kong and China. Several of us were "China Hands" and continued the longstanding tradition of China-watching at the consulate general. We had a small team of Chinese researchers who worked for us to understand China and ongoing developments.

Some people in the State Department suggested that since we now had offices in China itself, we could seriously cut back on staffing at the consulate general; we didn't need to look for good sources of information in Hong Kong. However, I argued, Hong Kong had become an even more useful China-watching post. Many Hong Kong people, Americans, and others were now traveling frequently across the border and were often willing to talk about their experiences of living and working on the mainland. Isn't that why we send trained officers overseas to learn directly what is happening and keep the secretary of state and president informed? The new Shenzhen Special Economic Zone next to Hong Kong offered numerous insights into a changing China. No longer did we do the China-watching of old, such as measure the oil levels in the trucks of train cars coming across the border to make guesses about the availability of petroleum supplies in the PRC.

Hong Kong turned out to be a wonderful tour for family life. Jon and Eric were happy at Hong Kong International School and received an excellent education. The teachers were mostly from the United States and had significant teaching experience. Aside from academics, the boys were involved in sports, music, and various clubs. HKIS became a source of friendship with many families as did attending Lutheran Church of All Nations. We never lacked fun things to do on weekends. Hong Kong and British friends regularly invited us to dinner as well as day-long yachting expeditions to New Territories beaches and coves, a favorite Sunday activity.

We also took advantage of vacation travel to visit Thailand, Malaysia, and Singapore. The boys were exposed to the wide variety of Southeast Asian cultures and histories, and the beach resorts offered a fun antidote to the often frantic, bustling Hong Kong. At a Cha-am resort in Thailand, I found a Galaga game machine of old and would head down after dinner to try my luck at destroying the opposing fighters. I was not a world-class gamer.

One of the highlights of our three years was the September 1985 official visit by Vice President George H. W. Bush and Second Lady Barbara Bush. The consul general asked me to be the senior visit control officer, which I was happy to take on. I could use all the earlier good learning about official visits in the Executive Secretariat. I got to work appointing consulate general staff for different responsibilities, preparing guidance on what such a visit would entail, and holding endless meetings to keep everyone on the same page. We even had an advance group from the vice president's office come out to review schedules and preparations. A highlight would be a visit to the huge Exxon-invested, coal-fired power plant west of Hong Kong. The vice president would also highlight the strong support of the United States for Hong Kong and express confidence in its future under the high degree of autonomy promised by China.

The vice president's staff promised a photo op with the Mueller family, including Jonathan and Eric, after he met with the consulate general staff at the Hilton Hotel. We chatted with the Bushes while waiting for the official photographer to show up. He was a no-show. Barbara Bush graciously said they would be in their hotel room and would come back for a

photo later. Without thinking, I blurted out that Jonathan had a bas-
ketball game later so we couldn't come. (Not even for the vice president of the United States?!) Suddenly, Art Kobler, a colleague from the
consulate general, came into sight. He had a camera and so was asked
to take a picture of the six of us. It now resides in the family archives.

We never imagined that the next time we met the Bushes would be
when they came to Hong Kong as ex-vice president when I was consul
general. That's another story for later.

Hong Kong International School

A professional and fun highlight of the tour was being asked to
become a member of the HKIS board of managers as a trustee,
which I happily accepted. The school was founded in the 1960s by
the U.S. business community, the American consulate general, and
the Lutheran Church Missouri Synod (LCMS). It was my first serious
introduction to governance of a non-profit and educational institution—eye-opening and satisfying. The board worked well together, led
by David Rittmann, head of school.

While on the board, we dealt with a wide range of issues. They
included building new facilities to support the hiring of excellent
faculty and staff and planning for the longer run. With 1997 and the
handover to China, we needed to think hard about positioning the
school. One decision was betting we could fill up a new high school,
so we held our breath and launched the project on a second campus
in Tai Tam. Another issue was whether to teach Mandarin Chinese or
continue with Cantonese. After much discussion, we opted to change
to Mandarin. Not everyone was happy.

The most consequential decision we made was deciding to build a
new high school building on a hillside overlooking Tai Tam cove. It
was on the southeast side of Hong Kong Island. When we first were
shown the site, I asked where the buildings would go. The answer?
Straight down the hill from where we were standing, with many levels. I was gob smacked. Hong Kong's exceptional ability to build on
mountainsides made the subsequent beautiful design a possibility.
My architectural contribution was to urge that the entrance at the top
be through a big, round plaza with gardens and benches, opening to
walkways down from level to level with views of the harbor and ocean.
To this day it is an exceptional building for a school.

Serving on the board of managers was the beginning of real insight on how non-profit schools and other organizations are run. It was the beginning of my deeper learning about the importance of good governance. If the institution was governed well, starting with the board, other programs were more likely to be successful. Our head of school was broadminded. He had run the school for two decades and had been instrumental in building its excellent reputation. He was a top-down leader. It was not a unique situation I witnessed over the years; differences within the community could lead to unsteadiness in the institution.

As our three-year assignment moved along, Burt Levin asked if I wanted to extend for a fourth year. Claire and I thought long and hard and finally decided that as much as we loved Hong Kong, we would try our luck at new assignments.

The assignment I set my eyes on was the director of the Secretariat Staff in the secretary of state's office, overseeing the staffing of papers, policies, and overseas trips for the secretary. It was the head of the same office I served in 1972–1974.

It was a much sought-after position. My longtime friend and mentor, Ambassador Nick Platt (who was the executive secretary and personal assistant to the secretary) would make the decision. I had a chance for the job. Many others were also interested. On Thanksgiving Day, Claire, I, and the boys were at home preparing to head for Macau for the long weekend. The telephone rang. I will never forget holding the receiver, looking out over Hong Kong harbor, and hearing the voice of Nick Platt: "Richard, Happy Thanksgiving. I'd like you to join me and be the director of the Secretariat Staff." Wow! I was overwhelmed, but found the voice to say, "Yes! Thank you!"

Again, Nick Platt helped determine the course of our future careers. Thanks, Nick!

Summer 1986 to Leningrad (St. Petersburg) by train and on to Paris, London, and Washington

For years I had dreamed of crossing Asia and Europe by train, specifically by the Trans-Siberian route. My father's love of trains helped stoke my interest. Claire was a bit more skeptical of six nights on the train, but she willingly signed up. Our good friends assigned to Taipei, Phil and Jane Lincoln and their three children, agreed to join us.

We were allowed to travel on our diplomatic passports. Visas were issued by the Soviet Embassy in Bangkok. We opted to fly to Beijing, where we spent a few days visiting sites newly opened to foreigners and catching up with friends at the embassy. Revisits to old haunts were fun for Jon and Eric: a new section of the Great Wall; the Ming Tombs; the Summer Palace; and of course, the Forbidden City and the fabulous treasures of the national palace museum.

The contrast with our experience living in Beijing a decade earlier was mind-bending. Commercial enterprises were everywhere. Cars and trucks filled the streets. Many new restaurants were open. Political slogans were few and far between. Hu Yaobang, chairman and general secretary of the Communist Party, 1981–1987, seemed to be allowing continued political experimentation and openness. That was exciting. He then lost his position in 1987 for too much willingness to allow a more open society. The CCP reacts badly to any hint of possible loss of control—witness the 1989 Tiananmen crackdown and massacre. By 1986 the U.S. Liaison Office had become the U.S. Embassy, which now was many times the size of our earlier thirty-five-person staff. Deng Xiaoping's reform and opening to the world were bearing fruit—a lot of it. Communists turned capitalists seemed to be everywhere, enthusiastically embracing Deng's supposed maxim capturing the spirit of the times even if he never said it with those words: "To Get Rich is Glorious!"

And then we arrived at the huge Beijing train station and our waiting train. All aboard!

Eric climbed up and moments later came running back to Claire, still on the station platform to shout: They have doilies! (He meant antimacassars). Claire, thus reassured, also climbed aboard.

Pulling out of the station, I felt a rising excitement for a week's adventure ending thousands of miles on the other side of Eurasia. We were on the so-called "Chinese train" with Chinese attendants, a step up from the Soviet train. Among other things, the food was better, and the attendants did not monitor our picture taking. The passenger cars went through to Moscow; the locomotives changed from Chinese to Soviet.

We traversed the North China plain, crossed Inner Mongolia of China, and then reached the Mongolian border. There we stayed for several hours while the passenger cars were lifted, and the trucks replaced to fit on the different gauge of the Mongolian and Soviet tracks. We had left Eric sleeping in the compartment; when he woke up, dismayed at being alone, the Chinese attendant reassured him and then handed him down to us.

We crossed Mongolia, stopped at Ulan Baatar, the capital, and continued north to the border with the Soviet Union. As we rolled along, we gazed at the vast territory of inner Asia, all lightly populated. One could almost imagine the hordes of Genghis Khan flying over the nearest hill on their way to establishing the greatest contiguous empire in human history.

Years later the State Department offered me the position of ambassador to Mongolia. That would have been fascinating. I turned it down twice, ultimately opting for ambassador to Cambodia and then instead becoming head of school of Northfield Mount Hermon School in Massachusetts, my high school alma mater.

In the middle of the night, the train stopped at the Soviet border. The border patrol looked at our passports and visas and then instructed Phil Lincoln to go with them. What was that about? We were in the hands of our sworn enemy, the Soviet Union. Quite some time later, Phil boarded the train just before departure and said the date on his visa issued in Bangkok was wrong—it should have specified the date of entrance into the Soviet Union and not the date of arrival in Moscow. A huge collective sigh of relief. The next train through wouldn't be for several days, and how would he have corrected the date? I'm sure the border patrol had no desire to take care of an American for days while figuring out what to do with him.

We continued our journey, passing Lake Baikal, stopping in Irkutsk, and then on to the west. We were far to the north in the summer so there was daylight very late. The kids played games and ate snacks we brought with us. We played Trivial Pursuit late into the night. We would also visit the dining car when hungry. The menu was many pages long. Every time we pointed to a dish, the answer was that it wasn't available. We finally caught on—there was only one dish for each meal; order it or else go back to our snacks.

One dominant memory for Claire and me: a very old, sad-looking Chinese man sat at the end of the dining car, seeming never to move for the six-day journey all the way to Moscow, *peeling potatoes!* To this day, we see him clearly and wonder about the many things he must have experienced through the decades of China's twentieth-century revolutions.

As daylight continued late into the evening, the result was hours of gazing out at the unending landscape of tundra and steppes of Siberia.

It brought home how large Eurasia really is. Periodically, we passed tiny villages and, not infrequently, caught views of people in bathing suits (and bikinis) stretched out in the warm sun. One can only imagine how long and daunting the dark winters far away from larger cities were. Periodically we stopped briefly at small stations, stretched our legs on the platform, and smiled at the ever-present children with food to sell.

In one of the large cities, Yekaterinburg, we stopped for an extended time. I hopped off with my camera. Claire followed. We walked for some exercise and then she aimed her camera at a group of marching troops. A policeman showed up and gestured he wanted her film—she committed a "no-no." She politely refused; she didn't take a picture because a train had blocked her view. The policeman, irritated, indicated he would go to get someone to speak English. As he did so, our Chinese train attendant ran over and told her to just get on the train. We pulled out of the station before Claire could be detained or arrested. The rest of the trip she feared someone would board the train and tell her she violated Soviet law!

Six days later we reached Moscow and made our way to the Intourist Hotel. I noticed that Tuborg beer was on sale. One dollar a can. Claire climbed into the bathtub (no bath on the train), lay back and gladly accepted a cold Tuborg. Heaven in Moscow thanks to Denmark.

The next several days we explored sights such as Red Square (no Lenin tomb), parks, museums, music events. To the layman's eyes and ears, the level of cultural professionalism was high. While waiting in line to enter a theater, I was accosted by a man who claimed he could take me to a basement church service that evening. I could meet many dissidents and people who were not happy with the Soviet government. Of course, it was obvious to me that he was a government person who would be happy to compromise and expose me as an American diplomat and spy. He seemed mightily disappointed he couldn't reel me in.

On to Leningrad (now Saint Petersburg) and all the historic buildings and sights. We took full advantage. A clear memory as we toured the beautiful Hermitage Museum: Eric had an upset stomach and suddenly, without any warning, he vomited on the polished floor. Our poor tour leader was distraught, not for Eric's illness but for the fear she would be chastised by her superior for not controlling her tour group.

An observation about a communist country: we ended up making our own arrangements for transportation and sightseeing because the Intourist personnel were totally uninterested in helping us. It was clear they had little motivation to be helpful—they were paid whether or not they made suggestions or arrangements for visitors. It reminded us of the adage in communist countries: "They pretend to pay us, and we pretend to work."

We had seen the same ethic in Beijing when assigned to the U.S. Liaison Office, 1976–1978. There was often little motivation even at the Friendship Store where foreigners had to do most of their shopping. Recall my earlier story about getting service only after we called out, *"Mao zhuxi shuo: Wei Renmin Fuwu"* ("Mao Zedong said: Serve the People!") We quickly had a gaggle of clerks converge on us.

Our flight from Leningrad was on Pan American, directly to Frankfurt. As we boarded, the smell of an American breakfast was in the air. It hit the spot. In Frankfurt we boarded a train for Paris and another round of visiting, with lots of walking. We fondly recall Jonathan and Eric walking behind us, good friends, talking at length about how they would design theme parks that were fun for kids.

And then we had to split up, I directly to Washington because Nick, my boss, needed me early, and Claire and the boys to London for one last round of sightseeing.

What a trip halfway around the world by train, plane, and automobile!

The Seventh Floor Heights of the Department of State: Executive Secretariat (S/S) and Legislative Affairs (H), 1986–1993

It felt like old home week as I got off the elevator on the seventh floor of the Department of State. My previous tours in the Executive Secretariat had been three fascinating years (1971–1974). I had arrived as a young officer from Embassy Saigon, unmarried, and in those next three years met my wife-to-be, traveled with Henry Kissinger, served again in Vietnam for seven months, received the State Department's award for outstanding analysis and reporting (the "Director General's Award"), and so much more.

Now I was married with two children and was a solid, promising, mid-career FSO with much hard-earned foreign policy experience, including a year of Vietnamese language training, two assignments to Vietnam, service in the Secretary's office, two years of Chinese language training, two years in Beijing at the USLO, three years in East–West Trade, two years on the China desk, and three years at the consulate general in Hong Kong.

The proverbial icing on the cake was being promoted to the rank of counselor in the Senior Foreign Service that fall. Reaching this rarefied height gave me permission to work even longer and harder.

Claire had been totally supportive all those years as we both balanced family life with foreign service work. She had proved her professional self and was rising rapidly up the career ladder. Without a strong family, success in the Foreign Service becomes much less likely or at least much more difficult. In the next several years, Claire also found great assignments: Director General's Office (all human resource and personnel issues) and African Affairs. Jon and Eric settled into life and school in the United States. Before we knew it, they became pre-teens, teens, and then young men.

As I arrived on the seventh floor that July day for a plum assignment, it was now time to jump into one of the hearts of foreign policy-making. It was a perfect position from which to work closely with the senior leaders of the State Department and participate in the country's policy-making process.

The seventh floor is physically the highest floor of office space at 2201 C Street and hosts the highest-ranking officers, including the secretary of state, the deputy secretary, and undersecretaries. The Executive Secretariat, headed by an executive secretary and personal assistant to the secretary and his/her two deputies, is physically wedged between the secretary's and deputy secretary's offices. It is responsible for supporting those top officials and ensuring development and coordination of U.S. foreign policy both within the Department and with the White House, NSC staff, Department of Defense, and other agencies.

My new position was as director of the Staff Secretariat, Office of the Secretary of State (S/S-S), but for years it has been known as the "Line." (State Department lore suggests the name came from the fact that the offices were lined up along the corridor opposite the secretary's office.) About twenty-five FSOs and civil servants coordinate policy priorities with State Department offices; work with bureaus to prepare high quality action, briefing, and info memos to the secretary; and plan and coordinate trips by the secretary overseas and travel with him/her on the plane. As I noted above, Kissinger, twice in his memoir, gave his staff—particularly Claire and me—a nice shout out for our support during our travels with him!

A successful "line officer" is one who has broad and deep foreign policy experience as well as an understanding of how the State Department and U.S. government are organized and managed to support our national security. The office was divided into teams and each team was staffed with foreign service people who knew well the issues their team's bureaus handled. Understanding the issues and being able to engage with assistant secretaries on policy was essential. The teams also needed to be able to negotiate with more than one bureau to know how to get them on the same wavelength and avoid end runs around other bureaus in pushing their preferred policies.

The secretary *must be able to trust* s/he is receiving factual and complete information and options as alternative policy approaches are considered. The "line officers" are literally on the front lines of ensuring the secretary is so served.

For example, a good line officer will require a bureau to "clear" its memo to the secretary with other offices to give them a chance to express their policy perspectives. Policy recommendations from the East Asia and Pacific bureau on economic relations with China would be coordinated with the economic and business bureau, or a memo on military issues would be coordinated with the political-military bureau. Some wide-ranging memos could have several "clearances." The bureaus are not required to agree to a lowest common denominator; if there are differences, they are laid out and the secretary chooses which policy approach is pursued.

Henry Kissinger when joining the State Department declared he was "onto" the ways of State: he claimed to have divined that the bureaus send action memos with three options—two at opposite ends of the spectrum and the (highly preferred) or moderate option in the center. He decreed they must all be reasonable options for consideration.

Yes, this policy-formulating process can be intense and even cumbersome at times. It is also more likely to produce informed and coordinated foreign policy. As the amount of information available skyrockets and communications proceeds at the speed of light, there is an increasing premium on producing coordinated and intelligent foreign policy information and priorities.

It was a joy to work with and supervise so many talented people. Many went on to become known as the best and brightest of the Foreign Service.

Secretary of State George Shultz

It was also a joy to meet Secretary Shultz again. By 1986 he had earned a well-deserved reputation as a steady and trustworthy statesman in support of American interests. Shortly after my arrival, he came across the hall and paid our office a visit. He thanked everyone for work done on behalf of the United States, chatted with several of the staff and talked with me about Hong Kong and China. He reminded me of our earlier conversations in Hong Kong.

Shultz's visit was a good example of the type of "people person" he was. He genuinely appreciated good work and wasn't shy about saying thank you. At the end of every trip overseas he organized a dinner on one of the last nights for all in his traveling party as a fun way to thank them.

Shultz also was a believer in being a good steward of an institution he headed. He aimed to leave it a better institution than when he arrived. He felt that way about the Department of State. He cared about people and was comfortable in relying on career staff, both foreign service and civil service. An important goal was ensuring the organization he headed was fully capable of the best service possible in support of its mission to our country. Other secretaries of state often brought longtime colleagues and created a bubble within which they worked. Shultz fought for and won increased resources for hiring needed people and training them. He was always the strongest proponent of good training and skills improvement throughout one's career—whether in languages, area studies, cross-cultural learning, history, administration, consular training, and so on. In recognition, the State Department created the George P. Shultz National Foreign Affairs Training Center and located within it the venerable Foreign Service Institute.

Shultz's personality, unlike other leaders I've known, such as Henry Kissinger, was comfortable dealing with people from many walks of life. He often had a twinkle in his eye and a kind word to share. He listened to you. On one of our trips, I wrote him a note urging him to speak out forcefully about Singapore's sentencing of an American student for what was a minor infraction of the law. Shultz asked me to come in, listened to my argument and then shared his perspective about the importance of Singapore to the United States and his desire to work more quietly behind the scenes. I didn't entirely agree with him, but he was willing to listen and explain.

Shultz could also be tough as nails. When President Reagan was persuaded in 1986 to require all national security personnel to undergo lie-detector tests, Shultz declared his total opposition on the grounds that he wanted to build trust and that lie detectors were too often just ineffective. He announced that even though Cabinet colleagues like Secretary of Defense Casper Weinberger and Director of Central Intelligence William Casey said they would comply, he would resign if the executive order went into effect. The order died a quiet death.

One of the strengths Shultz brought to his office was his wide range of experiences in different walks of life. He was an academic, a businessman, secretary of labor, director of the Office of Management and Budget, and a world traveler. He had experience working with Americans and others around the world from different backgrounds and experiences.

He was able to build bridges of trust, a critical ingredient in most endeavors. Shortly before his death in 2021, he published a perceptive article in the *Foreign Service Journal* on what trust means and how he used it to work with others to resolve even the thorniest of issues. In working closely with him for three years until 1989, I never once felt in any way that he dealt with me or anyone else in less than a trusting way—no flim-flam. Straightforward and honest.

Shultz was always keenly aware of the context within which he operated as secretary of state: the president; White House officials; other government departments, particularly Defense, the Treasury, and Commerce; Congress; the media; etc. Often it took longer to get things done than in other walks of life.

On one of our trips together, he told me how frustrating it was when criticism came his way because he wasn't more aggressive in trying to get things done. He observed that a venture capitalist or other businessman could fail nine times before hitting the jackpot and being hailed for the accomplishments. As secretary of state, if he failed nine times, he'd be thrown out of office—in fact, he would be out well before he reached nine. Thus, he demonstrated the need for care and patience in preparing the way forward and reaching decisions.

Shultz would often say that nothing in Washington is ever definitively decided. Even when a decision comes down, someone is always attempting to overturn it.

And then there is Shultz's favorite way of describing diplomacy: it's like gardening! It is a fully apt metaphor for the need for constant and focused vigilance in attending to relationships, identifying coming challenges, and creating options to protect national security while building bridges to other nations and peoples.

My experience was that Shultz was always steady and even. He did not have the emotional ups and downs of other senior leaders I've known. He kept his emotions under control. There was perhaps one exception I witnessed. On a visit to Manila, we added a trip across Manila Bay to Corregidor Island. During World War II, the Japanese finally overcame a determined Filipino and American defense and completed their takeover of the Philippines. Shultz was visibly moved on several occasions that day when we visited the Pacific War Memorial and the untouched ruins of many buildings left, as is, to memorialize the conflict. Shultz undoubtedly recalled his service as a Marine in the Pacific during World War II and the terror of the war. Adding to the emotion of the visit was the reaction of Mrs. Shultz (O'bie to her friends), who had been a First Lieutenant in the Army Nurses Corp and part of the invasion force to re-take the Philippines from the Japanese in 1944.

Then there was a celebrated "national security" leak of information. Rumors had been around that Shultz had a Princeton tiger tattooed on his backside. In response to questions, he would always flash his enigmatic smile and neither confirm nor deny. But reporters can be crafty. A journalist on one of our trips thought to ask Mrs. Shultz. She smiled and let the tiger out of the bag, confirming that the tattoo was real! The press had a field day with the story.

When we traveled overseas, Shultz always aimed to add stops to tend to his diplomatic gardening. Returning from Asia on one trip, we landed for several hours for ceremonies and dinner in the Republic of the Marshall Islands and another time in Western Samoa. As a Marine assigned to the Pacific during World War II, he retained a strong interest in all those Pacific Islands. He often added Hong Kong—one of his favorite cities—to the itinerary. He was keenly interested in how reversion to Chinese sovereignty was working out.

In 1988 we were approaching Hong Kong, ahead of schedule, and I thought to tell him we had finished a spectacular new residential complex on Victoria Peak for the consul general and senior officers: "Would you and Mrs. Shultz like to visit?" He said, "Sure!" So, I picked up the airplane's phone to call Don Anderson, consul general. I asked if it would be convenient for us to come up. He said, "Sure!" I can only imagine how much scurrying around ensued to greet the secretary of state. It was a pleasant visit. The secretary and Mrs. Shultz stopped to chat with Don Anderson's visiting mother during the tour.

Mrs. Shultz was a pleasure to be with. Always friendly, with a smile. Never demanding. A good traveling companion.

I admit to wondering what it would be like to live in Hong Kong.

It never occurred to me that five years later, Claire and I would take up residence in that magnificent house on the mountain overlooking Hong Kong harbor to the north and Aberdeen and the South China Sea to the south. Nor that we would entertain the Shultz's there for dinners when I was consul general. Or Secretary of State James Baker, or Secretary of the Treasury Robert Rubin, or Secretary of Commerce Ron Brown. Or British governor Chris Patten. Or many others.

We need more George Shultzes willing to serve as our political and moral leaders.

A Promotion within the Executive Secretariat to Deputy Executive Secretary

For much of the 1986–1987 year, I filled in for Ken Quinn as deputy executive secretary in the front office when he was traveling with the secretary or otherwise out of the office, all in addition to running the Staff Secretariat. I was comfortable enough with the long hours and frequent travel (thanks, Claire!) and heavy workload that I was able to put my hat in the ring to replace Ken permanently in 1987 as deputy executive secretary. There were dozens of qualified candidates.

I was fortunate to be chosen for the position, which ranked as a deputy assistant secretary—a higher position than I ever thought I might attain, and higher than the great majority of FSOs do attain.

Executive secretaries and their two deputies occupied three small offices between the secretary's and deputy secretary's suites. Three administrative assistants worked with us. The offices faced south, overlooking the Lincoln Memorial, the National Mall, and Potomac River. We spent countless mornings and evenings watching the sunrises and sunsets.

The three of us supervised hundreds of people who constituted "command and control" for the secretary and the State Department. They included the operations center (staffed 24/7 monitoring the world and helping American citizens), the "line," information (handling and storing papers, info), and administration (supporting all of us, human resources, logistics for travel, etc.).

We had conference facilities we used for classified meetings with NSC staff, the White House, and other agencies and facilities to create and oversee task forces to monitor ongoing crises. One of them, for example, was the 1988 Lockerbie terrorist bombing of Pan Am 103 over the United Kingdom, ordered by Libyan dictator Muammar Gaddafi and resulting in the death of hundreds. Or coup attempts in the Philippines or the violence in Tiananmen Square in May–June 1989. The task forces were staffed by representatives of concerned bureaus and were responsible for following all issues and coordinating with us to make sure U.S. government agencies were sharing information and taking necessary action, whether informing the secretary or coordinating efforts to support American citizens.

The two deputies also shared responsibility for principal liaison with all the Department's bureaus, knowing the assistant secretaries and the issues. I was responsible for East Asia and the Pacific, Near East and South Asian affairs, and African affairs, plus functional bureaus such as Economic and Business Affairs and Intelligence and Research.

A typical day looked something like this. The "early" deputy arrived by 6:00 am to be briefed on overnight developments, collect urgent cables and memos, organize priorities for the day, and then brief the executive secretary and senior Department officials at the secretary's early morning meetings, and others. The "late" deputy would usually arrive by 7:00 am. The day was filled with knowing the issues, tasking the bureaus with action requests (e.g., asking for a briefing memo updating the secretary), coordinating with the NSC staff, reading through the volume of memos that came for the secretary, and either signing them in for distribution or returning them to the bureau for substantive changes or further clearances. One of the three of us usually attended the secretary's meetings with the bureaus and others to ensure follow-up and coordination.

The pace was always brisk and usually intense. Keeping track of fast-moving crises and myriad other ongoing issues required one's full attention. I regretfully gave up smoking my pipe, a habit more suited to leisurely activities. Undoubtedly, though, my body thanked me.

The "early" deputy was fortunate to leave for home by 8:00 pm. The late deputy could be there much longer. These were not jobs for the faint of heart. But they did put one in the middle of the action in the making of American foreign policy.

The executive secretary when I first joined the office was Ambassador Nicholas (Nick) Platt and the two deputies were Ken Quinn and Lynn Pascoe. Nick was one of my favorite senior FSOs who became a real mentor and friend over the years. He chose me for key positions in the State Department, encouraged me into the China field, and in 1996 he chose me to be executive director of the Asia Society Hong Kong Center after I was consul general. In S/S, Nick handed the reins to Mel Levitsky, Lynn was replaced by Jim Collins, and I succeeded Ken. All of us went on to become chiefs of mission/ambassadors.

And then there were the trips with Schultz. He visited many countries, some repeatedly. Our job was to do the policy planning for the visits' objectives, including creating background and policy books, sending out advance teams to work with each embassy, and ensuring good coordination with all State Department bureaus as well as the NSC and other agencies. Truth be told, the trips often were a welcome change of pace from the Washington grind.

Shultz was one of the most traveled secretaries up to that point. I saw him when he visited Hong Kong in the summers of 1984, 1985, and 1986 while he was tending his "diplomatic garden" in Asia. Reviewing all his overseas travels, the ones that stood out were those that addressed the Soviet Union, NATO, Middle East, and East Asia. Here are trips I went on with him in 1987 and 1988.

- June 11–June 22, 1987 — Iceland, Philippines (I attended a luncheon for Cory Aquino, and went on the aforementioned visit to Corregidor, Singapore, Australia, Western Samoa.)

- October 16–20, 1987 — Israel, Saudi Arabia, Israel, Egypt, United Kingdom.

- February 25–March 4, 1988 — Israel, Syria, Jordan, Israel, Egypt, Israel, Jordan, Israel, United Kingdom, Belgium, United Kingdom, Israel, Syria, Egypt.

- April 1–8, 1988 — Italy, Vatican City, (I participated in audience with Pope John Paul II and Easter Sunday Mass in Saint Peter's Basilica), Israel, Jordan, Syria, Egypt, Jordan, Saudi Arabia, Jordan, Cyprus.

- June 3–10, 1988 — Cairo, Amman, Tel Aviv, Jerusalem, Cairo,

Damascus, Cairo, Luxor, Madrid.

- July 6–20, 1988 — Bangkok (Association of Southeast Asian Nations Post-Ministerial Conference), Kuala Lumpur, Jakarta, Manila, Hong Kong (July 13–14), Beijing, Seoul, Tokyo, Majuro (Republic of the Marshall Islands), Honolulu.

- August 19–21, 1988 — Cairo, Islamabad, Cairo. The trip to Pakistan was for the funeral of President Muhammad Zia-ul-Haq, killed in an air crash, and to bring back the remains of U.S. Ambassador to Pakistan Arnie Raphel, also killed in the crash. His widow, Nancy Ely-Raphel, returned to Washington with us.

George Shultz's relationships with Soviet leaders, particularly Minister of Foreign Affairs Eduard Shevardnadze and Soviet General Secretary Mikhail Gorbachev, helped set up the post-Soviet Union era in U.S.-Russia relations, which Bush and Baker later built on successfully. My colleague Lynn Pascoe accompanied Shultz on trips to other capitals, such as Moscow, Brussels, London, Bonn, and Paris as the United States pursued arms control, NATO planning, and other agreements with the Soviet Union and Europe.

The reader might ask the reasons for all this travel. In a nutshell, personal and direct diplomacy can have great value. Developing trust in one's interlocutors can be paramount. You will recall Claire and I accompanied Kissinger as he flew back and forth between Israel and Syria for five weeks in 1974 carrying ever-evolving proposals for dis-engagement. He might get President Assad locked into one key point and then in Jerusalem get Israeli Prime Minister Yitzhak Shamir to buy into a related key point. Then Kissinger would return to Syria and work to build on those points. The Israelis and Syrians did not trust each other, so Kissinger would have to put his own credibility and that of the United States on the line to move the negotiations forward as they built toward an agreement both sides would support. Knowing both parties and their national security objectives intimately was critical in bridging gaps.

Similarly, you will see in the above travel schedule Secretary Shultz engaging in Arab-Israeli exchanges in 1988. The First Palestinian Intifada brought violence to the fore in the region. In a nutshell, the Shultz and Reagan Peace Plan envisioned direct talks between the United States and Yassar Arafat of the Palestine Liberation Organization. Shultz was tough in laying down preconditions. Arafat only came part way. Shultz didn't budge. In the end, Arafat met the U.S. conditions, clearing the way for next steps in the George H.W. Bush administration. All along the way Shultz would call on other leaders in the Middle East to bring them around to supporting the plan.

U.S. Ambassador to Israel Dan Kurtzer, with whom I worked closely in 1987–1989, was a key adviser to Shultz on Middle East policy. He traveled regularly with us to the region. In homage to Shultz after his death in 2021, Dan wrote in a U.S. Institute for Peace publication about the negotiations and Shultz's tactical and strategic approaches. Dan's comment:

"His (Shultz's) diplomatic garden could appear unchanged for extensive periods only to bloom dramatically under his creative diplomatic flair and instinct."

Since we're on the topic of "diplomacy," here is another foreign service colleague's description of the profession:

"Diplomacy...is by nature an unheroic, quiet endeavor, less swaggering than unrelenting, after unfolding in back channels out of sight and out of mind" —Bill Burns

Bill Burns worked with Secretaries Shultz and Baker and traveled with us in 1987–1989 in that elusive quest for peace in the Middle East. In 2021, he became director of the Central Intelligence Agency. Bill, Dan, Aaron Miller, Charlie Hill, and other highly competent professionals were a great pleasure to work with.

Here are two of my favorite definitions of diplomacy:

"Diplomacy is letting someone have it your way."

"Diplomacy is telling someone to go to hell and make him feel happy to be on his way."

High points for me on all these trips were both the substance of the foreign policy objectives, which you will read about in the history books, and the seating arrangements on the aircraft which facilitated those conversations! A cabin with two worktables and seating for six was reserved for Secretary and Mrs. Shultz, Charlie Hill (special assistant), the deputy executive secretary (me), and his personal secretary. It was a privilege to share conversations with the Shultz's on those long flights. They were always gracious and friendly. My lifelong admiration for George Shultz is grounded in my observations in different settings of his personal and professional demeanor and actions.

My point in providing some detail above is to give a better understanding and flavor to what I was privileged to experience and learn.

It might also help the reader develop an inside view of the making of foreign policy and how much goes on behind the scenes, out of sight, but is nevertheless intense and consequential.

Transition to President George H.W. Bush and Secretary James Baker

President Bush and Secretary Baker took office in early 1989. I continued as deputy executive secretary. We had prepared significant briefing books in the fall of 1988 for the new secretary. We had organized a slate of presentations and meetings to get Baker's team up to speed. As it turned out, the Shultz-Baker relationship was not close. All our prep work was undoubtedly useful to Baker's team, and we provided more of what they asked for as necessary. But the transition was low-key, plain, and simple.

Baker brought with him many of his own people. Margaret Tutwiler as spokesperson and assistant secretary for public affairs (very close to Baker); Bob Zoellick as counselor; Bob Kimmitt as undersecretary for political affairs; Dennis Ross as head of policy planning; Larry Eagleburger as deputy secretary (a State Department veteran); Janet Mullins as assistant secretary for legislative affairs, for whom I would work in six months.

Yes, some people thought it was too much of an inner and closed circle. But in my experience, they were all smart people, some younger with fresher ideas, trusted by Baker and dedicated to good policy as well as politics. I saw them open up to career people who had experience that served the secretary and public policy.

Baker himself came with broad experience and considerable strengths: a close relationship with the president; a knack for dealing with Congress and the press; an instinct for putting together deals; and an ever-present keen eye on domestic U.S. politics.

Our office continued to do what it did best, namely, providing command and control for the State Department at the direction of the secretary. It was clear that with Baker's close relationship with the president, the State Department would be a leader in foreign policy formulation.

Baker's first trip was an early one to many allies in Western Europe. The emphasis was on connecting with allies and friends. President Bush was regularly on the phone with leaders around the world. There was much talk of a "new world order" with the United States as an active leader.

When we learned that Japanese Emperor Hirohito had died and the state funeral was scheduled for February 24, 1989, the president quickly announced he would travel to Japan; Baker would accompany him. That meant I would join the delegation. Preparations went into high gear. South Korea and China were added to the itinerary, so the trip became more complex. It was a golden opportunity for the new president to meet with leaders of three key countries.

We flew first to Tokyo for the funeral. I was on Air Force Two, the backup plane for the president, along with several members of Congress invited to join the delegation. The funeral went as planned and the meetings with Japanese officials were timely.

A personal observation about diplomacy and history: when I thought beyond my hours of work to support the secretary, it was a strange feeling having traveled halfway around the world for the funeral of a man who became the Japanese Emperor in 1926 and who was complicit in the attack on the United States at Pearl Harbor on December 7, 1941. A day of infamy, as President Franklin D. Roosevelt called it. I was born three years later. For most of my professional career, I was involved in the ongoing effort to nurture our alliance with Japan against the Soviet Union and China and to build back Japan's peaceful economy. It was a worthy professional effort and an homage to the cultural, economic, and social achievements of the Japanese people. Hirohito was spared charges of war crimes to preserve the Japanese reverence for the institution of the emperor and his ability to provide social unity. Again, it was a practical decision not to prosecute, most likely, but one that still left me thinking about how strange international affairs can be. Do we truly have no permanent friends? Only permanent interests?

On to Beijing: our two days in Beijing were less smooth. But first, shortly after arrival, I found myself and Secretary Baker on a landing in a villa in the Chinese Diaoyutai state guest house where we were all staying. I conveyed not only information about the upcoming discussion but the important nonpolitical Texas news that Jerry Jones had just bought the Dallas Cowboys. Baker laughed and said he knew Jerry well, they were both Texans, and that Jerry finally got what he wanted.

Baker pointed out again that President Bush wanted the Beijing visit to be a celebratory "homecoming" since he had been chief of the USLO years before. He and Barbara Bush had fond memories. He also wanted to continue to build the much-needed bridges between our two countries.

On the second night in Beijing, Bush hosted a large dinner for senior Chinese leaders and other community members in the Great Wall Sheraton Hotel. The theme was Texas and Texas barbeque.

As the clock counted down to the dinner, word leaked out that one of the invited guests was Professor Fang Lizhi, a well-known dissident and critic of the CCP. In order to deter him from attending, the government had detained him. This was big news. Questions from journalists came thick and fast, diverting attention from Bush's otherwise successful visit and Texas barbeque dinner about to begin. Bush was furious, assuming the guest list had not been vetted to foresee the possible crisis. The NSC staff pointed fingers at the embassy and U.S. Ambassador to China Winston Lord. The embassy pointed back: Fang Lizhi's name was on the list approved by NSC staff.

The recriminations continued back in Washington. Winston Lord had hoped to be chosen by Bush (a fellow Republican) as a senior national security official. That never happened. Lord would have to wait for the Clinton administration to receive the call as assistant secretary of state for East Asian and Pacific Affairs.

But that contretemps was just the first firecracker signaling that Bush's desire to build bridges to Beijing would be fraught in the coming months.

As spring blossomed in Beijing, so did the number of "visitors" to Tiananmen Square. As the weeks went by, the protests escalated. Hu Yaobang, former general secretary of the Party, died on April 15, 1989, leading to tens of thousands of students who loved his reformist ideas to flood the square. As the days passed others joined them, including workers, government employees, teachers, and rural residents. While the CCP claimed they were seeking the overthrow of the government, the vast majority were in fact demanding an end to corruption, an increase in government transparency, better wages and working conditions, and more social freedoms. Even though some built a replica of the Statue of Liberty, in reality few were demanding a full and open democratic, "one person, one vote," political system.

The PRC government suffered a huge embarrassment when they had to alter plans to receive Soviet General Secretary Gorbachev. At the same time, more and more protesters were congregating in cities around China.

The inevitable came to pass: Deng Xiaoping, despite not holding a formal senior position in the CCP, issued the order to clear the square. There was no instruction to do so peacefully. On June 4, the tanks and infantry moved into the square with deadly results. Thousands were injured and killed. The exact number is unknown; the government's published figures were demonstrably low.

The reaction in the United States and around the world to this bloody massacre of Chinese citizens was one of shock and horror. So much for peaceful reform and opening up that had been the mantra. Professor Fang Lizhi, who had been barred from President Bush's dinner four months earlier, took refuge at the American Embassy in Beijing. U.S.-China relations plummeted and remained in deep freeze for at least half of the Bush presidency. National Security Advisor Brent Scowcroft made an unpublicized visit to Beijing, drawing negative domestic criticism; Baker avoided visiting Beijing for two and a half years until November 1991.

I was not entirely surprised at the violence unleashed in Tiananmen Square. Not only were Chinese leaders seriously embarrassed, but they convinced themselves that the protesters were counterrevolutionaries and needed to be dealt with firmly. Some of us had the impression that if Premier Zhao Ziyang had been allowed to make the decisions, he might have been able to promise some actions in response to the crowd's demands and ultimately clear the square peacefully. He certainly had established a reputation for a "moderate" approach to reform and opening up, willing to continue to experiment with alternative approaches to transforming Chinese society. I'm willing to believe he would not have ordered in the tanks and soldiers. We will never know. It was certainly another reminder that many Chinese leaders were consumed, first and foremost, with maintaining social control and the primacy of the Communist Party. Deng's decision represented a major strategic challenge to the world order and led to a long-term souring of U.S.-China relations. Beijing's iron fist came down again in 2020 in Hong Kong when Xi Jinping tore up China's Basic Law and the Sino-British Joint Resolution on Hong Kong that had promised fifty years of a high degree of autonomy. Never forget: authoritarian leaders see "black hands" behind citizen protest and usually do not refrain from using force to counter them.

A Move Down the State Department's Seventh Floor Corridor To Be Deputy Assistant Secretary for Legislative Affairs (H), 1989–1992

As summer 1989 came into view, and with it the end of my three-year assignment to the secretary's office, the question of my next assignment came front and center. I had been assigned for a year to the prestigious Senior Seminar at the Foreign Service Institute. The class of senior FSOs was to spend a year of learning: travel, study, presentations, writing, visiting different government departments, and more. It was also designed as a change of pace, and for that I was enthusiastic.

But then fate and the infamous "needs of the Service" intervened. Every assignment memorandum contained, for example: "Richard W. Mueller is assigned to the American Embassy in Saigon as political officer subject to the needs of the Foreign Service." That meant you could be assigned anywhere at any time, and that happens to this day. It gives the State Department great flexibility.

Secretary Baker wanted Janet Mullins, his assistant secretary for legislative affairs, to have one career FSO as one of her deputies. She was new to the State Department and fresh from an active senior role in the Bush presidential campaign. What better way to connect her office to the rest of the building than to appoint a career person as deputy assistant secretary?

I had mixed feelings, knowing it would be another brutally difficult position right in the middle of hardball politics on Capitol Hill. Both the House and Senate were solidly in Democratic hands, thus making the implementation of the president's agenda more difficult. I had several talks with her. I liked her obvious professionalism and knowledge. She was also reserved and wary of the vast U.S. State Department and government she was entering. Could we, working together, each learn from and trust the other?

With Claire's strong support, I decided to go for it. I have no regrets.

My new position as deputy assistant secretary for legislative affairs made me feel as though I had entered the belly of the beast. Rarely do FSOs have the opportunity to deal so intimately with the U.S. Congress and U.S. politics. The legislative process is complicated and difficult to comprehend, let alone influence and direct.

Never has there been a truer comment than: *"There are two things one never wants to see being made: Sausage and the law!"*

During my three years in the position, I learned firsthand how complex the legislative and political processes can be. They are infused with widely differing interests, the influence of vast amounts of money, rapid fire communications often necessitating quick decisions allowing little time for reflection, and the need to cut deals to get things done. All the while, members must keep one eye on what's right for the nation and our citizens and the other eye on their own re-election interests. Sadly, their own futures often seem to take precedence over what would otherwise be good for our country.

And now, as I write looking back thirty years, our politics have become even more corrupted by personal agendas often driven by the search for power, money, and influence. People too often run for office for the wrong reasons. The "Gingrich Revolution" of 1994 broke the Republicans out of the Democratic lock on Congress and began the march to scorched earth politics to this day (Donald Trump, Kentucky Senator Mitch McConnell, the Freedom Caucus, Fox News, talk show hosts, and on and on).

But during my three years of 1989–1992 in Legislative Affairs, there was some degree of our representatives working together, particularly on national security and foreign policy issues such as the three-year response to the June 4, 1989, Tiananmen Square massacre and subsequent rebuilding of U.S.-China relations; the Gulf War to drive Iraq out of Kuwait and save Saudi Arabia; and the successful navigation of the unexpected and potentially dangerous breakup of the Soviet Union. The social and economic issues were another matter.

Secretary Baker, of course working closely with President Bush, deserves much credit for skillfully building bridges to allies and friends around the world, working with the Congress, and using successful media communications. The professionals in Baker's circle also deserve credit.

It was the beginning of the so-called unipolar world, a "new world order" led by the sole superpower, the United States. What this would mean was still unclear. One day I received a phone call from a member of Congress who wanted to better understand what the administration meant by a new world order. I gave him a few ideas and undertook to explore the question more fully. I did not meet with much success; it was mostly an ephemeral idea that sounded good.

I believe now that deeply planted seeds of that era led to vast overreach by the United States, whether through George W. Bush's ill-conceived and ill-fated invasion of Iraq to bring democracy to the Middle East (and find nonexistent biological weapons), or our long-term commitment to waging war on terrorism in Afghanistan, or investing even more heavily in military spending, or ignoring or downplaying potential challenges such as the "rise" of China and threats posed by Putin's Russia.

We also ignored supremely relevant lessons from post-World War II foreign policy, in particular, our ill-conceived and ill-fated war in Vietnam. It was driven by far too much "swagger" in U.S. foreign policy, a term popularized by Secretary of State Mike Pompeo decades later as he claimed he sought to empower once again American diplomats.

My role in Legislative Affairs? I was asked to take charge of the State Department's work with the Congress on State Department budget authorizations and appropriations (the lifeblood for our continued operations plus the many policy issues attached to the bills) as well as our intelligence interests with the foreign affairs committees, the Senate Select Committee on Intelligence, and the House Permanent Select Committee on Intelligence. A focus was on the highly classified "compartmented" intelligence work, including "Presidential Findings." These included the classified programs around the world designed to support U.S. national security interests.

I spent much time on Capitol Hill meeting key staff people, members of Congress, and lobbyists. I also learned how the process worked—and often didn't work. Just connecting the dots and discovering what was happening was key, followed by the need to devise effective responses to further the administration's agenda. As always, it was vital to learn whom I could trust and who was shoveling BS. There was always much of that to dodge.

I crossed paths periodically with Bob Gates, my old roommate from William and Mary who was now deputy director of the CIA. Early on in my legislative affairs tenure, I went up to a highly classified special compartmented intelligence briefing on U.S. programs. I saw Bob across the room. He came over and we chatted before and after the briefing. Shortly thereafter he had me over to lunch at CIA headquarters. We talked about foreign policy and our families. He was also interested in any "intelligence" I might share on what Secretary Baker was up to!

Back in the State Department, I was responsible for rallying all the offices that had responsibilities for each issue. For example, I worked with the undersecretary for management and his staff on appropriations, the bureau for administration, regional and functional bureaus on their respective budgets, etc. We often went up to the Hill to discuss the administration's positions on issues, looking for support first from friendly members of Congress and staffs, and then broadening our strategy.

I would keep Janet Mullins informed as well as the other deputies who followed the Senate and House. She generally liked to brief the secretary, unless I sat in for her during Baker or Deputy Secretary Larry Eagleburger's morning staff meeting.

She and I had in fact developed a good relationship. She had concluded she could trust me with the administration's business. In turn, I had learned to work with her at times unique style. She could turn on her frosty face, terrifying some in the building, and then turn around with a smile and her softer way. She dated Maine Senator George Mitchell, Democratic Majority Leader, which made for interesting Washington gossip. She assured us she had made sure President Bush knew of the "nonpartisan" relationship.

On the trust front, she paid me a high compliment one day when I told her what I had learned that an assistant secretary was doing. But I said it should be okay because he was an administration appointee. Her response? I don't trust him at all; he has his own agenda that's often not aligned with the president's; I far more trust you and other career officers who I find usually play things much more straightforwardly. One can't ask for more than that.

Some of the many, many issues that demanded attention included:

—U.S. support for National Union for the Total Independence of Angola leader Jonas Savimbi in his fight against the leftist government. There were other programs around the world that were sensitive and highly classified.

—U.S. support for Afghanistan in the wake of the Soviet Union's withdrawal. I took regular trips to Capitol Hill with Special Envoy Peter Tomsen, a career FSO I first met in Vietnam. Peter was tasked with supporting factions in Afghanistan who might be more aligned with U.S. interests. Much later the film *Charlie Wilson's War* was a well-done portrayal of our relationship and how a member of Congress worked to support Afghanistan. It showed how the United States made fatal strategic mistakes by turning away from the country after the Soviets left.

—Hong Kong Policy Act creation to recognize Hong Kong's high degree of autonomy under China's system of "one country, two systems." I was asked to lead State negotiations with the Hill to pass the Act unanimously in 1992. Subsequently, as consul general in Hong Kong, we worked to implement the act to support Hong Kong's autonomy and differential treatment from its sovereign, the PRC. See my *Foreign Service Journal* article (FSJ, December 2017, pp 33-34) explaining what the act did and why it was an important plank in our foreign policy toward China.

—Building support in Congress during the buildup to the Gulf War and the president's decision to send a hundred thousand troops to drive Iraq out of Kuwait. Baker traveled seemingly continuously to produce a broad coalition that opposed Iraq's brazen invasion. Saudi Arabia was undoubtedly in Saddam's gunsights after taking Kuwait. Saudi leaders, at their peril, forget that the United States almost certainly saved them.

—I give President Bush much credit for refraining from sending U.S. forces into Bagdad after driving the Iraqis out of Kuwait. The coalition of allies put together had one aim, namely, to save Kuwait, not take Iraq. Importantly, the United States and other countries had done little planning to administer Iraq, something that we found out was almost impossible when President George Bush invaded years later.

Briefing members of Congress over a weekend that gas masks were being provided to U.S. troops on reports that Hussein intended to use chemical agents. There was urgent need to inform our allies.

—Yearly renewal of Most Favored Nation (MFN) treatment for China, the never-ending battle to broaden trade relations that were constricted by the Jackson-Vanik amendment to the 1974 Trade Act. Every year, members of Congress threatened to withdraw MFN. The Chinese and the U.S. business communities would mobilize to oppose withdrawal. China would make some "concessions" and/or announce the award of some big business contracts. MFN was "saved" again. Looking back, some argued we should have continued yearly renewal to give us some possible "leverage" with China. Also, China was far from being a market economy country even though its economy was remarkably more open than it had been. The contrary argument had considerable merit: encourage China to continue to free up trade relations and "join the world."

This subject of MFN for China prompts me to note again, *"Words Matter!"* Many Americans, on hearing "most favored nation," assumed we were giving China exceptional and favored treatment. In fact, MFN is extended to virtually all our trading partners. So, the newly coined term "Permanent Normal Trade Relations" far better explained the attempt to improve relations with China. It was the normal thing to do! *"Words Matter."*

—Rebuilding the American embassy chancery in Moscow that had been seriously compromised by Soviet intelligence intrusion. The undersecretary for management had concluded that a "top hat" solution was needed: lop off the top floors and rebuild with American workers a "top hat" addition isolated from the rest of the building. There were huge Congressional concerns and recriminations.

In the seemingly tornado-sized swirl of issues and events, I also supervised more than fifteen Foreign Service and Civil Service officers who each followed designated regional and functional issues. They were the workhorses who kept tabs on developments and helped us coordinate with staff on the Hill and within the State Department every day. They were all part of a group of "unsung" heroes willing to work hard on behalf of the American people and *whichever* party was in power. Some people would uncaringly refer to them as bureaucrats or staffers. I prefer to emphasize the *"Service"* in Foreign Service and Civil Service.

Experienced staff on the Hill are key to getting anything done. Writing clear legal language is an art and it takes time, which often isn't available. Agreements worked out in committee meetings often aren't clear and are not written. So, staff goes back to paste something together. No wonder legislative meaning and direction are often opaque.

Staff regularly admitted that the federal budget was out of control in the sense that no one truly understood its full dimensions and content. No one could identify all the consequences, good or bad, of a particular piece of legislation.

Some staff members would welcome House or Senate recess and tell me: *"Well, the Republic is safe for another few weeks!"*

These observations were from thirty years ago. I appreciate how much more difficult (and at times impossible) legislating has become in an era of even bigger budgets and deficits; now pervasive and instantaneous digital communication; and the realization of the many challenges we face to fund adequate education, medical care, and many other needs to bring fairness to U.S. society. Political gridlock is often frustratingly insurmountable.

What Next after Service in Legislative Affairs?

Claire and I began to think seriously about our next assignments. It didn't take long to put consul general to Hong Kong on the list, a chief of mission assignment reporting directly to Washington and not to the U.S. ambassador in Beijing. It was a city we knew well and loved with a good school for Eric (Hong Kong International School), good family life, and undoubtedly fascinating coming history in the years leading up to Hong Kong's reversion to China in 1997.

I talked with Janet to ask for her support with Deputy Secretary Eagleburger and the director general. She said she would support me. I made my own preferences clear to decision makers. I was a credible candidate with my Asia, China, and Hong Kong background. The fact that I had put in six intense years on the seventh floor in two demanding positions and was known to many was also a plus. But it was far from a slam dunk assignment. There were other qualified candidates.

At the last minute, a senior official questioned whether the position should go to a political appointee—something that had not happened in recent history. Fortunately, in the twentieth century the personnel system and the secretary disagreed, and my assignment went forward.

An interesting fact: former Civil War Confederate officer, Jon Singleton Mosby of the Mosby's Raiders cavalry unit fame, was appointed by President Grant as American consul to Hong Kong, 1878–1885.

It was a big deal! We were gratified and ecstatic. Friends were happy for us. It was a fascinating ambassador-level, chief of mission professional assignment ranking with a four-star military officer. Had Hong Kong been an independent country, the position would have been as a confirmed ambassador. But we couldn't pack right away since the assignment was for 1993. Since my three-year assignment in Legislative Affairs was up, it made sense to join a refresher Chinese program at FSI, which also gave me time to prepare for the assignment by consulting with the many entities I would be working with, including U.S. government agencies, Congress, the U.S. business community, and others.

Family Life During Our Seven/Eight Years in Washington, 1986–1993/1994

Our years in Washington were filled not only with professional accomplishments, but also much good family time, with Jonathan and Eric growing into mature young persons on the verge of "young adulthood."

Claire worked for Ambassador Bill Swing and Ambassador Hank Cohen in the director general's office of the State Department, (personnel affairs) 1986–1989. Both men were among the best and brightest of the Foreign Service and became good friends of ours. She and I observed firsthand the interest of Secretary Shultz in supporting and nurturing the Foreign Service and State Department as quality institutions for the long run.

Claire then moved in 1989 to work for Hank Cohen, who became assistant secretary of state for African Affairs when James Baker became secretary of state under President George W. Bush. Africa was a whole new world for her, and she was fortunate to learn about it from one of the country's foremost specialists on Africa, namely, Hank Cohen. One of the highlights was meeting Nelson Mandela of South Africa and being forever struck by how he looked her in the eye and smiled, unlike other politicians who looked over your shoulder as they shook hands to see who else was more worthy of meeting. One of her proudest possessions is a personally autographed picture of the two of them meeting in the State Department on his second visit to State. Hank took it to South Africa on one of his trips, where Mandela graciously agreed to autograph it. Read her memoir *A Collection of Life Stories,* published by StoryWorth.

Jonathan and Eric both made smooth transitions to their new schools. HKIS had prepared them well. Jonathan attended Shrevewood Elementary followed by Kilmer Middle School. Eric went to Haycock Elementary and then on to Longfellow Middle School. All Fairfax County, Virginia schools.

We made a point of always trying to arrange our work schedules to allow us to attend teacher conferences, after school plays, oversee homework, orthodontic appointments, Little League baseball games, and many other special occasions. Of great help was having new State Department wireless phones so we needn't always stay close to a landline on evenings and weekends. They were the size of a brick and just as heavy, but they brought a newfound freedom. And today our Apple iPhones fit easily in a pocket.

Baseball was a big hit with both Jon and Eric. We were fortunate to find a team that valued both boys and that had a coach who was happy to stop by the house to pick them up for practice before we got home. Weekends in spring and summer were often devoted to games. Much anxiety on their parents' part! In one game, Jon was lifted as pitcher and replaced by—Eric!—who had little pitching experience. Claire was so nervous she promptly walked the third base foul line out beyond the fence.

These days we relive those experiences with grandson Jackson who loves catching and pitching. His sisters (Clara and Gillian) chose soccer, volleyball, and gymnastics over baseball.

We saw Mother and Dad regularly in Williamsburg or at our place in northern Virginia. They promised to visit us in Hong Kong, even though they had already been to Asia to see us in Beijing in the 1970s and Hong Kong in the 1980s. We also saw my sister Lynn, her husband Bill, and their daughters, Jennifer and Andrea, periodically for special occasions.

Summer vacations were a highlight. Kiawah in South Carolina was our favorite. We also went to Pipestem State Park in West Virginia, Vermont, Rhode Island, Cape Cod, New Hampshire, and elsewhere. Our lives would have been very different, filled with even more anxiety, if we had not been able to legally sponsor Dolly, a Filipina lady who worked for us in Hong Kong, to come to live with us in Washington.

And then it came time for high school. While we liked our longtime house at 7209 Gordons Road in Falls Church, we had concerns about the quality of the high school Jon would go to. As we looked at houses in the area, we became keen for Jonathan to attend Langley High School in Great Falls, a well-regarded public school with a strong curriculum and faculty. We also liked the feel of Great Falls. It was less crowded and easily accessible along the George Washington Parkway from the State Department.

We were fortunate to find a house in Great Falls we liked, 9813 Thunderhill Court, and made the move in 1990. We and Jonathan feel he did get an excellent education at Langley in preparation for his university career.

For Eric, we wanted a high school that could support his strong and gifted bent for STEM subjects. He applied to and was accepted at Fairfax County's nationally recognized Thomas Jefferson High School for Science and Technology. It was just what he wanted, and he enjoyed his freshman and sophomore years there before we moved to Hong Kong.

During the year I was in language training, we wrestled with the question of when Claire and the boys would join me in Hong Kong. I was due there in summer 1993. Our ultimate decision for them to join me in 1994 would allow Jonathan to graduate from Langley High School, allow Eric to do two years at Thomas Jefferson High School, and allow Claire another professionally rewarding year to work on African Affairs.

The boys were keen to stay for another year. We made a deal: they promised to help Claire and keep up the house and yard. It worked. We would no longer have Dolly's support once I went to Hong Kong. She was an immense help to us and the boys for the years she was with us. We appreciated her friendship as well. She later married a retired U.S. Army veteran and moved to California.

During the summer of 1992, after I finished up in legislative affairs, I accompanied my parents on a three-week driving visit to Germany. We visited relatives on my mother's side (Maack) in Zeven in northern Germany and in Hamburg. We visited Mueller relatives in Coburg in the south, ones Dad had stayed in touch with over the years. Coburg was an interesting city with its Veste Coburg castle, where Martin Luther hid for an extended period. I've recorded the relationships of the relatives we met.

For old times' sake we visited Bad Homburg, Bad Godesberg, and Berlin, where we had lived in the 1950s. We also visited Jena and the university where Dad had studied as an exchange student in the 1930s. Among many other memories, Dad recalled attending a Hitler rally and being pressed hard against a fence by the surging crowd of admirers of *Der Fuhrer*. He thought he would not survive. All in all, it was a memorable visit. There was also poignancy as they recalled events in their lives and of course realized they were unlikely ever to visit again.

We saw my parents and Linda and Bill periodically. We hosted a fiftieth wedding anniversary for Mother and Dad in October at our house and at other times visited them in Williamsburg. It was great to be close enough to spend holidays and special times together. They promised they would visit us in Hong Kong.

Another highlight of that year was the weeklong Ambassadorial Seminar designed for chiefs of mission. It focused on learning ambassadorial responsibilities and introduction to some of the key challenges in U.S. foreign policy. As part of security briefings, we went to West Virginia to learn to drive an automobile defensively and then practiced firing a variety of rifles and handguns. Jean Kennedy Smith (sister to President Kennedy), who had been appointed ambassador to Ireland, sat out the visit to the gun range, not surprisingly.

As the year went by, I worked at bringing back my Mandarin Chinese (spoken was reasonably strong, reading was rusty). No teachers were left from my year of language training 1974–1975. I worked hard at recalling and broadening my abilities, even though the brain was not as supple as it had been before. I also spent several weeks learning some Cantonese. While the Hongkongers and other Cantonese use similar characters as Mandarin speakers (traditional versus simplified), the spoken language is significantly different.

And, of course, I consulted in the State Department and elsewhere on my coming consul general responsibilities. Since I would have legal oversight responsibility for fifteen government agencies represented at the Consulate General, including the intelligence agencies, I visited with as many headquarters' staff as possible in Washington.

Before I left in June, we agreed Eric would fly out in July for a visit and that Claire and Jonathan would follow in August. It was a fun several weeks exploring this unique part of the world together. They would all be back in Virginia in time for school and work.

Chapter Four

Hong Kong, Here We Come Again!

Our United Airlines 747 entered Hong Kong airspace and flew straight toward the red and white checkerboard on the mountain, banked sharply to the right just hundreds of feet above Kowloon's rooftops, and settled down on Kai Tak Airport's single runway stretching into the harbor to the east.

I looked out the window at the lights of Hong Kong and the harbor. It was a homecoming.

It was also the beginning of many more intense, productive, and fun years of life and work in Hong Kong before and after its reversion to China in 1997. Eric—our aerospace engineer-to-be—and his friends in future years would climb the checkerboard mountain and watch the planes fly straight toward them and then, almost within touching distance, bank away at the last minute.

Mike Hinton, our management officer, met me at the bottom of the disembarking ramp to welcome me to Hong Kong and take me to the VIP reception room. I was now a VIP! I almost missed the usual swirl of passengers in the aging arrival hall.

And then came the drive through the cross-harbor tunnel, up the mountain to the Peak and 3 Barker Road, and up the driveway to the consul general's residence to be greeted by the staff, including Cholin. Of course, I never imagined that Cholin and her future husband, Cecile, would become lifelong friends and move to the United States with us to work at Northfield Mount Hermon School for more than two decades.

Jeff Bader, deputy consul general, also met me at the residence that evening. We talked for quite a while about the coming days' events and the current political and economic atmosphere. Jeff was deputy for two years. He was a perceptive analyst of Hong Kong and China and a steady colleague in guiding the broad range of work of the consulate general. We became friends and colleagues.

It was a restless night after flights halfway around the world into an altogether different time zone. My mind said, "Sleep!" My body said, "It's daytime!" As I lay there, I kept rehearsing my remarks to the next day's full country team of representatives of fifteen different U.S. government agencies.

What a different job this was going to be. Eyes inside and outside the building would be on me all the time.

The country team was warmly welcoming as we gathered. I talked about who I was, challenges we would face in the coming years, and my strong support for their work and responsibilities. Creating a sense of teamwork in furtherance of U.S. policy goals was my number one goal. They each gave a short overview of their current work. Some stayed behind to chat. In the following days I visited each office to meet the two hundred members of the staff, both American and Hongkonger.

And then we were off to make endless rounds of introductions to Governor Chris Patten, Hong Kong government secretaries and officials, business and community leaders, prominent Americans, and consuls general from other nations. The sooner I was able to meet informed people, the sooner I would personally have a much better sense of the lay of the land in these formative and critical years leading up to 1997 and after.

What Were Some of the Realities of Those Early 1990s?

In China, politics and foreign investment had seemed to freeze up after the June 4, 1989, Tiananmen massacre. From a foreign perspective, a black cloud had covered China and lowered expectations for increased development of relations. The Chinese government was resolute in controlling news about the events and imprisoning perpetrators. Clearly, political struggles were intense behind the scenes. Senior leaders of the last decade were gone, including Chinese General Secretaries Hu Yaobang and Zhao Ziyang, among the more open and seemingly progressive reformers.

And then Deng Xiaoping made his move. In January 1992, he made an extended trip south to Shenzhen and Zhuhai, the special economic zones, to make clear they were the vanguard of economic development.

Deng famously wrote a motivational inscription, simple but hugely effective: *"Shenzhen Hao!"* ("Shenzhen is good!").

He also wrote, according to *The People's Daily*, "The first point is: Don't be afraid of making mistakes; the second point is to quickly rectify problems when they are found."

And then this: "You should be bolder in carrying out reform and opening up; dare to make experiments; you should not act as women with bound feet."

Deng's comments began to lift the black cloud and signaled full speed ahead for economic growth.

In September, Barton Biggs of Morgan Stanley Asset Management visited China and then exclaimed: "After eight days in China, I'm tuned in, overfed, and maximum bullish!" His comments were widely circulated and helped create a feeding frenzy among foreigners. In the coming months, we hosted a stream of American businesspeople interested in opportunities for getting in on the action.

I confess to some skepticism even in the face of this excitement. Difficult Chinese business practices were still everywhere, and the hard practices of the Communist Party and its security services were always present even if they were invisible to many. It took many more years for accumulated negative experiences of American business to begin to tip the scales against overly committing to investment in China and to sour U.S. views of China and its "rise."

In Hong Kong, the establishment welcomed the new signals from Deng and other Chinese leaders. They were eager to amplify them to boost Hong Kong's growth and their business prospects in China. Many in Hong Kong, however, maintained a quiet reserve, knowing their families and businesses were still potentially vulnerable after 1997. Many were busy allocating assets outside of Hong Kong and China, knowing that the Chinese Communist Party line or policy could change overnight.

I learned the term "astronauts" to describe those who bought homes abroad and installed their wives and children in local schools in Canada, Australia, the United States, and the United Kingdom. The fathers would fly back and forth as if they were astronauts. The term for them in Chinese was *"tai kung ren."* It means "astronaut" and was also a double-meaning pun: "the place of the wife is empty." The Chinese language can be wonderfully amusing and inventive in its use of language and its characters.

But business was beginning to boom and over the next three years, more and more Americans caught the fever of "endless" opportunities for trading and investing. The optimism recalled the view of long-ago British traders to the effect: If every Chinese person wore their shirt one inch longer the mills of Manchester would grind forever.

From a U.S. perspective we felt an *extremely cautious hopefulness* that Beijing would take steps in its words and deeds to be reserved in its actions toward Hong Kong in order to maintain its promised "high degree of autonomy." The United States certainly believed it was in China's interest to maintain autonomy and prosperity in Hong Kong, but we also were realistic: China, at any point, could change those arrangements. Sure, the United Kingdom, United States, and others could challenge such an action, but they could not reverse them. Beijing held the power and so it ultimately fell to China to keep Hong Kong stable and prosperous. That proved the case until June 2020, when China imposed a crushing national security law on Hong Kong and unleashed its security services in the city. But that all came later.

. In the meantime, the United States continued to work with Hong Kong, Britain, and China on post-1997 arrangements and to imple-ment the U.S.-Hong Kong Policy Act. When I was in legislative af-fairs, I worked to coordinate the executive branch negotiations with Congress in 1991 and 1992 at Secretary Baker's request. China had made it clear it wanted other countries to respect its "one country, two systems" constitutional arrangement and therefore to treat Hong Kong differently from its sovereign in areas such as trade, finance, immigration, export controls, law enforcement cooperation, etc. Each of these areas needed to be examined and arrangements made under U.S. law with relevant Hong Kong entities.

Hong Kong Governor Christopher Patten

Governor Christopher Patten was, of course, a key player and col-league. He had been a member of Parliament but lost his seat in the last election. He accepted the post of governor in 1992 with the expectation he would stay until 1997 and then perhaps be in position to become British prime minister.

Patten's gift of dry humor and eloquent presentation had been on full display when I attended a Brookings dinner for him in Washington. He was asked about his political future and the possibility of becoming prime minister one day. He smiled and then claimed he hadn't given much thought to the question, but he had thought of the title for the first volume of his autobiography, *Hong Kong: The Formative Years.* We all appreciated his humor.

Patten had upended the traditional role of Governor. He did not come from a diplomatic background nor have any direct experience with China and Hong Kong. Famously, he arrived in Hong Kong wearing a business suit rather than the longstanding uniform that included a hat decorated with ostrich feathers!

Patten's focus was on preparing Hong Kong for the July 1, 1997, handover to China and introducing ideas and mechanisms that would reinforce for the longer-term Hong Kong's open society, protections for a free press and free expression, a solid, common law legal system, economic and trade openness, and protection of its promised high degree of autonomy.

Patten arguably got off on the wrong foot with China in some of his early days with statements that unsettled and angered Beijing. Neither side ever backed down. Patten never visited Beijing as governor, and Beijing never stopped belittling him. Could the atmosphere and results have been different had there been some cooling of the rhetoric? It's possible, but in reality, each provided a useful foil for the other as each set the stage for their long-term legacies on Hong Kong.

I developed a good relationship with the governor. I met with him regularly, and we crossed paths frequently. We also did a great deal of work with his immediate staff, particularly his political advisor, Bob Pierce.

Up close Patten was always congenial and friendly; deeply intelligent and experienced; and articulate in analyzing and describing any situation. He was very much focused on dealing with China in ways that would help protect Hong Kong's long-term stability and ward off the long arm of Beijing as much as possible.

Patten believed deeply in democracy and in open societies. He was a fan of Karl Popper and quoted him frequently. While Beijing and its supporters criticized Patten for talking about democracy in Hong Kong when the United Kingdom had never given up its colonial control, Patten would shrug off the criticism. He would insist that the democratic reforms he was proposing (e.g., in the makeup of the Legislative Council of Hong Kong) would help involve Hong Kong people in local issues and create a feeling of having a stake in society. He minced no words about the importance of a continued strong legal system, free speech, and a free press.

I supported this approach. I had no problem getting the Department on board. While the Sino-British Joint Declaration and China's subsequent Basic Law left some room for political development, such as eventual universal suffrage, it was not possible to imagine one person/one vote without Beijing demanding a mechanism to guide the outcome to its liking.

It's worth noting the Clinton administration in its early years was focused on many other issues, leaving the consul general and assistant secretary for East Asian and Pacific Affairs, Winston Lord, in charge of U.S. policy. Our ambassador in Beijing, Stape Roy, a good friend and longtime colleague, was fully supportive. Among other issues on which we cooperated, we recommended to the State Department that after July 1, 1997, the consul general should continue to report directly to Washington as chief of mission, not to the ambassador in Beijing as is true elsewhere. The point was to continue to support the consul general as a major leader in U.S.-Hong Kong relations and to demonstrate that our Hong Kong Policy Act fully supported the high degree of autonomy promised to the city.

We of course understood China's historical grievances around foreign subjugation of the country, its pride in its long and rich history, its desire to improve the lives of its people, and its fear of loss of governance control and resulting instability as had happened repeatedly throughout its history. We did not begrudge in any way the improvements the Chinese people felt in their personal lives. We also understood the huge challenges China faced with a population as large as it was. Still, the immediate question was how a tiny entity of Hong Kong's seven million people could keep PRC internal practices at bay for an extended period.

At the U.S. Consulate General

At the consulate general we hosted a steady stream of members of Congress, executive branch officials, and business leaders in those years. All were eager to see Hong Kong before 1997. They all wanted to know what we thought would happen post–1997. Here was our answer:

1. What will happen after China takes over? Good question. A lot can and will change over fifty years up to 2047. *If* China continues to open up to foreign trade and investment; if it continues to emphasize economic development and improvement of peoples' livelihood; if it moves to greater reliance on market forces and downplays inefficient state enterprises; if it allows a more open society in which citizens have more room to make personal and professional decisions; if it loosens control over the broad reach of the Chinese Communist Party; if it allows citizens more latitude to create nongovernmental groups to deal with social issues, to criticize corruption, and government malfeasance; and, importantly, if it shows real restraint in imposing its policies in Hong Kong and allows Hong Kong people some genuine space within which to make decisions affecting their political and other choices, *then* there might be some chance that Hong Kong could maintain for an extended period an important role as a dynamic, highly autonomous city contributing to the Chinese motherland and the world.

2. However, *if* China began to restrict its citizens' interactions with the world; turn inward; tighten the reins held by the CCP; assert more and more control over citizens' lives and ability to form nongovernmental groups and speak out against corruption and malfeasance; dictate more policies affecting Hong Kong; begin to erode the guaranteed protections of the rule of law and its freedoms, *then* Hong Kong's future would be less bright.

3. We fervently hoped that the U.S.-Hong Kong Policy Act would serve its role as a reminder to Beijing and its vast governmental entities to be restrained in its interactions with Hong Kong. If Beijing was not careful, then the things which mattered to Hong Kong's dynamism and made it an extremely attractive city for American investment and business—such as a solid, trusted, and independent legal system, openness, and freedoms of speech, of the press, etc.—could be lost. The United States and other countries might be required to end their special treatment of Hong Kong as it lost its autonomy. That would be highly negative all-around.

I argued loudly and consistently both as consul general and in succeeding years that the United States should keep Hong Kong on the agenda of every bilateral interaction with Beijing, and every secretary of state and presidential meeting. Doing so would continuously remind Beijing (even if the Chinese official did not want to hear it) that the United States had strong interests in Hong Kong's continued stability and prosperity. I'm afraid my goal was only partly achieved as other events pressed in.

Looking back now from the vantage point of 2023, after Beijing imposed its national security law in 2020 and unleashed its own security services to arrest and jail people who fought for Hong Kong's future, we were pretty much right in the above analysis. In the last year, Hong Kong's high degree of autonomy has been severely undermined. Hongkongers and foreigners now see clearly that the CCP has reached more deeply into Hong Kong, ostensibly to bring stability, but in reality, to turn Hong Kong's people into "patriotic" citizens to serve the state, not make trouble, and not question Beijing's decisions.

But in the years leading up to 1997, there were signs and glimmers of hope. We all wanted to believe this new system of "one country, two systems" could work for a reasonably long period even if in general PRC influence would be greater in Hong Kong. Could a Zhao Ziyang or Hu Yaobang and similarly minded people have sustained more continued experimentation with more open systems? I choose to believe it might have been possible. China for 150 years has debated and experimented with numerous paths to good governance systems and ways to unleash their citizens'and country's enormous potential. Sadly, by 2023, CCP leadership has clearly turned to a strict, top-down approach to governance.

Beijing's current approach to Hong Kong and throughout China in 2023 may be sustainable for a period of time, but eventually China's many challenges and need for less top-down management may well force governance changes. With newer leadership in the coming years, combined with the limitations of the current system, we may see beginnings of new openness. We need to be alert to when foundations for new bridges across the Pacific might be built, particularly between China and the United States.

What was the role of the American Consul General in Hong Kong in the 1990s?

First and foremost, the consul general, as chief of mission—*by law*—was responsible for protecting Americans and American interests and coordinating the work of all U.S. government agencies.

Within the consulate general, the consul general led and managed the two hundred staff—half Americans and half Hong Kong Chinese.

The fifteen different U.S. government agencies reported to the consul general and looked to him for support of their activities. For example:

—the economic/political section's analysis and reporting on Hong Kong and Chinese trends and developments;

—the FBI's liaison with Hong Kong security services in law enforcement cooperation;

—the Department of Commerce and Foreign Commercial Service's support of American trade and business;

—the consular section's assistance to American citizens, issuance of visas to travelers to the United States, or renewal of passports for American citizens;

—the Agriculture Department's support for American food exports;

—the U.S. Information Agency's responsibility for public communication and educational and cultural activities;

—the U.S. Custom's work with Hong Kong and China to enforce trade laws;

—the Defense liaison office's interactions with the British military and in better understanding of China's defense policies and capabilities;

—our management section's task to allocate and manage our funds, our residences, and our consulate general building (which underwent fundamental renovation during my three years, with all of us suffering regular eviction and another move to a temporary office).

Obviously, I could not be on top of all these every day. Our team needed to develop trust that as a team we would stay true to our mission and support each other. My deputy, Jeff Bader, was invaluable in day-to-day management. I particularly appreciated his firm hand on the tiller in working with other agencies and his talents in analysis and reporting. His judgments were almost always on the mark.

I chaired regular "country team meetings" and met frequently with agency leaders. I spent much time brainstorming with our economic/political section and others to understand developments and to direct our efforts to dig deeper where necessary. I enjoyed drafting, shaping, and editing our analyses and reports.

Making sure we were responding to requirements from Washington was a high priority, as was making sure we pushed hard on recommending policy initiatives. For example, I was interested in the possibility that negotiating a free trade agreement with Hong Kong could be good all around, including for support of Hong Kong's long-term autonomy.

Regrettably, too many people in Washington were skittish about opening even more doors for Hong Kong and Chinese exports.

There were times I disagreed with Washington and stuck to my guns. For example, the Treasury Department wanted to station an officer at the consulate general at a time when we were trying to slim down our presence. Legally, I could turn down or agree to the Treasury request. Repeatedly, I asked for what they needed that was not already being reported. They had no convincing answers. So, I denied the request. Years later I met a former Treasury official who, when realizing I was the former consul general, said "Oh, you're the guy who turned us down!"

I also enjoyed the "external" requirements of the job and spent many hours each week outside the physical confines of the building to "show the flag" and to learn about developments.

One aspect of the job was to understand the community and what was happening, so we could share our judgments with Washington. (Analyses and reports went not only to the secretary of state and White House, but to a vast number of U.S. government agencies who used them in their own assigned areas of responsibility, for example the Department of Commerce to support U.S. business.)

What better way to learn what was going on than meeting and talking with knowledgeable people? These could be Hong Kong officials, American and Hong Kong businesspeople, other consuls general, officials at Chinese-related institutions, and visitors to Hong Kong.

The easy characterization of the diplomatic life as endless, fun cocktail parties could not be farther from the truth (except for the "endless" part).

My days were often filled with breakfasts, meetings, lunches, meetings, receptions, and dinners. Stamina was a precious asset. Many events were held at our residence. That is why the government spent heavily to build a nine thousand square feet residence at 3 Barker Road on the Peak that accommodated everything from a small breakfast to a reception for two hundred. In those days, an invitation to the American consul general's residence was a coveted thing, because guests could be assured of meeting others of interest who could share information, rumors, or interpretation of the latest pronouncement from Beijing.

I enjoyed being host, introducing people to others, networking, listening for important insights, and honoring the achievements of a guest. Claire was an invaluable ally.

Events outside our home that needed my presence included meetings with Governor Patten, Hong Kong officials, the U.S. business community, and local Hong Kong businesspeople. A day could start with a small breakfast for a visiting senator, lunch with a Chinese emissary from Beijing, a meeting with a state delegation from Kansas or another state or city looking for trade opportunities, a briefing from Hong Kong government officials on security issues, a reception commemorating the Textile Council's anniversary, capped by a dinner at the home of one of Hong Kong's billionaires.

Aside from learning from others, these were all opportunities to get out the American message on issues of the day. These could be presidential speeches, or U.S. policy toward Hong Kong and China, or the latest American economic news.

My job gave me a chance to regularly give speeches about Hong Kong, China, and the United States. They all contained a common theme of what attributes made Hong Kong the prosperous, attractive business center it was, and therefore how good execution of the promised high degree of autonomy over the longer run would help to maintain that stability and prosperity.

Speeches and remarks also addressed specific issues of interest to the United States. For example, enforcement of intellectual property rights was a perennial theme and one that remains to this day a point of great concern to America. U.S. firms often found they were being manipulated or coerced by Chinese companies, losing something to the tune of tens of billions of dollars in proprietary information every year. We saw how Chinese companies would acquire specific knowledge of technical processes to improve their own products and then supplant U.S. products and squeeze the company out of the market. Many Chinese firms were adept at using Taiwanese firms and managers to build and run factories in China. Those Taiwanese managers and factory builders were contributors to China's economic success.

The American consul general's regular and loud speaking out helped draw attention to important U.S. interests, such as building bridges to understanding.

We also had our more sensitive times with military issues. For example, two of our consulate general defense liaison office military officers who followed PRC military developments legally entered China and were detained outside a military base not far from the coast facing Taiwan. The Chinese government claimed they were in violation of China's laws about how close they could come to the base itself. The men staunchly maintained they were outside the limits. Still, they were held incommunicado for several days, not allowed to contact the American Embassy in Beijing or us in Hong Kong. Their families in Hong Kong, unsurprisingly, were gravely concerned, as were Washington agencies. The embassy and the State Department pushed the Chinese government hard to release them immediately. It seemed very unlikely to me that the PRC would hold them for an extended period, but rather would look for propaganda points and then let them go. In fact, after several days, they were released with the "most stern" warnings about never trespassing again and violating Chinese sovereignty. As you can imagine, they were warmly greeted as they returned to Hong Kong.

Such was the military component of American diplomacy and a clear reminder of the high stakes both countries faced as they developed various facets of their relationship.

We also experienced an extremely tense time, 1995–1996, as Taiwan's president, Li Tenghui, sought to visit his alma mater Cornell University, and China went to great lengths to warn against issuance of a visa. The U.S. Congress overwhelmingly passed resolutions urging President Bill Clinton to allow the visit. He relented. Li made his visit as planned. But there ensued what is now called by some the "Third Taiwan Strait Crisis," with China firing missiles north and south of Taiwan and conducting assault training exercises in the run-up to Taiwan's March 23 election, followed by the United States sending carrier battle groups through the Strait to show our opposition to China's use of military force. In the end, President Li was re-elected. His margin of victory was almost certainly boosted by China's actions.

To this day, the question of whether China will try to take Taiwan by force is front and center in all diplomatic and military minds. The fast-approaching 1997 Hong Kong transition was unsettling as people repeatedly asked the question of whether China would live up to its promises of allowing fifty years of a high degree of autonomy. China's military moves and firing of missiles toward Taiwan in 1996 were not a good sign for many in Hong Kong.

Other more fun events in the life of a consul general and his family could be a day on a Hong Kong person's yacht, which would sail to a bay on the coast, there to anchor so guests could swim, water ski, have lunch, and talk, talk, talk. The guests were usually involved in interesting activities, so the day was not just about fun but also work. I was learning all the while about Hong Kong and China.

Everyone kept a wary eye on the calendar as the days ticked down to July 1, 1997. Beijing helpfully erected a huge "countdown" billboard in Tiananmen Square to remind everyone of the glorious "recovery" day approaching. There was no doubt that Beijing would continue to use the recovery of Hong Kong as a sign of the CCP's resounding success in re-uniting the country.

Macau Is Still Portuguese

I was also accredited as consul general to Macau, across the Pearl River Delta. The Portuguese years before attempted to return it to China. However, Beijing declined for fear it would raise too many questions about the future of Hong Kong and unsettle its future.

We enjoyed traveling to Macau, where we could relax as well as pursue business. I would call on the Portuguese governor of Macau for insights into plans for the return of Macau to China in 1999 under its own "one country, two systems" arrangement similar to Hong Kong's. He would periodically include us in a dinner or a Portuguese cultural event such as Fado—the soul of Portuguese music.

Once a year we organized "Macau Day" to show the flag. We offered visa services, assistance to Americans, advice on doing business with the United States, and hosted a large reception.

We enjoyed visiting historic sites which afforded glimpses of Macau's history back to 1557, when it became a Portuguese colony. This Macau was a backwater with a slower pace of life and was fully controlled by Beijing and Chinese interests behind the scenes. We would visit the Protestant Cemetery, which contained the graves of Americans and others who had died in Macau. One headstone recorded that a man from Sag Harbor, Rhode Island (should have been Long Island), fell from the yard arm of his ship. A cousin of Winston Churchill's was buried there. Once a year, the U.S. Navy chaplain assigned to the consulate general would organize a visit for us to commemorate the continuing American relationship with the church and cemetery. I was the designated formal representative of the U.S. government.

We would often visit with Father Lancelot Rodrigues, Society of Jesus, the Jesuit priest who had lived in Macau for years and ran the Catholic Relief Services. He and his colleagues welcomed Vietnamese refugees and, through a contract with the U.S. government, gave them safe haven until they moved on to the United States or elsewhere. He loved to tell stories and give tours around Macau. He passed away in 2013 at the age of eighty-nine.

We usually stayed at our favorite small hotel, Posada de Saotiago, as a wonderful getaway. The gambling didn't much interest us, but it did interest Claire's mother. When we went to Macau in 1985, she made a bee line for the slot machines on the ship taking us across the Pearl River!

There were numerous interesting events during our time in Hong Kong. Here are a few.

—A life-changing lunch meeting: in my first year, I received an invitation to lunch from Antony Leung, Citigroup's representative in Hong Kong. Bill Rhodes, vice chair, wanted to meet the new American consul general. He made a point of meeting chiefs of mission and finance ministers. We had a good conversation. Bill asked if I would excuse him a bit early because he had a plane to catch; he would chair a meeting of the board of trustees of a New England boarding school. I asked, "Which one?" "Northfield Mount Hermon," he said. "Do you know it?" Richard: "Not only do I know it. I graduated from Mount Hermon in 1962." Bill looked at me with incredulity. I'll never forget his astonishment. He himself was a 1950s graduate and was now chair of the board. He wondered why NMH had not told him the consul general was a graduate. We stayed in touch over the next years, and Claire and I hosted events for the NMH head of school.

Thus began my reconnection with NMH and eventually the beginning of a second career.

—High Level Visits: Governor Patten made an official visit to Washington and the United States to keep Hong Kong in the public eye. I went to the United States to join the official meetings, which culminated in a visit to the White House and a meeting with Vice President Al Gore. A hoped-for "drop by" from the president did not materialize, but there was good discussion about the status of the transition. The vice president and others pledged to do whatever we could to support Hong Kong's promised high degree of autonomy, particularly as recorded in the Hong Kong Policy Act.

—Winston Lord, assistant secretary of state, in turn made a high-level visit to Hong Kong. It was designed to have high visibility, again to emphasize U.S. interest in Hong Kong and support for China's constitutional approach to "one country, two systems." We had an extended meeting with Governor Patten to review developments. At the beginning, Patten helped write my performance review for the year. With a big smile, he pointed to me and then said to Winston Lord, "He's great!" We hosted a reception for Lord at the residence. He was so taken with the residence and the view of Hong Kong that he asked me how much I was paying to the State Department to serve in Hong Kong. All tongue in cheek (I think!).

—Becoming an Honorary Naval Aviator. Each year, sixty to eighty U.S. Navy ships visited Hong Kong. We entertained some of the visitors and visited the ships. To show the flag, the Navy allowed us to invite up to twenty visitors to fly out to an approaching carrier on a small plane dubbed the Carrier Onboard Delivery (COD). Claire and I would accompany the group, as did Eric and Jon periodically, and we felt proud. These flights were an important concrete sign of U.S. presence in Asia.

I was particularly proud of the pilots who have ice water in their veins. As we gathered at Kai Tak Airport one morning for a fly out, I remarked that we had three generals going out that day: a brigadier general, an attorney general, and a consul general. The two pilots came over with their helmets under their arms to brief us. One of the visitors whispered to me, "You mean they will fly the plane? Two women?" I said, "Yes, women can fly just as well as men!" He shook his head in wonderment—old school. The pilots landed us safely on the carrier and then later took us back to Kai Tak.

When Admiral Archie Clemens, commander of U.S. Naval Forces in the Pacific, came on a later visit to Hong Kong, I pitched the idea of my flying off a carrier in the back seat of an F-14 fighter jet. I knew the Navy did that sort of thing for the right "VIP." When he saw I was serious, he said, "Okay, Richard. I'll make a deal. You do the two-day water safety training, and I'll make it happen."

When I next visited my parents in Williamsburg, Virginia, I went to the Naval Air Station in Norfolk for a physical, tests of swimming ability, and prowess in using a life vest to keep from drowning with seventy-five pounds on my back. The required maneuver: take a deep breath, sink to the bottom of the pool, pull out a breathing tube, blow air in to inflate the vest, and thus, bob to the surface. I avoided drowning and passed, thank God.

When the USS *Nimitz* was scheduled to visit Hong Kong, in December 1995, I was notified they would schedule the F-14 Tomcat flight. The COD landed us on board the carrier in the morning. The next hours were spent getting suited up with my G-suit and getting endless instructions. At lunch, I asked the sailors what I should eat before a flight. Chili, they advised. It goes down easily. It took me a minute to realize the joke; chili also comes up easily when you encounter 6.5 G's in an F-14.

Finally, they strapped me into the back seat of the F-14 lined up on the catapult. The pilot, Chevy, twice made me confirm I understood that *under no circumstances* was I ever to touch the handle between my legs. Pulling it would eject both of us through the canopy above. He assured me he would do the ejecting in the unlikely event it was necessary. Not to worry. The seat I was in would automatically deploy the parachute, we would land in the water and float, and a helicopter would be there to pluck us out. Sounded straightforward. But what a way to come back down to earth.

There we were on the catapult. What a unique feeling, sitting in this shaking and shivering metal tube as we went to both afterburners for takeoff. The "Catapult Officer," better known as the "Shooter," once assuring all was clear, dropped his arm, the restraining hook released us, and we were slammed backwards into our seats—145 mph within three seconds! I could feel the plane sink toward the water as we left the deck but then as the air provided lift under the wings, we accelerated toward the clouds.

We were aloft for more than an hour. The pilot demonstrated a variety of maneuvers. First, we approached the long trailing gasoline hose of the aerial refueling tanker and nosed into it. Then the pilot demonstrated a variety of rolls and loops and full vertical flight. We approached full supersonic flight. Then he asked if I was ready for maximum G-forces of 6.5Gs. I said I was. From high above the South China Sea, he nosed the plane down, and increased acceleration. We screamed toward the ocean and then before we hit the water, he put the plane into a hard starboard turn to pull out of the dive. At that point we reached maximum G's. I felt the G-suit squeezing my arms and legs. I felt my vision narrowing as if I were entering a black tunnel and thought I was about to black out. But then the G forces lessened. I was still conscious. I passed the test—no blackout and no lost lunch!

On the carrier, Claire was perched in the air traffic control center between the "big boss" and "mini boss." She saw us screaming past the carrier just above the water, at which point she told the controllers to bring us down. They asked her who I was. "My husband, please get him down," she instructed.

Landing was another thrill. We lined up miles behind the carrier, which was just a speck in the distance. As we neared the ship, I fully appreciated how tricky such landings are. We sank lower and lower, slowed to 165 mph, hit the deck and then, counterintuitively, the pilot went immediately to full throttle. Why? Simple. If the tailhook missed the wire, the F-14 had enough speed to climb back into the air and go around again.

What an adventure. I was still flying high a week later, even months later! Half of Hong Kong seemed to know I'd had the high of a lifetime. What could possibly top it?!

I have the pictures and the U.S. Navy certificate to prove I'd experienced a carrier F-14 Tomcat takeoff and landing. What more can I say than, "Hats off, double hats off," to those pilots and the U.S. Navy and *all service members who do their jobs every day to keep the nation safe.*

There's the important word again: *service. Also, as in Foreign Service and Civil Service.*

More earthbound activities were numerous.

—Governor Patten always came up to the residence for our annual July 4 celebration. It included remarks and a toast to the Queen and the United States President. One of Patten's favorite quips was that if the United States had not succeeded in its revolution against Great Britain, today he might be governor of, say, Texas rather than Hong Kong!

—An important emissary. Every several months, Liu Chuwen, a graduate of Saint John's in Shanghai and now an emissary from Beijing, came to Hong Kong to assess the atmosphere and recent developments. He always accepted an invitation from me for lunch at the residence, one on one. We traded standard Chinese and U.S. talking points, then gingerly talked about some of the more difficult issues around the transition such as how to maintain confidence in Hong Kong when its new sovereign had a very different, and stricter, governance system. He was a kindly man, easy to talk with, and a good representative of his government.

An anecdote: at one of the lunches, Liu looked out the window and down at a group of recently built homes. He laughed and said that many years before, he stayed at a building on that site belonging to China. He recalled looking up at the American flag and the consul general's residence, never imagining that one day he would dine with the consul general in his home. I admitted that in the 1960s, when I first started visiting Hong Kong and saw the residence, in no way could I imagine being consul general and dining with a Chinese government official.

—Anson Chan Fang On-sang, chief secretary for Hong Kong (second highest position) under Patten and then under the new chief executive, C.H. Tung, was our regular guest. We also agreed to host a delegation led by the president of Tufts University to confer an honorary degree. Forever after, Anson would often thank me again for hosting. Her family spent time in Anhui Province restoring the family homestead, local temple, and schools. I liked Anson's straightforwardness and enjoyed her and Archie's dinner parties. She became increasingly outspoken in her defense of Hong Kong and her strong desire for a determined move toward a more open, democratic governance system. She was elected to the Legislative Council but was increasingly marginalized by the establishment and China. I loved her mother's paintings of traditional Chinese scenes in bold strokes and colors.

—In Zhou Nan's public appearances, the most senior PRC official in Hong Kong, there was no question about his strong loyalties. At one point, he invited me to dinner at the New China News Agency, the cover headquarters of the CCP in Hong Kong. Just the two of us. As with Liu Chuwen, he was on a fact-finding mission. Of course, Hong Kong's transition back to China was front and center and he did not hold back in reciting China's historic grievances against Britain and other foreigners.

At one point, as we discussed historic governance systems in China, I said I was interested in whether, given its huge size, some form of de jure federalism might serve China well. The United States found many positives in its federal system. Zhou almost gagged on his soup. He quickly responded that *lianbangzhi* (federalism) in China is seen as *fenliezhuyi* ("splittism"). Anyone advocating splittism is trying to weaken China. I pointed out that China already has a de facto federal system whereby provinces and localities often pursue differing approaches and policies but all within the context of one China. China had already placed in its constitution a "one country, two systems" provision about to be launched for Hong Kong. Why not formalize the system and allocate authority? He would have none of it and continued to push back. I'd love to see the report he sent to his bosses.

—Martin Lee was and remains one of the most well-recognized advocates for democracy in Hong Kong. I saw him frequently as he tirelessly fought for the best deal for Hong Kong as China's Basic Law was drafted (based on the Sino-British Joint Declaration on Hong Kong of 1984). Some thought him too rigid and unwilling to compromise. I found him principled and a fervent believer in democracy and open societies. He knew he was up against the behemoth of China. He periodically came to lunch and dinner. We invited him to a Thanksgiving dinner; he sat next to Claire and smiled about the fact that it was the first time he had been invited to the residence for Thanksgiving. Martin hired Americans (e.g., Tom Boasberg, Minky Worden), which gave China a reason to suspect the United States was one of the "black hands" behind riots and instability meant to destabilize Hong Kong. Still, he believed in many of the values I believed in, so I admired his unstinting efforts to help shape good governance systems for Hong Kong.

—Jimmy Lai, publisher of *Apple Daily* and one of Hong Kong's most outspoken advocates for more democratic systems. As with Martin Lee, I appreciated his outspokenness on behalf of Hong Kong and even his willingness to poke the establishment and China in the eye. Since 2020, Beijing and the Hong Kong government have gone to great lengths to close down his newspapers and bring charges against him. As I write in 2023, he remains in jail facing more charges. It's shameful.

—A Midwest governor's request. A governor from the "Heartland" led a trade delegation visit to Hong Kong. I invited them to the residence. As we looked at the view of Hong Kong below, I made a comment about how useful it was to have governors and businesspeople visit. Not only could trade be good for the state, it built bridges of better understanding across the Pacific. He said he agreed but asked if I understood how much pushback he and others often receive from voters, "They think these trips are a boondoggle." I said I'd be glad to write a letter to him he could use to show the benefits. He smiled. "Would you do that? It would be very useful."

—Commerce Secretary Ron Brown visits Hong Kong. Secretary Brown came to Hong Kong for an update on the transition and to learn of future business opportunities. His visit was also important in the context of making clear to China and others why Hong Kong was so attractive to foreign business, e.g., solid legal system, openness, civil liberties, etc. Brown met with a good range of Hong Kong officials and business leaders. We put together a widely attended reception for him at the residence. Interestingly, he wanted his arrival to be low-key, so he entered through the back stairs and stopped in the private family room, where Eric was doing his homework. He was interested in what Eric was working on and spent some minutes engaging with him.

—Supreme Court Justice Anthony Kennedy and his wife Mary Kennedy visited Hong Kong and stayed with us. One day we received a cable from the State Department alerting us that the Kennedys would be visiting Hong Kong for meetings and speeches sponsored by the Law Society.

Would we be able to invite them to stay at the residence for three nights and support their visit? We sent back an enthusiastic "yes."

I saw their visit as a unique opportunity to share views with Hong Kong and PRC people about the importance and role of a strong legal system and why it undergirds a favorable business climate and an open, free, and democratic political system. During his visit he addressed those questions with great success and received considerable public attention.

During Kennedy's visit, I had the idea of asking him whether he had visited the PRC and had a chance to share views on the role of law in society. He had not, he said, because he did not want to lend legitimacy to a "legal" system that was dominated by the CCP. I pitched this idea: work with our U.S. ambassador to China, Stape Roy, to set up a visit that gave opportunities to address what an independent judiciary can do for a freer society and economic development. China was educating many lawyers, including at American law schools, so there might be some fertile ground for his ideas. China was still "opening up" and seemed to be experimenting with many ideas.

Subsequently I wrote to Stape Roy and put him in touch with Justice Kennedy. The idea worked. He did visit Beijing and had a platform to talk about the role of law in society and the value of a solid, independent legal system. Years later, he sent a message to me via a friend visiting Hong Kong saying how much they appreciated their visit with us and the idea of engaging with Chinese "lawyers" in Beijing.

On a personal level, we enjoyed having the Kennedy's as visitors. They were gracious and down to earth. They had several meals with us, and Claire and Mary Kennedy took walks to the Peak every day. The Kennedys took an interest in Eric's high school experience at HKIS. When he learned of Eric's interest in bridge, the Justice taught him a short form way of playing the game.

—Kansas Senator Nancy Kassebaum accepted my invitation for breakfast at the residence. It was just the two of us. I found her a gracious and down-to-earth guest and interlocutor, one of those so-called "moderate" "Rockefeller" Republicans we remembered from the past. She was keenly interested in Hong Kong and China as I shared my views. She was totally supportive of U.S. policy. We also discussed U.S. politics, which even in the 1990s were becoming more fractious and difficult. She clearly was frustrated with the difficulty of bringing politicians and parties together to govern effectively. She shared that she woke up every morning almost heartsick, knowing that for re-election she needed to raise, on average, something like $50,000 a day. That meant getting on the phone with potential donors, making deals and promises. That weighed heavily on her. (I will not vouch for the exact amount each day, but it was a large sum. The sums required today are far higher.)

Such a get together with a sitting senator or member of the House of Representatives was one of the privileges of serving as consul general or in another Foreign Service position. One could exchange candid thoughts out of range of an open microphone and appreciate how human such icons are in real life.

—Lunch with former Secretary of State Henry Kissinger. We had at least two lunch discussions during my term as consul general. Imagine sitting alone for conversation with one of the icons of twentieth-century national security policy. He was deeply interested in Hong Kong and China. He listened to my descriptions of developments. He could use those with the business he was accompanying to China. His thoughts about Hong Kong were mostly filtered through the lens of his history with China. Bottom line was that the important priority was keeping the United States relationship with China on an even keel. That would support a good transition for Hong Kong back to Chinese sovereignty. He listened more than I was used to when working for him years before!

—All of these visits showed us again that even highly placed people, whether elected, appointed, or otherwise, are still human and not mythical creatures of some kind with superhuman powers. They have foibles, weaknesses, emotions, abilities, and brilliance all humans have in varying degrees. We need social and political systems that channel all those facets in constructive and decent ways for the benefit of all of us.

—Visits to China provided periodic changes of scene, including to Gansu Province to see the "Silk Road" and other historic sites. In October 1995, I felt the need to see more of China than Beijing and other destinations I was familiar with. China Travel Service was more than happy to arrange a tour for the consul general. For a fee, of course. It turned out to be refreshingly free of rhetoric and bombast about the CCP's achievements. I flew directly to the capital of the province, Lanzhou, to see the historic sites in the area. The city has been a center for Silk Road trade for centuries.

I was met by a driver—he was a retired military officer—and a woman who spoke some English to help with interpreting. I'm sure the government was more than curious whether I was up to something more than tourism. I wasn't. As a presumed "China Hand," I was just interested in learning more about China.

After visiting numerous Lanzhou historic sites and the Yellow River, we took a train northwest along the historic trade route, stopped to see the western end of the Great Wall, which I hiked, and visited the city from which Laozi (reported originator of the philosophy of Taoism) rode off to the west beyond the western edge of the Empire. He and his donkey were reportedly never seen again.

After a couple days in Dunhuang, it became perhaps my favorite China destination. Claire and I were fortunate to visit in 2001 while leading a Northfield Mt. Hermon alumni group. The Dunhuang Caves, or Mogao Caves, are now a UNESCO World Heritage site and number well over five hundred in the area, dating to probably the fourth century AD and after. They contain spectacular murals and sculptures of Buddhist art as well as tens of thousands of historic manuscripts. One could spend days visiting only the ones already open. The local Chinese abbot knew of some of the caves and in 1900 began to attempt preservation. In 1907, Aurel Stein visited and told the world about the fabulous "treasure." He "bought" large numbers of manuscripts to take home for study. Today, preservation and research are full-time jobs for many.

Nearby are sand dunes one can climb and the Singing Sands oasis. Camel rides and sled runs down the dunes are encouraged.

We flew back to Lanzhou and then drove up to the Labrang Tibetan Buddhist monastery just on the edge of the Qinghai plateau, at about ten thousand feet of altitude. The government had helped rebuild the monastery to attract visitors after it burned in 1985. It was a spectacular piece of architecture. A monk invited me to visit his quarters, where he showed me numerous Tankas he had painted. I bought one. Beautiful. Will hope to keep it in the family. We also visited the main city of Xiahe, which is part of the Gannan Tibetan Autonomous Region.

We visited numerous other historic sites in southern Gansu, including the Hui Muslim areas. All in all, the trip brought home again the vast richness and history of Chinese civilization.

I will repeat one of my favorite questions about China. Does its long and rich history with many world views over the centuries help it to deal with twenty-first century challenges? Or does it hold China back from adapting to new ideas and events as necessary?

—Treasury Secretary Robert Rubin visited Hong Kong in 1996. He was interested in understanding Hong Kong as an international financial center and, as with all our official visitors, helped to draw attention to what made Hong Kong uniquely successful financially and economically. He helped get our message across publicly and privately that practices such as its legal system, openness, and personal liberties must be preserved. It was a message that resonated as we came closer and closer to 1997.

Claire and I offered to host a dinner for Secretary Rubin to meet Hong Kong notables. He accepted. But then we found that we could not accommodate the number we needed to include. Our big round table (my preference) and long rectangular table (which I disliked) just wouldn't do it. Our administrative section had a brilliant idea: our carpenters constructed a large *oval* table to seat about twenty. The evening went spectacularly well. The conversation was spirited and dealt with all the challenges which Hong Kong, China, the United States, and the rest of the world faced as the transition neared. Secretary Rubin in his meetings expressed specific support for Hong Kong's financial stability as it prepared for its transition.

—Wynton Marsalis, one of America's most famous jazz musicians and trumpet players, visited with his group. He was gracious and friendly at the reception we hosted. I told him Eric was a trumpet player; would Marsalis sign Eric's special wallet? Sure, he said, and wrote, "Eric, Practice! Wynton Marsalis."

—Seijei Ozawa, the Boston Symphony, and Tanglewood Chorus sang happy birthday. They came to the residence for a reception. What a collection of musical talent. It was December 1, 1994, my fiftieth birthday, and Claire confessed to Ozawa she hadn't gotten me a present. Would the group like to sing "Happy Birthday"? With gusto, he gathered the Tanglewood Chorus around the grand piano in the living room, sat down at the keyboard, and conducted the roomful of guests in a robust rendition of "Happy Birthday." It was my most notable birthday. Their public concert the next night was just as rousing.

—Bon Jovi. The famous band led by John Bon Jovi accepted our invitation. It was a popular event with acceptances of our invitation at a record level. Band members worked the room like professionals, to the particular delight of the twelve Hong Kong International School students we had invited. (For appropriate events, I'd let the head of school know we'd be happy to include ten to twelve students and faculty members in hopes of further broadening their educational horizons.)

—Former President George H. W. Bush and Barbara Bush visit Hong Kong. As a courtesy, even though the Bushes' trip was a private one—he was flying to China with an ARCO (Atlantic Richfield) delegation—Claire and I went to the airport to meet them and accompany them to their hotel. Claire rode with First Lady Bush, and I rode with President Bush. We both found our visitors down-to-earth. With me, the former president was candid about his disappointment that the U.S. media would not credit him before the election with reviving the economy. Within months of Clinton's election and Bush's defeat, it was clear that the economy was doing well. That development before the election would have swung the election his way, President Bush thought.

I asked Bush about the book he and Brent Scowcroft were co-authoring. He said it was going well, but Barbara Bush was his toughest editor. For example, she couldn't understand why he praised a certain person, when in fact that person "stabbed you in the back." He admitted to me that she was right, so he went back to the drawing board.

Later, when I was executive director of the Asia Society Hong Kong Center, we crossed paths with the Bushes again as they stopped in Hong Kong overnight while heading to China. The host kindly included us in a small dinner in their honor.

On these Bush visits, I was able to brief him about events in Hong Kong and China and urged him to raise Hong Kong and the importance of a firm and continuing commitment by China to fully respect its "high degree of autonomy." He said he understood and expressed appreciation that the U.S.-Hong Kong Policy Act, passed with his administration's strong support, was still front and center in U.S. relations with China. I did tell him that I'd played a role when working for Secretary Baker in leading legislative negotiations with Congress on the Hong Kong Policy Act on behalf of the Bush administration.

Family Life in Hong Kong

After my solo year in Hong Kong, sinking deeply into the all-consuming work of consul general, I flew back to Washington to attend Jonathan's graduation in June 1994 from Langley High School in Northern Virginia and to help Claire pack up our house in Great Falls. Jonathan got the excellent education at Langley that we had hoped for in making the move to Great Falls. His commencement speaker was his classmate's father, Supreme Court Justice Antonin Scalia. Eric said goodbye to his friends of two years at Thomas Jefferson High School for Science and Technology where he, too, got an excellent education in his two years.

Claire finished up her assignment working for the assistant secretary of state for African affairs, George Moose. All in all, it turned out to have been a good decision we made for the family to stay in Washington for that one year.

On our way to Hong Kong, we stopped for a short visit and vacation in Hawaii, where we saw Claire's sister, Joan, and toured the island—including a visit to the USS *Arizona* memorial. I spent a day at CINCPAC (Commander in Chief Pacific Area Command) consulting on policies toward Asia, China, and Hong Kong. There was great interest in Hong Kong and China, including whether China was likely to continue to allow sixty to eighty U.S. Navy ship visits a year. One of my priorities as consul general was to reach an agreement with Beijing to continue to allow those ship visits after 1997, even if there were issues in other areas of U.S.-China relations. My reasoning? While the PRC would assume defense and foreign relations responsibilities after July 1, 1997, allowing ship visits could be interpreted as another signal that Beijing was willing to acknowledge Hong Kong's high degree of autonomy. It was a good idea in principle, but not surprisingly Beijing would not agree.

Foreign Service officers and the U.S. military have worked closely together over the years and developed respect for each other's professional abilities. That doesn't mean we always agreed, but such respect does increase the potential for diplomats and the military to work in sync in service to U.S. national security objectives.

And then from Hawaii we were off on the last leg of our return to Hong Kong. Our trusty United Airlines 747 banked sharply to the right and settled down safely on Kai Tak's single runway. The lights of the city all around us were familiar and welcoming. It felt like another homecoming and the start of the next chapter of our lives.

Although on leave without pay from the Foreign Service, Claire went quickly about the work of becoming "Mrs. Consul General." In the coming weeks she organized the staff, made living arrangements and furniture decisions, and threw herself into the waiting diplomatic social calendar. The State Department does not pay spouses for this essential job; it did pay to hire a "residence manager" to help with the work. In the end, Claire decided it was just quicker and easier for her to do the work herself.

At summer's end we reluctantly drove with Jonathan to Kai Tak Airport and hugged him goodbye as he headed back to Virginia. He had decided to enroll at the University of Virginia as an Echols Scholar, a distinction that allowed him to create the major and educational program of greatest interest to him. (He was accepted at Cornell University and my alma mater, the College of William and Mary as a Monroe Scholar, but his heart and head were at the University of Virginia.) While we felt the pangs of sending our first born off alone, Jonathan was full of high spirits and energy for his newest adventure. We breathed a sigh of relief when we heard he had reached Charlottesville and was settling into college life.

Meanwhile, Eric headed off to Hong Kong International School as a junior. We were utterly confident he would get a fine academic education. Teachers and staff we had known from the 1980s were still there. Jim Handrich, his elementary school principal had become the high school principal and David Rittmann was still head of school. Eric had superb science/astronomy, English, history, and math teachers. We strongly supported the values and principles which undergird the moral, ethical, and spiritual education of HKIS, so we were happy he had the opportunity to live in Hong Kong again.

We began to attend the Lutheran Church of all Nations (CAN), associated with HKIS. We became friends with Pastor and Mrs. Temme, a dynamic speaker and leader. Some of Eric's good friends were members of CAN. When the Temmes announced they would be returning to the United States, we were happy to host a dinner for them at the residence, part of our desire to reach out to many different segments of the community.

The next two years of my tenure continued in the directions set in my first year, carrying out traditional activities of reporting on Hong Kong and China, assisting U.S. citizens, and increasingly assessing what China was doing and saying about Hong Kong's coming return to the Mainland. Importantly, we followed closely how the community was reacting and adjusting to coming changes. The "Establishment" publicly expressed confidence while privately worrying about the many uncertainties ahead. Many Hong Kong families continued to spread their assets outside Hong Kong and provide alternative residences for their families. The less well-off Hong Kong population was somewhat resigned to the return, but they also knew that their accustomed way of life and the openness that marked Hong Kong's unique society was potentially threatened by the very different and heavy-handed Communist Party and government just across the border.

Many of the events described above occurred during these two years. We were delighted that Mother and Dad agreed to visit us in October/November 1994. It was a joyous opportunity to show them the Hong Kong of today (Dad first visited in the 1950s) and to show them what their son and family were up to. They certainly appreciated that their son was now the senior U.S. diplomatic representative. I know they were proud of us. They participated in social occasions with us, for example, a cooking presentation and dinner with celebrity chef, Martin Yan, of "Yan Can Cook." They also visited China. In Guangzhou Mother tripped and injured her foot. But they gamely continued to Sichuan and then boarded a steamer to experience the Yangzi River cruise through the famous gorges to the Three Gorges hydroelectric dam.

When they returned to Hong Kong, they found me in the Adventist Hospital. Eric had noticed one evening that my left ankle and leg were seriously swollen. Off to see Dr. Gloria Pei the next morning. She quickly diagnosed a deep vein thrombosis (DVT), which can be dangerous if it moves up into the lungs and brain. I stayed in the hospital for days while the blood thinned, and the danger passed.

During one visit my parents made to the hospital, my mother and I were each put into our wheelchairs and allowed to spend time together outside in the sun! Regrettably, I missed the annual Marine Corps ball honoring the Corps and the detachment of Marines assigned to Consulate General Hong Kong. Claire and Eric did the honors as the senior guests.

What Next after Consul General Hong Kong? Asia Society

By 1995, a year before the end of my assignment, we began to ask, "What next?" I was told in Washington that an ambassadorship was in the cards. I was not keen to walk the corridors of the State Department lobbying for my next post.

And then Richard Boucher, our good friend, was named to replace me. He wisely had the idea to have Claire come off leave without pay and work for him. He knew she had broad experience and knowledge of Hong Kong and could help him settle in quickly. She was intrigued, but asked: What do we do with Richard?

Coincidentally, the Asia Society began to look for a director of the Asia Society Hong Kong Center to replace Burt Levin, who had run the Center for several years. My old friend, Nick Platt, now president of the Asia Society in New York City, encouraged me to take the position. Bottom line: with State Department approval I could go on leave without pay and become Claire's dependent!

We were happy to stay beyond the July 1, 1997, handover; Claire was happy to return to work; and I was interested in broadening my horizons working for a nonprofit organization. So we did the deal and worked out the many logistical arrangements to move to a new apartment building—Harbourview on Magazine Gap Road with a beautiful view of Hong Kong and the harbor. It was an apartment owned by William Fung, strong supporter of the Asia Society, of the well-known Fung family headed by Victor Fung of Li and Fung.

When the news of my moving to Asia Society Hong Kong Center was announced, we were heartened with the warm reception from many who were glad to have our familiar faces and presence remain in Hong Kong with a respected organization.

Finishing up as Consul General

The final months were a whirlwind of "farewell" events (even though we weren't really departing town) and of my final public addresses about Hong Kong and the U.S., as well as my private, classified, "end of tour" personal analyses to the State Department. Interestingly, my views remained essentially as described earlier: *As China goes, there goes Hong Kong.*

We also looked forward to Eric's high school graduation in June 1996. He was finishing up well academically and growing into a well-rounded young man. He was selected for the HKIS Honor Society. I was asked to speak at the induction ceremony. An honor, for sure, but not an easy task to speak to anxious seniors headed for the door. We made it through, with Eric undoubtedly relieved that it was over. At commencement, Principal Jim Handrich, whom we had known since 1983, handed Eric his diploma. Eric began his school career at HKIS as a kindergartener in 1983 and finished as a graduating senior thirteen years later.

Eric was off to Princeton University in the fall to study engineering. We were proud of him. While he also had been accepted to the engineering school at the University of Virginia as a Rodman Scholar, Princeton seemed like the best fit for his interests.

We flew out of Hong Kong for a summer of visiting family and friends: Hawaii to see Joan, Alaska to see Deb and Chris and to give the boys a good taste of our largest state, Jon to New Jersey and Eric to Atlanta. We all met up in Kiawah for a family get together with my parents who drove down to meet us. After we visited with the McCormicks in Rhode Island,

Claire headed back to Hong Kong, I spent time with the boys in New York City, dropped Eric off at Princeton, and escorted Jon to Dulles Airport for his flight to Beijing for his latest adventure: a semester to study intensive Chinese at Capital Normal University.

I skipped visiting the Department of State and instead spent some time in New York with Nick Platt and Asia Society officials preparing for my own new adventure in the private sector.

Did I regret not being consul general in Hong Kong on the night of the handover just a year ahead? In a word, no. I would still participate in handover ceremonies thanks to my previous position but also would be embarking on something new and unique at Asia Society Hong Kong Center.

Hong Kong: Here We Come, Again!

It was time for another red and white checkerboard approach and landing at Kai Tak Airport! The new apartment in Harbourview was great and signified our next chapter of life and work in Hong Kong. No Eric or Jon, but Cholin had agreed to move with us to our new place. She had been married a while before and was now expecting her first child. She told us she would have to return to the Philippines. We suggested she, Cecile, and baby stay with us instead. They accepted, so our family grew again, and they all settled in with us for the next two years.

Claire was already deeply engaged at the Consulate General. I jumped into the Asia Society with enthusiasm.

The Society was founded in New York City in the 1950s by John D. Rockefeller to educate Americans about Asia. It had small offices and a museum and was essentially an upper East Side cultural landmark. Under Nick Platt's decade of leadership, it broadened its focus to what I called "building bridges of understanding across the Pacific between Asia and the United States." The entire region needed to understand others much better. To that end, Asia Society established its first center outside the United States—the Asia Society Hong Kong Center. With Burt Levin's and Nick Platt's deep experience with Asia, they drew strong support from Hong Kong's leaders and businesses. Attracting another former consul general with long Asian experience also helped. With other Centers established later, it was a dynamic and thriving organization, helping to satisfy a hunger for more learning about the Pacific region.

We satisfied that hunger in two ways. One was to present economic, cultural, or political programs by a consul general in town, an author or an artist, a government official, or a film series. Hong Kong was well-located to take advantage of visitors passing through or someone locally resident.

By featuring a wide range of topics we aimed to draw a broader audience of people who might make new contacts in areas of mutual interest. Learning was the goal; and networking was the name of the game. We also produced a regular newsletter that summarized interesting presentations and contained informative Asia Society materials.

We were always on the lookout for big names who could help us draw a large audience for, say, a dinner. Henry Kissinger was popular, as was Bill Gates. The president of Pakistan gave a luncheon presentation on doing business in his country.

Since we were a private, nonprofit organization, increasing the membership was imperative. We needed to balance the budget and not rely on Asia Society New York.

I understood nonprofits but had never run one. It was a good learning experience and certainly set me up well for the next fifteen years as I ran three different schools that each required charitable donations in addition to tuition revenue. Over the next two years in Hong Kong, we more than doubled the number of programs and the membership, so we felt we were meeting a need in the community.

Ronnie Chan, who was well-known in Hong Kong and ran his father's company, Hang Lung, was the chair of our board. Quite a few distinguished and deep-pocketed Hongkongers and a few Americans served on the board and helped us to grow. Ronny was deeply committed to Asia Society. We started looking for larger premises at which to expand our operations. Ronny, to this day, has continued to build the Asia Society Hong Kong Center into a powerhouse cultural center.

Much later, Asia Society fortuitously acquired a prime site above Pacific Place near downtown, an overgrown former British ammunition storage site, and built a beautiful set of facilities for art exhibitions, community presentations and gatherings, and a restaurant. It's now a prime draw for visitors and is still carrying out its original goal of building bridges of understanding.

We took time in the fall for a quick trip to Beijing to visit Jonathan. He was deeply enjoying his time studying Chinese and traveling within the country. He took us to some of his favorite haunts. One was the well-known "Uyghur-ville"—a part of town where many Uyghurs had settled and opened wonderful small restaurants. Signs of Uyghur culture and life were everywhere. Sadly, not long after our visit, the government brought in its bulldozers and leveled the entire area. Two consequences emerged: many Uyghurs were driven back to Xinjiang, and more open land became available for new building. I wonder how many of those people forced back to Xinjiang languish today in China's new and vast labor and re-education camps.

By expanding and solidly grounding Asia Society Hong Kong Center, I'm glad I was able to contribute to Asia Society's long-term success both in Asia and in the United States

With China's new national security law of 2020, the Hong Kong Center will need to choose its programs and speakers carefully. New ways of building bridges of understanding will need to be devised if the Asia Society is to fulfill its historic mission of bringing peoples together.

Hong Kong International School

A brief word about HKIS. Claire mentioned to a board member that I would probably be willing to join the board in the summer of 1997. I was known and could help settle in the new head of school, Chuck Dull, and his wife Joanne. In fact, I took over as chair of the board until we left Hong Kong in 1998. It was a time of settling down and re-aligning the governance infrastructure. It also began a lifelong friendship with the Dulls. Chuck had a business and educational background. He was what the school needed in this new era—a breath of fresh air and new ways of thinking about education. He was immensely successful in helping lead the school in positive ways. He led us through a strategic planning process that put a new stamp on what was already an excellent school: a new mission statement, new learning goals (I insisted we include "academic excellence"), and a new-found commitment to supporting more students with learning differences. All of those remained in place through my head of school tenure and continue today.

It is worth remembering that HKIS was and is an important asset to the United States government and business community. It provides world class, excellent education as well as preparation for U.S. universities—drawing business and other leaders who set high educational standards for their children. The Hong Kong government over the years has also recognized the service HKIS provides in drawing international firms and investment, and thus has been a strong supporter in many ways, including providing precious new land and facilities.

And Then Came the Long-Awaited Hong Kong Handover

For many Hong Kong people, the formal "Handover" which came at midnight on June 30, 1997, was the long-awaited "return to the motherland." After 155 years of British colonial rule beginning in 1842, the sacred soil of Hong Kong was returned to its rightful sovereign.

For others, the Handover was caricatured as the Great Chinese Takeaway—with a pair of chopsticks making the snatch.

Here are some facts to ponder:

—China has rightfully felt aggrieved for many years that other countries, whether in the West or in Asia, felt entitled to invade the country and rule directly with their own laws and practices in different regions of China.

—China was angry that Britain and others used military force to dump huge quantities of opium into China, against Chinese law, to create millions of addicts and drain the country of silver, all in the name of trade.

—China was proud of its long and rich history and culture, yet was unable to stop the foreigners. It knew it needed to change. Many new ideas of governance, education, focus of investment, etc. (some of them Chinese and some foreign) were widely debated. "Mr. Science and Mr. Democracy" of the New Culture Movement seemed promising to many. Principles of science and democracy could help China evolve and prosper in the twentieth century. In the end, it was dictatorship in the form of Communism, Leninism, and Mao Zedong Thought that drove the Japanese and other foreigners out and won the civil war. The price of those victories was high, in the form of great famine and disruption in the Great Leap Forward and great killing and destruction in the Great Proletarian Cultural Revolution. China was saddled with a vast and ineffective governmental bureaucracy and inefficient economic system. Deng Xiaoping led efforts to undo many of these disastrous policies and put in place a more stable and somewhat freer political and economic governance system. Hong Kong would be allowed to continue to serve the country in its own way and was given fifty years to make the full transition back to China.

—On British minds was a sense of pride that they had led Hong Kong to become a thriving and unique world-class city and a center of business and finance. British minds also focused on thoughts of "loss." Loss of the last jewel in the crown of empire. Loss of respect for Britain and thus loss of influence around the world. And in a much larger sense, it was the end of a unique era in British history, one in which Britain would change the world. Such an era would not come again.

Many of these thoughts were prevalent in the immediate days before the official ceremonies as many notables made their way to Hong Kong, including British Prince Charles, Chinese President Jiang Zemin, Secretary of State Madeleine Albright, Margaret Thatcher, and others. It was an important and solemn occasion.

It was also an occasion for companies to sponsor lunches or dinners with well-known scholars or other commentators and invite their clients. Everybody had produced commemorative booklets, pictures, special cans of beer, cans of "pompous British air," 1997 umbrellas, Jiang Zemin's written phrase of *"Xiangang tian tian geng hao"* (Hong Kong will be better and better every day), and on and on. We had boxes of them. Stories of "End of Empire" filled newspapers around the world. The British brigadier, commander of the garrison, included us as guests in the military's "retreat" at his house on the Peak, with music and military formations.

The weather gods poured down their rain for days before the ceremonies. Inevitably, the Chinese penchant for sour prediction was that the continuing rains were washing away chances for Hong Kong's well-being in future years. Maybe they were right.

The British held their final "farewell" ceremonies on the afternoon of June 30 outside by the harbor. The rain continued its downpour. Many of the notables were drenched. Prince Charles had raindrops in his eyes (or were they tears?). The speeches and bands and military formations continued, resolutely.

Claire and I put up our 1997 commemorative umbrellas seated next to Senator Frank and his wife Lisa Murkowski of Alaska. They had forgotten theirs so the four of us did our best to huddle under just two umbrellas. For ever after, I have felt a special *guanxi* (relationship) with the Murkowskis for enduring such an afternoon together.

All in All, It Was a Dreary Time

We then headed to the dinner in the barely finished convention center, looking like turtles in the harbor. There were myriad guests. We weren't hungry. We went through the motions.

Claire soon left as she was not invited to the formal ceremony itself. As she walked to the consulate general to get a taxi home, she realized that Governor Patten's executive assistant, Jenny, with whom she worked and went to lunch with periodically, was walking alone ahead of her. Claire decided not to try to catch up. Claire felt emotionally drained by the day's events and could only imagine how Jenny, her professional colleague, must be feeling at this historic and deeply moving moment.

The formalities of the ceremonies were stultifying—and dreary. Everything was stiff—the two delegations walked in stiffly; they stood stiffly; the speeches were stiff and pro forma. The Chinese and British flags were stiffly "waving" on their flagpoles with one waiting to go down, the other to go up. There was little obvious emotion or joy from the Chinese, despite the historic occasion; no life from the Brits.

At least we were dry.

I believe that both sides would not have minded the simplest of ceremonies, such as: acknowledge that it had been 155 years; British representatives' hand over the keys and the golden goose; China signs the receipt accepting the goose and promising "one country, two systems" for fifty years; and Prince Charles and Governor Patten head for the royal yacht *Britannia* waiting in the harbor. Such a simple gathering could have dispensed with all the dinners, social gatherings, foreign visitors, dignitaries, and fireworks.

China wins this round.

But the full script had to be acted out for the sake of "history." After all, it was an historic occasion.

At the end of the ceremony, the British delegation exited and headed for the royal yacht. Two tugs pulled the ship slowly away from the HMS *Tamar* pier in Central so it could aim directly for open water and depart Hong Kong waters before midnight. My guess is that the bottles of spirits were opened and poured long before the ship reached international waters.

C.H. Tung, scion of the famous C.Y. Tung family, longtime Boston resident and Boston Red Sox fan, was now in charge as chief executive of Hong Kong. We had come to know him and his family well over the years and liked them on a personal level. The common wisdom from the establishment was that C.H. Tung was trusted by Beijing's leadership and in turn should be trusted by Hong Kong people because he was like the friendly grandfather wanting to do the best for the country and city. Sadly, C.H., as everyone called him, and his successors, found they did not inherit a truly workable Hong Kong governance structure. There was no effective way to build political legitimacy and to satisfy Beijing's leaders.

Nick Platt came for the historic event. He and I watched the departure from a balcony of the convention center. Two Hong Kong cooks joined us for air and a cigarette. We asked them what they thought. They looked at each other, then one said in broken English:

"Old boss go. New boss come. Not like new boss, I quit!"

That about sums up Hong Kong people's dilemma after twenty-five years of "one country, two systems" and a promised high degree of autonomy. The dragon has arrived and is settling in.

The question remains: Who stays? Who quits?

What Next for the Muellers?

After all the ceremonies and fireworks of July 1, 1997, it was time for a change.

The four Muellers decided to fly to Australia, squeezing a visit to a continent-sized country into two weeks. We visited the west (Perth and Fremantle), the center (Alice Springs, Uluru/Ayers Rock—yes, we climbed it before it was closed to visitors), the north (Darwin, Kakadu Yellow Water National Park), and the south (Canberra, Sydney). We visited friends as well as places I had lived many years before. It was a wonderful visit and a great change of pace for the four of us. It also brought back many memories of where I began my Foreign Service career at the U.S. Embassy in Canberra. Since then, Australia has become a far more cosmopolitan and interesting country. I wouldn't mind living there one day.

We returned to a Hong Kong with a new flag and new sovereign. On the surface it seemed to be the same Hong Kong, but one we knew behind the scenes was a swamp of activity. C.H. Tung and the Hong Kong government were scrambling to adjust to its new leaders across the border and new ways of doing things. There wasn't often a clear road map, so companies and other institutions plowed ahead as in olden times, hoping to stay online and out of trouble. PLA trucks, tanks, and other gear had rumbled into Hong Kong early on July 1 to former British bases. They deliberately drew attention to themselves, to make a point, and then disappeared behind the barbed wire. But Hong Kong *had* changed, in ways great and small.

Asia Society Hong Kong Center continued its quest to educate its members. Our programs continued much as before. We weren't overly worried about speakers who might utter some critical words about China. After all, free speech, free expression, and a free press were guaranteed by China, right?

The consulate general continued to operate more or less as before. Claire worked long hours as did Richard Boucher. Whether before or after July 1, 1997, the demanding work of the consulate general went on. Once Claire asked if I could attend a reception for a visitor. Richard nicely wrote up an invitation: Richard W. Mueller, former American consul general to Hong Kong, is invited to attend any and all consul general functions in which he has an interest.

It was nice to have such a close and collaborative relationship and to still feel valued. The relationship with Richard and Carolyn continues to this day.

Chapter Five

Northfield Mount Hermon School Comes Calling and Our Farewell to Hong Kong

O ver the years, friends have expressed interest and even amazement at how I ever went from a thirty-two-year Foreign Service career into a serious education career running three schools over fifteen years (Northfield Mount Hermon in Massachusetts, Hong Kong International School, and Shanghai American School). The account below is perhaps longer than it needs to be, but it answers many questions about how it all happened, what the process was like, and beliefs I shared. Nothing was ever a slam dunk; we worked hard each step along the way. Claire was a huge part of it and helped make it happen.

At some point during fall 1997, we spent the day on a friend's yacht. One of the guests had a connection with Northfield Mount Hermon School in Massachusetts. By chance I heard him say he understood that the current head of school, Jacqueline Smethurst, would be stepping down at the end of the academic year. I didn't know Jacqueline, and the information didn't register in a meaningful way. End of subject that afternoon.

In November I had a call from the assistant to Bill Rhodes, chair of the board of trustees of NMH and vice chair of Citibank. I had met Bill earlier at the beginning of my consul general tenure. His assistant explained that Bill would be in Hong Kong shortly. He recalled our meeting earlier and very much wanted to meet me again. I said sure, that was fine. She said he insisted on calling on me in my Asia Society office.

When I told Claire about the call, she wondered why Bill wasn't asking to meet the current consul general, her boss, Richard Boucher. I didn't know. We wondered what could be on Bill's mind. Was he looking for a private briefing on Hong Kong and China? A new director of international affairs for NMH? For a new trustee? Intriguing.

When Bill arrived in my office some days later, he said he had a question for me and "Please, don't say no right away!" What?!

He explained that Jacqueline was stepping down and that Russell Reynolds (a recruiting firm) had looked at eighty-some candidates for head of school. Some were pretty good, but he was really hoping for a candidate with serious experience internationally as well as leading large organizations. Having a graduate of NMH would be a big bonus. *Bill asked me directly whether I would consider becoming a serious candidate.*

I was truly dumbstruck. Speechless. Head of school? Me? My brain told me I had to respond.

I managed to say, "Bill, this is nuts. I'm a diplomat, not an educator."

His response, which has stayed with me so clearly over the years, "Believe me, Richard, diplomacy will go a long way in the world of education!"

With the benefit of hindsight, one can say that many times over!

We chatted about diplomacy and education, my background and experience, and overlapping skills a diplomat might share with a successful head of school. We touched on commitment to service and collaboration; bringing the community together around common goals; dedication to NMH ideals such as helping those who needed an extra hand; dedication to good learning and academic success as well as making a positive difference in the world; hard work; and willingness to fundraise.

We also chatted about some of the challenges faced by NMH, including being a large school on two campuses and the resulting financial and logistical challenges, a declining pool of high school-aged students from which to draw 1,155 students each year, an endowment too small for our needs. Those were just a few.

But there were many positives: A long-established and respected boarding school with an enviable underlying moral, ethical, and spiritual foundation; a large alumni body strongly supportive of the school, even if many were without the financial wherewithal to endow the school as it required; an innovative curriculum taught in extended blocks by high quality faculty; an historic commitment to international education and developing cross-cultural competencies. Those were just a few.

I admit to being close to overwhelmed. Still, I was intrigued, as I thought Claire would be, and so I promised to give his idea serious thought.

Bill urged me to fly to New York in December to meet with the school's search committee and recruiter.

A few days later, Claire and I flew to Bali for a change of scene and relaxation and to talk about Bill's visit. The deeper we dove, the more sense it made to travel to New York City and see how realistic this offer was. I could also assess the latest thinking by State's director general on my onward ambassadorial assignment possibilities after Hong Kong.

I proposed visiting the NMH campus for a day before meeting with the school's search committee in New York City. I hadn't visited for some time. "Good idea," Bill said. My trusty United 747 again delivered me to the east coast. The visit was an eye-opening experience. Where I remembered a smaller community of young men confined to the Mount Hermon campus, I found a very large community of young women and men—co-ed—on two campuses—Northfield and Mount Hermon—with busses running continuously between them. It had a much more open feeling than the cloistered experience of the past.

Jacqueline was welcoming and shared much about the school, its more recent history, and a new and unique approach to the educational program. Those highlights included a focus on two major subjects each trimester in a block system designed for intensive work. It also included more emphasis on dorm-focused life to create school spirit and loyalty within the very large, almost sprawling school community on two sides of the Connecticut River. Jacqueline was full of energy and seemed dedicated to making the school an even better one, even if it meant making major changes of approach.

The seed of an idea of leading such a community, daunting as it was, sprouted and began to grow. It was much later that I learned how challenging the issues in leading such an institution were, let alone making needed changes.

After a good visit to my alma mater, I headed to New York City to meet with the search committee made up of trustees, faculty, and staff. Bob McKinnon—trustee, lawyer, and Bill Rhodes's righthand man—chaired the committee. The Russell Reynolds recruiter told me beforehand that the committee was eager to hear from me. I was a unique candidate.

Still, I was a realist. The odds were high that I would feel such a position was not for me, while the committee would conclude that I was an interesting and unique candidate, but wasn't whom they were looking for.

They drilled down on governance issues such as board and head of school relations, my leadership style, and how I would build partnerships with the many far-flung constituencies.

We had a lively conversation for an extended period. It felt like a good, honest exchange. They clearly were interested in my international and leadership experience. Being a graduate was a positive.

Bob MacKinnon helped guide the conversation. From my perspective, knowing Bill Rhodes' interest in my candidacy, he gave me a chance to highlight foreign service experience that could be helpful to NMH. At one point, I realized my stock was rising when a trustee, Jane Gamber, who later became a big supporter, asked a question prefaced by, "If we were to be so lucky to have you at NMH . . . ."

When the meeting ended, search committee members made a point of coming over to thank me for coming and ask me to seriously consider throwing my hat in the ring formally. Bob MacKinnon asked me to come by Bill Rhodes' office later. And the Russell Reynolds search consultant, after meeting with the committee, told me they were very keen on my candidacy.

I confess I had gained more interest in pursuing the position while the meeting went on longer than I had ever expected. Later, Bill and Bob encouraged me to become a formal candidate. Would Claire and I be prepared to visit the campus for interviews and meetings? They hinted at my strong candidacy and being at the top of their list while avoiding making promises. I would have to prove myself in interviews on campus in February.

I called Claire to give her a readout and to say it went much better than I had expected. I was inclined to formally throw my hat in the ring. We would talk at much greater length when I returned to Hong Kong.

Home again, home again in our always trusty United 747. Here's how we thought about the pros and cons.

In favor of pursuing this brass ring: it sounded like a promising and extremely interesting professional opportunity. I felt I wasn't yet ready to be pushed out to pasture after Foreign Service retirement. NMH could be a multi-year position. Even if I stayed in the Foreign Service for a while longer, wouldn't I be looking for a position like this?

In favor of staying the course with the Foreign Service: I was at least five years away from mandatory retirement, maybe longer. I continued to be assured that an ambassadorship would be in the cards. Latest thinking was ambassador to Cambodia. Such a post would be another nice capstone to a successful career.

Mother and Dad were all for my becoming a formal candidate and seeing how the process moved forward. Both had been educators before the Foreign Service beckoned, and they still believed in the importance of a good education. They said, "Go for it!"

We Visit Northfield Mount Hermon for Interviews

In late January 1998, we flew to Hartford and drove up to Deerfield to overnight. Having seen that the head of school of Deerfield Academy, Eric Widmer, had a China background, I was in touch to ask if we could stop by. "Sure," he said. We had a good conversation about education and schools like Deerfield and NMH. I asked what kept him awake at night. His candid answer: "Nothing, really." His view was that being head of school at a prep school was still manageable and that good changes were still possible, unlike large, sprawling universities which verged on the ungovernable.

We were met at NMH again by a welcoming Jacqueline. She had invited us to stay at her home, Ford Cottage. Nice residence, we thought, not really believing we might reside there ourselves.

But before that could happen, we would be put through our paces over two and a half days. Twenty-five differing gatherings of students, faculty, staff, parents over that time. Grueling and exhilarating.

We joined an opening gathering with students at Memorial Chapel, one of my favorite places when I was a student. I loved their energy and outgoingness. Jacqueline introduced us as candidates for head of school. They clapped with energy. I was happy to hear them break into the school song, "Jerusalem," and sing with evident gusto. But I was taken aback by an unexpected twist: when the song reached, "Bring me my arrows of desire," the words were shouted out with even more gusto. It was a 1998 version of an old classic, with students delighting in their performance.

The search committee meeting in New York City weeks before was good preparation for the campus visits. Questions came by the hundreds. Tell us about your experience. What qualifies you to be head of school? What are your plans for the future of the school? How long do you plan to stay? What do you think of recent changes in curriculum and organization? Will you spend time with students and faculty and not just stay in your office? Like the Roman god Janus who with two faces looks in two directions, how will you balance the need to be on-campus to oversee education and operations with the need to be raising money and meeting alumni off-campus?

What was my approach to answering such questions and to talking about experiences that I would bring to NMH? I drew on much of the following as appropriate:

—I'm an NMH graduate, Class of '62, as is my sister, Linda, Class of '66. I have great respect for the school's history, ethical and spiritual foundations, care for others, traditions, and excellent education for thousands of graduates over the years. If I were to become head of school, my priority would be to maintain and broaden the excellence of the school for the long-term.

—I like the fact that NMH has maintained a different ethic and vibe from many other prep schools. We don't aspire to being considered "elite," but rather maintain a degree of modesty in our approach while maintaining strong academics and an emphasis on good character. Along with that approach we honor those who believe in service and in helping others. My entire life has been devoted to public service, and I would be pleased to continue as an educator also dedicated to service.

—I believe that quality education is what is needed to improve human society. My parents were educators. (My father was a Cornell professor and my mother an elementary school teacher in New Jersey). I have been intimately involved in our sons' education from preschool through university, and I have served on the board of trustees—including as chair—for Hong Kong International School. Schools are not alien places to me.

—An important goal at NMH would be to create a partnership with the faculty who are the recognized, career educators with the goal of continually improving the curriculum and the broader educational program.

I would create a partnership with the staff who make it possible to run such a large and complex institution.

—I do not have my own favored educational program that I would impose on the school. Rather, I would work with faculty and staff to resolve specific issues as well as find innovative best educational practices to improve student learning.

—I would work to create a partnership with the board of trustees, which has the ultimate responsibility to set the long-term course for the school and to ensure its continued success. A successful governance structure, which includes a cohesive board of trustees pulling in the same direction and a good working relationship with the head of school, provides a solid foundation for success.

—My thirty-two-year foreign service career means I bring experience in understanding other countries and peoples and how they can interact successfully—or not. I believe in strengthening global ties and in ensuring students develop cultural competencies that will allow them to live and work successfully around the world.

—I believe that Northfield and Mount Hermon were founded on the idea of creating an *historic commitment* to educating students from around the world, creating ties with other schools, and making sure all students developed a deep understanding of our world and its peoples. Call it *global competence.*

—I believe many skills from the world of diplomacy would help me to lead NMH, such as:

- Leading successfully larger organizations and groups of people, most recently as consul general of the U.S. Consulate General in Hong Kong.

- Listening carefully before rushing in to fix a problem or chart a new course.

- Collaborating with colleagues.

- Understanding and building trust with the different groups within our community and finding ways to bring them together to support the school.

- Showing that I'm a lifelong learner who is deeply interested in new areas of learning, such as what it means to be an educator and how teachers ensure that students are in fact *learning.* I would look forward to faculty and staff teaching *me!*

- Learning that leadership is about *followership.* One cannot lead if those in your organization do not *follow* (Garry Wills). So how would I best help to create a strong sense of working together successfully toward common ends? It starts with careful listening, collaborating, and identifying issues or obstacles, and then together creating options. The leader must decide *when* the time is right to make a decision and not draw out the process.

- When I do make a decision, I hope there is enough trust among my colleagues that one of the reactions, other than "great decision!", might be: "Well, I don't think I would have chosen that option, but I had a chance to have my ideas discussed. I'm willing to trust and support Richard in choosing the right way forward."

- Demonstrating that Claire and I are "people persons." We enjoy meeting people—we met many in our foreign service careers. We would aim to be out and about on campus to see what students are experiencing and how the faculty and staff are going about their jobs.

—We would be eager to travel within the United States and internationally to meet alumni and parents. A strong "people network" is vital. Fundraising is an important part of that outreach, and all heads of school need to learn the art of balancing on-and-off-campus time. I had learned at the Asia Society Hong Kong Center, a non-profit, that fundraising wasn't about twisting arms but rather about showing people who often are already philanthropically inclined how their donations can make a positive difference.

Those were a few beliefs I shared in varying ways during our February visit.

Most of these twenty-five gatherings over two and a half days were friendly. People seemed invested in the search process and interested in learning more about me. I chose to be the last of three candidates to speak, on the theory that the good points they saw would be fresher in their minds when decision time came.

I was keenly conscious there was some undercurrent of concern about recent changes in curriculum and organization led by Jacqueline. I was aware of those who questioned the changes, called *Educational Innovation at NMH,* and the way they had been implemented, but those faculty feelings were muted for now. Jacqueline was clear with me why the academic block system of two major courses each trimester was a better way to learn; why academic departments had become curriculum teams; why dorm life and loyalty helped to improve student connection with others and the school; and why she had expanded the office of international education and added resources. I appreciated they were designed to bring new ideas and life to the school.

If I came to NMH we would examine what was working well and what might be adjusted. But that was for much later.

My favorite meeting was with students to talk about their differing experiences and their favorite books. They were articulate and deeply interested, both in the school and the world. Students from Hong Kong were intrigued that their new head of school might have close connections with Hong Kong. Students pressed me on a favorite author. I talked about why I was so enamored of Wallace Stegner: great writing, keen insight into human nature, and good stories that pulled one along.

While I was being grilled, Claire was having fun on her own separate schedule arranged by Grace Robertson, secretary to the board of trustees and athletic teacher going back to her Northfield School days. I would end up working closely with her for seven years. Claire visited the classroom of Glenn Vandervliet, American history teacher. The two of them hit it off as they talked about history and our diplomatic careers. He became one of our biggest supporters; he told us he suggested to the search committee they should hire Claire!

And what about the all-important reaction of the faculty? I remember clearly the meeting with the full faculty toward the end of our visit. While I seemed to have connected with individuals and small groups, how about a large roomful of well more than one hundred faculty members? A potentially make-or-break meeting? School faculties can be known for their strong and often idiosyncratic ways. From my perspective, not surprisingly, my presentation and the many questions went quite well. I saw quite a few smiling, nodding faces. I noticed several people, previously identified to me as "curmudgeons," with perhaps some skeptical looks but also nodding as if in agreement.

The high point came when a senior and iconic member of the faculty stood up and said, "Richard, I believe most of us judge that you would bring many useful skills and experience of great use to NMH. Now, I think many of us would be interested in hearing your thoughts about an area you are well familiar with: China and Hong Kong. Would you share some thoughts about China's development and the U.S. relationship with China?"

Bingo! I was told later that the comment and question were a capstone of our conversation and that it would carry weight as consequential faculty feedback.

But we weren't quite home free. It still wasn't a slam dunk. The Board would meet in New York shortly. Nevertheless, Claire and I were enthusiastic and prepared to accept if offered the position.

The Board of Trustees Takes Action in New York City

Two days later, Claire and I were asked to be available for a call with the outcome of the board's deliberations. We chose to wait in a bookstore close to the Citibank meeting place.

When the call came, Bill Rhodes asked us to come to his office. He greeted us by saying, "Congratulations. The board has just voted unanimously to offer Richard the position of head of school, beginning July 1, 1998. We hope he will accept." Of course, we accepted on the spot and then were ushered into the meeting room to receive warm congratulations.

We stayed for a while hearing the board discuss issues and plans. My clearest recollection was of a trustee who made the point there was a missing $100 million in the endowment. That's what should have been raised in recent years. Claire kicked me under the table and whispered, "That's meant for you." The trustee made clear that I—and the board—needed to get to work. Welcome to a new world.

Bill Rhodes wanted to go back to the campus in a day or two to introduce me to the full school and community. Claire drove up from Pawtucket with Janet and Jim; I made my way separately from New York City.

We convened at the Auditorium on the Northfield campus—full student body and faculty at hand. It was Dwight Moody's favorite place from which he, in his booming voice, without a microphone, addressed students at Christian rallies and many other events. Just a bit intimidating. Jacqueline and Bill spoke and introduced me. I made some remarks, since lost to history and my memory. Some years later, I met an alumnus who said he remembered being at the occasion. All he remembered was, "You looked a little nervous."

Yep. He was right. I was reminded to be careful what you wish for!

The rest is history.

Back to Hong Kong and Preparation for a New Future

The next four months were a whirlwind of events and logistics. I wrote to the director general of the Foreign Service, Skip Gnehm, a good friend, that we had decided to retire because of this promising leadership position at NMH. We were ready for a change. He was flattering in saying that he was distressed for the Foreign Service to be prematurely losing two senior experienced and talented diplomats. The offer of a prominent ambassadorship, Cambodia or another one in Southeast Asia, did not tempt me to change my mind.

We attended to myriad tasks of wrapping up projects, penning "end of tour" thoughts with analysis and predictions, giving a last public speech with my observations about China and Hong Kong, attending numerous generously offered farewell lunches and dinners, and of course packing and shipping.

I came up with the idea that we should visit Tibet before we departed post. I had dreamed for years of visiting and, in particular, driving up to the Everest base camp on the Tibet side. Claire said she really wasn't interested. Jon and Eric accepted with enthusiasm. The next thing I knew, Claire decided she would in fact join us. Good. It would be a fun and unique visit.

Asia Society arranged a big farewell reception to invite many of the people we had worked with and known. It was held in the function room of our apartment building, Harbourview, and people came in droves. We were astounded at the turnout. Betty Tung, wife of C.H. Tung, chief executive, prominently represented him since he had another mandatory meeting. The traffic on Magazine Gap Road was clogged up and down the road with cars dropping off and picking up guests. We were gratified that so many were willing to take the time to say goodbye. Guess we did some good things representing American taxpayers over so many years and building bridges to understanding across the Pacific.

Tibet: Visiting the Roof of the World

We put in our applications, flew for an overnight in Chengdu and successfully obtained our permissions. The American consul general in Chengdu took us to a Sichuan restaurant. Authentic Sichuan cuisine was far fierier and tastier than we ever imagined it could be.

The next day we landed in Lhasa, Tibet. The elevation is just about twelve thousand feet. Doctors cannot predict who will react badly or well to that elevation. We remembered members of Congress who passed Chinese medical tests when we were at USLO and yet did not do well. We were hopeful we would acclimate quickly. After twenty-four hours of fatigue and some nausea, we were doing better. Jonathan and Eric were eager to try the yak burgers.

Our guide was a Tibetan Buddhist. He was knowledgeable and friendly and accompanied us for the duration of our stay. Inevitably, when out of earshot of Han Chinese, the conversation turned to Tibetan-Han relations. His stories were deeply distressing and confirmed what we knew from different sources. The CCP and government were pressing hard on Tibetans to make them conform more to Chinese ways. Less education in the Tibetan language. Increasing restrictions on practicing their religion. Fewer good jobs for Tibetans.

Sadly, these Chinese practices have only become more heavy-handed and menacing in the years since. Not only does the government want to change traditional Tibetan ways of life, but it is determined to keep the "country" united, with Tibet as an inalienable part of the People's Republic of China. In 2023, we find Beijing's actions equally unacceptable with the Uyghurs in Xinjiang, Hongkongers in Hong Kong, Mongolians in Inner Mongolia, Christians around the country, and others.

We spent several days in Lhasa visiting the main Tibetan Buddhist sites. The Jokhang Temple was vast with innumerable passageways and rooms. Tibetans were ever-present in circumambulating the temple on their knees in reverence for the Buddha. The Potala Palace, home to the Dalai Lama, constructed as a fortress in the seventeenth century, sitting imposingly high up overlooking the city, was equally vast and intriguing. Our Tibetan guide took us to visit other outlying temples and villages. I was fascinated observing a group of trainee monks in pairs discussing religious concepts. One would stand, ask a question, and deliver it to his seated colleague by winding up his arm, bringing it down, and then clapping with his other hand. After the seated monk answered the question, the two would discuss it and then exchange positions.

One object of the trip was to see other areas of Tibet, including the Mount Everest base camp. We drove through Gyantze and then climbed steep, narrow, curving mountain roads with no guard rails and drop offs of thousands of feet. The driver drove fast, demonstrating his sports car skills. It's fair to say we were terrified. I wondered the reaction at

NMH if they were to learn their soon-to-be head of school and his family had tumbled far down a Tibetan mountainside. Twice I asked the driver to stop and had our guide explain that while he drove these roads frequently, we were not used to them and would appreciate his driving slowly. Understood. But before long speeds crept up again.

When we got to Shigatse, we came up with a plan. The guide arranged for Claire to stay at a guest house and take her meals at a restaurant just down the street. We would pick her up on the way back. She was more than agreeable. Jon, Eric, and I continued with some trepidation.

We were taken by the unbelievable mountain views as we descended to valleys and then climbed up the next mountain range. Finally, we arrived at a huge rocky plain—base camp! No trees, no amenities, no other tourists, or climbers—only stupendous views of the north face of Mount Everest right in front of us. In Tibetan, it is known as Chomolungma.

The elevation at base camp is 16,900 feet. The peak is 29,031 feet. We could feel the thin air and the need to breathe deeply and move more slowly.

We walked around, getting different views of Everest and the surrounding mountains. At one point, I did a double take: A lone—and lonely?—yak meandered slowly across the huge plain, paying no attention to us. Where he was headed and where he found food were a mystery.

Our Tibetan guide and his team set up camp. We continued to gaze at Everest, which looked so close, as if we could reach out and touch it. As the sun set, we were enveloped by the deepest black of the sky with thousands of points of light. It was the most stars and constellations I have ever seen. It was easy to see how many people feel a spiritual/religious experience in such a setting.

I slept fitfully and decided the next morning to take some oxygen. It helped. Jon and Eric were okay.

The scene that morning was altogether different from the night before: the sun's rays filtered through the canyons and lit up snow, ice, and the vast fields of rocks. Another spectacular scene. I could have stayed for several days just thinking and meditating and wondering whether there were other forms of "life" out there. And if there were, would they be "friendly?" Would we really want them to visit us?!

Looking at the steep slopes of Mount Everest also made me appreciate the intrepid climbers who made it to the top. It was by far the most difficult and dangerous route on this northern side. What is it about the human spirit that propels some people to the edge and even beyond?

But the real world called. We couldn't linger. The truck with our supplies had gotten stuck in the rocks and water around us. Jon and Eric helped save the day by taking the initiative to build a rock dam to divert the water and free the truck so we could be on our way to rescue Claire in Shigatse.

We stopped to pick her up and found that she enjoyed her sojourn for a couple days, without the terror of mountain roads.

Our trip to Tibet, with its majestic mountains and inspiring Buddhist pilgrims, culture and religion, will stand as one of our most treasured visits.

Northfield Mount Hermon: Here We Come!

Our ever trustworthy 747 again carried us home.

Claire and I landed at Bradley Airport in Hartford, Connecticut in the early hours one day in July 1998. We rented a car and drove an hour north to Northfield Mount Hermon in Northfield and Gill, Massachusetts. We made our way to a guest house on the Northfield campus known as The Birthplace. It was where Dwight Lyman Moody, founder of the Northfield and Mount Hermon schools, was born. I remember so clearly the utter silence surrounding us and a clear sky with myriad stars and thought, "what a contrast to Hong Kong!"

The Birthplace was old and creaky. Maybe even creepy. Some asserted that the ghost of DLM, as he was affectionately known, was often sensed or even seen by visitors. We did not have the pleasure of meeting him the two nights we stayed before moving to the Hermon campus to our new home, Ford Cottage.

Not surprisingly, there were reports that the ghost of Elliot Speer, the headmaster murdered in the house in the 1930s (presumably by one of the deans who was not chosen as head of school) would periodically roam Ford Cottage. It turned out that my predecessor helped keep the story alive. Even our son Jonathan, as levelheaded as he was, swore that he and our future daughter-in-law, Kim, could sense a presence. One evening we returned to find lights on in every room; Jon swore that "something" was present. Kim agreed with him. Regrettably, we missed out on making acquaintances with any "presence" during the seven years we called Ford Cottage home.

Ford Cottage, a lovely three-story brick Georgian house built in 1911, was under renovation. Claire took charge of the house and plans to furnish it while I set about learning about the school and meeting the four hundred plus faculty and staff. Claire and I were dedicated to furnishing it comfortably so we could do what we particularly enjoyed, namely, sharing it with the community and visitors. We didn't know at that point all the many guests we would have—for example, the president of South Africa, Maya Angelou, the folk group Peter, Paul, and Mary, and so many others.

Getting to Work

I had two very clear goals for the coming months: 1) meet as many people as possible and visit every building on the two campuses and 2) learn about the current state of the school—its many positives as well as challenges—so we could begin to plan for the school's future.

To that end, I put on my listening and learning cap and went to work. It almost felt like a new foreign service assignment of getting to know one's new country, peoples, and cultures. A critical skill.

I teamed up with differing staff to walk the two campuses, visit the buildings and chat with those still there for the summer. I felt a warm welcome from everyone, perhaps not surprisingly. I smiled a lot and took time to listen to those I met.

I was struck by the beauty of the two campuses and their unique architectural styles, particularly on Northfield. The graves of Moody and his wife were on Round Top, a hill overlooking the Connecticut River Valley. The Birthplace was just above them, and Moody's lifelong home, The Homestead, was just below, now serving as our admissions office. There were beautiful views of the Valley from Round Top, and I was happy over the years to see the many students drawn to it at sunset to chill, make music, and chat with friends.

The Hermon campus was beautiful as well, but in a different way. It was perched on the western hills, overlooking the river and valley. Buildings were mostly built in an oval pattern around large open green fields with the beautiful stone Memorial Chapel "standing high upon her hilltop" overlooking the campus. Ford Cottage was just above the chapel with its own lovely views of the campus and to the east.

I came to learn that these idyllic settings tended to root people to the campuses and led them to choose not to leave for any extended period such as overseas travel or professional development. Many did not have passports. That came to concern me because people could become too settled and not expand their horizons. Later, one of my creations was to establish an exchange program with Hong Kong International School for faculty willing to trade teaching positions for a year or semester. What great learning that provided.

I was impressed with the size of the operations and the logistical complexities of supporting so much infrastructure on our limited endowment. There was much more deferred maintenance (a phrase I heard repeatedly) than desirable—particularly with the much older buildings, some dating back to the nineteenth century. The buried steam lines were a century old and needed replacing. The Russell Sage Chapel on Northfield had serious foundation problems. Sadly, many donors weren't as interested in supporting deferred maintenance.

Hats off to David Bolger, one of our most generous alums, for funding needed maintenance and repairs. One day he showed up in my office; he said he had been inspecting Memorial Chapel and noticed numerous areas that needed attention. He gave me his list, asked me to get estimates, and promised to donate the needed funds.

The logistical complexities of the schedules were equally a challenge. Buses ran back and forth regularly, and it was not unusual for a student to have classes on both campuses the same day. Our registrar had to design a unique scheduling system to accommodate all the details and literally get the buses to run on time. No educational company produced an adequate system for two campuses.

One of my first meetings was with the senior staff, all experienced and knowledgeable, both about the school and education more generally. I learned a lot from all of them. One was our dean of faculty, Lorrie Byrom, longtime NMH leader, a steady hand to work with, a figure trusted by the faculty, and a strong supporter of international education. One was our new dean of student life, Randy Stevens, just hired from Cornell, with a wealth of experience dealing with educational issues and young people. One was our dean of curriculum, Janet Durgin, who had helped design significant portions of the curriculum contained in *Educational Innovation at NMH*. One was Bill McMahon, our director of planning and communications who was the steadiest and most creative of strategic planners. One was our director of admissions, Pam Safford, among the most energetic and effective advocates for NMH; and one was Michael Bronnert, who, as CFO, held the finances and campus operations together. Later we were well served by Joe Ribeiro, interim CFO; Rick Wood, CFO; Deb Wright, dean of admissions; Pete Ticconi, dean of development and alumni relations; Nicole Hager, dean of students; and Tom Sturtevant as associate head of school.

Let me also give a shout out to three educators who helped immeasurably in serving as executive assistant in the head of school's office during my seven years. They taught me about schools and the current generation of young people. Their contributions helped to make each school year successful, including our strategic transition planning to one campus. Liz Resnick served for one year, was succeeded by Kyp Wasuik for three years, who was then succeeded by Carol Lebo for three years. Each made invaluable contributions to leadership of the school and became our good friends.

I listened intently to everyone and asked questions. I was alert to subtle—or perhaps not so subtle—messages being passed to me. I could hear their careful questioning of what my plans were for the school. Did I have some preconceived ideas or other instructions from the board of trustees? I reminded them of my consistent statements during the interview process that I would come with no specific plans to impose. We also discussed the important and demanding priority of getting school up and running in August, a truly demanding feat needing to be repeated every year.

My goal was to understand how we could work together as partners to make NMH an even better school.

I began reaching out to trustees to get to know them and understand what their priorities were for the school and for me. A high priority was to stay close to them and work with Bill Rhodes to keep the board functioning well together and toward agreed ends. Interestingly, they had never put together an "entry plan" that would make clear at least their short-and-medium-term expectations. Such plans can be an important component of good governance, providing support for the head and reducing the likelihood of miscommunication. But Bill Rhodes and the board were not day-to-day managers and assumed I would figure out best ways forward.

I met with all the campus deans to hear from them. The school was organized not as two separate schools but rather as one school. For example, the dean of student life oversaw both campuses rather than having two deans, one for each, with the subsequent difficulty of ensuring clear and consistent policies for both. The very large span of control for each of these leaders for so many students and four hundred faculty and staff on two campuses was breathtaking.

It became clear as I met with faculty and staff in the following weeks how many questions and concerns there were. Would we continue with the academic program of the "block system" of two major courses every trimester, condensing a normal year's work into an intense three months? What about the new student life curriculum with improvements to dorm life and new counselors known as "DLs" (from Dwight L. Moody)? What about doing away with academic department heads and replacing them with curriculum directors? Were we going to adjust the admissions funnel so we could fill all those beds? What about funding to bring needed salary levels up in order to hire the faculty and staff the school needed? Who would replace the advancement director and, of course, how often would I be on the road to raise money? There were other questions.

I had a memorable introduction to school life during a meeting with a longtime dean before a larger meeting. After telling me about the school, she said she should alert me that she knits during meetings. I assumed she meant using knitting needles to produce a sweater or some such. But that seemed odd, or at least unusual to me. My mind quickly told me maybe she nit-picks (hence nits) during meetings to keep people on their toes. But as the meeting started, she indeed took out her knitting bag and began to knit, following the conversation carefully. It turned out that her knitting helped her to concentrate. It was an unexpected piece of learning I hadn't known before, but one I subsequently observed on other occasions on campus. It was all fine with me.

I tried to imagine taking out my knitting in the office of the secretary of state or Governor Chris Patten.

Different cultures! No disrespect intended, but yes, the academic world can be effective while being unique in so many ways.

Opening Faculty Meeting—Should I be Worried?

I understood faculties can have their own personalities and priorities. They can be "prickly" and not easy to deal with. I learned much later that NMH faculty in the school world had a reputation of being among the more "prickly" ones!

My first encounter with all the faculty came at the end of August. I needed to "perform"! I had pondered at length. Then serendipity struck. My study in Ford Cottage was piled high with boxes from our move. I pushed myself to open them. In one of the first boxes, my scrapbook from Mount Hermon days seemed to leap into my hands. I don't think I had looked at it in decades. It was filled with memorabilia: laundry slips, my cum laude certificate, school bylaws and rules, letters from girls at Northfield School across the river, grades, and notices (not many) that I had transgressed some rule or other.

Bingo! My scrapbook turned out to be a perfect bridge to the faculty. I paged through, commenting on the humbling experience of having to sort and wash fellow students' dirty underwear (yuck) and the order to help clean up the Chateau in punishment for my roommate and my tying a rope to a chair and lowering it out our dorm window one evening, breaking a window below. It was retribution for some provocation from the nether region, but what exactly has been lost in the mists of time.

An important point was showing the rule book from my day. It was small, maybe the size of a three-by-five-inch index card with only a few pages. On the inside cover was a statement to the effect: this booklet contains fewer, rather than more, rules for daily life at Mount Hermon on the presumption that good and polite manners and civil behavior will best guide most personal interactions in the community.

I then compared it to the current book of rules and instructions, a thick eight-by-ten-inch brochure with many detailed instructions of do's and don'ts. The contrast was stark. How much had society changed over the decades that we needed to provide detailed guidance on proper behavior?

The point was not lost on the faculty.

The scrapbook served me well for weeks as an icebreaker at student assemblies and gatherings of parents and alumni. Claire, my best critic, finally told me it was time to drop the scrapbook theme and move on.

Of course, the faculty meeting was also a chance to share some info about Claire's and my foreign service careers and world experiences, some hopeful plans for the school for the next year and beyond, and my intention to listen carefully and learn well from them and the staff. I felt the school had a good foundation in the strategic plan that had led to many good changes. We needed to be alert to what might need some adjusting.

All in all, I think the faculty meeting got my first year of leadership off to a good start. The faculty laughed and smiled. They listened. They asked questions. They saw me smile, and they exhaled. And the bottom line, I believe, is that I came across as human, accessible, open to new ideas, and most importantly, didn't act as if I had my nose in the air. I just needed to show I could make the transition from the realm of diplomacy to that of education.

Similarly, Claire and I went to great lengths to talk and meet with the large staff that kept this huge place running: dining and kitchen workers, plant and property staff who did the maintenance, plowed the roads, etc. Claire was particularly good at building those relationships, with many staff believing they had a good ally in her in Ford Cottage.

And Then Came 1,155 Students to Two Large Campuses

It is an eye-opening experience to observe the myriad steps needed to open a boarding school. Details matter. Instructions for first time students. Another set for returning students. Rooms and dorm assignments. Sign-ups for classes, sports, clubs, international travel. Financial payments. Planning enough food for perpetually hungry adolescents. Orienting new faculty and reviewing their syllabuses. Planning fall speakers, concerts, sports schedules. Ordering, storing, distributing textbooks. Assigning work jobs. And on and on.

I observed with great respect how experienced people went about their jobs with dedication. I supported wherever I could. I prepared sets of remarks to use for myriad gatherings in the next weeks. My goal was to avoid unnecessary intrusion, even while observing, learning, and guiding.

Claire and I established a routine of greeting parents and students as they lined up to enter the gym for signing in and signing up. It was too busy a time to chat for long, but it did send a signal that we were out and about and very much present. We needed to decide which campus to visit first and then dash to the other.

Strolling around the campuses always gave us a chance to meet students, faculty, and visitors. It was always energizing. I was impressed that students were friendly, willing to smile and say hello. I often enjoyed going to the cafeterias on both campuses and would randomly ask students if I could sit down with them. Nobody turned me down. I heard all sorts of interesting stories and feedback over the years.

I asked one young man what he had done for the summer. He said he took a computer course which also taught the basics of how to breach firewalls for email and other systems. He gave me a big smile. I was tempted to warn him I would toss him out of school if he used those skills. He obviously already knew the possible consequences.

So many people to meet, so little time. My natural inclination to spend time meeting and talking to people was a God-given gift that served me well in the Foreign Service and in leading a school.

Then came opening convocation in the auditorium on the Northfield campus. The entire school fit in without a problem. It was used by Dwight Moody to address the student bodies and the many religious conferences he hosted. The acoustics were excellent. He used his booming voice. The rest of us used a microphone.

There was an engaging and fun program, with a ceremonial opening by the Franklin County "sheriff" who banged his staff three times and called for order, followed by singing of the national anthem and later the school song, "Jerusalem." Then came Bill Rhodes' "installation" of me in a simple, fun way, followed by my "homecoming" address. I had worked on it for several weeks. I tied together my time at Mount Hermon and the Foreign Service to 1998, and then to our hopes and dreams. Claire and I reread it recently. We both agreed, biased as we are, that it hit the spot, maybe even with a degree of eloquence. I recently unearthed a letter from Charlie Tierney, then a new dean and now deputy head of school, who wrote how impressed he was with the program and my address.

I introduced family members. Jonathan and Eric. Mother and Dad came up from Williamsburg and seemed to just keep beaming. It was so good to see them obviously proud of their family. Others included Linda (my sister) and Jennifer (her daughter); Claire's mother Alma; Janet and Jim and other McCormicks; favorite retired teachers; and some 1962 classmates. Bill Morrow, the school librarian and iconic campus presence I worked for my senior year, was a lively participant. We had lunch with him a short time later and reminisced about how the world, the school, and I had changed over the years. Sadly, he passed away shortly after. I was pleased that NMH remained very much a singing school with music constantly on tap.

I knew there was much work before us both to successfully educate 1,155 students every year and to lay foundations for an even better school ahead.

And then we were off—to classes and the new academic year!

The School Year Moves into High Gear

The fall raced by. Claire and I made it to many student activities, classes, and sports events. We had assumed students would not much notice that we were there. In any case, we did not want to distract them. How wrong we were. In fact, just the opposite was the case. We got positive feedback about how thrilled faculty and students were when we stopped by to observe and learn.

Early on we drove into Boston for a girls' varsity soccer game. I never expected the wonderfully positive response, which I was told reverberated around the campus. The good news was that Claire and I enjoyed getting out of the office and Ford Cottage to see the students. We agreed to a proposal that we host dinner at Ford Cottage for the members of a team that went undefeated for its season. It was another occasion to engage with students.

We created a Head's Advisory Committee with a carefully selected range of students from both campuses and from different grades and backgrounds. When they arrived at Ford Cottage, before dinner, we used various paintings and artwork on our walls to tell them about other countries, cultures, and our own experiences. We fed them a specially prepared Dining Services meal around the dining room table and encouraged free discussion. Few held back in sharing their opinions. I encouraged them to ask about rumors around campus and ideas to make NMH an even better school. One student, David, was an ardent proponent of letting teenagers sleep longer in the morning and start classes later—better for their health. Another student was focused on building a fully modern ice hockey rink. He promised that when he earned a big salary, he would underwrite the project.

We were truly overwhelmed by the huge range of activities on campus in each of our seven years: Dennis Kennedy's students' Irish literature presentations; Tim Seeley's mock trial on capital punishment; Sheila Heffernon's music groups; Hughes Pack's astronomy students, who discovered a new celestial body in the Kuiper Belt out at the edge of our solar system, later named KBO 1998 FS144 (a huge deal in the astronomy world!); faculty and student music performances; the annual jazz concert; the full range of sports contests on Wednesday and Saturday afternoons; chapel services on Sundays led by Reverend Betty Stookey; international students' day, culminating with dinner serving food from around the world, cooked by students; and on and on. We attended so many.

The important point of such contact was that it reinforced what I believed, namely, that students and their learning and welfare must be at the heart of almost every decision the board and I made. *I learned a great lesson that served well: When facing a conundrum or obstacle, if we put student learning at the center, good solutions usually appeared. For the rest of my education career at three schools my mantra became: It's all about our students!*

It's All About Our Students!

The fall board meeting on campus in November came off without a hitch. The board reviewed and discussed reports from me and school leadership about my transition to the school (good) and progress on several ongoing initiatives as part of the strategic plan. I was impressed with the amount of detail available and the energy that had been expended. The board quickly picked up that the atmosphere was collaborative; faculty and others seemed to be settling well into my style of leadership.

We made sure the board understood that two high-priority educational goals would be pursued: review and revise the student life curriculum (focused on student learning outside the classroom including life in the dorms) and further implementation of schoolwide outcomes, namely, learning objectives for students in all major areas of their experience.

Otherwise, no major decisions. There was a gathering energy around building the board (now down to fifteen trustees) and beginning to think about our future. What priorities should NMH be pursuing?

By the time of the board meeting, Claire, with some unsolicited assistance from me, had decorated Ford Cottage with our artwork and furniture, supplemented with some things purchased by the school. It was a warm and attractive home we were happy to share with others, including Bill Rhodes, our board chair. He was the first of many visitors we hosted over seven years. For every board meeting, we hosted several trustees overnight at Ford Cottage and had a dinner in Ford for all trustees in what was always a relaxed occasion. I think they appreciated our willingness to open our home for such special occasions.

Claire always said she thought she might want to run a bed and breakfast in New England. At Ford Cottage, she fulfilled her desire in spades over our seven years.

One of our biggest efforts that lasted the entire first year was to invite, every week, a group of ten to twelve members of the faculty to dinner. Our goal was to have all faculty up to the house; we succeeded. We billed it as a listening and learning opportunity for them and for us. While we were happy to describe our work with the Foreign Service and life overseas, the reality was that they did much of the talking and we did much of the listening. In the Foreign Service, we learned firsthand that most people, including friends and family, don't relate easily to lives lived in other countries and so fall back quickly to describing their own lives and what they are doing.

In the setting of Ford Cottage, most faculty members were anxious to share their views of the school, what they liked, and concerns about school changes of recent years. I had picked up on some of these ideas and concerns during the interview process, but they ran deeper and were more openly expressed now that they had a new head of school.

Here were some of the themes.

—Faculty members maintained a strong loyalty to NMH over the years. They felt a commitment to its values and the types of students it draws.

—Despite that loyalty, they felt they were well behind other independent schools in compensation. Some of the benefits of sabbatical leave, more freedom to arrange programs and curriculum, and life in the Connecticut River Valley were high points for many.

—Some faculty members felt the school was so large on two campuses that students did not get the support and mentorship they deserved. There was also anxiety and stress among both adults and students in dealing with the school's size and complexity, including frequent worry about making it to the bus on time.

—The *process* of implementing the wide-ranging academic and organizational changes contained in *Educational Innovation at NMH* could have benefited from more inclusive and serious discussion. Some faculty felt they should have been more involved in the process. There were also strong supporters of the changes made. They argued the school needed to up its game to provide the best education possible.

—Many liked the opportunity to teach in a block system of two main courses each trimester. It emphasized learning skills rather than coverage of facts and accorded with evolving educational research. Those who were not as supportive argued it was unproven. It lacked the "marinating" time for learning and absorbing that could be so important. Also, faculty had to significantly retool their teaching approaches; it was onerous and time-consuming. There was less time for coverage of material, important to many.

—School leadership style from senior leaders was mostly top-down. It could have been more collaborative and transparent.

—Many facilities were older and in need of serious updating. We needed to invest in both people and facilities.

It was clear from my first three months that between the size of the school on two campuses, the number of students, and the size of the faculty/staff, I had my work cut out for me. How would I allocate my time and what would be my priorities? The board had not provided answers, so I would have to figure them out myself. That "figuring out" included collaborative work with a talented senior staff.

The fall semester raced on. Just before Thanksgiving, we had an open house at Ford Cottage for all faculty, staff, spouses, and partners. It was well attended with many saying they appreciated seeing their colleagues in a new setting. The gathering was also a reminder of how large an institution we were. Two teachers who began talking to each other realized they had been in regular contact by phone and email, but because one was based on Hermon and the other on Northfield, they had never met!

Thanksgiving was a good break and chance to slow down. Jonathan came from Chicago where he was working for A.T. Kearney, and Eric came from Princeton. We were joined by Cholin, Cecile, and Celine, who had moved from Hong Kong to Holyoke, where she was taking a yearlong course in culinary arts at Holyoke Community College. Looking back from 2023, they have now worked at NMH for more than two decades, becoming valued employees and supporters of students. Cecile has earned the "student choice" award on multiple occasions. Celine attended NMH, benefited from its rigorous curriculum, and then graduated from Suffolk University in Boston. I'm happy to say they have become our good friends and not just "employees." They exemplify immigrant dreams of working hard, contributing to American society, and making a good life for themselves.

The time between Thanksgiving and Christmas was wonderfully busy with Christmas preparations, celebrations, and one of two iconic NMH traditions, Christmas Vespers. I had such wonderful memories of Vespers from my student days. It was held twice on the same day, once at Northfield at Sage Chapel and once at Hermon at Memorial Chapel. The music was interspersed with readings from the Bible about the birth of Jesus. I had the privilege of reading the account in Luke 2:1–20. For decades, the chamber orchestra played the opening music, followed by the Introit, *"Veni Emmanuel"* ("O Come, O Come, Emmanuel") with student soloists, and then the processional, "Sing We Noel." The closing hymn was *"Adeste Fideles"* ("O Come all Ye Faithful") and the final closing of *"Stille*

Nacht" ("Silent Night") with a student soloist filling the chapel with song as the candles filled it with light.

The only sadness I felt was that attendance at this wonderful music celebration by students was no longer appreciated by all students. Attendance was not mandatory. The explanation was that we wanted to be "sensitive" to those of other religions. I disagreed with that reasoning. Vespers was an important and historic school tradition, and students throughout their lives would be in situations with those of different backgrounds; they would not be "protected" from different points of view. Attending Vespers would importantly help them learn about people of other cultures and traditions. I decided not to take on the uphill challenge of changing this way of thinking in my first year as head of school.

I was coming to understand how much the school had changed over the years. Betty Stookey, chaplain, (married to Noel Paul Stookey of Peter, Paul, and Mary fame) had shared with me how frustrating she found it that so many people on campus were shunning the Christian traditions and elevating those of other religions. Betty held an ecumenical Christian worship service every Sunday. We were religious about attending every week. Sadly, only relatively small numbers of students and adults joined us.

Part of the problem I discerned was that through lack of knowledge, many equated all Christians with the very conservative theology of some churches and of the U.S. political right who, for example, did not favor gay and lesbian rights, gender equality, or women's rights. They were unaware of the very progressive Christianity of my Evangelical Lutheran Church in America or Betty's Church of Christ.

Echoes of the so-called "culture wars" were evident at NMH.

The extended Christmas break was a much-appreciated chance to exhale and ponder the many things we learned in the first half-year of our new life at NMH.

The Second Semester—1999: Even More Adrenaline!

The second half of the year was even busier than the first half, with day-to-day running of the school, new learnings, and new challenges.

"Show Me the Money!" Philanthropy moved up my list of priorities as the head of school. As with other institutions, the school needed to stay in touch with its alumni and friends, whose yearly donations were an important source of revenue for each year's budget. We also cultivated larger donations for specific needs. For years, the school appreciated that many alumni had jobs that were service-oriented or philanthropic, and thus did not have the "big bucks" to help. The endowment per student was much smaller than a school our size needed to continue to compete in a very competitive market.

A brief comment on fundraising which was always on our minds and one of the biggest changes from our lives in the Foreign Service. It's not about twisting arms. It's about the opportunity of making a positive difference. If you believe in your school, you have a good story to tell about how their help can make a crucial contribution to the school's success in educating the next generation.

My colleague in the Foreign Service, Bill Luers, who was now president of the Metropolitan Museum of Art, told me his best advice was, *"Don't be afraid to ask."* Too many fundraisers cultivate and cultivate a potential donor and then shy away from making the needed specific ask. Opportunity lost.

In the "nice surprise" category: a parent we had met and built a relationship with told me his son loved track and field and was having such a good experience at NMH. The parent wanted to talk about contributing to build a desperately needed new track. For years, runners had to compete on an old cinder track. Other schools often declined to compete at NMH. Thus was born the Miller Track in 1999. Construction of a state-of-the-art, eight-lane track, between the chapel and the gym in the heart of the campus, was a visible shot in the arm for the community. Claire, I, and Mr. Miller were happy to sit on the first bulldozer for pictures. Thanks, Miller Family!

It was also time to get off campus and visit alumni. Winter was a favored time for such a trip because so many snowbirds sheltering in Florida were happy to meet the head of school and his wife. Sometimes we met in homes, other times in country clubs or restaurants. Everyone was interested in the school, its students, and its future. Much of the effort was directed to building relationships, which in future meetings could lead to discussion of specific projects they might be willing to support.

In addition to the fundraising, we were interested in "friend-raising." We were always on the lookout for potential new students as well as new trustees and people who had expertise or professional networks to support NMH. We were not shy about asking alumni or parents to serve on committees or participate in other ways.

There was one thing I needed *not* to do on these winter trips, namely, sit on a beach getting a tan. I didn't want to return to winter's grey, overcast New England skies looking as though I'd been on vacation.

Boston and New York City were both stocked with alumni and parents, so we organized regular shorter visits. During the seven years at NMH we visited dozens of U.S. cities, some many times more than once.

And of course, there were many overseas trips. That first year, we visited Tokyo, Seoul, Taiwan, and Hong Kong. Many of our international students were from Asia. Parents were hospitable and often went well above and beyond in hosting us. Other destinations included Germany, Turkey (the deputy prime minister's daughter was a student), the United Kingdom, and Dominican Republic.

The most unexpected encounter was when a man came to our admissions reception (in an unnamed country) with his child, pulled me out of the room, and showed me a briefcase full of cash. He wanted to make sure his child was accepted. For the record, I was not tempted and explained how our system worked. If his child was qualified and entered, we would be happy to have him donate openly to our annual fund.

There was another positive result from all our travel. I had the opportunity to describe to students and others some of the things happening around the world. Even though the Pioneer Valley was beautiful, we all needed to become more comfortable with learning about the world and "global competence." That message played directly into the considerable effort the school made to boost the whole range of international education learning activities.

Spring 1999 and Culmination of the Academic Year

The cold and snowy New England winter gave way to mud season and then to a glorious spring. There was no end to the beauty of the two campuses nestled in the Connecticut River Valley as the leaves burst out and the flowers bloomed. Life seemed to move outdoors as students engaged in sports, made music, or just found a comfortable spot under a tree to read a good book. My favorite tree was a magnificent dawn redwood on the Hermon campus across from what I planned for a new arts center. I knew who our benefactor might well be.

There was palpable excitement as the end of the school year came into view. Seniors looked forward to commencement and their new beginnings as they headed off to college. Numerous favorite traditions dotted the calendar, including Founder's Day, honoring both Dwight Lyman Moody and Martin Luther King, Jr. I noted that in both cases, the bulk of the remarks honoring both men focused on ideas other than the important Christianity that animated both men.

Parents' Council gatherings, faculty meetings, prize assemblies for students and faculty, visiting speakers, athletic banquets, International Food Festival, and on and on. They seemed to be endless—also endlessly satisfying in talking with students. Claire and I were always privileged to attend. I often had a place in the lineup to welcome attendees, share some stories, describe school policies, or encourage the group in their endeavors. It seemed there were eyes on us all the time.

And then we all did a double take when the April 1 edition of *The Bridge,* the student newspaper, came out with a big headline: "AP Biology Class Clones Richard and Claire Mueller!" The news account revealed the reason Richard and Claire were seen so often everywhere at student and other events—the biology class had cloned them! We had a good laugh at the April Fools' insight.

I enjoyed Cum Laude ceremonies every spring. Students were elected by a faculty committee for their academic achievements. Parents and friends attended. It was a big deal. I would open the huge book with signatures of Cum Laude graduates going back decades and had fun turning to the page with my signature from spring 1962. I would tell them I believed one of them might one day be on stage as head of school handing out Cum Laude certificates. Students' heads would shake in disbelief. Did he really say that?

Of all the traditional celebrations, my favorite was Sacred Concert in the auditorium, with many alumni and visitors making their way back to the school. The music was drawn from many sacred traditions and religions, and beautifully performed by students. Unlike other areas of school life, music from Christian traditions was featured. Attendance was required. The alumni choir, which had little time to rehearse, always helped reinforce the idea of NMH as a singing school. The alma mater was sung with a degree of solemnity; "Jerusalem" was sung with great joy and gusto.

On the social front, Claire and I confirmed we wanted to host the senior prom, known as "The Chat," in mid-May in a big tent outside Ford Cottage. It would be an elegant occasion. We asked students to arrive at the front door where we greeted them and then let them walk through the house and into the tent.

For each of our seven years at NMH, we hosted "The Chat." We encouraged students when they wanted a break to stroll around the house, sit for a bit, and ask questions about art works or other treasures. It was a great way to connect with students more personally and to talk about other countries and our Foreign Service and international lives.

As midnight approached on that first Chat evening, so did one of the deans, who asked me to join them in our kitchen. All the deans were gathered, including the dean for student life. They informed me that a "cutting" incident had taken place. Four students had been fooling around; a sophomore said he liked the music group, Queen. The oldest student said he must be gay. The younger denied being gay, at which point the hotheaded, older student wrestled him to the ground, took out a penknife and scratched the letters "h-o-m-o" on his back. There was some bleeding. They all then helped him up and cleaned off his back. The deans learned of the incident and investigated. I asked what they recommended. They weren't sure. There was concern that reporting to the police could be negative for the school. I wasn't concerned about the school; I was concerned about the illegal act of violence against a student. "Call the police," I said.

The police came and took the perpetrator into custody. We called the father, who later suggested it was not such a big deal; kids were just fooling around. The student had been headed to the U.S. Naval Academy until he was denied his NMH diploma and later convicted.

All hell broke loose the next day as word got out nationwide of the attack and "carving" on the back of a gay student. Gay and lesbian communities, politicians, and others around the country understandably expressed great concerns. Making it even worse was the memory of the previous October's horrific murder of Matthew Shepherd in Wyoming.

My instruction to the staff was to be transparent and tell the truth. We became proactive with the press and the NMH community. The perpetrator was arraigned and charged. As word got around that it was a "scratching" and not a "carving" and that it was *not* a crime against a gay student, public attention slowly shifted.

But it was a searing moment for all of us and a dangerous moment in the school's history. Continuing press attention and public opinion could have seriously damaged the school's reputation.

We learned that the victim's parents had visited the campus soon after the incident, seen the bloody T-shirt, and yet agreed to let their son deal with it himself. No word to the school.

The student elected to remain at the school for the next two years, accepting our unstinting academic and other support. His back healed quickly, so that within a short time there were no signs of the scratching. Right after he graduated, the parents launched a lawsuit making claims against the school; they accepted an insurance company settlement.

So much was at stake; I was glad my instinct to call the police immediately was the right one. I was deluged with messages congratulating us on how we handled it. Our board of trustees was fully supportive. I had messages of support from numerous heads of school, all essentially saying, "There, but for the grace of God, go I."

The Academic Year Sprints to a Close

The end of the semester was almost upon us. Final exams, final celebrations, goodbyes, baccalaureate service, and finally commencement all came to pass.

Remembering Reverend William Sloane Coffin from my student days as an eloquent defender of human rights, including gay and lesbian people, I had invited him to be our commencement speaker. After the cutting incident, I called him in Vermont to describe our incident of violence. He readily agreed to address the issue. He arrived the afternoon before commencement and accepted our offer to stay at Ford Cottage. He was friendly, but we wondered whether he would be up to the task the next day. He took his drink to his room and settled into watching an NBA playoff game, his favorite New York Knicks.

The next day, Reverend Coffin appeared with his full pastoral robes, looking quite imposing. We processed with the seniors to the ceremonies on the Hermon football field. I introduced him at the appointed time. He rose like an old war horse to a final challenge. He began slowly and then gradually cruised into an eloquent rhythm, challenging those who violated the human rights of others. He described our challenge of violence and called on everyone to stand up for what was right and just. The crusader, with his booming voice, delivered just what we needed. The audience was strongly receptive. Undoubtedly there also were parents in the audience who weren't sure what to make of the reverend and his remarks. I hoped all learned something about treating *all* individuals with decency and fairness.

In a fun twist to the ceremony, seniors of the class of 1999 handed me small mementos of their time at NMH as I handed them their diplomas.

I have a boxful of them, with lots of notes written on cards or napkins, pictures, a Chairman Mao button, thank you's for a great school and education, and so forth. One student handed me a fork with one tine to remind me of the school's tradition of working hard, namely *"eating soup with a one-tine fork."*

I will never forget, as we slowly dispersed after the ceremony, Claire asking a senior faculty member how they handled saying goodbye to students they had taught, nurtured, and supported for four years. Her simple answer: "We grieve."

Claire and I came to experience similar feelings over the next years as we got to know students and adults and then at some point had to say farewell, knowing that chances were slim that we would ever see or hear from them again. This included many parents we had come to know and enjoy talking with while their daughter or son attended NMH. To this day we not infrequently think about individuals we knew and wondered where they might be now.

But the school year wasn't finished for us quite yet. Within a couple days, we pumped ourselves up again for several days of intense reunion activities. Again, we worked at being everywhere, meeting the oldest alums in their nineties and the very youngest, just a few years out of school and university. They all recalled their good and not so good days at Northfield, Mount Hermon, and NMH. Almost all expressed that their days at school were special and had made a formative difference in their growing up.

On Sunday after the Alumni Worship Service, we mingled at lunch in Alumni Hall as the final attendees prepared to depart. We then were free to take our leave and head for Ford Cottage and collapse. Inevitably, a trustee or two would want to hang around for a while to chat.

How Did We Feel About Our First Year at NMH?

It had been an extraordinary year of taking on an entirely new venture, learning about boarding school life and the many rhythms, successes, and even lowlights of an educational institution. I began to make some decisions that seemed necessary and were welcomed, such as improvement of the dean and dorm director system and negotiating the termination of the school's lawsuit against a former staff member. The decision whether students could paint the inside of one dorm pink I left to the dean of student life.

Claire had taken on an important role in the community with great success and satisfaction, connecting to people, listening, and making them feel comfortable as a part of our school community.

Meeting so many different people from literally around the world was as energizing as one could ever hope for. From the many extremely positive letters and comments of students, faculty, parents, and trustees, we felt proud to be a part of such a vital and successful educational endeavor. We were directly helping to inform and guide the next generation in so many good ways.

We marveled at the extraordinarily different worlds we had experienced in our lifetimes: the beautiful rural New England campuses of a large, premier boarding school, NMH; the corridors of power in the Department of State in Washington, DC; the dense and adrenaline-crazed world of one of the world's great cities, Hong Kong; the cold, forbidding, intriguing city of Beijing as China came out of its Cultural Revolution insanity; war and peace in Vietnam and Southeast Asia; the summer of riots in the "City of Lights," Paris; the wonderful family vacations on the beaches of Southeast Asia and Kiawah, South Carolina; and the hometown anchor of Claire's youth, Pawtucket, Rhode Island.

In the spring, we had received a warm letter from long-time friend Parker Borg who had visited with his daughters considering boarding school. He wrote, "We were all extremely impressed by NMH and the work which you are doing to maintain high standards. Of all my foreign service friends who have moved on to different lives, I think you have definitely found the most extraordinary and probably the most rewarding second career."

Indeed. We were fortunate.

Coming down from our year-long high as we kicked back in Ford Cottage that Sunday after reunion, we agreed we had no regrets retiring from the Foreign Service when we did, after thirty-two years, and moving to NMH for that next seven-year chapter of our lives.

I feel a huge rush of nostalgia as I write this account in 2023 of our seven years at NMH, 1998–2005.

Chapter Six

Northfield Mount Hermon School: The Journey Continues

That summer of 1999, we had a chance to escape to Cape Cod for a couple weeks. Claire loves the ocean, so it was a good time for mental and physical refreshment. Family and friends came to visit as did Bob and Ilsa MacKinnon who had a place nearby. He was a strong supporter of the school and of Claire and me, helping to navigate board and community issues.

We were happy to be back in the United States and close enough to visit Eric at Princeton periodically. And close enough for him to surprise me by driving up one night unexpectedly for Father's Day. His club sport of co-ed ultimate frisbee was always fun. He was doing well, finishing up his junior year studying mechanical and aerospace engineering; Princeton turned out to be a good fit for him.

Speaking of ultimate frisbee, here's a footnote to NMH history: loving the game of ultimate, one of my achievements at NMH was shepherding ultimate into the sports program as a varsity sport. We had a great team and many fans. We even made it to a national finals tournament.

Jonathan was still in Chicago working for A.T. Kearney. He was learning while earning a good salary. But there were no mountains to climb, and he was getting restless. How about hiking the Appalachian Trail for a change of (hiking) pace? Stay tuned.

While Cape Cod was a good change, my brain would not turn off. There were too many issues needing attention in the coming year.

One issue was the need to launch a strategic planning initiative that included an assessment of our educational program and of our facilities on both campuses. How would we organize our work and who would lead it? What would be our priorities? How much could a capital campaign raise to pay for it?

A second issue was how best to stay on top of the vast operational and logistical demands of a $100 million, two-campus school such as ours. We were not nearly as well-endowed as competitor schools, so every dollar counted and was stretched to the limit. Howard Jones, former Northfield Schools president, went to bat for me with Bill Rhodes, arguing for a strong deputy head of school. It would be four years before we found that person and brought him or her on board. In the meantime, I relied on strong members of the senior staff. Still, the span of control could be overwhelming at times.

A third issue was impacted by number two above. I wanted to develop relationships of trust, without which initiatives and success often falter. Trust can be nurtured by visiting as often as possible with people on both campuses. Visibility would help. Hearing people out and sharing thoughts was critical. So being strategic in my "showing up" was imperative.

Over time, I came to realize how I hoped to build trust with the community. What would be my touchstone? I would work to have enough people interact with me to conclude I was working in good faith to maintain and build the very best school. Even if they didn't often see directly what I was doing or deciding, they were much more likely to say something like, "I'm willing to believe that Richard will do his best to make good decisions affecting me and NMH and not decisions good only for himself."

That sentiment was what I continuously worked to cultivate. For the most part, I believe the community wanted to trust. I believe I had more success than not over my seven years as head of school. Smiling whenever appropriate was all to the good.

Where is NMH Headed? Longer-Term Visioning for Northfield Mount Hermon

Over the next two years, we carried out an intensive planning process to examine options for the future of NMH. We hired an educational consultant and a firm that looked carefully at all our facilities and operations. The board was entirely supportive except in one area. One trustee suggested we include looking at the option of moving to one campus. Our board was reluctant to go that route. They preferred an effort that would not require us to leave either campus.

I appreciated that Jacqueline's strategic planning was designed to keep two campuses, deal with the large and complex organizational and financial issues and implement the best of current educational thinking. This included the "block system," an enhanced student life program based on dorms to provide solid student support, replacing departments with curriculum teams, enhanced international education, and other innovations. I believe the hope was that an invigorated school and educational programs would draw more students and lead to better educational outcomes. The two-campus conundrum was still there.

Our top priorities in this new round of planning included:

1) Updating and refining the features of the previous plan, including our unique educational program.

2) Increasing support and financial aid for underserved students, an historic commitment by the school for capable students who often were not welcome at other boarding schools. Dwight L. Moody was a towering Christian evangelist, both in "saving souls" and in creating good education for all. He found young women and men in towns in the Connecticut River Valley, Black and Native Americans around the United States, Black students from Africa, and Chinese students from southern China, all of whom he recruited to come learn at Northfield and Mount Hermon.

3) Adjusting faculty and staff compensation packages to make us more competitive.

4) Investing in extensive renovations to existing buildings and the building of new ones.

All our work in the next year led to recommendations for investment in the above priorities, designed to create a tighter knit community. Strategically located small cafes and collaborative meeting areas would enhance the sense of gathering and collaboration.

We had many good pictures and descriptions of what we were considering unveiling on the fundraising road. We began putting a campaign together.

We would have a difficult time in the coming months to slim down our priority investments to fit our likely fundraising constraints.

Show Me the Money

The board worked with us on the plans and was exceedingly supportive. The response of the community was positive.

As we fleshed out our plans, we asked where the money would come from to finance such an ambitious program.

Claire and I began to travel more frequently. Domestic stops included Maine, Boston, New York, DC, Florida, Chicago, San Francisco, and Los Angeles. Internationally, we visited Seoul, Tokyo, Beijing, Hong Kong, Taiwan, Cambodia, London, Munich, Istanbul, and Ankara.

We loved traveling and meeting of so many alumni and parents. They were consistently supportive of the school. We also found what our predecessors always found, namely, that real mega-donors were relatively few and far between.

In March 2000, the stock markets began to go bust in what was called the tech bubble or internet bubble—an insane speculative fever within the rapidly exploding tech industry. Over the next two years, many of the markets lost upwards of seventy-five percent of their value. Naturally, our endowment also plummeted.

We didn't lose faith, but it was clear the headwinds were becoming more challenging. Stay tuned.

An Interesting Issue of School Rankings, Briefly

NMH was part of a "Group of Eight" well-known boarding schools. It included Exeter, Andover, Deerfield, Hotchkiss, Lawrenceville, Saint Paul's, and Choate Rosemary Hall. It later evolved into a more formal Eight Schools Association (ESA) for closer collaboration in a wide range of educational programs. The Heads of School met in the fall and again in the spring with trustees. I enjoyed the collaboration with fellow educators.

I will make a strong statement here about how difficult, if not impossible, it is to assess and rank schools. Not all schools (or teachers) are right for all students. Unfortunately, Americans can be obsessed with who is number one. Rankings also send the misleading message that there can be an objective measurement that will apply to all schools and students. There is no such measurement.

The editor of *U.S. News and World Report* approached the ESA in 2000 to create a ranking system for boarding schools. We all said, "no, thanks." The college ranking issues of the magazine did not appeal to any of us. The editor persisted over many months and continued to make promises of non-ranking and non-comparison. Eventually, the eight heads of school agreed to strict ground rules and visits to each campus by writers. The final product did not endear any of us to *U.S. News*. Traditional prejudices showed through. The NMH write-up did not capture the true spirit of learning and education at the school. It was neither positive nor negative for our recruiting efforts. Denouement? The editor apparently ran into his bosses' buzz saw and left the magazine shortly thereafter.

I recall all these thorny issues of rankings and performance as the education world continues to wrestle with the legitimate public interest in assessing and comparing different schools of many kinds. There is no one-size-fits all for students. My best advice? Start with a clear-eyed understanding of the educational needs and interests of each young person: academic, social-emotional, particular passions, etc. One can then focus on schools promoting values and offering programs that meet those needs.

A Political Watershed on the Pivotal 2000 Election Preceding 9/11

The presidential election of 2000 was a watershed in American history: Vice President Al Gore versus Governor George Bush. It was an experienced leader in the mainstream of our politics versus a former Texas governor who had limited experience in governing a huge, complex society. There was also an extended legal process concluding only on December 12, 2000, when the U.S. Supreme Court handed George Bush the presidency by overturning a Florida Supreme Court ruling on how to count the ballots.

Many students on campus were excited about the election and followed events closely. On the night of the election, the Northfield gym was decked out as "election central." Students dressed to express their views. Blue, for Democrats, was the dominant color. But it was to be a close election. Gore was considerably ahead in the popular vote, but it was the electoral vote that mattered. Finally, it came down to one state. Whoever won Florida would be president. But the vote was extraordinarily close and came down to several hundred votes in Broward County. There were some ambiguities about the validity of certain votes, particularly so-called "hanging chads."

The issue became whether to continue the counting and which votes to count. The question went up to the Supreme Court, where a conservative coalition of five justices decreed that the vote counting should stop. It handed the presidency to Bush.

To me, it was a travesty that halting the counting of all votes expressing citizens' preferences put George Bush in the White House and further roiled our politics. The five conservative justices chose a legal interpretation they knew would decide the election for Bush.

The election outcome was another example of how the person with the most popular votes (Gore) lost because it was electoral votes that counted. Gerrymandering was becoming a true political art, still being practiced and perfected, particularly by Republicans, as I write in 2023. More recently, in 2016, Hilary Clinton had the most votes, but Trump became president because of the Electoral College's bias. It pains us.

At NMH, the 2000 election was an important "teachable moment" that educators are always on the lookout for. *We needed then, and still need in 2023, a serious national debate on creating fair rules in all states to ensure each person gets a ballot, and that each person's ballot is counted.*

Fun and Much Needed Change of Scene and Pace—Asia Here We Come

Two trips to Asia in those early years at NMH were great changes of scene and perspective.

Cambodia: Siem Riep and Angkor

After traveling with NMH music groups on visits to Asian capitals in 2000, Claire and I spent several days exploring Cambodia's ancient city and Khmer capital of Angkor with its wonderful old temples, including the famous Angkor Wat. It was hot and humid, but we were determined to be intrepid learners and visitors.

We visited dozens of temples as the lighting changed from early morning to late afternoon. Angkor Wat and the small, more distant Ban Serei were among our favorites. The huge sculptures of Buddha heads on the towers and the many stone carvings telling stories were fascinating. It was a photographer's delight, and I took full advantage.

There were few visitors, but many disabled Cambodians who had suffered through the recent wars and under the Khmer Rouge. Landmines all over the country continued to kill and maim every day. Many of those we saw sat among the ruins, hoping for a small handout. It was a heart-rending scene and again, we witnessed man's inhumanity to man. Quite a few young girls repeatedly offered us beautiful pieces of hand-woven cloth; each was "only one dollar!" They were a bargain. Our purchases, which to us were so cheap, clearly helped feed a family. But our meager help meant so little in comparison to the compelling need for honest and effective political leaders who put the welfare of citizens at the top of their priorities.

As I mentioned earlier in this memoir, so many people in the United States have no understanding of the extraordinary civilizations that were built over the millennia in Asia, the Middle East, South America, Africa, etc. To walk among the many temples in Angkor allowed one's imagination to consider the peoples who often ruled in luxury over a vast territory of workers, farmers, artisans, and religious leaders. As with Chinese dynasties over thousands of years, rulers and governors sooner or later flagged, the empire weakened and eventually died, to be replaced again by others who accumulated power. The entire game was about power, who had it, and what they did with it.

Although we did not know it at the time, a group in the Middle East that did not wish the United States well was planning a deadly attack on the "American Empire"—an attack that shook our foundations and made us ponder our own civilization's future.

An Extraordinary China Odyssey: West on the Silk Road and Return Via the Yangzi River

The summer of 2001 included a wonderful change of pace: leading an alumni group to China and the Silk Road. NMH travelers led by an alumnus and his wife, Jim and Billie Babcock, had asked early whether Claire and I would help organize and lead the group of about twenty. This was fun! We met up in Beijing for orientation and visited the highlights such as the Great Wall, Tiananmen Square, Forbidden City, and others.

While I spoke to the group every day about various sites, Chinese history, economics, politics and answered numerous questions, Claire was the real star of the trip. She interacted as a friend with everyone, always helped a lady who needed assistance, and gave feedback on what people were thinking and wanted. Her energy and enthusiasm never flagged.

We flew to Xian to see the terracotta warriors, then on to Urumqi in Xinjiang, which looked mostly like a Chinese industrial city. We drove up to see the famous Tian Chi Lake (Heavenly Lake) in the mountains. Regrettably, fog and rain had descended, so we did not get the full experience. Still, the ethereal scene was captivating.

We were entranced with artifacts from hundreds to thousands of years ago. A highlight was the so-called Loulan Beauty, the perfectly preserved mummy of a woman who lived in the area four thousand years ago. DNA analysis showed she had European origins, then Siberian, and finally Xinjiang (but not Uyghur).

The museum brought home to us how vibrant and diverse many of the societies in Central Asia were over the millennia. It was a blending of peoples from many points on the compass. The so-called Silk Road was truly a highway, not just of commerce, but of migration of people and religious and cultural traditions. In Urumqi, we also bought, for a pretty penny, a small beautiful handmade silk rug. We hope it stays in the Mueller family for future generations.

Then on to Kashgar, the traditional home of the Uyghur people. The Sunday market, bringing people from a large area around Kashgar, was unique, with the most amazing range of animals, food, textiles, and people. With so many people gathering, one can see how the market served as cross-roads of communication and news among the Uyghur community. It was also another photographer's paradise.

Sadly, in 2021, it was clear the Han Chinese were slowly clearing it away to make room for "modern" buildings. The same was occurring with where we stayed, namely, the remaining buildings of the old Russian Consulate from which Russia directed many of its moves in the Great Game of Central Asia. The old buildings now have all been torn down. Our best souvenirs were tee shirts with beautiful, hand painted scenes of Silk Road life and commerce painted by the hotel's resident Uyghur artist.

We then drove quite some miles south to get a good feel for the vastness of inner Asia. Had we continued, we would have traveled the

Karakoram Highway through the mountains to Pakistan. We would have loved to do that.

We then worked our way back to the east via bus and train to visit oasis towns like Turpan, Jiaohe, Gaochang, Bezeklik, and the surrounding areas. We had a wonderful stop in Dunhuang, in western Gansu Province, far to the west of the country. It truly was, and remains, one of my favorite places in China. (I had visited and learned of its importance as consul general in Hong Kong.) There is lots more to write about its importance. What art in all the caves; what history! We rode camels to the Singing Sands oasis and climbed part way up the huge sand dunes and slid down on sleds.

We flew to Chongqing to see one of China's largest cities. We visited the General George Stillwell Museum, which honors United States and Chinese cooperation during World War II and documents Stillwell's legendary history in China. Then, it was on board a river boat to float down the Yangzi River to the Three Gorges Dam, one of the largest in the world. We saw many of the new towns built higher up on the mountainsides above the traditional towns, below which would be flooded by the rising waters as the dam was finished. It was an impressive feat of planning and engineering to see how Chinese engineers had planned out the enormous project of transplanting huge numbers of people to higher ground to provide hydropower and to lessen the traditional floods that often devastated downriver towns and fields.

And then we finished up with three days in our favorite city, Hong Kong. The travelers loved it. An NMH Hong Kong family hosted our entire group at their home overlooking the ocean.

During our seven years, we often included Hong Kong on our Asia trips. We always found people welcoming and friendly. On one trip, we accompanied music students and Sheila Heffernan on a musical tour of Tokyo, Seoul, Beijing, and Hong Kong, performing for parents and friends. In Hong Kong, we put on a concert for students at Hong Kong International School and met with former Chief Secretary Anson Chan. The Hong Kong students were overjoyed to have a chance to meet such a prominent and popular Hong Kong leader. Anson had become a good friend and outspoken advocate for the uniqueness of Hong Kong and its continued full autonomy within China's "one country, two systems" framework.

Our return from our iconic Silk Road trip in 2001 with the alumni was a good homecoming to Ford Cottage and NMH to unpack and regale family and friends with stories of our three-week odyssey. We also began the serious planning for the beginning of the 2001–2002 school year.

But there was one critical event in September we never had reason to plan for: terror from the skies.

The Bush Administration Is Slow to Respond to Terrorist Warnings

Vice President Dick Cheney, a neoconservative with hawkish foreign policy views, played an outsized national security role in the George Bush administration. He pulled many of the foreign policy strings and was ultimately responsible for getting us deeply into a major war in Afghanistan and subsequently in Iraq.

One of the great tragedies was that knowledgeable people in government, from the beginning of the administration, were warning of likely terrorist strikes very early on in Bush's presidency. Richard Clarke, the NSC's counterterrorism official with whom I worked in the 1980s in State, was in the White House in 2001 but could not get the attention of the Bush staff to be much more vigilant about counterterrorism. There were straws in the wind suggesting some kind of terrorist action was afoot. Frankly put, the president and his team were asleep at the switch and distracted by other things on their minds, such as how to use the U.S. military to subdue enemies in the Middle East and bring democracy to Iraq. Diplomacy never seemed in the cards, although Secretary of State Colin Powell gave it his all in his four years in Foggy Bottom.

And Then Came Terror from the Skies

New England, the morning of September 11, 2001, dawned with a crisp blue sky and cool premonition of fall.

I was in my office in Kenarden Hall on the Northfield campus when I received word that an airplane had crashed into one of the World Trade Towers in Manhattan in New York City. I jumped in the car and drove fast to Ford Cottage on the other campus to join Claire in front of the television.

The commentators were speculating about what kind of plane had crashed into the building—an errant Piper Cub whose pilot lost his way or decided to end it all in spectacular fashion? —when suddenly a passenger plane appeared on screen and crashed into the other World Trade

Center tower. Could our eyes have deceived us? Heavy smoke and fire poured from both buildings. How would it be possible for fire fighters to put out such intense blazes so high up?

We sat staring at the television. Senior staff members joined us. Disbelief among us all was an understatement as the blazes became more intense. People poured out of the buildings. With horror, we saw some who could not make it down jump to their deaths. Commentators speculated whether the buildings could withstand the fires' furious assault on the towers' internal structures.

And then, horrendously and unbelievably, one of the towers began its collapse upon itself. It pancaked into a colossal mass of steel and concrete. The second tower held on longer, but then followed suit in spectacular fashion. Photographers captured it all. Smoke and ash filled the surrounding streets. Panicked people were running for their lives. Injured people were collapsing and dying on the sidewalks.

And then, equally astounding, news came of a plane that had flown into the side of the Pentagon in Northern Virginia with similar disastrous death and destruction. And then came word of another passenger plane crashing in an open field in Pennsylvania. Were there other attacks occurring or planned elsewhere around the country?

We sat in Ford Cottage, in the peaceful surroundings of the verdant Connecticut River valley. It was impossible to relate to what we were witnessing.

Quickly we turned to the most urgent task: the safety of the NMH community. What did we need to do, to understand, to console, and to comfort? Could we possibly experience such attacks near us? There was a large nuclear power plant just up the river. We had to initiate our emergency evacuation plans. Law enforcement announced that anthrax powder was being found in spots around the country. Was it connected to the aerial terrorists? What do we do about the white powder found on a sidewalk on campus? Was it anthrax spread by the terrorists? Our plant and property director bravely scooped it up. Baby powder. How many parents, relatives, friends might have worked in those World Trade Center buildings or close to them? What was the emotional and psychological impact on young people and adults?

This was crisis management of the first order. It was as though I'd been trained in the Foreign Service for responding to just this kind of crisis event. I recalled leading the task force formed in the wake of the terrorist bombing of Pan Am 103 over Scotland in 1988. Even as we watched the flames and smoke from the towers, we began to reach out to law enforcement, political leaders, our trustees, and others. We assigned deans to assemble relevant information on how to speak and respond to students and adults as the community needed answers and comfort.

By early afternoon, we had gathered students on each campus. Claire and I went to Alumni Hall on the Hermon campus; Randy Stevens, dean of students, went to Northfield.

As Claire and I walked to Alumni Hall, we met a student leaning against one of the columns, sobbing and crying. We stopped to talk with him. He said his father worked in one of the towers and of course, he was deathly afraid that his father was lost or injured. We tried to comfort him as best we could and took him inside with us. The good news was that by the end of the day, he learned that his father had decided to stop at an electronics store on his way to work and thus was saved from becoming one of the many victims.

I told the assembled students what we knew about the terrorist attacks and cautioned against believing all the inevitable stories, "facts," and conspiracies that would soon circulate. I urged them to speak with teachers and deans if they had concerns or reactions. I was able to assure them we were in touch with relevant law enforcement, and that there were no known threats in our area.

Days later, a teacher told us that she knew things would be okay because she had observed Claire and Richard walking hand in hand on the campus. True story.

Peter, Paul, and Mary Come to NMH for a Concert After 9/11/2001

At the end of September, as we began to settle into an uneasy fall term with 9/11 dominating the news and much of our school life, the iconic folk group, Peter, Paul, and Mary, arrived at NMH for a long-scheduled concert at the auditorium.

How did we arrange for their concert? Serendipity! Betty Stookey, our chaplain, was married to Noel Paul Stookey. He arranged for his fellow singers to put the school on their calendar. We worried just a bit that most students wouldn't know the group and thus might find it less than exciting.

As it turned out, it was a wonderful concert with huge energy from both the group and the audience. In the wake of the 9/11 terrorism attacks, the afternoon was fully cathartic. Students joined in the singing and the energy clearly fueled Peter, Paul, and Mary. A concert planned for one hour extended for almost two. Afterwards, we entertained the group under the trees outside the auditorium. It was the chance of a lifetime to meet one of America's true cultural and musical icons and to receive a signed copy of our poster for the event.

Betty and Noel became our good friends during our seven years at NMH—people of the same generation who shared similar values and with whom we could share confidences. I hope our grandchildren will learn PPM's music of love, kindness, and speaking out against war and violence. They were among those who prominently during the Vietnam war called on all of us to rethink our actions and policies.

Our Foreign Policy Turns to War in Afghanistan

Our infamous "9/11" changed America and our historical course forever.

In the weeks after the terrorist attacks, our politics, press, and citizens' urgent questions all turned to "What now?" How do we respond to a horrific act perpetrated not by a nation state but by individuals associated with the notorious Al Qaeda terrorist network?

The Bush administration prepared for significant military and other responses. Many Americans expected and supported hard military force. Historical accounts are instructive of how we mobilized friends, allies and public opinion around the world and vowed to track down Osama Bin Laden and crush the Taliban in Afghanistan. The following months saw the entry of CIA intelligence officers riding into Afghanistan on horseback and B-52 bombers indiscriminately unloading their bombs on the Taliban. Various Afghan forces sided with us to hunt down Osama Bin Laden, who eventually escaped from encirclement at Tora Bora, Afghanistan, to Pakistan. The Taliban were driven from power. Even as Afghan, U.S., and other armed forces increased troop strength and operations, reconstruction and development got under way.

In the coming years, the Bush administration expanded its and NATO's aims and troop commitments to adopt broader goals of creating more far-reaching political, economic, governmental, and societal change in Afghanistan. The goals of a more democratic and open life for the country including equal rights for women in a deeply patriarchal society were admirable. But even as we sent in more troops, the Taliban began to gain strength and stymy both Afghan and United States forces. The conflict progressively became America's "forever" war.

The Bush administration, in its mistaken decision-making, did not recall lessons of our involvement in Vietnam. These lessons included mistaken reliance on unreliable and incapable Vietnamese while our "enemy"—the Viet Cong and North Vietnamese—stood for fighting the colonialists and protecting Vietnamese traditions. The United States had also broadened its goals in Vietnam, hoping to create more long-lasting and deeper change in society.

Similarly in Afghanistan, after ousting the Taliban, the Bush administration broadened the goals. It made some progress in urban areas, but then it over-reached. We had to rely on incapable and weak Afghan leaders and partners, deal with corruption, and address other issues. All the while, the Taliban progressively gained support. The Taliban were rooted in Afghan culture and society and stood for fighting the invaders to protect Afghanistan's political, religious, and social traditions.

Years later, my old friend Bob Gates (who became President Bush's secretary of defense in 2006 and stayed on under President Obama until 2011) acknowledged that the United States had set too-broad goals in Afghanistan. Both Bush and Obama ultimately felt trapped by the war in Afghanistan. They couldn't win, but politically, they felt they couldn't withdraw. Does that description sound like President Johnson's dilemma years before in Vietnam? It took President Biden to make the hard decision to withdraw troops by September 2021. Do I grieve for millions of Afghans? Absolutely.

America Turns to War in Iraq

The Bush administration, not long after sending troops into Afghanistan, turned its sights on Iraq in 2002 and 2003.

In Afghanistan, we were seeking Osama Bin Laden and terrorists who perpetrated the 9/11 attacks, but our mission morphed into a multi-year military, political, and economic effort to defeat the Taliban and build a new Afghan society. In Iraq, by invading and driving out Saddam Hussein, we hoped to create an Iraqi democracy that would spread its wings throughout the Middle East and transform the region.

How did that work out for us? Disastrously, I believe. All the lessons that came out of our disastrous war in Vietnam were ignored. Hubris and hopes for personal and political victories on the part of our politicians took over.

In retrospect, the administration from the beginning was seized with the idea of engineering Saddam's ouster. As above, I believe they convinced themselves that removing him would lead to a democratic Iraq that could create waves of other democratic transitions around the Middle East and block the spread of terrorists groups such as ISIS. Vice President Cheney and Secretary of Defense Rumsfeld were willing to use U.S. forces to drive Saddam out if we could find a plausible reason. That reason turned out to be the suspicion that Saddam was developing weapons of mass destruction, particularly biological weapons.

Cheney and Rumsfeld went round and round with the intelligence community trying to pin down the evidence. They convinced themselves there were just enough crumbs of evidence that Secretary Powell was willing to go to the United Nations, put his credibility on the line, and declare there was sufficient evidence and that we needed to remove Saddam. I believe Powell forever after regretted that he made those promises to the international community.

While there was widespread concern and opposition around the country about expanded war, Bush nevertheless issued the order: the U.S. invasion began on March 29, 2003. Combat operations continued for more than a month. The Iraqi army collapsed, Saddam disappeared, and chaos and violence broke out around the country. It would continue unceasingly while various political, religious, and tribal factions—all armed—strived for control and influence. The surge of some twenty thousand U.S. troops in 2007 helped to quell some of the violence and increase security, but it was not a long-term solution. Later, U.S. forces arguably helped save Bagdad, Iraq, from the attacking and fast-moving ISIS fighters who were sweeping through the country.

The administration never had game plans for exits from either Afghanistan or Iraq. Nor for setting up governance structures that would work for the Afghans, and later the Iraqis, after Saddam and the Baathist Party were eliminated. Donald Rumsfeld, as defense secretary, ran everything, and even tossed out the State Department study and game plan for post-Saddam Iraq. The fighting in Iraq was bloody, violent, and continued for years.

My longtime friend L. Paul Bremer III, who came into the Foreign Service with me in 1966 (whom we all knew as Jerry), went to Bagdad early on as the American "czar" to oversee the U.S. effort to bring order out of chaos. He was the one who announced the capture of Saddam Hussein hiding in a hole in a village outside Bagdad, "Ladies and Gentlemen. We got him!" The ill-considered decisions in Washington to disband the Iraqi Baathist Party and the Iraqi army eliminated potentially useful organizational and national structures and led to more chaos. Sadly for Iraqis and Americans, it was mostly downhill from there for the years-long American effort to build democracy, build a new Iraqi society and counter Iran.

You might think that our unsuccessful Vietnam experience might have induced some caution and restraint. Wrong. We deluded ourselves in misguided and inept invasions of Iraq and Afghanistan, thinking large-scale military involvement was the right strategy. The economic development was both insufficient for the task and often subject to corruption. There was no strong hand of restraint in the Oval Office. Cheney, Rumsfeld, Wolfowitz, and others grabbed the national security reins and essentially sidelined Secretary Powell and National Security Adviser Condoleezza Rice. Have we yet learned our lessons?

Please ask yourselves, as above: are America's lessons about war and American foreign policy receiving the critical study and consideration that such "teachable moments" demand? My view is that our politicians and other leaders must better analyze and debate these questions if our body politic and country are to move away from the highly militarized approach of the last quarter century.

Back to Our Northfield Mount Hermon Bubble: A Diplomat in Partnership with Faculty Negotiates a Successful Outcome

International travel had not distracted me from leading a great school of 1,155 students. A huge academic issue needed to be addressed and decisions made about our academic program. No easy answers were available, but a good former diplomat needed to find a way to move forward.

The signature academic innovation from the previous strategic plan was to divide the school year into three trimesters and have students take two major courses—each equivalent to a year's worth of study—each trimester. It was designed to give students a deep dive into the subject, with an emphasis less on content coverage and more on development of skills and understanding. In principle, there was merit to the design of such a "block" system. I was basically in favor of this approach, although I had a feeling a few more weeks for each trimester would be beneficial.

Teachers had had to adapt their teaching approaches to make best use of the extended time available. That was difficult for some. And others argued for more "marinating time" that comes from extended immersion in the subject. It was an issue that caused continuing tension among our faculty.

I decided we needed to put this issue to bed. What would constitute effective change management? After considerable consultation and consideration, I appointed a faculty committee and charged it with digging deeply and coming up with objective pros and cons on the options, but not a recommendation. I said I would put the results to the faculty for a vote. I could not promise I would accept the outcome, since the head of school needed to retain the authority ultimately to make such decisions, but I would give serious weight to their input.

The committee did good work and came up with a good report with options. After sharing the report widely, I called for a faculty meeting where the committee presented the results. I asked for a secret written vote. The respected dean of faculty, Lorrie Byron, and several others counted the ballots.

The outcome was a solid vote to continue on our current course. While some faculty remained skeptical, the reality was that my decision to accept the faculty vote was based on a consensus for continuing to refine our program and not going back.

The outcome confirmed my strong belief that a governance system relying mostly on top-down decision making is often not the best way to create effective and lasting change. In this case, listening to faculty and being seen as working with them on options in support of our most important objective, namely, good student learning, could settle an issue and allow us to move forward together. *It was a follow on to my promise in the interview process to create a collaborative partnership with the faculty.*

Some Well-Known Visitors Come to Campus

We were fortunate to have a steady stream of visitors to the school during our seven years. The Auditorium was a welcoming venue. The visitors included:

—Maya Angelou, the world-renowned writer and poet. I met her in the green room of the auditorium before she spoke. She was warm and engaging, both toward me and the student body. She read from some of her books and had students captivated. I still have the personally inscribed book she gave me, *I Know Why the Caged Bird Sings.*

—Ken Burns, the famed documentary filmmaker. He came to dinner at Ford Cottage first, held forth answering questions about his filmmaking from the guests, and then addressed the community in the auditorium. He spoke particularly about the importance of history and understanding its relevance to today's world. An insightful man and speaker.

—James Carville and Mary Matalan, political practitioners and pundits married to each other. He is a Democrat and she a Republican. They came to dinner first at Ford. They had gained prominence on the political circuit and spoke knowledgeably about the upcoming election between George W. Bush and John Kerry. We were in the middle of wars in Iraq and Afghanistan; the electorate was becoming anxious about the continuing conflict. Regrettably, Bush squeaked through, perpetuating the increasing divisions in our country. Mary was as even as could be, James was full of energy. He talked with Jon, who was visiting, and then excused himself to watch his beloved Redskins (now with the new name of "The Commanders") on TV.

—John Updike, foremost American novelist of the twentieth century. His writing contains brilliant portraits of people and human relationships. We had lunch for him at Centennial House in Northfield. He was an easy conversationalist and presented Claire and me a signed copy of his recent book *Seek My Face.* He wrote: "For Richard and Claire Mueller. Old China Hands become Northfield Mount Hermon Hands. Best Wishes, John Updike. 2/2/03"

His informal, almost avuncular presentation to students of his insights into human nature and reading of excerpts from his writings were a hit.

—Fareed Zakaria, a journalist and creator of GPS (Global Public Square) on CNN, talked about world events and the importance of understanding history and what is happening now. The United States was deeply engaged militarily in Iraq and Afghanistan; our country was divided. He urged students to dig into the issues and make their own judgments about the conflicts. After his talk, he held an impromptu Q&A in the Gould dining room with twenty-five-to-thirty students. To this day he is among the most knowledgeable and balanced foreign affairs commentators we have.

—Howard Zinn, famous for his *People's History of the United States*, expounded on his thesis that history is told ultimately by the victors and not the victims. It gained widespread notoriety, both because he wanted to re-shape the narrative about the rise of America (e.g., how white colonizers decimated Native American tribes), and because some historians felt he had his facts wrong and was unbalanced. There was truth in the criticism, but we wanted our students to hear alternative views and realize they themselves would have to make their own judgments.

And of course, there were many others bringing diverse voices and viewpoints to our academic mixing bowls.

—President Thabo Mbeki of South Africa visited for a day, breaking away from his United Nations meetings in New York City. How did that visit come about? It started in Hong Kong when I was director of the Asia Society Hong Kong Center. Mbeki and I sat next to each other at a lunch. I told him I was headed to NMH to be head of school and hoped he might pay us a visit sometime. I described the school's long tradition of enrolling students from Africa and one in particular, Pixley Ka Isaka Seme from South Africa, who later went home to found the African National Congress. Mbeki smiled and said everyone in South Africa knows of Pixley Seme.

Fast forward. At NMH I learned that the daughter of the South African ambassador to the United States was a student of ours. The wheels began to turn. I issued an invitation to Mbeki to visit; the ambassador seconded it; and Bill Rhodes, our board chair, who served on a U.S.-South Africa business council and knew Mbeki, put in a strong endorsement.

His visit resembled what I had experienced and had organized so many times: a secretary of state visit. We had a wonderful lunch at Ford Cottage. As we broke up to head to the auditorium and greet the full student community, Mbeki pulled me aside and said he wanted to take a few minutes privately to ask me more about the school. He had a speech his staff had prepared, but he wanted more.

What I told him about the school and its acceptance of students from around the world, Pixley Seme being an excellent example, became the basis of his remarks. At the auditorium, the student choir led by Sheila Heffernon sang the South African national anthem. Mbeki complimented them on how well they sang it: "It's not an easy anthem to sing well. You sang beautifully, much better than most South Africans can sing it!"

I will never forget the words he used as he started his remarks:

"I wanted to come here today because Pixley Seme is still a revered figure in South African history. I wanted to know what it was that this young African boy learned at the Mount Hermon School a hundred years ago that later propelled him to first found the African National Congress that changed South Africa and who then went on to change Africa!"

Mbeki continued on to talk about current change in South Africa and the urgent need for all countries to work for greater racial harmony and equity.

It was a proud moment in our school's history and a moving testament to how education plays a crucial role in instilling the right values for the next generation.

We Tackle Head-on the Elephant on the Campus—How to Create a More Closely-Knit, Academically Excellent, and Financially Sustainable School

Yes, NMH had a proverbial elephant in the room. It would take all my learning, experience in governance, and work to build coalitions to find ways forward and rally the community. The elaborate longer-range plans we painstakingly put together over two years were unlikely to be realized. Successful fundraising was doubtful given the economic downturn and lack of deep-pocketed alumni ready to step up. And we were feeling the acute stresses and strains of maintaining a close-knit large community on two campuses while searching for the investment dollars we needed.

An important observation, particularly in retrospect, is that our difficult, extensive first round of planning for two campuses and subsequent fundraising highlighted the magnitude of the task before us. It helped convince trustees that considering a one-campus solution was a necessary option.

The senior staff and I spent many hours discussing options for the way forward. Part of me resented having to spend so much time on these questions. As important as they were, I would much rather have spent more time interacting with students.

But we needed to deal with the elephant that no one really wanted or dared to tackle. In September 2002, I spoke with our board chair, Bill Rhodes, and told him I was drafting a memo to the board that explained current realities facing the school and recommending a reopening of the strategic plans and putting all options on the table. I sent him the memo, and Bill agreed, but he was wary of where such planning might go.

The memo was comprehensive in documenting our situation and the need for the board and the senior staff to work together expeditiously. I proposed a "Small Group" led by Don McNemar, trustee, to include trustees and staff. We would provide information, analysis, options, and regular discussion at board meetings.

Importantly, the memo argued for all options to be considered, including whether to remain a two-campus school, ninth through twelfth grades; or hold ninth and tenth on one campus and eleventh and twelfth on the other; or become a one campus school on either the Northfield or Mount Hermon campus. I truly did not know where I might come out on these options, particularly the question of two campuses versus one. It was a huge conundrum. But the first priority was to inform and educate the Small Group and the board so the discussions and decisions were rational and defensible.

The trustees met on campus in October 2002. I picked Bill up at the airport. The board discussion was vigorous and engaging, neither angry nor antagonistic. Trustees understood the need to move forward. They also understood the sensitivity of their decision. The research plan was approved unanimously, including not constraining the options to be considered. Bill as chair worked to keep trustees focused on our research priorities. Don McNemar was willing to take the reins for the board and work with us. He had been head of school of Philips Andover, a well-known boarding school, and then-president of Guilford College in North Carolina. He knew schools and institutional issues well, and his guidance turned out to be invaluable.

As we began our work, my most important instruction was to start with considering how best to deliver an outstanding education, both in academics and student life, and to create a closer-knit boarding school community. All else should flow from that: facilities, finances, reputation, etc.

The goals set out were a tall order. We wanted to recommend real improvements to our educational program without undermining our current program and do so in practical and achievable ways.

Among the many factors we noted were: 1) many competitor boarding schools over the years had merged with a nearby girls' school, suggesting that a two campus model could be problematic in the twenty-first century; 2) demographic projections predicted a decline in the high school population over coming years; 3) we needed much more investment to correct deferred maintenance and insufficient faculty compensation if we were to remain an excellent and attractive boarding school; 4) the size and complexity of our school operating on two campuses put exceptional pressure on our staff, particularly given perennially tight budgets; 5) the NMH endowment was considerably smaller per student than almost all our competitors, giving us fewer dollars to spend on programs; moving to a smaller student body on one campus would be one option to increase the resources to invest in each student.

The next year saw a steady stream of meetings and analyses while students experienced a great education every day. Don McNemar was a wonderful leader of the "Small Group" in partnership with us. Normal, traditional rhythms of school continued. We opened with convocation, Junior–Senior Rope Pull at Shadow Lake, Mountain Day, Pie Race, maple sugaring, Thanksgiving, Vespers, Christmas, Dwight Moody's Birthday, International Food Festival, Martin Luther King memorial, the head of school's student advisory council, innumerable athletic events, music and art presentations, Sacred Concert, baccalaureate, and finally, a glorious commencement. Oh, and don't forget reunion weekend.

I could have used two or three clones of myself. Claire and I participated in all events. Students were being well-educated even while we sketched out a new future for NMH behind the scenes.

As the end of 2003 came into view, it was clear that the board was coalescing around an educational and student life program in the context of a closely-knit community of about 650 students on one campus. Would it be the Northfield or Mount Hermon campus? I initially favored Northfield because it was a beautiful setting and was the heart of Dwight Moody's legacy, containing his birthplace and home.

Rationality favored Mount Hermon in the end: it was also a beautiful campus centered around a big green heart of open space; there were more facilities, more room for building expansion, and less deferred maintenance. The Northfield campus could potentially be better used by a future owner for multiple programs and activities.

In the fall of 2003, we held a gathering of select trustees, faculty, alumni, staff to share analyses and discuss possible future directions. Dick Peller, senior member of the faculty, at one point stood up and painted a compelling picture of the many positives of what a revitalized school on one campus could do for students, academics, and the community. His picture made an impact.

It was truly a heart-wrenching conclusion to create a smaller school on the Mount Hermon campus and find a purchaser for Northfield. The huge upside was that if we executed the transition successfully, we would find that educationally and financially, the advantages all added up for us to become a sound and sustainable school with a much more closely-knit community while maintaining our deserved reputation as outstanding and among the best of the New England boarding schools.

As we moved through the fall of 2003 toward a January 2004 meeting to make the momentous decision, you might wonder if there were stresses and strains within the board of trustees as we made progress. The short answer is yes. But they revolved around some personal agendas and not around the fateful decision to move forward.

The specifics no longer matter. Most of us have moved on and are pleased to see the school doing so well.

In December 2003 I wrote a detailed set of recommendations for the board based on the work of the Small Group. The most important was to consolidate the school on the Mount Hermon campus and to find a buyer for Northfield. In the end, the board voted almost unanimously at the early January meeting to move to one campus. One trustee abstained for personal reasons.

After the board meeting, we all went up to the Mount Hermon Memorial Chapel, where faculty, staff, and some students heard us announce and describe the coming changes. At one level there was little surprise, since the stresses facing the school were well-known. But of course, it meant a big change, emotional and otherwise, for everyone over the next several years.

The reactions more broadly, in the alumni and surrounding communities, were varied. Many alumni said they weren't surprised. They had wondered how long we could sustain the current operation. Many said they liked the outlines of what we intended to create. Many confirmed what I had decided early on, namely, it was imperative to take effective, if tough, action from a position of relative strength rather than wait until we might be perceived as a declining institution. At that point it would be much more difficult to make changes, keep up enthusiasm, and maintain admissions.

Not surprisingly, the people of the town of Northfield were concerned about the fate of the Northfield campus and the impact on the town. I met frequently with the town council to hear their views. I assured them the NMH board would take the possible impact on the town into account in any proposed sale to a new entity.

I understood the reaction of female graduates of Northfield (as well as young women and men who resided on the Northfield campus after the two schools went co-ed in 1972) who emotionally wrestled with the "loss" of *their* campus. Many understood and came back over the next few years; others have not. We knew that would be the case, as we had purposefully chosen the long-term health of the educational program and a focus on financial sustainability to address the existential questions surrounding the elephant on campus.

Some alumni thought we should have announced the need to raise the money required to remain a two-campus school. They said they would have helped. The reality was that the school, for decades, under many different leaders, had worked hard at fundraising without the success needed. We judged that a campaign in 2004 would also not have had success. But the decision was not just about money. It was also, importantly, about creating more sustainable and even better educational and student life programs.

I was gratified by the number of people over the years who congratulated me for "saving *our* school." While that was not the description I used, I'm glad they felt we did the right thing. There were many who worked together to make it happen. To be candid, I believe deeply that our insights, willingness to name the issue and take it on, and then our leadership working with the board and the community were crucial to putting NMH on a long-term track for stability and success.

It took some fortitude, leaps of faith, and just plain hard work by Bill Rhodes, the board and Small Group, and the school community to do what needed to be done.

In the following weeks I worked with the board on how best to provide the strong leadership needed on campus to implement the decisions. I proposed that I become president of NMH, with overall responsibility including a focus on our external relations, while my deputy, Tom Sturtevant, would become head of school with day to-day-responsibilities. It was a sensible move and had precedent in NMH history.

Looking back eighteen years later, I feel satisfied that our difficult decision and move have in fact fulfilled our goal by strengthening the school and paving the way for an even better educational experience for the next generations of young people. In addition, the school finally found a permanent occupant for the Northfield campus, Thomas Aquinas College, which is investing in the buildings and grounds and recruiting students. A separate, nonprofit Moody Center has been created to maintain certain parts of the campus and uphold Dwight Lyman Moody's profound legacy to humankind.

In the end we identified the elephant on campus. We tamed it and made it our friend!

School Year 2003–2004 Races to Conclusion

After our historic announcement to create a smaller school on one campus, we raced to the finish line of Sacred Concert, final exams, commencement, and reunion. It had truly been a momentous year, certainly one of the more momentous ones in my professional careers.

That summer we took off on our third driving vacation to Canada, this time to Quebec City, Saint Lawrence Seaway, Gaspe Peninsula, and back south through New England. It was another wonderful trip. We particularly enjoyed experiencing the two cultures of Quebec: French and English Canadian. Canadians are good people.

In previous years we had made two other fun driving visits to Canada. One was to the Canadian Rockies, where we rented an apartment in Canmore, at the base of the Canadian Rocky Mountains. Jonathan and Eric joined us for several days for really good family time. We took in the Calgary Stampede rodeo and visited Lake Louise and other mountain spots. Without doubt the Canadian Rockies are a world treasure. We drove north to see Jasper National Park and found Angel Glacier, which my father visited when he was a young man. We noted the glacier had been much bigger in his day. It is melting rapidly as average temperatures rise around the world. We spent a day in Edmonton and found it an attractive city. In fact, Calgary and Edmonton both rank high on the list of livable cities.

Our third trip was to the Atlantic provinces. We took in Campobello Island and Roosevelt's summer home. I recalled that on our 1964 home leave trip across the United States, Dad as consul general had to break off and fly back to attend the opening of the park and museum because the First Lady, Lady Bird Johnson, would represent the United States.

We ventured north to Saint John, where Dad served as consul general for four years, 1961–1965. We crossed the bridge over the Reversing Falls (thanks to the high tides) of the Saint John River, and I eagerly looked forward to showing Claire our home in Rothesay outside the city. To my surprise, the house was gone and there was just a big open grassy lot.

Our trip continued for several days on Prince Edward Island and then all along the Nova Scotia coast. We found the small villages and ocean scenes wonderfully inviting.

We also made a visit north to Cape Breton Island, another very pleasant visit. A highlight was the home of Thomas Edison, now a museum devoted to his research and many inventions.

All three trips were far more attractive and easier than flying and braving the enhanced security and terror threats in the wake of the 9/11 attacks.

Our Capstone Seventh Year at NMH

The 2004–2005 academic year began auspiciously and with much energy. Everyone in the community realized there was change coming in the next several years as we moved to just one campus. There was excitement and of course trepidation.

The year proceeded as it always did, with convocation and all the normal academics, sports, and traditional gatherings.

I launched into my new priorities as president of NMH: providing overall leadership and concentrating on external bridge building, also known as fundraising, and finding a buyer for the Northfield campus. In September we had a nice installation ceremony in the Auditorium to show me off as the new president.

"President" had a nice ring to it. I set out with my deputy, Tom Sturtevant, to create a working relationship. There was no clear dividing line on responsibilities, but I plowed ahead.

On the fundraising front we organized a board retreat led by a noted fundraising consultant we had used before. Many of us thought it went quite well. Some trustees were not enamored of being told, convincingly and correctly, that trustees needed to show confidence in the future by taking the leadership in the coming fundraising campaign and, in the meantime, being vocal and visible advocates for NMH.

I went to New York to ask our board chair to consider a $10 million pledge toward the new arts center we committed to building and naming after him. The good news is that the fundraising moved forward. Ultimately, after I left, we realized the dream I had kept for several years—to build a beautiful arts center where Recitation Hall had once stood. Claire and I loved the arts programs and attended every music program, play, dance concert, and arts exhibit we could.

The Center is named the William R. Rhodes Center for the Arts and was the envy of the school world. Thanks, Bill!

The future of the Northfield campus was also at stake. We worked with an upmarket real estate company and put it on the market for $40 million. We knew that was a stretch but didn't want to discount it too early. The selling job went on for multiple years after I left. Carol Lebo, who had worked closely with me, was one of the "keepers of the keys" as the transition went forward. There was scant demand for such an entire school campus, and the yearly upkeep for NMH was substantial. Finally, the foundation created by the owners of Hobby Lobby, a national craft store, agreed to buy it for $100,000 with commitments to preservation of Dwight Moody buildings and legacy.

Hobby Lobby looked for a Christian school to take over the campus. Finally, Thomas Aquinas College in California became the ultimate owner and now has done much preservation work and started an undergraduate program on the campus.

Although I was saddened that the Northfield campus was no longer part of the Northfield Mount Hermon School, I was overjoyed to see how the downsizing of students, faculty, and staff (carefully spread over three years) and the move to one campus had provided a far more solid foundation for the school's long-term future. It is thriving.

I am grateful for all the people who contributed to the work that was needed to get to where we are today, in 2023.

Chapter Seven

Along Came Hong Kong International School

Our friends in Hong Kong in the summer of 2004 alerted us to the departure of the head of school three years into his five-year contract. There were too many differences and too much tension among the head, the faculty, and board of managers (trustees). We were sorry to hear about the continuing governance problems exacerbated by differing approaches in operating styles and priorities.

In the fall our old friend, Jim Handrich, formerly elementary principal and later high school principal, was in touch asking about our plans and how long we might stay at NMH. It was more than an idle question. As the recruiter put forward candidates' names, Jim decided my name should be near the top of the list. Why? I was a known commodity: two assignments to the U.S. consulate general; a stint at Asia Society Hong Kong Center; two boys who attended the school; former board member and chair of the board; seven years as head of school at NMH.

Jim encouraged me to apply. Claire and I were intrigued. We needed to consider seriously where our future lay: back in Hong Kong which we loved, or at a school we strongly supported as the new president of NMH with the satisfaction of pursuing new directions. But that also included all the guaranteed headaches of taking the school to one campus, particularly after seven years of hard work getting to this point. I polished up my application and resume but held them until the November deadline.

While there was no guarantee of being chosen, we were good candidates. I say "we" deliberately because Claire was also fondly remembered at HKIS (and she had worked at the middle school).

Jonathan and Eric were fully supportive of our application for the position. Jonathan gave me good tips on updating my resume. Clearly, vacations in Hong Kong were more exciting than coming to Northfield!

I pushed the "send" button on my computer just before the deadline. I felt a sense of excitement. We could see ourselves in Hong Kong, happily settled in. Jim, who was acting head of school for the year, promised to move the application along smartly. Claire and I drove to New York to meet with Bill, still chair of the board, and told him we were exploring a move to HKIS. We talked about some of the reasons. He understood.

Then began the selection process. The recruiting company was not practiced in working with international schools. The process was at times painful, with long-distance interviews on equipment that kept breaking down. But ultimately, the board asked me to be a finalist and invited us to visit in February of the new year.

We flew to Hong Kong again on our trusty United Airlines 747 to begin the grueling multiday rounds of interviews. The first day on the ground was Sunday, so we attended services at Church of All Nations on the HKIS campus. We were greeted by old friends who were surprised and happy to see us. It was like old home week.

The next few days of meetings reminded me of our three days of interviews at NMH. Everyone wanted a nod from me about the importance of their favorite issue or program. The lower primary principal was particularly disappointed that I did not have elementary age education experience. "How will you learn?" she asked. I laughed. "You will be my teacher," I proposed.

And so it went. I could sense the tension not far below the surface among differing groups. The Lutheran Church Missouri Synod (LCMS) would name the new head of school based on the board's recommendation, as long as he or she was a Lutheran, even if not LCMS.

The best question came during the parent night gathering. The parent opened by saying:

"Mr. Mueller, you seem well qualified for this position. I would like to say, diplomatically, you seem closer to the end of your professional careers than the beginning. Do you feel you have the energy for such a demanding job?" (I had just turned sixty). "Of course," I assured him.

My health and energy levels well-matched my experience levels to lead HKIS.

That same parent night had begun with an extraordinary surprise. As we greeted parents, there were Henry and Lisa Tang. He was Hong Kong's chief secretary (number two in the government), and they had children in the school. We had known them well. We were delighted to see them. Henry was upfront with us: they supported my candidacy and decided to come to the meeting to let the board and the community see they supported me!

It can be nice to have friends in high places, but I still had to perform well.

I learned I had two strong competitors: one was from a Concordia Lutheran University in Wisconsin, and another from a Lutheran K–12 school in Australia.

Decision time for the board came some days later. We received a phone call; Doug Henck, chair of the board, was on the line. He cut to the chase and said the board had voted and was pleased to offer me the head of school position. Would I accept? My answer was quick and to the point: "We accept!"

What a great feeling it was to again have succeeded in something we had worked for, as had already happened with Consul General Hong Kong and head of school, NMH. We promptly went down the street to get something to eat at McDonalds and then called Jonathan and Eric. They, too, were excited and happy for the family. They began planning their own Christmas activities in Hong Kong.

Once again it was back across the Pacific via United's trusty 747.

One more step remained to make me officially the head of school. I had to fly to Saint Louis to receive approval of the LCMS, which was one of the founders of HKIS in 1966.

First, I took a psychological test. The psychologist who analyzed the results said he saw no reason I couldn't adjust to life in a new city and culture. Say what?! Surprised by the observation, I laughingly asked whether he knew my background as a thirty-two-year FSO who had lived and worked in other countries. His answer? "No," he said, "we only analyze the test results." Sigh.

I also met with President Gerald B. Kieschnick of the LCMS and had a friendly and upbeat conversation. I encouraged him to visit Hong Kong and learn about the city and school as well as observe how we upheld the Christian foundation of the school in an international city with people of many faiths and backgrounds. He was receptive. We met again a couple years later in Hong Kong when he visited to try to calm a storm created by the church.

Separately I met with one of the deputy LCMS presidents, who would cross swords with HKIS trustees several years later, helping to muddy our future and prevent both the school and LCMS from moving forward in a rapidly changing Hong Kong and China.

At the end of April 2005, I flew by myself back to Hong Kong to learn more about HKIS and coming issues. Jim Handrich and I also flew to Phuket, Thailand, for a several-day-long conference of heads of school in the Asia Pacific region. It was well worth the time invested to catch up with school and regional trends. I also saw firsthand the devastation of homes and buildings caused by the recent tsunami that had roared ashore. I learned that our human resources director and her husband had been caught in the waves. She had severe injuries, but they were fortunate to survive. Again, Mother Nature had her own plans for hu-mankind.

HKIS provided a very nice apartment at 127 Repulse Bay Road, a new building with a magnificent view of the Bay. Not only did we enjoy it for the next five years, but we used it to great advantage in entertaining for school purposes. We contributed significantly to the monthly rent. It was well worth it. Claire told me I did well in selecting it.

The NMH Spring Term Races to Conclusion

We were in the final months of our seven years at NMH. The time was racing by as we participated in the end-of-year traditions and made plans for the move to Hong Kong.

The May NMH Board meeting went smoothly enough. The board gave me a rocking chair and several nice farewell plaques to hang on my wall to remind me of seven good years. I was overwhelmed with the number of trustees who genuinely praised Claire's and my efforts to lead and improve the school and who wished us well as we prepared to return to Hong Kong.

I agreed to be the commencement speaker even though I knew such talks were not easy to carry off successfully. I spent many hours drafting and revising a talk designed to get them thinking of the connection between their time at Northfield Mount Hermon and their futures. I called out a couple seniors who might one day be standing where I was as head of school. Raucous laughter. It was an emotional ceremony and an even more emotional round of farewells over those final weeks.

The final faculty meeting of the year was similarly emotional, with warm thoughts from many members. Claire and I appreciated the many genuine sentiments about our tenure and the progress the school had made. The one I most appreciated was from David Dowdy, senior English and religious studies teacher, who praised what he and colleagues saw as one of my big accomplishments: from the beginning, in my actions and words, he described how I taught the faculty to again listen and again talk with one other, thus bringing the school together as a community. We all learned to work together in much needed ways.

It was a successful and hugely enjoyable run of seven years. We had lived in Ford Cottage longer than anywhere else. And bottom line, thousands of young people received an excellent education while the hard decisions we made left the school in far better shape for the long run.

Yes, we probably helped "save our school." And yes, our NMH sojourn was about as good a "retirement endeavor" as we had hoped it would be.

Mueller Family Life During Those Northfield Mount Hermon Days

Before describing our return to Hong Kong and HKIS in 2005, let me bring the reader up to date with some of the stories of Mueller family goings-on in those years.

My mother passed away in October 2004 in Williamsburg at the age of ninety-one. She had been in the hospital for a urinary tract infection. The doctors were not clear about what caused her final hospitalization and death. We were with her in Williamsburg until the end. We buried her in Woodlawn cemetery in New York, where her parents were buried. She was a wonderful person who was fiercely devoted to the family. Even as she aged, she maintained her determination and grit not to be housebound or be shunted off to a nursing home. She maintained a sweet and warm smile even when I think she did not at times fully follow conversations or activities around her. We had a nice memorial service for her at Saint Stephen Lutheran Church in Williamsburg, which I attended regularly when at William and Mary and that she had attended during their years in the area. Jonathan was able to attend the service and give heartfelt reflections about his grandmother.

My father stayed on at 120 Holly Road in Williamsburg for two years after Mother died, being mobile enough to live by himself. I know he became more and more lonely. On one visit he and I drove to the Outer Banks of North Carolina to stay overnight, a favorite vacation spot for Mother and Dad. He also flew up to New England, spent some days with us at NMH, and visited his sister, Betty, in Berlin, Connecticut. He finished up the brilliant six-thousand-page memoir he left us, which Eric spent innumerable hours digitizing, editing, and binding in 2014. In 2005 as we headed to Hong Kong and HKIS, we urged Dad to come and live with us. Sadly, he just wasn't up to such a move halfway around the world.

In October 2006 Dad came down with stomach cancer. He declined all treatment. Claire and I flew back when we knew he was failing. Fortunately, he did not suffer for long. He was in hospice care for several days and was alert and engaged with his visitors. His spirits were good, all things considered, and he talked about the many positives and successes of his life and family. Jonathan and Eric came to spend some time with him. They talked about Lake Tahoe and Eric's and Jonathan's careers. When the chaplain came to visit and asked him whether he believed in an afterlife, he smiled and said he was curious to find out.

We organized a memorial service for him in the chapel of the Wren building on the William and Mary campus. My freshman year English class was in a classroom adjacent to the chapel. Our niece Andrea played the organ. As with Mother's service, Linda, Bill, Jennifer, and Andrea were with us (they were still living in northern Virginia). Dad expressed the desire for his ashes to be scattered both in the James River in Virginia, and at Zephyr Cove at Lake Tahoe, which he had visited years before on his transcontinental rail visit across North America. Later, Jonathan and Kim (who were living in Reno) and Eric and Susan (who were in San Francisco) went together to Lake Tahoe to scatter his ashes as he had wished.

As I look back, I appreciate how much both Mother and Dad were very much a part of our lives for so many years. They were with us for the great majority of our growing up years and our foreign service and education careers—sixty-two-some years. They were always encouraging and supportive. They visited whenever they could. They loved all the pictures and letters Claire sent them regularly. They loved her as their daughter-in-law.

We still feel their absence. They very much live on through powerful memories and pictures which remind us of them every day.

At NMH, Claire was a stalwart and enthusiastic supporter of the school, engaging in all facets of our involvement with school activities. She enjoyed meeting parents, alumni, faculty, students, and trustees. She was as much a presence on campus as I was, sometimes more. Travel was usually a nice change of pace for both of us, whether driving to board meetings in New York City or flying halfway around the world.

A huge bonus of our going to NMH was her being able to drive to Pawtucket once a week to spend a day with her mother. She was also available for family time such as reunions, or when brother Roger was sick and subsequently passed away.

In 1999 we were fortunate in buying a nice pied-à-terre in Boston on Beacon Street, facing Boston Common. It was small, in a historic building, and had a certain elegance. It overlooked Frog Pond in Boston Common and was just down the street from the Capitol. It was a wonderful getaway spot. Sadly, I did not get there nearly often enough. So many weekends were devoted to on-campus athletics, arts programs, etc., all of which I wanted to attend.

Claire did take advantage of spending weekdays in Boston for a year to give her a break. She also took courses at Boston University. Her favorite was about the 1970s in America, which she of course lived through, to the delight of the professor. She always came back on Fridays for the weekend. When people expressed concern for Richard, her standard line was that he was so busy he never missed her.

In fact, she was wrong: I did miss her!

Throughout, she shared her keen insights into people and situations. She was and remains my toughest critic—and strongest supporter.

Claire was also a terrific "communications center" for the family. She wrote regular notes and sent pictures to my parents in Williamsburg. They loved her being in touch with so much news. She also was regularly in touch with Eric and Jonathan. She would feed me the day's news when I came home.

A year before we left NMH, we bought a townhouse in Tiverton, in a new community with a magnificent view of Sakonnet Bay, The Villages at Mount Hope Bay. It was to be a getaway destination for us and perhaps a retirement spot, well-located between Boston and New York City. For our time in Hong Kong, Tiverton was our summer home, since we had sold our place in Boston. We sold it in 2010. We made some money on our Boston place—on Tiverton, not so much.

Eric graduated in 2000 from Princeton University with a degree in mechanical and aeronautical engineering. Serendipity in the spring introduced him to a visiting researcher from NASA's Ames Research Center in Mountain View, California, just south of San Francisco. Ames offered him a position, which introduced him to a broad range of NASA programs and turned into a full-time job he enjoyed for almost two decades before going into private industry with Uber and then Joby Aviation. During those years, he earned his master's and PhD degrees in aerospace engineering from Stanford University. It was a huge accomplishment.

Early on he worked on developing flight controls for the mission to the moon. He invited NASA astronauts to Ames to fly the Vertical Motion Simulator with the programs he was devising to guide them to the moon. Regrettably, the moon program was shelved. Even as he worked on a variety of programs, he focused increasingly on how to fly drones safely in the national airspace, which become a focus of his academic research.

Eric had the same travel bug Jonathan had inherited from his parents. Over the years, they included travel to NMH, Europe, Cuba, Madagascar, Sri Lanka, Mexico, China, Vietnam, Malaysia, Finland, Russia, the Baltic states, and of course Hong Kong, as well as others.

But I'm getting well ahead of myself.

Jonathan had gone to California for a while after graduating in 1998 from the University of Virginia. He accepted a position in Chicago with the consulting firm A.T. Kearney. He shared an apartment with a friend and certainly learned a lot about the business world. His lament was that there were no mountains nearby to climb, only tall buildings.

Before we knew it, Jonathan had declared he needed a change of scene and that he and his friend, Dimetri, planned to hike the Appalachian Trail from Georgia to Maine. That was a surprise. He moved to Ford Cottage on the campus and settled in, making plans and buying supplies. He and Dimetri packed boxes we would mail to them at pickup points along the trail. (Advice to other hikers: do not include laundry sheets with perfume that ruin the rest of the contents of the box!)

In the spring of 2000, they made their way to Springer Mountain in Georgia, their jumping off point for the Trail. Were we worried? Just a bit. It was the unknown. I read Bill Bryson's book, *A Walk in the Woods*. Everything seemed okay and doable until he quoted himself as worrying about coming home with a bobcat attached to his head.

Jonathan and Dimetri started off walking quickly, thinking they might do the hike in four months. But then they realized how much they were enjoying themselves, and they decided to slow down and enjoy all the rituals and meetings of other hikers along the trail. We learned that hikers gave other hikers nicknames which replaced their real names. Jonathan became "Pig," short for "pigpen" which described his living style at college (of course, not in his growing up years with his mother and father)!

Jonathan came off the trail in June 2000 and joined us for Eric's Princeton graduation. He looked like a wild man, with long hair and full bushy beard. Then, it was back on the trail. He stopped at Ford Cottage as he went north. And finally, in September, we drove to meet him and Dimetri as they came down from the summit of Mount Katahdin in Maine, the official northern end of the trail. Back to Ford Cottage for some downtime.

Jonathan will have to expand on his many ensuing adventures. Later in the year, he headed to California for his job with a tech company, Savi Technology, working on strategic planning and traveling to all six continents. Two plus years later, his itchy feet took him to Africa—Tanzania—to work for a British nonprofit, Mondo Challenge, providing microloans to individuals. He traveled in East Africa and to Zanzibar and the area, and then to northern Africa, including Morocco. Finally, he hiked the Spanish pilgrim's path of *Camino de Santiago* ("The Way of Saint James"), for a pilgrimage to the Atlantic Ocean ending at Compostela di Santiago. We were happy to welcome him safely home after a year of travel. His stories about these adventures kept us entertained for months.

Subsequent landing points included working for Pali Mountain Institute in Los Angeles in 2004, and then for Great Basin outdoor school in Reno in 2005. Then came his great accomplishment of founding Sierra Nevada Journeys (SNJ) in northern Nevada, an outdoor school teaching about science, technology, engineering, and mathematics (STEM) and the environment, both in local schools and then at Grizzly Creek Ranch in the Sierra Nevada mountains. Over the next five years, he nurtured and grew it into a mature and influential nonprofit providing excellent learning for young people.

Hello Hong Kong!

Home again, home again to Hong Kong on our trusty United 747. It felt like old home week in mid-July of 2005. Sam, our always loyal and trusty HKIS driver, met us at the airport and took us directly to our new home at 127 Repulse Bay Road. Claire confirmed I had made a good choice of housing for our newest "assignment" in Hong Kong.

The next morning, we caught up with one of my favorite colleagues—Josephine Wai, who worked for the head of school; she would be a terrific supporter in the next five years. Claire and I spent the next few days visiting every division and reaching out to friends we knew from our earlier years in Hong Kong. It sure felt refreshing and was a real change of pace from rural Massachusetts and campus in a bubble. The furniture we had sent ahead was arriving in August and by coincidence, Cecile, Cholin, and Celine would be visiting Hong Kong on their way back to the United States from the Philippines. They generously offered to help us get settled so we could host an introductory dinner for the board of managers in the function room. No reason not to get started early in making connections.

It was great seeing Jim Handrich again, who was acting head of school and to this day has remained a best friend. He had agreed to stay on for a while as deputy head of school. I have met few people who have a heart for students as big as Jim's. He always saw the good and the potential in young people. He, like I, felt strongly that we had to always put students at the heart of all we did.

We felt good seeing how the school had grown and expanded over the years. It certainly deserved its reputation as one of the very best international schools in Hong Kong and Asia, perhaps the world. We toured the lower primary school where both Jonathan and Eric had been students, 1983–1986, and then the high school from which Eric graduated in 1996 when I was consul general.

Even though it was summer, there were many people to talk with and learn from about the school and particularly recent events that had caused such upset. In a nutshell, we learned:

—The board and head of school wanted to make some changes to compensation and other policies that were potentially controversial.

—The board's and head of school's approach could have benefited from more preparation with the community and faculty.

—Some members of the community were accused of undermining the head and the board.

—In the summer of 2004, the head suddenly announced his resignation with immediate effect. He said he was unable to complete the transformation he had been hired to carry out. Jim Handrich was appointed acting head of school.

Bottom line: HKIS needed a new head of school by the summer of 2005. It needed someone who could calm the waters and lead the school in a more collaborative and effective way. The school also needed a new understanding of what good board and school governance looks like and demands. It sounded as if some of these clashes of the last three years could have been avoided.

Claire and I also spent the summer visiting with many long-time Hong Kong friends, Americans, and other foreigners alike. We engaged with many important groups such as the American, international, and local business communities; Hong Kong government; the American consul general; and other school heads.

By the end of July, the familiar rhythms of school preparations for the next academic year began in earnest. I worked with Jim Handrich and our board chair, Doug Henck, to sketch out goals for the year: educational, financial, and operational. I very much looked forward to Doug's leadership of the board. I had known him earlier in my Hong Kong consulate general assignments. The four principals on the two campuses were key players. As with NMH, having two campuses on the southern side of Hong Kong Island provided multiple challenges.

I met with a group of trustees in August to discuss the big issue going forward of how to create a differentiated salary system for faculty. It was to be some form of "pay for performance." The board had hired a consultant the year before who oversaw what I concluded to be a flawed process. I had seen a draft in the spring and felt it did not reflect the reality of schools and teachers. I asked a senior faculty member who had participated in the committee what she thought. She just shook her head and said neither the consultant nor the administration would listen to her and others.

I committed to the board to put together some new ideas for a way forward. (For the reader's information, so-called pay for performance has had at best a checkered history in education—with few, if any, significantly successful systems. But boards tend to be obsessed with the idea.)

We planned for opening celebrations and convocation at the Church of all Nations, with board members participating and a convocation of faculty and staff. The themes revolved around coming together as a community and working together for our students—upwards of 2,600 among the four divisions of lower primary, upper primary, middle school, and high school. The not-so-openly stated messages addressed the need to move on from the turmoil of the previous years and aim for a new future.

It quickly sank in that the board, in hiring me, hoped to put to work my experiences of bringing communities together and getting people to work together. A top priority was working with the board to help it provide important leadership in ensuring good governance.

I learned repeatedly during my educational and diplomatic careers that such good governance by the board—following agreed, ethical rules and practices, based on solid research—is one of the most powerful tools to create a well-organized and well-functioning institution. The benefits are felt throughout the organization.

I'll make the comment here that good governance has a critical role to play in how nations organize and govern themselves. What are the constitutional underpinnings, the laws, the organization of government, the unwritten and often traditional expectations of behavior by leaders and citizens alike? Often, they depend on individual forbearance and generosity of spirit by leaders.

For example, I often write about the challenges China faces today. These include environmental, economic, demographic, climate warming, corruption, lack of investment in medical and elder care, and many others. But I think the biggest challenge is how China's leaders can effectively *govern* a country of 1.4 billion people, particularly given the widely varying regional histories, cultures, languages, and traditions which pull the country in differing directions.

A Chinese reference may say it all: "The mountains are high, and the emperor is far away." That's as true in modern Marxist-Leninist China as in the time of emperors.

Sadly, HKIS's governing principles had been drafted in the 1960s and had been little updated in the years since. They were often incomplete or not precise. The imbroglio that led to the school head's departure drew attention once again to the need to update them for the twenty-first century. This issue and all its ambiguities would prove vexing throughout my five-year tenure as head of school and even to this day.

The Academic Year Lifts Off and Gains Altitude

Classes got underway, and one could feel the energy of so many students and adults. My office was located in a very public place in the center of the middle school. Transparent glass surrounded it so I could watch with a smile as students ran to classes, played games, and even came over to wave at me. I learned so much about those middle years as students grew from callow sixth graders to young adult high schoolers. What transformations in minds and bodies! And I learned to deeply respect middle school teachers, who had special talents and patience to support such young people.

I spent a good bit of the fall visiting all four divisions to better learn about all age groups and the varying approaches to educational programs. It was instructive and fun. It also gave me a chance to meet teachers and staff and build relationships. I loved visiting classrooms and talking with students. Seldom were they shy. Often, I would read storybooks and then we would talk about them. In the Chinese classroom, I could use my Mandarin Chinese and see the students smile in amazement that a non-Chinese person could speak Chinese.

As with NMH, I felt the constant tension of needing to deal with "big" issues or appease board trustees to the neglect of visiting classrooms or events close to students. I relied on Jim Handrich to help sort out priorities and often to represent me.

Welcome to the usual tensions experienced by most administrators whether heads of school, superintendents, or principals. Today's leaders spend much of their time dealing with parents, legal issues, fundraising, recruiting, and so much more. Still, it was exhilarating being in Hong Kong and dealing with the widest possible range of people. But I felt comfortable.

Lutheran Church Missouri Synod Comes Calling in 2005—The "Ablaze" Summit on Campus Lights the Fires

The LCMS held an "Ablaze" summit in the fall on campus to gather the faithful and set Christians "ablaze."

I agreed to participate and give a talk on China and U.S.-China relations. It covered the waterfront of the state of China's economic, political, social development and where the United States stood in building relations with China. I described China's antagonistic approach to foreign religious activity and encouraged the church to downplay the planting of new physical churches and emphasize people learning about Christianity through the good works and actions of Christians.

Many people said they had learned a lot from my talk.

After the day's conference, Bob, the senior international representative for the church, took me aside to reveal recent decisions by the church board in Saint Louis. They included a request that HKIS tithe a percentage of its "profits" each year to the church and provide $5 million to support the founding of schools like HKIS in China and Asia.

I was astounded. This had never happened before. Why had we not been told this was an agenda item and asked for an HKIS response? What did they think the reaction of parents would be? Why did they think the school, a nonprofit institution, had "profits"?

Bob was a bit chagrined and said the church was in difficult financial straits and had asked our "sister" school in Shanghai, Concordia, to also provide financial help.

This was the beginning of what became, in my experience, continuing tensions between the school and the church. In retrospect, we should have done what David Rittmann, the head of school at Concordia, did, namely, just say plainly the school was not able to comply and move on.

We decided the way forward was to 1) collect all the ways in which the school already served the church's interests in Asia; 2) explain why we couldn't respond positively; and 3) state our willingness to work with them in other ways.

The flames died down, but the embers remained alive, threatening to reignite at any time. Unfortunately, they did. Read on.

The School Year Rolls Along

While principals took care of the day-to-day running of their divisions and the school, I tackled some of the longer-run issues waiting to be dealt with.

Jim had pledged to stay on for at least a year, perhaps two, while I launched a search for a deputy head of school. A strong deputy was imperative to help carry the leadership load of such a large school on two campuses. A sticking point was the role of the LCMS. While at one level they expressed interest in helping, at another level they did little to identify promising Lutheran candidates even within their own educational system, or to even work with us collaboratively. We cast the net much more widely in the coming months.

In the end it would be a long two years to find the right deputy, DJ Condon, and another year to settle him in so he could help move the school in the right direction. DJ and I became good friends. We complemented each other's skills. We both shared similar views about global education and teaching students about cross-cultural learning and understanding. His positive and even temperament helped us, together, to build good relationships with the community.

In a nutshell, all senior administration and teacher hiring searches brought up questions of "fit" and particularly of experience in international schools, quite different from LCMS and even other U.S. schools. Finding and hiring the right teachers was a continuing challenge and one I was keenly focused on.

HKIS has had a foundation of Christian beliefs and values but has never refused to accept non-Christian students nor required students to receive Christian religious instruction. The same is true with faculty. What it has believed is that demonstrating Christian beliefs in action would often be a strong motivation for people to want to learn more about what it meant to be a Christian. In fact, that was the LCMS approach to evangelism more generally in China and Asia, unlike long-ago missionary practices. What we hoped students would learn in their religion and ethics classes was—yes—to appreciate Christian teachings but also to have a chance to be exposed to a wide range of religious and spiritual inquiry.

A foreign service colleague who was Jewish had expressed some reluctance to accept an assignment to the consulate general in Hong Kong because of HKIS's Christian traditions. I persuaded him that the school was open-minded, as above. At the end of the year, Bernie told me that HKIS had been the best place for his son. Not only did he learn about other religions, but he had a reawakened interest in his family's own Jewish faith.

The bottom line was that HKIS was a school and not the outpost of a religious missionary church. Therein lay one of the sticking points between LCMS and HKIS. LCMS headquarters were far, far away in Saint Louis and often did not have much understanding of Hong Kong or our parent community.

There were other serious decisions to make around senior staffing. I had not inherited a well-functioning and effective team. The chief financial officer stepped down. After some searching, I hired the American founder of Pacific Coffee, a coffee chain in Hong Kong. He was energetic and hardheaded, able to go toe-to-toe with our finance committee. I offered Joy Okazaki, a staff member in upper primary, a position in the finance office. She had a background in finance and business from Sheraton, and she turned out to be a wonderful addition to the leadership team, short and longer term. Later she became director of human resources. (I preferred to call her the "director of the office for people.") She helped to measurably improve the way we communicated and worked with both faculty and staff. (As I write, the current head of school has made her deputy head overseeing human resources, finance, operations, and more.)

A New Faculty Performance and Salary/Benefit System

Early on we tackled what a new "performance management" system might look like. The work done earlier was far off the mark of accomplishing what we wanted, namely, to encourage faculty to deepen and broaden their skills, have them apply them in the classroom, and then reward teachers as they demonstrated they had done so.

The new system would have to help create strong bonds between teachers and principals to produce a positive atmosphere of working together. Most teachers do want to learn and grow and apply that learning for the benefit of students.

It was not an easy task because there were few successful systems to draw from. It often requires years of learning the profession and the craft of teaching. A teacher can't just stand in front of the class and talk. They must understand each child's needs and learning style, know when the child isn't learning and in response know how to boost their success. There is a plethora of skills and experience a teacher needs to be effective in doing so, including course content, social-emotional learning, empathy, flexibility, creativity, and many others.

The craft and art of successful teaching is on par with other professions such as engineering, law, diplomacy, accounting, etc. And ultimately, it is outstanding and humane education that the world so desperately needs.

Of course, teaching is not like a factory, where if you produce so many widgets, we'll pay you more. It is mightily difficult to assess student learning and then assess what an individual teacher's contribution is to that learning. In fact, it may ultimately be impossible. At the October meeting of the East Asia Regional Council of Schools (EARCOS) in Southeast Asia, I described our endeavor to a seasoned head of an international school. His heartfelt advice? Stay away from the plan; it's a fool's errand. Boards think they know what they want but don't appreciate that success is virtually impossible.

Despite the many complexities and obvious difficulties, we plowed ahead with our idea of a "career ladder." We developed a list of important skills needed by a teacher in different roles. We described what a beginning teacher would need to demonstrate in each skill area, followed by a developing teacher, mid-career teacher, and finally a master teacher. The school would provide strong support for each teacher including feedback and professional development. As the teacher progressed up the "ladder," salary and benefits would improve. The principal and other supervisors would play a critical role in both supporting and assessing the teacher's effectiveness.

That's it in a nutshell. While easy to describe in one paragraph as above, it was a difficult and at times perilous journey. We included teachers in the deliberations and held endless brainstorming sessions. It was two steps forward, one back. We drew on good work done by Professor William Odden at the University of Wisconsin. Our new board chair, who was otherwise supportive, kept encouraging us to move the process along faster. The enterprise was derailed at one point. The best progress began when DJ Condon, our new deputy head of school with deep educational experience, arrived with his insights and helped us to refocus.

The faculty was intrigued and wanted to believe a new system could be fundamentally positive. There were many jokes about the "career ladder" and how to climb it. But the positive news was that there was a fair amount of collaboration with a willingness to see whether we could break new educational ground.

I was much impressed with Daniel Pink's book, *Drive,* about human motivation. He debunked most of the supposed understanding of what motivates people, particularly teachers and other "knowledge workers." Just paying a person more for working harder or producing more widgets of some kind is usually not motivating. Instead, he focused on *autonomy, mastery, and purpose.* Teachers (and others) like autonomy/space to expand and control their professional craft and not have someone tell them what to do each step along the way. They like to learn and master new skills. And they like to work for an organization whose purpose or mission they believe is making a positive difference. *Provide teachers a decent salary and compensation package, provide appropriate autonomy, mastery, and purpose and you have the makings of a dynamite cadre of dedicated and motivated educators.*

The Bottom Line? Very Likely Better Student Learning

The bottom line for this most thorny of educational issues was that by our last year at HKIS, we were able to begin piloting versions of the scheme we had been working on for more than four years. The initial implementation was ready for the year after I left, followed by a variety of adjustments, many centered around the supervisory support and feedback of principals and vice principals. The more there was of the latter, the more teachers would learn in a collaborative relationship with administrators. Most importantly, it put the spotlight squarely on what can improve teacher effectiveness and in turn improve student learning which, after all, is the ultimate goal.

I understand that while the scheme has gone through a variety of adjustments over recent years, many useful ideas and goals still survive to help ensure the best possible learning for students.

A brief footnote about the considerable time we spent on two other vexing administrative and personnel problems. One was to create a new salary and benefit system applying to all staff and faculty employees. The existing system treated employees hired locally differently from those hired overseas. The new system, which we worked on for a year, established equity and was widely applauded for its fairness and attractiveness to employees.

The second major change was to move away from always providing HKIS housing for faculty and instead providing a housing allowance. This was at least a two-year project of research, design, and board approval. The Hong Kong housing market was wide, deep, and provided many options. I felt strongly that by providing a housing allowance, we could give faculty greater choice about size, location, and quality of housing. The allowance was generous enough to satisfy most people. Importantly, faculty could choose to spend all their allowance, top it up, or even spend less and save the difference. That was fine with me because it gave people more control over decisions affecting their lives. One family, for example, chose to live in a very small house across the bay from the school. They hired a boatman to ferry them back and forth. All the savings went into the college fund for their children! They were happy, and I was happy they could make an important choice that worked well for them.

A happy and effective employee who feels decently treated is one of an organization's best assets.

What Was Going on with Students?

I write all of the above because it encompasses many of the issues the board, senior administrators, and I spent a great deal of time on, all designed to create an even better foundation for an excellent school for the long run. It was not necessarily my preferred focus, but it was an important one.

Just to remind the reader: we had about 2,650 students on two campuses who came to school every day to learn. I involved myself as much as possible in visiting classrooms, attending concerts and plays and competitions (and there were many of them), as well as athletic events both in Hong Kong and around the region.

Every day I was surrounded by youthful energy and even shenanigans. Lower and upper primary on the Repulse Bay campus, and middle school and high school on the Tai Tam campus all provided endless student contact. Just walking out of my office and strolling about observing young people was always the best tonic.

Time with students was precious. I would meet periodically with high school students to talk about the world and how to bring about effective change. I gave each student leader the book *Our Iceberg is Melting* by Jon Kotter, which provided good food for thought and learning. I shared my experiences on change and leadership from my diplomatic and education careers. An important starting point was, "Identify your goal or the issue to be solved. What do you want to accomplish? Then work backwards and plan steps and actions that can lead you there. Be clear-eyed about bringing differing groups together around working toward the objective." Sounds simple, but it isn't. It is a conceptual framework to get one started.

This same group of high school students one day came to my office with a "snack." They proudly and laughingly presented me with a grilled cheese sandwich! Why in the world...? Well, I had told them how in college I was thrifty and always hungry, so I would wrap two slices of bread and cheese in aluminum foil and put a heated iron on each side for a couple minutes. Presto. A perfect grilled cheese sandwich!

We had a good laugh and then good conversation.

On another occasion, I was asked by middle school students to conduct one of the band's selections in an upcoming concert. I initially protested, saying I wasn't a musician. So, they taught me how to simply wave my arms to conduct in time with the band. When I asked how I would know when to stop conducting so the band would stop, my student teacher smiled and said, "No problem! When we stop playing, you stop conducting!"

Such moments are priceless. Heads of school live for them.

We were blessed with interesting speakers and performers. A favorite was Erik Weihenmayer who had attended HKIS in his younger years, and who had gradually lost his eyesight. He was building a reputation as a climber of mountains. Yes, the blind climber. Not long before, in 2001, he had summited Mount Everest with his team, not seeing but feeling his way. He stressed he wanted to be a full participant in the ascent and not just carried up and spiked as if he were a football. It was an extraordinary experience he recounted. His book on the adventure is *Touch the Top of the World.*

The best question to Erik from younger students? "Where do you go to the bathroom on the mountain?"

Jane Goodall visited with our younger students and told them about the chimpanzees she had lived with and studied in Tanzania. She is world famous for research and teaching. The highlight was teaching students some words in the chimpanzee language. She taught the students how chimpanzees greet one another and humans in the morning, to the great delight of students.

The richness of the academic and cultural offerings made HKIS an outstanding school from pre-K through high school.

Likewise with the teaching of important values such as respect and kindness for others. One day I joined high school students sitting in the gym waiting for a speaker. Suddenly, a boy popped up from the stands and danced his way across the open space to the other side of the gym and sat down. Probably seeing a quizzical look on my face, a student told me:

"Oh, that's James. He has some kind of condition so does unexpected things sometimes. We understand and try to help him when he needs us."

Travel from Hong Kong

We were fortunate to be able to travel around the region during those five years. Every fall, there was a gathering of all EARCOS school heads and staff in a different Asian city. Claire accompanied me. We caught up with colleagues on educational developments and participated in numerous workshops, presentations, and social events.

The spring saw a gathering of heads of school for more exchanges about the profession. It was good to be reminded that most schools and their heads faced many similar problems and opportunities. Wives/husbands/partners participated, adding to the experience.

Cities we visited over those five years included: Kuala Lumpur and Kota Kinabalu (Malaysia), Bangkok (Thailand), Siem Riep and Angkor (Cambodia), Manila (Philippines), Saigon/Ho Chi Minh City (Vietnam), and Singapore.

In early January, we would head to faculty and administrator recruiting fairs in the United States, particularly in the Boston area and San Francisco. In the summer, we visited family and enjoyed our townhouse in Tiverton, Rhode Island.

These were all enriching and illuminating gatherings which inevitably supported new ideas for our home schools. The changes of pace and new adventures were also much needed refreshment and an important replenishment of spirit.

Truth be told: classroom teaching is exhilarating, worthy of respect, and exhausting. Leading the school is equally exhilarating, worthy of respect, and exhausting, 24/7.

Hong Kong's Evolution Under China's Sovereignty and Its "One Country, Two Systems" Constitutional Provision

During our five years in Hong Kong, 2005–2010, we began to feel the increasing changes to the city, both planned and unplanned. Millions of mainland Chinese visitors came as tourists as well as consumers to take home scarce goods (e.g., baby formula). Their spending helped power the economy. They brought Mainland cultural and personal habits, including demanding that Hongkongers speak Mandarin to them. Hong Kong people felt disrespect and even contempt from their supposed "compatriots," who treated them as leftover colonials from the British empire. The differences between the visitors' and Hong Kong's own histories and cultures and Cantonese language traditions were profound and ultimately unbridgeable.

Hong Kong and its business and social elites not surprisingly turned more seriously toward China. Investment opportunities abounded. Political bridges were built across the border to provincial and national leaders and institutions. Hong Kong's international financial connections and tradition of rule of law helped power economic and business development. Hong Kong remained, for the most part, an open economy with free access to information and the internet, with a still solid legal system trusted by many. The international community allowed itself to feel reassured.

On the surface, "one country, two systems" was functioning, and Hong Kong appeared to still have its prized high degree of autonomy.

But not far below the surface, the tide of Mainland influence and control was running ever higher. China, of course, had already been building its own networks throughout the city over the years. It now engaged in ever more intense united front work to capture the loyalties of key Hong Kong people and sectors of the economy and the press. It invested in key businesses, such as the airline Cathay Pacific, in order to ensure Beijing's ultimate influence and control. It planted official Chinese government institutions, which operated openly. Few if any significant Hong Kong government decisions were taken without a positive nod from Beijing.

An important continuing issue was the shape of the city's future political development. Over the years, Britain and Governor Patten in the lead up to Hong Kong's reversion to China had provided only limited introduction of political and civic opportunities for Hong Kong people to choose their leaders and participate in their own political governance. The newer practice of Legislative Council and District Council elections was a start. Sadly, chief executives such as C. H. Tung, Donald Tsang, C. Y. Leung, and Carrie Lam had no real political *governing* experience. No wonder it was easy to fall short in their leadership of the city, particularly as Beijing looked over their shoulders. In turn Hong Kong people did not develop the skills and interests required for effective civic participation.

Still, there was intense interest in how China's promise of *universal suffrage* would be implemented. Would Hong Kong have some genuine control in choosing its leaders, first by allowing an open process of proposing candidates and then allowing a genuine one person, one vote election? Or would China only allow people to vote for one pre-approved Beijing candidate, thus ensuring China's full control?

A full, open, democratic system for Hong Kong. let alone a vote on independence from the PRC, were never in the cards, although the city had the population, economy, and educated citizenry that could have supported those developments—as happened in other former colonies around the world, for example, Singapore.

The standoff on political development continued, creating divisiveness and ill will. Other important issues pushed by China and the Hong Kong government met with strong pushback from citizens, such as a national security law and later an extradition law allowing the sending of Hong Kong people to China for "trial." The later demonstrations in 2014—the so-called Umbrella Revolution—and then again in 2019 and 2020, were a direct result of China's continued push for control combined with Hong Kong people's strong desires to keep a genuine high degree of autonomy and control over their lives. The "pro-establishment" elites and businesspeople were unwilling to take any strong stand in favor of preservation of that high degree of autonomy.

Most establishment leaders knew that Hong Kong's divided society needed serious healing, both within Hong Kong and with Beijing. Might they have been smarter about working with the Hong Kong government to address a variety of economic and other problems that might have calmed the waves? I think there were possible windows of opportunity had there been more creativity and willingness to break some traditional practices (e.g., the tight constraints on land creation in order to keep prices high). But when it came to dealing with Beijing, there was little power they had in the face of the CCP and its vast intelligence agencies. Even billionaires were reluctant to speak out or act; they saw how Beijing invited chief executive officers of huge companies and billionaires to "have tea" and in the process let them know CCP officials would be watching to ensure they followed the CCP line. They also knew they risked their families, businesses, and even their lives if Beijing turned on them.

The later demonstrations revealed the deep divisions in society and with Beijing. They gave Beijing the excuse in July 2020 to finally impose its own draconian national security law and all-but-crush Hong Kong's promised high degree of autonomy. Beijing's brazenness and even callousness in doing so, effectively throwing out Deng Xiaoping's Sino-British Joint Declaration and much of China's own Basic Law for Hong Kong, was a clear sign both of the CCP's willingness to use brute force and the paucity of its creative abilities to understand Hong Kong's peoples and work together with them.

So, a "one size fits all" CCP rule of Hong Kong essentially changes forever a unique city participating productively in the world. The idea of a diverse and creative society co-existing peacefully with its sovereign has been snuffed out. To what end? To show that Beijing brought law and order and control to deal with citizens' mostly peaceful protests? To claim credit in the eyes of history for having reunited the empire? All of Hong Kong's people now have the privilege of receiving a "patriotic education," of having "rule by law" instead of "rule of law," and a police force that has been taught to goose step like its Chinese counterpart across the border.

Beijing's actions torpedoed Deng Xiaoping's vision that a constitutional provision of "one country, two systems" could be a solution to bringing Taiwan back to the motherland.

Sadly, American policy and statements had little positive impact on Beijing. The United States Hong Kong Policy Act of 1992, which I had helped to negotiate with the U.S. Congress while working for Secretary Baker, proved unable to have much influence with Beijing. The Act was designed to support the Beijing-designed constitutional approach of "one country, two systems" and a "high degree of autonomy," at least until 2047. The Act's only "punitive" policies were to treat Hong Kong the same as the rest of China, thus pulling down the pillars that had helped make Hong Kong prosperous and ultimately successful as an international center for business and economic growth. In the end, of course, Beijing held all the cards and angrily rejected all criticism on the grounds that the United States and others were the "black hands" fomenting violence and instability.

The above history skipped ahead to 2023 to record the demise of a unique city that so many of us treasured over the years, despite rule by Britain and now by China.

Fortunately, during the time we were in Hong Kong at HKIS, 2005–2010, we continued to enjoy what the city still offered, and we hoped for the best in wise leadership from Beijing.

A Mueller Family Hong Kong Potpourri

Our five years in Hong Kong were marked by family events and travels, gatherings with friends, visits from relatives, and of course endless HKIS-related meetings, planning sessions, crisis avoidance actions, and on and on. Overall, we felt as satisfied and settled as was possible. Here are a few memories.

—Dad had passed away in October 2006. We decided that we and Jon and Eric would spend Christmas in Bali and use it as good family time. We had a fabulous time playing games, having happy hours at various times of the day, visiting favorite sites on the island, and getting in some swimming and beach time. It was a memorial week in honor of Mother and Dad. Particularly rewarding was having good and even fun relationships with our adult sons. We feel fortunate in the extreme that those relationships continue to today in 2023.

—For another Christmas Jon, Kim, Eric, and Susan all came to visit. It was a fun time in Hong Kong but even more fun when we all went up to Shanghai for a few days to see the city. Jon loved sitting in the front seat of the taxis, chatting away with the drivers in Chinese. Susan was the adventurer who tried so many different foods and snacks in the old city. Of course, Claire and I had no inkling that we would spend three years of the next decade in the city at Shanghai American School.

—Wonderful news came in 2009 when Jonathan called with the news that he and Kim had just gotten married. They went to the courthouse and exchanged their vows. We couldn't have been happier to hear the news. We agreed to visit Reno the next February when they aimed to hold a wedding reception for family and friends.

—The American Chamber of Commerce in Hong Kong invited me to become a governor (trustee) of the organization. It was a good match. I had been a strong supporter of the Chamber over the years and was able to provide history and advice in dealing with China and Hong Kong. It was a great opportunity to meet business and other people who would candidly tell me about their experiences doing business in the PRC. They were a good source of information to help understand trends and issues. I also chaired a Chamber committee to revise and clarify its *governance* bylaws, a neglected task desperately needing attention. It again reinforced my understanding of "good governance" and its fundamental importance to an organization.

—Claire and I became good friends with the new American consul general, Jim Cunningham, and his wife, Leslie. Jim had spent most of his career in Europe and the Middle East. He was an eager student of China and Asia and had a willing ear for my observations. In turn he kept me informed of developments that might affect American interests including HKIS and our community. His two daughters both enrolled at HKIS and graduated during his assignment. Later he headed to Tel Aviv as the American ambassador to Israel. Jim's three successors over our last two years were all good friends, Chris Marut, Joe Donavan, and Steve Young. It was nice to be invited periodically to events at "our" residence on 3 Barker Road on the Peak.

—Another crisis unfolded when it became public that the HKIS yearbook contained a picture depicting the Muslim Prophet. Students had created a timeline with pictures of world events. Not knowing how strongly some Muslims felt about not depicting the Prophet, they had included the picture that a magazine had published, creating some worldwide criticism and now a focus on our school. We received emails and letters of criticism. Cognizant of the volatility of potential terrorist responses, we released a strong statement both apologizing and explaining how inadvertent the timeline was. Some faculty members began to cut the pictures out of the yearbooks. We were fortunate that one of our religious studies teachers had a good relationship with the Hong Kong Muslim community and arranged meetings for me to explain what had happened. I also explained to our own community how unintended this had been. The controversy quieted down as Muslim leaders and we broadcast our explanations. None of us had any desire to find jihadis descending on Hong Kong as had been threatened. The Hong Kong government was supportive in its security responses.

—In August 2008 I succumbed to another DVT (deep vein thrombosis) in the leg which led to a severe PE (pulmonary embolism) in the lungs. My two doctors fortunately diagnosed the problems quickly. They kept me in the Adventist Hospital for days to recuperate. I had no idea that DVTs and PEs cause many deaths each year. I was fortunate. Claire was in Rhode Island at the time. She flew back immediately. Later she would say that she was relieved that Richard must be okay when Sam, our driver, met her. Had the pastor met her, she would have feared for the worst.

—The following January my aging hip finally demanded remedial surgery after almost two years of increasing discomfort and then pain. Claire and I flew to San Francisco for my hip replacement at Stanford University Hospital. Dr. Huddleston was terrific. I had thought about "hip resurfacing," but he was persuasive in recommending full replacement: "If you were my father, that's what I would recommend." The operation was a success, and they had me up and walking within a day. After a week of recovery, I was able to participate in two San Francisco education conferences. And now, thirteen years later, the operation continues to be a success.

—I was still in the hospital when Barack Obama was sworn in as president of the United States. We were overjoyed to have, for the first time, an African American as president. He and his wife, Michelle, were intelligent, well-educated, and made up a thoroughly decent and moral family with their young daughters. Although he had little political governing experience, he had skills and presence that could make him an exemplar of presidential leadership. Many of the ideas and policies for which he advocated were ones we supported. Some Americans speculated the United States was now a post-racial society. Personally, I had my doubts. Subsequent history, particularly eight years later, with Donald Trump as president, proved we are in for a long-run struggle against racism, violence, and insurrection.

—It was in this time frame I informed our board chair that I would look to retire from HKIS in 2010. I was accomplishing much of what I came to do, starting with helping change the mood within the school and by getting us collaborating toward broadly agreed goals.

I was also becoming somewhat weary of working with those who were increasingly skeptical of the relationship and were willing to adopt a harder approach to negotiating.

In retrospect, I should have insisted at the time of the search committee's formation that its work be entirely open to all board members and subject to regular board oversight. From a *good governance* perspective that would have helped forestall personal agendas and a devolving relationship with LCMS officials.

HKIS-LCMS History that Illuminates Working with Other Cultures

There is much history that illuminates the many ups and downs in the HKIS-LCMS relationship in recent years. During my tenure there were a few tough times and several hopeful steps forward.

In the tough times category—reported above—was the LCMS Board resolution in 2005 (voted on without knowledge of or input from the HKIS Board) that HKIS provide, among other things, ongoing monetary contributions to the church and a lump sum payment to support the establishment of new schools in Asia. Regrettably, that request was something that produced a negative reaction within our board and beyond.

It led to a serious discussion at a board retreat on the future of the relationship with the LCMS. The board chair, by lot, asked me to go first. Personally, I strongly supported a continuation of the relationship. I argued that we must address critical changes in governance if there was to be any improvement. Without those changes, we were guaranteed continued frustration and ineffective governance. I was hopeful that that could be accomplished with goodwill on both sides of the Pacific. While others agreed with my presentation, some were adamant that more fundamental changes were needed, including a split if necessary.

The vote at the end of the day was for working with the LCMS to improve the relationship, by-laws, and governance mechanisms.

In the hopeful category of events was the visit of LCMS President Kieschnick to Hong Kong. In a meeting with our board, he said he came to "apologize" for the LCMS Board's actions. Our chair said we accepted the apology.

I think President Kieschnick learned a lot about the context of sponsoring a school in another country and culture with a diverse student body. What worked in the United States must often be adapted to be successful in another culture. He was impressed with HKIS facilities and its broad educational program. He even laughingly said it was the first time he had seen a picture of the Buddha in a Christian school.

I described our efforts to recruit Lutheran teachers who could communicate well across cultural and religious divides. It had been an uphill campaign. Several LCMS people had helped with the outreach, including Dave Birner, Jim Handrich, Chuck Dull, our Church of All Nations Pastor, and others. I also described my experience with David Rittmann, LCMS-trained and rostered educator and longtime Head of HKIS (and later at Concordia School Shanghai), who had recruited and trained a good balance of Lutheran teachers and experienced international teachers. Flexibility and a balance of backgrounds were the right approach.

President Kieschnick pledged a positive and flexible future relationship so the board of managers would have the authority it needed to manage the school, including the flexibility in choosing both teachers and the right head of school, even if not LCMS-rostered educators.

That pledge never saw reality. Sadly, it was not observed by others in the church, thus adding to governance frustrations that came to a head when looking for my successor in 2009–2010.

That's another story in this saga. The negative and extended exchanges it led to between a minority on the board and the representatives of the church still strongly colors relations today. It is the reason the school has seen an extended period of interim and short-term heads of school. That's not good for long-term institutional health.

A Crisis in Leadership Transition

The chair of our board formed a search committee to find my successor. It was small and not transparent. It had little public visibility within the school community and our board. The chair communicated with the chair of the LCMS International board with supposed oversight of HKIS. Their relationship slowly, and then quickly, devolved into a divisive series of exchanges over the months. I was appalled and heartsick.

Two groups of LCMS visitors came to Hong Kong for discussions. We introduced them to a variety of HKIS families and others who knew Hong Kong well. While our exchanges were friendly, they were not productive, particularly with the antagonistic atmosphere.

The far deeper problem was that from a Saint Louis perspective, administrators and pastors in the church could not relate well to the needs and realities of an LCMS-connected school in Hong Kong. Our parents were from all points on the compass. We were not located in the religiously and politically conservative Midwest. From the HKIS perspective, we could not figure out how to satisfy church leadership far, far away.

After some weeks board members learned that I was being excluded and pushed to open the process, first by getting me fully involved. That was good, correcting a mistaken tactic that excluding the head of school would be a productive step.

As we looked at candidates, a few were in the ballpark. Still, the bottom line was that no candidate received broad support. One "stealth" candidate who was an experienced head and was currently head of an Episcopal school was brought out just for a weekend of interviews. We met him and his wife for lunch and concluded he was a strong candidate. But, no, he was hung out to dry.

In parallel, we heard that LCMS had hired a law firm to examine Hong Kong law. HKIS similarly sought legal counsel to help clarify Hong Kong law on ownership. It was complicated. The Hong Kong Education Bureau said it had no desire to take a position of any kind but made clear it valued the school's contribution to Hong Kong and urged that both sides find a mutually agreeable way forward.

Finally, after all the swirling arguments and bad feelings engendered by them, the board decided to choose DJ Condon, my deputy, as my successor to be the new head of school. He was well-qualified and favorably known by the school community. He was not a member of the LCMS Church, but hadn't we received a pledge of flexibility from President Kieschnick?

Sadly, the LCMS pushed back. Our board asked DJ to visit Saint Louis to engage in dialogue. Church leaders would not meet. DJ came back with deep sadness that the way had not been better paved beforehand.

Weeks of deadlock ensued. The situation was not good for DJ, LCMS, the school, or the community. Finally, the board decided to appoint DJ as interim head of school and promised to work harder at making the match permanent.

DJ did well that one year of leading HKIS. LCMS still did not budge to allow him to continue permanently. A loss for the school and our students' education.

After DJ, two successive heads of school each served only three years and in between each there was an interim head. Under current Head of School Ron Roukema, the school has done well and worked to maintain its good reputation. That can't continue indefinitely. As with most schools, a long-serving head is a key to a strong, sustainable school. Frequent turnover undermines confidence and consistency.

Why do I include such detail in this section?

One is to document again the importance of *good school governance* and perhaps provide some guidance for others experiencing similar challenges.

Two is to describe one type of crisis a head of school lives and deals with, taking precious time away from students and the educational program.

Three is to preserve important history for future HKIS and LCMS leaders who will eventually need to reach some type of effective agreement on the future of the school.

Four is that Claire and I care about the school and want it firmly planted on a solid foundation for the indefinite future.

The HKIS experience with governance so far is not promising for the future. Only when trustees and other significant stakeholders transparently work together toward common ends, based on clear, agreed-upon bylaws and rules will the school have the strong foundation it needs.

We Create a Blueprint for Rebuilding Repulse Bay and Tai Tam Campuses and Expanding in the New Territories

In my last two years at HKIS, we worked to develop a long-term facilities plan for both campuses. Some of our buildings were dated and needed serious investment. We also needed to think about the future course of education practices and how we could provide flexibility for future use.

As we were working on options, the Hong Kong government announced the availability of a good-sized piece of land in Sai Kung in the New Territories for school use. I was intrigued and went to look. It was a lovely parcel not far from the water. It was large enough to build a second elementary school.

For a long time, I had felt that as populations grew in the New Territories, HKIS would need to make sure it did not suffer a declining admissions stream from the southern side of Hong Kong Island as people moved north to cheaper housing and proximity to Shenzhen and China. A full pre-K–high school institution was not feasible; an elementary school was. If HKIS built a new school, it could draw from expat and local Hong Kong populations in the New Territories.

I worked to build support on the board to do a feasibility study. The board chair agreed the board should discuss the possibility. After some debate, trustees narrowly voted down even doing a study. The majority argued our future was on the south side of the island. I argued otherwise. It was a lost opportunity.

We turned to a plan to invest in our two existing campuses without acknowledging we needed a longer-run strategy that included a broader admissions funnel. The international school that did acquire the land built a nice facility and quickly filled it with students from the area.

We decided to start our new facilities investment at the lower primary school that had been the elementary school for years. Jonathan and Eric were both educated in that building. The plan was to tear it down and completely rebuild it with flexibility for the youngest children. We would include a good size "auditorium" that also served well as the Church of All Nations.

The plan was launched and when I visited in 2017 for the fiftieth anniversary of the school, I was able to visit the almost-finished building. It was beautiful.

The second stage of the facilities plan was recently finished. It involved rebuilding and modernizing significant parts of the upper primary school. And twelve years after I left HKIS, the third part of our plan was launched on the Tai Tam campus. It is an extensive athletic and community facility that takes advantage of a good parcel of land that we finally received control of after years of petitioning the government. The last part of our plan was to rebuild the central core of the high school to give us a much better theater and other spaces.

From my admittedly distant vantage point of 2023, I question the wisdom of continuing to invest large sums at a time of such uncertainty about future developments in Hong Kong. The foreign expatriate population is already shrinking. If empty spaces are filled with Hong Kong students, the government, under the thumb of Beijing, might demand that HKIS provide them a "patriotic" education or even forbid their attendance. There is even the possibility that the atheist CCP could forbid international schools from having any religious or other international ties. That could finally force the issue of any LCMS links to the school.

There are a number of options. At the top of the list is following through on the church's request of 2005 to HKIS for monetary support. Perhaps the offer of a substantial donation might help lead to an agreement for formal separation and assuage any feeling that LCMS has "lost" an asset. Words and ways could be found to maintain a friendly Christian-to-Christian relationship, with full control and ownership clearly in the hands of the school board.

Since the American consulate general and the U.S. business community were all instrumental in establishing HKIS, not the LCMS alone, the three groups should gather to discuss and agree on a good future for the school now facing existential threats with the CCP takeover of Hong Kong.

We Sing Our Swan Song

Our final months in Hong Kong in 2010 were a blur. So many farewells. So many expressions of "thank you." So many promises to keep in touch.

The school's spring gala of hundreds of people was a nice occasion for us to share thoughts about our years in Hong Kong and association with

HKIS. Mitch, board chair, shared some very nice words of appreciation, as did others. I believe the positive reactions were genuine. The board had earlier hosted a farewell dinner. Many made a point of expressing appreciation that we had come back in service to the school during a difficult time.

Today, we feel good about our many years in Hong Kong both as diplomats and educators. We had good family time and many friends. We believe we contributed to providing an excellent education for thousands of young people. We helped grow Asia Society Hong Kong Center with its many links among cultures and countries. And we represented our country well and seriously, including building more bridges to understanding and collaboration between the United States and Asia.

Where to from here?

People were curious about where we were headed. If we said Reno, Nevada, many would express puzzlement. What's in Reno? If we said we were headed to the Lake Tahoe area, most would smile and tell us how beautiful the area was.

We were happy to explain that this next chapter of our lives revolved around family and the imminent arrival of our first grandchild in August. His parents happened to live in Reno, where Jonathan had founded Sierra Nevada Journeys, a non-profit outdoor science and experiential learning organization serving young people.

Our leaving did not feel like a retirement. We did not feel washed up. Rather, we felt exhilarating energy, pursuing our next adventure in the life of the Mueller family.

We spent our last night in Hong Kong in a hotel in Stanley. We were in bed when Claire suddenly sat up and exclaimed: We didn't say goodbye to Tommy, our favorite American Club staff member! We got dressed and took a taxi to the club. It was a heartfelt and personal moment.

The next morning Joy and Josephine sent us off to the airport with farewell hugs and waves.

Our trusty United 747 awaited to take us home again.

Nevada Becomes Our Latest Destination and Adventure

We were genuinely excited about our new home in northern Nevada and even more excited with the anticipation of Jackson's arrival at the end of August. Kim and Jonathan met us at the airport, took us to Rose's restaurant for luncheon sandwiches, and then straight to our home at 3760 Boulder Patch, Reno, Nevada.

It was a delight to move straight into our home in the Village of Monte Rosa which was already furnished and livable. We were right off the Mount Rose highway leading up to Lake Tahoe only twenty minutes away. The views all around, including Mount Rose to the west, and the sunsets were spectacular. I was particularly enthusiastic about my new den, converted from a stand-alone garage. It was a great place to work, giving Claire her space in the house and her den.

We set about helping Jon and Kim get ready for Jackson's arrival and getting to know our new surroundings. It was much like a new foreign service assignment. As it turned out, northern Nevada, Washoe County, and the nearby Sierra Nevada mountains had much appeal.

We also were about a three-and-a-half-hour drive to San Francisco, so we would be able to see Eric, Susan, and family often.

Jackson made his entrance on August 30, 2010! He was, of course, a delightful little boy. Claire and I dusted off our parenting skills and helped as best we could. Grandparenting is a notch more fun than parenting. As was caregiving for Mac and Athena, Jonathan's and Kim's beloved, aging dogs.

The follow-on weeks and months pretty much revolved around Jackson. These were new and happy routines for us. The first big challenge came a few months later when Kim and Jon were scheduled for a honeymoon visit to Europe for skiing. Kim had been nursing successfully. Would Jackson take a bottle from us? If he wouldn't, Kim was prepared to pull the plug on the trip. At almost the last minute the answer was: Yes! Kim and Jonathan went off happily for a good change of pace including skiing. We enjoyed our time with Jackson immensely.

Then came our big trip to San Francisco for Eric and Susan's wedding in October 2010. They chose Grandview Park in the Sunset District, with wonderful views of San Francisco, Golden Gate Bridge, and the Pacific Ocean. They asked Jonathan to officiate, which he did with aplomb and sensitivity. They were a good-looking couple. Coincidentally, as part of Fleet Week the U.S. Navy Blue Angels flew overhead as if to bless the event. We hung out for a while that afternoon, having fun, and then proceeded to a nice restaurant for dinner with the two families.

In addition to weddings and childcare responsibilities, I was on the lookout for interesting endeavors to challenge the mind.

One was joining the board of trustees of Chinese American International School in San Francisco (CAIS). Friends in Hong Kong had recommended me as a candidate for head of school. I met with the board chair for a good conversation. In the end, I demurred. It was time to take a break from the 24/7 routine. When they invited me to join the board instead, I was pleased to do so. They did not have any nonparent members, so they saw me as bringing alternative experiences and perspectives. It was another example of how a diverse decision-making body can be a stronger one. I was energized over subsequent years, working with talented and professional fellow trustees. The next years saw us heading regularly to San Francisco both for board meetings and to see Eric and Susan.

I was impressed with Jeff Bissell, whom the board subsequently hired to be head of school. He had extensive experience in China with excellent language skills. We got along well and, with the board, worked together to build CAIS and its Chinese language immersion program. We created a new mission statement for the school with clear values and goals and a strong emphasis on "good governance." I found that my nonparent status was an asset to bringing some of my experience to the board and its work.

I was directly associated with CAIS for the next twelve years. The school had continued to grow and improve under Jeff and the board's leadership to stand out nationally, with its noted Chinese immersion program. A huge, historic achievement came in 2020 as the COVID-19 pandemic spread: The Sisters of Mercy decided to sell their all-girls high school in San Francisco. We were eager to acquire it. We faced determined competition. To cut to the bottom line, board members and Jeff stepped up, did the analyses, created financial options, and met with the Sisters. In the end, we were successful. I was a strong supporter of stretching ourselves to make the deal. There is a much longer story to tell. Here, the important conclusion is that CAIS now has its "forever home," which it fully controls, rather than sharing space with French American International School. And we now have ample space for expansion and new programs.

CAIS has a bright future as it takes advantage of the opportunities ahead. Long-term leadership, as with Jeff's twelve years, demonstrates the great value of a steady hand on the tiller. Now, in 2023, CAIS must wrestle with two important challenges: 1) What can a well-funded independent school do, and what should it do, morally and practically, to support its broader community and the less well-off members of society? And 2) How will CAIS deal with the dangerous issue of deteriorating U.S.-China relations and the potential impact on admissions and on the school along with China's aggressive attacks on Chinese Americans and others who speak out critically against the PRC? I shared these views with trustees in much longer form. The board, as part of its responsibility to ensure long-term stability and success of the school, will need to dig into these questions.

I feel CAIS was another opportunity for me to contribute to the all-important education of young people in our country. Their learning was not just the Chinese language and the three Rs (reading, writing, and arithmetic), as critical as those are, but also the cross-cultural and global competence learning that comes with a good education.

I can't stress enough the importance to America of grappling with the critical need for improvement in all aspects of our educational systems. We must recruit our best and brightest to be educators, support them fully, and get politics out of the classroom and school board. Vibrant, healthy democracies, societies, economies, and political governance systems must rest firmly on an outstanding educational system *for all people.*

Back to 2010 in Reno. I was introduced to several former State Department and military professionals. We spoke the same language. U.S. Army Colonel (retired) Ty Cobb and I became good friends. He had also served in Vietnam. He started an organization called the National Security Forum, designed to educate the community on national security issues, and which brought speakers periodically to northern Nevada. Eventually, I worked with Ty to create the Forum as a nonprofit organization and joined the board, helping to create a set of governance documents and bylaws as the foundation of the organization.

I became the "China hand" who provided commentary and presentations on U.S.-China relations and developments in Asia. There were very few people in the area with a China background. My favorite presentation was playing the role of national security adviser to the CCP general secretary, analyzing United States actions and policies. I worked hard to put it in the vocabulary of a Chinese version of Marxist-Leninist ideology.

Wanting to help Jonathan out in any way I could, I agreed to join the board of trustees of his Sierra Nevada Journeys (SNJ) nonprofit education organization. Along with Ted Oleson, Jonathan founded SNJ a couple years earlier to provide outdoor science and technology education to younger children, particularly underserved students. I'm glad to say we worked together cooperatively while he worked to grow SNJ and plant deep roots. I will never forget the image of Jonathan, on one of his earlier visits to Hong Kong, sitting on Repulse Bay beach, creating his business plan for SNJ on the other side of the world. We were glad to be able to provide Jonathan and SNJ support as they learned to raise funds and establish a firm foundation.

SNJ began to gain altitude when Jonathan got to know the CEO of the Sierra Health Foundation in Sacramento, which owned a developed outdoor camp in the mountains, Grizzly Creek Ranch.

Jonathan and SNJ agreed to lease the camp and use it initially for summer, and later, year-round campers who came for science education as well as fun. Sierra Health had designed and built the camp to be able to serve kids with disabilities. Since then, Grizzly Creek has been at the heart of SNJ educational programs. We contributed to the capital campaign that just recently allowed SNJ to purchase the entire camp.

Claire and I were also on the lookout to meet and make friends with like-minded people in the area. We had some success. We also found that so many people, even those with whom we shared similar interests, already had full lives and calendars. Those with grandchildren and those who were still employed were among the most likely to be reticent to carve out time to invest in new friendships. It was a disappointing fact of life.

My advice to our friends and younger relatives is to make strong friendships in your school and working years. Work to keep them up, and then as you become a more "experienced citizen," as I have called ourselves, you might well find they remain reliable and good friends. We find that many friends whom we met and worked with many years ago are still those we consider among our closest friends.

During what turned out to be our three years in Reno, we were able to do a fair amount of travel to see our own country.

Claire and I took a trip to New England at the request of HKIS to pay calls on admissions directors of noted Ivy League and other universities. The goal was to share information about an HKIS education and keep the school on universities' radar screens. It was a successful and fun visit.

We took another trip through the southwest, including national parks in Utah, Nevada, and southern California. We loved the vast range of geologic formations and bold colors. Bryce Canyon is a treasure with its vast delicate stalagmite pillars. Zion National Park is different: huge mountain formations, which make visitors feel insignificant. It reminded me of the Chinese tradition of building vast complexes and huge structures (think Tiananmen Square and the Forbidden City) to make "the people" and foreigners feel unimportant in comparison to the power of the emperor and other rulers. We visited the Grand Canyon, Las Vegas, and friends in San Diego and Los Angeles. Highway 101 north along the coast to San Francisco is one of the world's great treasures.

We were getting a good view of our own country and its treasures as we had been doing for years abroad.

In 2011 we had a wonderful cross-country driving trip, stopping in Oklahoma to visit Deb and family; Churchill Downs in Louisville, and the Louisville Baseball bat factory where we purchased a specially made bat for Jackson; and other places. We arrived in Saratoga Springs, New York and met up with Kim and Jackson. Kim needed to spend a few workdays in London and couldn't manage it with Jackson. We had the fun of having him for a week. He was walking and very engaging. No problems missing his mother, fortunately. We also took him to Rhode Island to introduce him to Claire's family.

On the drive back west, we stopped to visit with Joanne and Chuck Dull in Sturgeon Bay, Wisconsin. Beautiful home right on Lake Michigan. They introduced us to Door County (the "New England of the West") and all its summer attractions of fish boils, art shows and galleries, wine bars, and brew pubs. We count Joanne and Chuck as best friends with whom we have kept in contact. Lots of common interests and good vibes among us.

Along the way home we stopped at Mount Rushmore for a view of the four presidents carved on the mountainside. Quite spectacular. Hard to imagine that kind of creation these days. Years later we laughed when the idea was bruited about by an acolyte to add Donald Trump's head to the collection.

At the end of the trip, I recall feeling much as I did after my long driving trip across the country in summer 1973 after our five-week Israeli Syrian disengagement shuttle diplomacy mission with Secretary of State Henry Kissinger. My trip then helped open my eyes to the vastness of the United States, its natural beauty, its history (good and bad), and the great diversity and often generosity and kindness of its peoples.

The highlight of the year was the wonderful news of the birth of our granddaughter on September 27, 2012, to Susan and Eric in San

Francisco—Katherine Elizabeth Mueller. She was our second grandchild, on the way to a total of seven by 2019.

Chapter Eight

Shanghai American School Comes Calling

In November 2012 I received a call from an international school recruiter I knew, Ralph Davidson, telling me about an interim head of school position at Shanghai American School (SAS). I perked up. "Tell me more," I said.

In a nutshell, the SAS board had decided not to renew the contract of its head of school. There was no time to find the right permanent head, so they sought a one-year interim head, beginning summer 2013.

I learned there was a complicated set of relationships on the board and some poor governance practices that had set off big fights in the community. The head of school, Kerry Jacobson, was well-liked and perceived as competent. Still, a slight majority of the board, led by the chair and his wife, wanted to oust Kerry and try their luck with an interim head. They were not sure who they were looking for, or what they wanted her/him to do, but someone with a China background and significant school leadership experience, like me, sounded right to them.

When the board moved not to renew Kerry's contract, it made a fatal mistake in not preparing the community. When their decision was announced, with little explanation for it, the community erupted. It was not pretty, with anger and confusion throughout the school. It also touched on ugly racial characterizations since the majority in the 5–4 vote was Chinese.

I told Ralph I was intrigued. I had experience dealing with community disruptions and governance failures. It sounded challenging, not something I shied away from. I would talk with Claire and get back to him.

The next step, if I decided to throw my hat in the ring, would be a digital interview and then a visit to Shanghai in January or February of 2013.

Claire, too, was intrigued. Jon and family had already left us to move to Golden, so that was one less reason for staying. We figured there was no reason not to pursue the opportunity to see where it would go.

Suffice to say, the interview went well enough for them to invite me to Shanghai. Our trusty United 747 awaited. In Shanghai I learned more details that fleshed out the history above. Kerry Jacobson was more than polite as well as direct with me: the chair of the board had assured him he would be offered a new contract. Shortly thereafter, the chair sprang the news of nonrenewal. It was a gut punch without explanation. No wonder the community reacted so harshly.

The board interviews were fine. Trustees were particularly interested in how I would pull the community together and improve educational programs. They liked hearing me talk about excellence in education. The chair was not much engaged and seemed disinterested. While still a candidate, I attended a board meeting that turned out to be a classic of confusion and incompetence. Trustees talked above and contradicted each other. One trustee, with some vehemence, pointed out two candidates were in attendance and that the board should get its act together.

Meetings and interviews continued for several days. By then I was familiar enough with such community gatherings that I knew what I wanted to say and what they wanted to hear. It turned out that my China experience and language combined with my diplomatic credentials and experience at Northfield Mount Hermon and Hong Kong International School hit the spot.

There were two other candidates. The board told us to go home, and they would be in touch. So, home again, home again.

Back in Reno, Claire continued to be intrigued with what life in Shanghai might be like. We would soon find out because the board called offering me the position.

Of course, our answer was an enthusiastic, "Yes!"

What a feeling. Three for three in applying successfully for head of school positions of three very large and complex schools, each with two campuses and each with its own governance and other challenges. Somehow, I had hit my stride.

The board offered a generous contract that helped to soothe any feeling of disruption of our lives and pulling up stakes from Reno. I recalled my father saying that when he went to the University of Alaska as dean, it was the first time he felt he had some financial security. The Great Depression had been a searing experience for him and my mother and then his Foreign Service career gave him and us a reasonable standard of living although far from a life of ease.

At the end of April, I flew to Shanghai to finalize the contract and to start the transition process. There was much to learn and decipher in dealing with the community. The good news was that voting for new board members that spring had brought in trustees who shared a desire to work with me to put the school on a new track.

One of those elected, York Chi Harder, became board chair and an invaluable ally in keeping the school on an improvement course. We worked closely for three years without serious disagreement. And she had the full respect of the community, which helped solidify the board's standing in making needed decisions. York Chi was from New York and a lawyer by profession, married to a lawyer, very active in the community, with one more child left about to graduate shortly from SAS.

While in Shanghai, Helene Reiter, human resources director, also became a strong supporter with her willingness to provide candid advice and move as firmly as necessary in dealing with difficult personnel issues. She also had experience dealing with the Chinese bureaucracy in getting needed approvals for visas, work permits, etc. Maria, my executive assistant from Malaysia, was similarly helpful, as she had developed connections with Chinese officials whom we needed to move our paperwork along. The Chinese system could be daunting and could often stonewall, so knowing individuals willing to help was a necessity.

An opaque and resistant Chinese bureaucracy was just the tip of the iceberg of serious governance issues in China, overlaid with corruption and personal self-dealing. Beijing's attempts to control corruption at lower levels often failed since the country was so large and "the emperor was far away."

Andy Torres would stay on as deputy head of school for one year. I appreciated his steady hand that helped calm the community and his creative ideas to move our educational program forward. Likewise, Jeff Rosen would stay as deputy head of the Pudong campus to provide continuity and stability. I became a fan of our new chief financial officer, Jorgen Hoeben, who was rock solid in his analyses and recommendations. We needed that in such a large and complex school with two campuses, with a budget of more than $100 million. I had interviewed him when I was still in Reno and liked what I heard. I was delighted that the board developed respect and trust in his work with me.

Jorgen's wife, Valerie, and Claire became friends. Years after first meeting, they still regularly play "Words with Friends" via the internet.

On the home front, before we moved to Shanghai, we were overjoyed to welcome the birth of granddaughter Clara Elizabeth Mueller on April 15, 2013, in Boulder, Colorado.

Our Tenure Begins . . . .

On our way to Shanghai in June 2013, we stopped in San Francisco to spend wonderful quality time with Eric's and Jonathan's families. We rented a house in Cole Valley and enjoyed a great family reunion.

Claire and I arrived in Shanghai in early July after deciding to rent out our furnished house. At that point, we fully expected to be back in a year. In Shanghai, we moved into a nice two-story apartment rented by the school for us in the Shanghai Racquet Club. It was in a quiet and green compound. That month the temperatures went sky-high, slowing the city considerably. For comfort, Chinese men switched to tee shirts and tied them up to expose their midriffs for some coolness. The international press latched on to the story. When shopping for furniture at Ikea, we laughed at the number of people who had gone to shop but instead stretched out on the beds and chairs in the cool air conditioning. Store employees were sympathetic: let sleeping shoppers lie!

In the next months we explored our two campuses, Puxi—west of the Pu River—and Pudong—east of the Pu River. They were at least an hour's drive apart, so learning to work in the car was imperative. We learned to fully trust Xiao Lin, our driver, who kept us safe during our entire time in Shanghai.

Xiao Lin also took us on tours of different sections of the city to orient us. We were seriously taken aback at experiencing the most modern of cities and transportation corridors (highways and subways) throughout. When we visited Shanghai a couple times while at the U.S. Liaison Office in Beijing in 1976–1978, the city often had the effect of a ghost town. Back then, standing on the Bund by the Huang Pu River, looking east, there was nothing on the opposite bank but warehouses, small piers, and farms.

Our visit to Shanghai from Hong Kong while at HKIS in 2006 introduced us in person to vast economic development. Now in 2013, not only was the eastern bank fully developed with huge buildings, with the second tallest in the world going up, but the entire area out to the ocean had been built up, with even the new main airport built out to the east. It was a phenomenal history, which we were of course aware of, but experiencing it was even more impressive.

Of course, we knew of the many far poorer people in various quarters of the city foreigners didn't often visit. They included marginalized migrants who lived on the outskirts and worked in the city but had few rights to education, homes, or medical care. Too many foreigners see only the tall buildings and unicorn billionaires and huge companies and thus assume everyone is well off. It was another example of how difficult and even dangerous it is to generalize about developments in China.

As we prepared for the opening convocation with faculty and staff and the start of school, it sank in that I had a lot more to learn about the school. I had had experience with NMH and HKIS and so had a head start on understanding traditions and even knowing staff, but with SAS I had a much steeper learning curve. I would have to work hard at learning.

The next weeks saw the expected and dizzying opening of school rituals and traditions in the classroom, divisions, and campuses, and even at the very top, namely the board of trustees and head of school. I tried to be everywhere all at once to cheer everyone on.

The board had scheduled a retreat to create cohesiveness and momentum after the last year's turmoil. We invited Ralph Davidson, our executive recruiter, who, along with York Chi and me, orchestrated discussions about good governance. We stimulated discussion of trustees' hopes and anxieties. With new members joining and divisive ones stepping down, I judged we did a reasonably good job of laying the groundwork for better working relationships.

The board also seized the issue of bringing head of school candidates to campus in the coming weeks. Helene orchestrated the travels and rituals around interviews. A very promising candidate whom I knew dropped out at the last moment. She wasn't ready to move halfway around the world. The remaining candidates arrived and were put through their paces.

When asked what I thought of them, I said the honest answer was that while each had good qualities, none seemed to fit the bill of a longer-term head of school of this huge and complex institution. It turned out many trustees had similar reservations.

I slowly came to the idea of making my contract a three-year one rather than one-year. That would give the school longer to heal and to decide whom they wanted as their long-term head. Claire and I discussed the possibility and agreed I should tell the board I would be willing to stay longer. We were enjoying Shanghai and were settling in well so far. I told York Chi we were willing to stay to get the school onto a good track. She was intrigued and planted the idea with the board.

Shortly after, the board, with what turned out to be enthusiasm, offered me a three-year contract in October. The community could exhale because I was now a semi-known commodity. And it solved the problem of finding, under pressure, yet more candidates and handling yet another transition with all that that entailed.

I'm happy to say there was a welcome reaction from both campuses. The reaction from the home front, namely, Jonathan's and Eric's families, was likewise welcoming. Asia was a part of the world they would enjoy visiting again over the next three years.

It was only natural that in a $100 million institution with over three thousand students on two campuses, the issues for discussion and resolution would come at us fast and furiously.

You might ask about the tradeoffs in priorities heads of school must make every day. Many times I regretted having to attend to non-classroom issues at the expense of interacting with students.

A classroom teacher enjoys day-to-day, hour-by-hour, direct interaction with young people. It can be the most satisfying job on the planet. It can command respect from the community. In China and Asia, teachers were historically accorded respect and held in societal high esteem. I found that to be generally true, even in international schools like HKIS and SAS. Unfortunately, in so many U.S. school systems, teachers are burdened with political fights in the community, a straitjacket "teach to the test" requirement, relatively low pay and benefits, and are often subjected to the latest new teaching "innovation."

I often told teachers that one of my principal jobs was to *keep the wolves away,* so teachers could teach the way they needed to and receive the support and recognition they deserved.

So, I reluctantly share with you that I had less contact with students than I wanted. We did go frequently to athletic events, music and drama presentations, community events, classroom events, and many others. We were recognized by parents, faculty, and many students. Still, it was not the type of close involvement in the direct teaching and learning as experienced by classroom teachers. This was not a surprise, but it was still disappointing.

I unequivocally respect the work of those classroom teachers. A strong and healthy society results only when its educators are among its "best and brightest."

It's also self-evident that good school leaders must deal with those big issues out there. They are usually the basis of a good institutional foundation that makes it possible to hire and retain excellent teachers, put in place an excellent curriculum, and in turn provide excellent student learning.

Here are a few of the issues I wrestled with as I settled into SAS.

—What would be some of my top messages to the school community in the coming months? *The first message* was:

"It's all about our students!" I wanted to emphasize to everyone that we were there to support and educate our students. Virtually nothing was a higher priority. Hiring the right faculty, providing a challenging curriculum, and constantly asking how issues could be decided to support students, first and foremost, were critically important.

The second message concerned the making of a strong and cohesive community, something we were working to create in the wake of the recent fiasco of adult infighting that roiled the community and ignored the impact on students. I was a fan of Roland Barth at Harvard University and frequently quoted from his book *Improving Schools from Within.* He had consulted with us at NMH. I repeatedly emphasized a key passage:

"My years in schools suggest that the quality of adult relationships within a school has more to do with the quality and character of the school and with the accomplishments of students than any other factor. In too many schools, personal relationships tend to be adversarial relationships: teacher against student, teacher against teacher, principal against teacher, and school people against parents. The most memorable schools I visit are ones that have begun to find ways of transforming these adversarial and "parallel play" relationships into cooperative and collegial coalitions." Roland Barth, Improving Schools from Within: Teachers, Parents, and Principals Can Make the Difference (San Francisco, CA: Jossey-Bass 1991): 163.

This message reinforced my own observations and experiences over many years. Collaborative and supportive relationships make students happier to come to school and work for common ends. Many people at SAS told me they agreed with the wisdom of these ideas. I kept repeating them as we rebuilt collaborative and productive relationships.

—Educational excellence. How would we address the issue of educational excellence for all students? A start was to embed within the institution a senior, empowered educational leader and a network of those who would work specifically with principals and faculty on curriculum alignment and in other ways to keep the focus throughout the school on *student learning.* We had curriculum "coordinators," but they did not have the authority to compel needed change. With Andy's help, we designed a network to do so, headed by a forceful deputy head of school, a new position. The board was initially skeptical about a new senior position, but I was able to convince them this would help move us in the direction they wanted. During the hiring season we found an excellent candidate, Jennifer Weyburn, who started the next year. She had deep educational experience, as well as work experience in China.

—We created our guiding "Themes and Priorities"—medium-term academic program and operational priorities. At the end of my first year, I put together an outline of our school priorities and how we would address them. The senior leadership liked them, added ideas, and then we presented them at the board retreat in August. The piece engendered good discussion about how we would be investing our time and resources in the coming years. I called the document "Our Themes and Priorities," focusing on:

- Building Educational Excellence: Build educational excellence in learning and teaching so students are challenged to learn to their maximum potential.

- Building Community: Build a strong community of educators, parents, and students.

- Building for the Future: Plan and build for our future.

Each section listed numerous specifics answering the question: "How will we do this?"

—Reaccreditation Committee of the Western Association of Schools and Colleges. Who would lead the effort to pull together the data and study needed for our upcoming accreditation review, an important periodic process to document the efficacy of the school's educational approach? Andy volunteered to take the lead and spent countless hours with the school's committee in a herculean effort to complete our input, which included our strategic priorities for the next few years.

We also used the process to address important questions around the past year's turmoil and the governance process overseen by the board. We needed to have the visiting committee understand and talk to the board about how to ensure that all future board actions would be in accordance with acceptable governance practices. The meeting in the spring was a useful placing of markers by the visiting committee to the board, building on previous warnings to the SAS Board in earlier years about its unacceptable approach to good governance. The accreditation team can recommend suspension of a school's accreditation if educational standards are being undermined—a clear negative signal to the community about school quality.

I'm happy to say our committee did a superb job, and we earned kudos from the accreditation team the next spring.

Lastly, a footnote. In many ways the Foreign Service and international education share similarities, in particular the regular movement to new "assignments" in countries in different parts of the world and regular path-crossing with good colleagues.

A case in point in Shanghai. An education colleague, Tim Carr, was head of the visiting accreditation committee. He and I started our careers as heads of school together in 1998 in the new heads' orientation session in Wellesley. Coincidentally, he chaired the visiting accreditation committee to HKIS when I was head of school and had to deliver similar admonitions to board and LCMS representatives for their "out of bounds" actions. Tim had to leave Shanghai early to return to his school to deal with Indonesian arrests of school staff, a series of actions that roiled the community and went on for several years.

—Building bridges to the surrounding community. What Tim dealt with in Indonesia was another example of life and work in another country and being subject to their laws and practices, no matter how outlandish or even dangerous. In Indonesia, the local authorities maintained that they had special "stones" that communicated to them actions of school employees.

Heads of school need to be continually attentive to surrounding cultures, laws, and governance practices that can aid or hinder the school's mission. Heads have the critical responsibility of building solid and positive relationships with local communities. If they do not, they leave their institution potentially much more vulnerable to adverse events or people who do not wish the school well.

What was true for international schools was also true for independent schools in the United States. I found that out at NMH, which was located in three different political jurisdictions. I worked hard to get to know the elected and other officials in each town so that we could more naturally work together as issues arose. Every Christmas Claire and I invited to Ford Cottage all those officials to a holiday gathering. They appreciated it, and one told me it was meaningful because it was the only time, every year, they all saw each other!

I also attended periodic town council meetings, a New England tradition. One evening I listened to the police chief of the town of Gill present his report on the performance of his office. He was questioned by an angry citizen. Amid the resulting turmoil, a man stood up and asked to speak. He said he was a scientist working at the nearby fish hatchery. He wanted to tell American citizens he hoped they appreciated their freedoms, in particular, for that evening's questioning of the police chief. "In my home, in Palestine, no one would dare cross swords with the police chief!" He received a warm round of applause.

The director of public works sitting next to me leaned over and asked, "Do you know why the lady doing the questioning was so upset?" I said I didn't. "She was mad because the police chief had pulled over her son for drunk driving," he told me!

At SAS we needed to make sure we knew and understood Chinese officials. As I learned more about Shanghai, it was clear that we needed to build better ties with the surrounding communities of both our Puxi and Pudong campuses. I shared with senior administrators my experience in how the Chinese governance system worked with interwoven CCP and government officials at most levels. With the help of a Chinese member of our staff (who was a CCP member), we identified key CCP and government officials with responsibility covering both Puxi and Pudong campuses. We came up with a game plan to invite them to visit each campus, have lunch, and introduce them to our educational practices.

Not only were most of them interested in learning more, they were also eager to arrange for their principals and faculty members to visit and understand international schools' approaches to education. In an interesting aside at one lunch, a visiting principal told me that one of the weaknesses of China's educational system was that there were just too many rules and regulations, which inhibited them from the type of creativity and experimentation she saw in our school.

With a senior Puxi official, we hit pay dirt: she was a former teacher and educator, particularly interested in building bridges. We found that while officials remained discreet, they would periodically drop hints and suggestions of policies being considered or not considered or which levels of government (local, municipal, national) were interested in what issues. Often, they suggested how to cut through red tape or with whom to liaise, for example, when we were unexpectedly notified of construction of a huge underground traffic tunnel just outside our Puxi gates that impinged on our campus.

We reached what I thought was a high point in my third year in 2016, when we dedicated a wonderful, newly completed theater on the Pudong campus. We put together a broad range of music and orchestral groups for an evening of performance and invited a range of local officials. Almost all came. I welcomed them in Chinese and described our continuing interest in building bridges and good relationships.

I can still see them sitting, smiling, and nodding in agreement. I was told afterwards that we had hit a home run in reaching out to these individuals.

A final, obvious observation. While all the officials were part of a Communist system, one I deeply disliked, they were not automatons or robots. They could still be very human and were not infrequently willing to respond to expressions of friendship. Fast forward to 2023, and I wonder how attitudes are changing almost ten years into Xi Jinping's policies of turning inward with concomitant skepticism of the West and the United States in particular. Without doubt those same officials are needing to be even more careful in their relationships with foreigners.

I also got to know the American consul general, Robert Griffiths, who some years before had written many of the school's bylaws. He and his wife were generous in including us in consulate general events. His deputy sat on our board. They were extremely supportive of the school, which at one point was housed in the garden of the consulate general after it reopened in the 1970s. It had originally been founded in 1912. A new consul general, Hanscom Smith, and his new deputy, Gwen Cardno, were similarly supportive. Gwen served on our board of trustees and was an active and engaged member. Hanscom subsequently moved to Hong Kong to become consul general. We corresponded frequently in the next three years about my favorite city. Coincidentally, it turned out that Gwen was the daughter of our good friends in the Foreign Service, Lynn and

Diane Pascoe. Lynn was a China hand and colleague who served with me in the Executive Secretariat. A small world, indeed.

Consulate General personnel were helpful in plugging us into our surrounding communities and sharing their observations. I also became involved with the American Chamber of Commerce, whose members worked all over China and frequently provided useful insights into developments. At one point the consul general helped me invite our ambassador in Beijing, Max Baucus, and his staff to a small luncheon at SAS to discuss China and U.S.-China relations. Before the lunch I gathered four students to meet and chat with the ambassador. I was impressed that he kept pushing me to share my experiences with China over the decades, rather than just lecturing me on his views.

This was all part of my desire to be a leader who did the necessary things, on and off campus, to allow the faculty and students to do what they do best: teaching and learning.

—Finances and declining enrollment. Shanghai American School was a well-resourced school. Money was generally available for worthwhile projects, even for the expensive, modern theater and music center I described above on the Pudong campus. Both campuses were modern and functional and the envy of many other schools. The issue we began to wrestle with during the 2013–2014 year was the beginning of a decline in applications to the Pudong campus. As we tracked the decline, it became evident that senior business executives were departing, sometimes to be replaced by a Chinese executive but often not replaced at all. The business climate for foreigners was souring and many firms could no longer justify the financial cost of an expatriate executive. Companies also shifted operations outside of China, citing an increasingly unfriendly business climate.

We needed to plan for reductions in enrollment and consequent reductions in employees. Such are never easy. Still, we grasped the nettle and over three years planned and carried out three rounds of downsizing. Jorgen, Helene, and others were masterful in proposing options and pathways for getting to our new goal each year. Planned enrollment when I first arrived was about 3,300 on two campuses. At the end of my tenure, we were planning for about 2,800 students.

I insisted that we be totally upfront with the community. Transparency in how we planned to make our adjustments was essential for keeping up morale. Faculty whose contracts were not renewed deserved to be treated with respect.

I also insisted that we look for reductions and adjustments on both campuses, not just Pudong. It was important to keep Pudong functioning and thriving. Interestingly, Puxi was filled and was the campus of choice for many Chinese families, partly because there was a critical mass of students from Chinese-speaking parts of the world that lived in the Puxi area. The PRC government had changed the rules about attendance at international schools. The student must hold a passport of a country other than the PRC. The government was not willing to allow international educators to educate a Chinese citizen. In years gone by there had been ways for PRC students to enroll, but the government had closed off that option. It also closed off the infamous Chinese *zou hou men* ("going through the back door") to gain admission or get things done.

—Creating a new school legal foundation. On arrival I learned that the full legal basis under Chinese law was under review by the Shanghai authorities. First, we would have to re-register as a Wholly Owned Foreign Entity (I laughed when learning it was pronounced "woofy" for short), but we first had to create a legal entity in the state of Delaware that would be our sponsor. Second, we needed to align that sponsor with Chinese law and, to ensure clear ownership, have all SAS trustees also serve on the Delaware Board. Third, we made some changes to our existing bylaws to align with China's required rules and policies. That was tricky, to say the least, but we got it done.

I'm happy to say that with hard and sustained work by the senior team, it was all approved by the Shanghai education authorities and the Civil Affairs Bureau. That work should keep the school's solid foundation under the Chinese system for the foreseeable future. It made the onerous work of getting there all worthwhile.

—Updating SAS internal governance and bylaws. In parallel with the new legal basis, we worked to update our internal governance policies, for example, adding two appointed members to the board, revising and simplifying the trustee election process, and changing the title of "superintendent" to "head of school." We had an intense education process for the community so they would understand what we proposed and why. In the end, we had a good majority vote in favor.

I was still not a fan of elected boards, whether for public schools or independent schools. In theory it might be a good idea. In practice parents often run for school board positions for the wrong reasons, e.g., to carry out a political objective, to be seen as an important presence in the community, or to gain the right to choose whichever teachers one wants for one's children or maybe get a better college recommendation for them.

—A new high school design center and maker space. In my second year we authorized four million dollars to completely rebuild Puxi High School science and other spaces. These would provide a state-of-the-art center for design, collaboration, and "maker" spaces. It gave students new opportunities to work with each other to create projects and experiment with different ways of making things and learning. It was part of an educational wave of the future.

We Explore Shanghai and Surrounding Areas

Our driver often drove us to historic sites and museums. Shanghai had invested heavily in museums and other cultural and historical attractions. I loved the small Photography Museum and tried to grapple with the overwhelming size of the China Art Museum. The Shanghai Art Museum housed a vast range of Chinese treasures. One could easily spend hours visiting. Another truly spectacular museum was the Shanghai Natural History Museum, opened in 2015. Both the architecture and the exhibits were compelling. Not surprisingly, modern technology intruded: on a rest break, a bench full of Chinese students in uniform were all staring at their smart phones and not the surrounding lifelike exhibits of extinct animals!

The Maritime Museum was particularly fascinating, of course featuring a full-sized replica of Ming Dynasty's "Admiral" Zheng He's long-range seafaring vessels. Zheng He sailed at least to the east coast of Africa, spreading Chinese influence and accepting tribute for the Chinese emperor. The Ming emperor ultimately banned all such voyages. Apparently, China had everything its people needed without such far-flung voyages. Such is the historical narrative surrounding Zheng He, whether fully true or not, created by succeeding Chinese generations to show how China received recognition of its powerful and central role from other rulers.

Hangzhou in the spring was a particularly lovely visit, as was Suzhou. All Chinese know the expression: "Above is heaven and below is SuHang (Suzhou and Hangzhou)." Those cities were deemed by Chinese as among the best. And Suzhou women were fabled to be among the most beautiful. Suzhou and its many gardens were genuinely spectacular. We school "administrators" loved the garden we thought was dedicated to us and known as the "Humble Administrators' Garden!"

The new I.M. Pei art museum in Suzhou, with its clean, white lines of architecture, was captivating. We experienced another example of ordinary Chinese courtesy: as we waited in line to enter the museum, two ladies came over and invited us to the head of the line. We said we were happy to wait our turn. No, they insisted they wanted foreign guests to feel welcome. We accepted their hospitality with thanks. That was neither the first nor last time that we experienced hospitality and friendship from Chinese people. It's a tradition of welcoming those from far away.

We also drove to many other destinations around the Shanghai area on weekends, particularly ancient towns along the many rivers and the "Grand Canal." Each was interesting, with many small shops, cafes, and often art galleries. People were friendly. A favorite visit was to an "art village" with overwhelming numbers of small galleries. In one of them we found and bought what is now one of our favorites: an unusual perspective of one of those river towns.

Tan Dun—"Water Heavens" Music Performance

One afternoon, at the invitation of the world-renowned musician and composer, Tan Dun, and his wife, whose child attended SAS, we drove to Zhujiajiao town in Qingpu District. We strolled along the river and then were greeted by Tan Dun at his purpose-designed music venue (a rebuilt old house on the river). He described how he rebuilt the house and composed his music. It sat across the river from a Buddhist Monastery, whose bells he incorporated into the program. It was a spectacular sunset/evening performance involving Chinese and Western instruments with water as a pervasive theme. It was truly a unique experience with great enthusiasm and energy from all the performers. Here's an excerpt from the program announcement:

> On a water-filled stage, Bach will dialogue with Buddhist monks, rock'n'roll will give way to strings and pipa duets, with water percussions reeling the audience with their virtuoso, climaxing pace throughout.
>
> An eclectically unique architectural style mixes traditional

Ming and minimalist Bauhaus characteristics in the performance hall. Designed by Tan Dun himself with Isozaki Studio Architects, the building acts as instrument too.

As we enter, we have the feeling that time has stopped, in a space where the sacred meets the unconventional.

Here's how Tan Dun described his vision:

One day I was walking along the riverbank in Zhujiajiao when I stopped to listen to the monks' chants from the temple across the river... what a beautiful moment. In this very tranquility I had a vision, it was as if in this sacred chant I was listening to Bach's melodies. At the core of this vision was the harmony between people and nature, East and West, which would become the central theme running through the architecture and music concept of the Water Music Hall. I wanted to let the river flow in and out the music hall, to create a strong metaphor where in a space that transcends time the audience's hearts and minds would be washed clean and purified.

Richard's question prompted by Tan Dun's vision: could we, citizens of the twenty-first century, find a way to put aside our antagonisms and differences and build a new vision of humankind based on appreciating our differences—cultural, historical—and working together for a peaceful world for all?

We Have Good Family Experiences and Visits Around Asia

An unexpected highlight of our time in Shanghai was the travel Claire and I were able to undertake. I include the destinations below as examples of the many opportunities we've had to observe and learn about other cultures and peoples. And of course, to share many of these experiences with grandchildren who might follow in some of our footsteps.

—For Christmas 2013 we invited both Jonathan's and Eric's families to join us in Kota Kinabalu in Sabah in East Malaysia. The Tanjung Aru was on a beautiful beach and a perfect place to stay to bond with Jackson and Katherine. We also flew to Gunung Mulu National Park, a fascinating protected rain forest. We walked at length and made our way along an elevated walkway, giving us an unusual view of the interior of a rain forest. A highlight was waiting outside the Deer Cave for huge numbers of bats to stream out at dusk. Estimates are that two to three million bats live in the cave and leave at dusk to find food. It was an amazing sight as we watched an endless stream of them flying out. As I write this years later, amidst the COVID-19 pandemic likely caused by bats in China, I recall the Deer Cave bats and wonder how many of them might also carry pathogens deadly to humans.

—For Christmas 2014 Jonathan and family met us in Thailand on the island of Cosa Mui. Eric and family were not able to join us. It was a good vacation with beach time, games, sampling restaurants, and driving around the island.

—For Christmas 2015 we met up with Jonathan and family in Kona, on the big island of Hawaii. Much fun with the kids on the beaches and exploring various historic sites. The Kona Brewing company and Lava Java bar/restaurant by the ocean were highlights along with the extensive Asian artwork featured in the nearby Hilton Hotel.

We also visited cities for international school conferences and personal travel at school vacation time:

—Kaohsiung, Taiwan, which we last visited on a trip in 1975 while at the Chinese language school in Taichung. Southern Taiwan was and is the stronghold of those who consider themselves Taiwanese, rather than mainlanders (or the Kuomintang). But over recent years, more and more people on Taiwan have become less and less interested in joining the PRC Marxist-Leninist state without democracy Taiwan currently enjoys.

—Bangkok, Thailand, the liveliest and most energy-infused city we know of.

—Two trips to Kota Kinabalu, Malaysia, where we always caught up with educator friends and exhaled.

—Singapore, Claire's stomping ground early in her foreign service career. The city has grown and expanded enormously. As China and Hong Kong became less hospitable to business, many companies moved their operations south. It still had the look of a clean and well-ordered city. We had a celebratory lunch and Singapore Sling (a cocktail invented at the Raffles) at the Raffles Hotel we both had stayed at in earlier days. We still did not catch a glimpse of Somerset Maugham sitting in the garden writing. The orchid garden was a highlight.

—Hong Kong in 2014, where we took the political temperature of the city as Occupy Hong Kong and the Umbrella Revolution (aka the Umbrella Movement) played out on the streets. We saw many old friends, visited HKIS, and were the guests for lunch of the American consul general at our old haunt, the residence at 3 Barker Road. We were reminded of why it has been our favorite city over the years with its truly unique blend of cultures: Cantonese, southern and northern Chinese, Western, British, Indian, Christian, Buddhist, Muslim, and many others.

—Cambodia, Siem Riep and Angkor, still one of the most stupendous civilizations we have visited. In addition to enjoying the conference, we made a point of visiting our favorite temples. A photographer's paradise.

—Hanoi, Vietnam, the capital of the enemy that France, and then America and South Vietnam, fought for years and then lost to. When walking the streets of Hanoi and observing people and bustling businesses, buying Vietnamese paintings, and attending a traditional Vietnamese water puppet show, I marveled at the course of history. As with Germany and Japan after World War II, the wheel had turned and now with one eye on China, we were building a new relationship with a former enemy, despite its Communist form of government we had sought to destroy. Ironic, isn't it?

The Vietnamese, for their part, also with one eye on China, wanted the economic and political support of the United States. Their economy was expanding quickly and becoming a manufacturing hub for American supply chains such as shoes, textiles, and garments. The majority of Vietnamese were born after our withdrawal in 1975 so had little direct experience of the war, as brutal as it had been.

In Hanoi we visited the lake into which John McCain, who years later became presidential candidate McCain, parachuted after his A-4 Skyhawk flown off the USS *Forrestal* was shot down. We saw the marker put up by the Vietnamese saying that McCain, U.S. Air Force, was captured in this lake. Later, McCain said he resented being identified as U.S. Air Force. In fact, he was U.S. Navy!

We stayed at our favorite hotel from the French colonial days with lovely Vietnamese decor, the Metropole. It had more character than almost any other hotel we knew. A factoid: air raid tunnels under the hotel sheltered guests when U.S. bombers passed overhead during the war. Folk singer Joan Baez was one of those guests in December 1972 when she and a delegation of "peace activists" stayed for a week. I still recall when I was working in the secretary of state's office in Washington that she was labeled a traitor for visiting the enemy. A month later the Paris Peace accords were signed. We learned she had visited the Metropole for a week in 2013 after the tunnels had been excavated and opened again. It was her first visit to Vietnam in forty years.

—Vientiane, Laos where we saw up close the increasing and unstoppable Chinese influence. Sadly, we had no time to visit Luang Prabang, which I had experienced as a quiet and beautiful backwater when visiting in 1970 from Saigon. I took one of my favorite pictures on top of a hill of three Buddhist monks contemplating the sunset. Luang Prabang was now a favorite tourist destination for its beautiful setting and its numerous Buddhist temples. In Vientiane we crossed paths, totally coincidentally, with our old friend Jane Lincoln. She was with a tour group visiting Laos and Southeast Asia. Another example of our planet: a small, small world.

I should add that we made it back to the United States a couple of times a year. A January trip would focus on faculty recruitment at hiring fairs and a summer trip to see family and exhale. While you might think we disengaged from the school, the reality was that school still occupied my thoughts and communications virtually every hour of every day. Email and smartphones kept me in touch continuously (for better or for worse).

Stay Longer at Shanghai American School—or Head Home Again?

As we got deeper into the 2014–2015 school year, some trustees began to encourage us to stay on for a couple more years beyond our three-year contract to provide continuity and continued momentum. York Chi said she would support our staying. The logic made sense and, truth be told, a part of me was interested. I felt comfortable with my relationships with trustees, faculty, and parents. I was sure we were on a good track of stewarding the school. And there was still far more for us to experience of Shanghai, China, Asia, and the world.

At the same time, we felt far from home and from our extended family, particularly our grandchildren.

In the end, Claire and I decided we had done our part to launch SAS on that new track. We were now in our early seventies, even though in good health. It was time to head home. Jonathan and family had settled into Golden, Colorado, and they encouraged us to come join them. Eric and family were still firmly rooted in San Francisco. The die was cast. Besides, could we not assume our trusty United 747 would be there for future trips?!

The board set in motion a broad search for my successor, both an exciting and onerous process. There were some good candidates around the world. Who wouldn't want to lead a large, excellent international school in China? Marcel Gautier, one of my deputies, threw his hat in the ring. I supported him with the board. He knew the school, was supportive of the directions in which we were headed and had the right personal characteristics to be a successful leader even though this would be his first head of school position. The board agreed. We would have many months together to cooperate on a smooth transition.

York Chi and the board were gracious in our final months to host a large farewell gathering for us, where many nice words were said. Students presented souvenirs and pictures. I believe there was a genuine sense that Claire and I had been good stewards of the school for our three years, had rejuvenated it and set it off on a good course.

Commencement and Our Homecoming

Commencement for our students in 2016 also marked the commencement of Claire's and my fifth and final retirement from active employment.

Every year at SAS we held two commencements for graduates, one for Puxi High School and one for Pudong High School.

In my three years and six commencements at SAS I handed out 990 diplomas to graduating seniors. At HKIS I handed out 1384 diplomas and at NMH 2,392 diplomas. All for a grand total of 4,766. I count all those graduates as proud representatives of three schools for which I had been responsible. We were sending well-educated young people around the world—imbued with good moral character, hopefully—destined to make our world—our "Pale Blue Dot" as Carl Sagan called it—a better planet.

A light-hearted note: today, our Colorado Public Radio played Sir Edward Elgar's Pomp and Circumstance March No.1—the music played (repeatedly) at virtually all high school graduations as students march in. Later, we listen to it again as they march out. I must have heard it thousands of times over the years. As a well-trained head of school, as the music began this morning, I felt an almost out-of-body experience as I rose on cue and then for the next few minutes marched several times around our living and family rooms. No diplomas to hand out or receive, but there were lots of good memories and smiles. Claire could only stare in amusement and wonder as her husband showed signs of finally heading into his dotage.

Back to Shanghai. At each one of these six SAS commencements, I shared a few words instead of having a formal outside speaker. My remarks were based on a theme of "Take Care." An excerpt:

Whatever careers or other paths you choose, I hope they allow you to reflect on the power of the ideas and values of the SAS mission statement, our core values, our EAGLES [the school mascot]. Such ideals as integrity, lifelong learning, passion, compassion, pursuing your dreams, and cross-cultural understanding will all help guide you in coming years.

It's up to you, the class of 2016 and those who come after you, to make a positive difference in another person's life, every day; and, in many persons lives, every day. My generation is rapidly handing the baton to you and cheering you on. Do not let anyone convince you that you cannot do it or should not do it. This is not a guilt trip. It's the opening of a door and an offer of a wonderful opportunity. That's my heartfelt plea.

Now just a simple request, one I've made of previous graduating classes. Just three words: Please take care.

Please take care of others who are less fortunate or who need a kind word or a helping hand. Please take care of our earth and all its creatures and inhabitants. And please, take care of yourself in this fast-paced, anxious, tempting, demanding—and yes, fascinating—world.

Have you ever stopped to think that with modern medicine progressing so rapidly that you have a good chance to live well past one hundred years of age—on into the twenty-second century? If you are eighteen now, you may have eighty-two years or more ahead of you. Hard to imagine, isn't it? You will do many things along the way. Make them good things!

So, work hard, be gentle with yourself every day, and save some energy for the twenty-second century.

That's my simple request.

Please take care of others.

Please take care of our earth.

Please take care of yourself.

Chapter Nine

A View from Shanghai: We Experienced a Rapidly Changing China as U.S-China Relations Hit a Slippery Slope

Before we pick up the narrative in San Francisco and Colorado, here are a few thoughts about China and our experience of it over many decades, including most recently from the ground up in Shanghai.

As we settled into Shanghai in 2013, it was clear from a "rice roots" perspective that China had continued to make progress in reducing poverty around the country by hundreds of millions of people. That progress was commendable, particularly when you understand that for so many years the Chinese people suffered under brutal conditions of poverty, political violence, famine, the Great Leap Forward, the Cultural Revolution, and social disruption. They did it with hard work, a lighter hand of control from the CCP and international economic ties. Still, there remained hundreds of millions of Chinese who were waiting to move up the income curve and come closer to a living standard enjoyed by so many fellow citizens.

What were some of the factors that led to such admirable improvement?

Do not underestimate the critical role international connections and relations played in China's impressive development, starting with the United States.

It's worth recalling that the United States' willingness to support China in the early 1970s was a game changer for China – and us. It was at a time when China and the USSR engaged in military confrontation along the Amur River in Northeast China. China also feared the Soviet Union had created a plan to attack and destroy the PRC's budding nuclear capabilities. Whether the Soviets would have launched an attack will never be known, but the Chinese leadership was sufficiently convinced of the threat that Mao was willing to turn to the long-mocked "paper tiger," namely, the United States. We were ready to respond.

That political opening has led to a sustained and substantial economic and trade relationship serving both countries and the world. What made a difference? Wide open markets in the United States and Europe; deep factory production experience from the United States, Taiwan, Japan, Korea, Germany; vast sums of investment from the United States, Hong Kong, Taiwan, Europe, Korea, and overseas Chinese; importation of a wide range of technology for computers, communications, manufacturing, energy and natural resource exploration, and many others. Russia over the years has contributed technology, military and otherwise.

For years the consensus was that the United States could not afford to keep its borders fully open for an economy like China's for an export-led development strategy, as we had for Japan and the Asian tigers of Korea, Taiwan, Hong Kong, and much of Southeast Asia. In fact, we did keep our trade borders open to China, particularly after we and the World Trade Organization extended "Permanent Normal Trade Relations," formerly called "Most Favored Nation" treatment, in 2000. We did it even though China was not close to becoming a market economy. We did it with an expectation that its trajectory was taking it to a more open economy and that doing so could lead to improving relations with us and the rest of the world.

China of course also contributed to its rapid economic growth.

Importantly, Deng Xiaoping's leadership in 1978 of "reform and opening up" loosened up restrictions on economic and social life. China was to develop a "socialist market economy." Farmers in Sichuan took more control of what they planted and were allowed to sell on the open market. Nian Guangjiu in the early 1980s, knowing of the Chinese love of sunflower and other melon seeds, started the Idiot Melon Seed Company. He became a nationally famous entrepreneur who was later praised by Deng Xiaoping, thus signaling to the country that entrepreneurship, hiring employees, and making money was welcomed in the new era. And then many Chinese were allowed to become "gloriously" rich (reportedly suggested by Deng Xiaoping) by starting and growing world class companies; witness Jack Ma and Alibaba.

China invested heavily in new infrastructure, particularly transportation, provided trained workers at relatively low wage cost, supported new foreign businesses with low-cost land, subsidies, favorable tax treatment, and security. It also developed integrated supply chains which afforded foreign and Chinese firms efficiency and speed of production in getting lower-priced products to Americans.

I wish I could say that China expressed some gratitude over the next years. What we are seeing now is the hard realpolitik of Chinese policy. China profited enormously. The United States perhaps less so.

What was the harder edge of Chinese business and government practice? Theft of intellectual property by Chinese firms for decades has been near or at the top of U.S. companies' concerns. Often, foreign enterprises were required to take on a Chinese partner who then had access to the foreign company's business plans, trade secrets, and privileged information. The Chinese partner also usually did not share a second set of financial books kept only by the Chinese side. Those books would often show a different view of the joint venture's operations and finances. Once the foreign company shared its proprietary information with its partner, the foreigner not infrequently was slowly or quickly squeezed out of the market. And then there was the sustained cyber hacking, particularly by government entities, to steal technologies and information from companies around the world, which Chinese companies then used for China's own purposes, including, importantly, defense technologies.

It's worth remembering that reverse engineering is not always easy or even possible, a lesson I learned during my years in the Office of East-West Trade as we sought to control technology products to the USSR and the Warsaw Pact countries. Still, having access to a variety of research and design information can give a good head start, particularly with China's growing technical prowess.

Some people might point out that the United States has its own cyber capabilities. That's true. It's important to recognize that China's government activities benefit both its national security and commercial interests while the United States does not similarly spy on behalf of its companies. Chinese companies now are intertwined with and, under Xi Jinping, increasingly subject to direction from government entities.

You get the idea. Effective intellectual property protection was something China promised, repeatedly, starting with the negotiation of the U.S.-China trade agreement in 1979. It seldom seriously delivered on those promises. The plain fact was that China increasingly saw the United States and other countries as zero-sum competitors. If it would benefit China, anyone and any technology were fair game.

Nor can we overlook the corruption within the society, CCP, and government. By 2013, foreign businesses were doubly set back by Chinese entities' demands—at times subtle, at times heavy-handed—for special deals, payments, or outright bribes. American companies were constrained both by the Foreign Corrupt Practices Act and their own sense of fair play.

Chinese leaders and most of its citizens are aware of corruption and the vast challenges it presents. Leaders, including Xi Jinping, have made fighting the practice a priority. They also use the fight to attack and remove political competitors.

It was an increasingly difficult business environment—one reason for the downturn in Shanghai American School enrollment beginning in 2013.

In fairness, many American firms have done well in China, particularly in the earlier years of trade, as lower production costs made goods for the United States market competitive and reasonably priced for millions of Americans, helping keep inflation low. Companies such as Boeing, Apple, General Motors, Tesla, and Kellogg thrived, as did smaller ones like Radio Flyer and Patton Fans. But even large ones such as Google and Uber did not. As China gained leverage, confidence of Americans and others in doing business headed downhill. The political impact in the United States has become increasingly hostile, particularly as Chinese companies bought American factories, dismantled them, and hired American workers to reassemble them in China. Additionally, Americans have seen the Chinese capture of entire industries such as textiles and garments, the solar industry, pharmaceuticals, rare earths, and others.

Further undermining confidence in the relationship and souring it was China's increasingly heavy hand in suppressing human rights and civil society around the country. Dissidents were routinely rounded up. Lawyers were not allowed to practice. Groups like Tibetans, Uyghurs, and Christians were continually faced with arrest and imprisonment. Chinese security officials routinely spirited dissidents out of other countries and back to China. They also worked to co-opt Chinese overseas whose support they wanted.

Much later, in 2020, so many of us were deeply sad and even angry to see Beijing's move to impose on Hong Kong a brutal destruction—via an imposed new national security law—of its many freedoms and openness and to end its promised high degree of autonomy. While Beijing asserts it is only doing in Hong Kong what a sovereign China has the right to do to preserve national security, many of us say its actions reveal how skeptical we must be of future CCP promises and agreements. Taiwan is watching closely.

Even as we experienced the national fervor of creating the China Dream led by Xi Jinping, we repeatedly met well-educated and successful PRC citizens (many of whom had been educated abroad) who did not fit the mold of a hardline Marxist-Leninist as exemplified by Xi Jinping. Little by little we picked up vibes from those we knew of their deeper concern about China's increasingly clear directions. Would they have a place in this new and more rigid society being crafted by Xi Jinping? Would they diversify assets and family abroad and be ready to move on short notice? They could learn from Hong Kong people about pre-1997 contingency arrangements. Without doubt, these debates were quietly underway across the country. I stress *quietly* because undue attention from ubiquitous security officials could cost them their lives and fortunes.

Some SAS employees acknowledged being CCP members. They were almost always helpful in supporting the school. Without doubt, they reported to superiors on their observations. My deliberate comments would usually revolve around the purely educational nature of our school and about American support for developing constructive and peaceful relations with China. I would drop in ideas about how open societies can thrive as citizens have opportunities to be creative and make decisions which directly affect and motivate them. I would describe how in a more open society, citizens could band together to tackle local problems, call out corrupt and incompetent officials, and start businesses, which provided employment and a greater variety of products for the community.

One Chinese acquaintance was not averse to telling me stories of his anger at the government and society. The medical establishment treated his father miserably as he suffered from throat cancer. Doctors and nurses would stand at the door and demand off-the-books "fees" before they would "treat" him. He was likewise angry at his son's teachers and principal, who would constantly demand that parents pay extra fees. He said many people he knew chafed under similar experiences.

Such has been the experience of other societies without a strong rule of law, ethical practices, and opportunities to work for a living wage.

Was China Serious About Reform and Opening Up? Was the United States Taken in by China?

I could write for days about China and U.S.-China Relations. Let me leave the reader with these additional thoughts for now.

The Chinese people over the centuries have created admirable traditions, intellectual ideas, scientific advancement, literature, culture, and art. They have contributed to learning around the world. Having had the privilege for more than five decades of living, working, and traveling in China, in learning the language, and in meeting so many Chinese people, I can only feel positively for them that so many today are doing so much better. They eat better, live better, travel around the world, make their own marriage decisions without permission of the "work unit," and in so many other ways. But there remain hundreds of millions who still have not benefited significantly.

Beginning in 1979, the heavy hand of the CCP *did lift somewhat* to allow more space for individual choice, creation, and innovation that led to the above advances.

Given the history of Deng Xiaoping and others who deliberately loosened the CCP's grip, and seeing the explosion of production and creativity, it was reasonable for us to imagine the continued lifting of hundreds of millions of people out of poverty. We could also imagine China's building of a more constructive and stable relationship with the United States. I was heartened that America's leaders, beginning with Nixon, have been willing to work for a reasonable and fair relationship that benefited both the Chinese and American peoples.

I bridle at American political leaders who today criticize those who supported building bridges across the Pacific and allege that we (mistakenly) believed China **would become a more open democratic and civil society** because economic development would **inevitably** lead to it. See, for example, former Vice President Mike Pence's speech in October 2018 at the Hudson Institute:

> After the fall of the Soviet Union, we **assumed** that a free China was **inevitable** . . . . Heady with optimism, at the turn of the twenty-first century, America agreed to give Beijing open access to our economy in the **hope** that freedom in China would expand in all forms—not just economically, but politically, with a newfound respect for classical liberal principles, private property, religious freedom, and the entire family of human rights . . . but that **hope has gone unfulfilled.**

Pence is not the only one. Even *The New York Times,* in an August 7, 2022, editorial pursued a similar line, saying, **"The United States also needs to move past the old idea that economic engagement would gradually transform Chinese politics and society."** (Emphases added above.)

Such assertions are misleading and even historically inaccurate. These are just two examples. There are others who have fallen into the same historical revisionism, particularly for political purposes by those who believe China has a one-hundred-year plan to destroy the United States and "rule the world."

Many of us who worked to build those bridges and supported trade were not naive. We knew China and its hardcore system. We deeply disliked it. I experienced its brutality first-hand while assigned to the U.S. Liaison Office in Beijing, when we were told that a Chinese man, even though mentally ill, was executed almost immediately because he attacked and slightly injured an American visitor, actor William Holden.

We believed that the only way China might slowly evolve politically was through its own internal decisions and policies, not ones imposed from outside. Economic growth and openness including through integration with other countries might facilitate that process, or it might not.

Interestingly, see Jonathan Spence's history *To Change China*, about all the foreigners over hundreds of years who went to China "to change

China" but ultimately failed. See also John Hersey's novel *The Call* (based on true experiences), which explored the work of an idealistic American missionary in the first half of the twentieth century. He sought to change China through Christianity, science, and technology—but ultimately knew he had failed.

During our own repeated experiences in China, foreigners had the good fortune to observe up front developments on the ground and make judgments. We were often intrigued with the loosening of controls and leaders who possibly were prepared to see further opening to the world, further reliance on the private sector, and further development of a civil society. Hu Yaobang, Zhao Ziyang, Zhu Rongji, Wen Jiabao, and others, as well as Chinese businesspeople who built very large corporations, e.g., Jack Ma of Alibaba, showed the possibilities of a more open and diverse China. Don't forget that many Chinese well more than a century ago were debating the need for a new, modernized society and one based less on controlling power from the top, whether an emperor or a CCP chief. For example, many years ago, "Mr. Science" and "Mr. Democracy" of the *New Culture Movement* were proposed pillars of a newly revitalized China.

So, the United States and other countries faced **two broad choices**, but not entirely mutually exclusive, as our relationship with China evolved since 1979:

1) We could have severely restricted trade, exchanges, and further development of relations to ***deliberately hinder*** China's economic and military development. The bamboo curtain would be up. Doing so would have been on the ***assumption*** that China ***would be*** an existential security threat in the coming years. But this course held its own dangers and could well have become a self-fulfilling prophecy leading to a hard confrontation in future years. Would such a policy have led China to give up its plans to modernize and grow? Could we re-erect a bamboo curtain of a previous era? Would other countries have gone along? The simple answer to each question almost certainly would have been "No."

2) Alternatively, we could have decided that the building of bridges held ***some possibility, even if not certain,*** not only of economic advantage for both countries but also China's integration into the international system and working at least reasonably collaboratively and peacefully with other countries. This approach required the United States to keep a close eye on American national security. This approach **could** reinforce China's own emerging, more open society with increasing choice allowed to citizens, even if the CCP still held the bulk of political power.

I make no apology for having supported the latter option, working to build a wide variety of bridges benefitting both Chinese and Americans, while ensuring that national security concerns received continuing attention.

A Picture of a Changing China in 2023 under Xi Jinping

In the last decade, we have seen significant events that changed China's trajectory and helped to put it on an ever more slippery slope toward U.S.-China confrontation. Here's a review of some of them. (The U.S. perspective follows.)

—Xi Jinping has become a commanding top-down leader who has seemingly neutralized any serious opponents. He holds the reins of all the organs of governance: Communist Party, Government, and People's Liberation Army. Trusted supporters now are in key positions.

—He has promised to realize for the Chinese people a "China Dream" that has elements of creating economic growth and "common prosperity;" maintaining stability and security internally and then, externally, restoring China to its historic position of respect and influence on the world stage—and ultimately unifying the country including bringing Taiwan back to the motherland.

—He has changed or swept away many of the Deng Xiaoping-era policies put in place after Mao's death to provide more stability and growth, more collective leadership, avoidance of a personality cult, checks and balances on leadership power, and relaxation of economic policies that have borne fruit. He has no identified successor, risking serious political struggle when he passes from the scene. This will be a tense period within China and other countries who will not know what or who to prepare for.

—He portrays himself as confident, in charge, and never wrong. Still, how often can he paint himself into a corner, as he did with insisting on three years of strict COVID-19 quarantining, and then when he could no longer hold the line, turn around and walk right back out over the fresh paint?

—He has worked hard to refresh the role of the CCP and put it back into the center of China's politics, economics, and daily life. The CCP is the important framework and vehicle for governance and control of the country. Communist party members are being inserted into many levels of government, business, academia, etc. They are selected for

CCP loyalty, not necessarily for competence in the work of the group. What will this do for creativity and initiative? How many Chinese are truly motivated by ideology study sessions and thus only pay lip service?

—He has pumped up Marxist-Leninist Communist ideology and put his own stamp on the ideology for the twenty-first century. We may see a new phrase: "Marxism-Leninism-Xi Jinping Thought," replacing "Marxism-Leninism-Mao Zedong Thought." It would be a bold step, but one confirming his view of himself as supreme leader on a par with Mao Zedong and his high degree of political control.

—He is restricting the personal rights and activities many Chinese have become used to by imposing an ever more restrictive Great Firewall and internal technology controls for surveillance and censorship systems; restricting many forms of music, movies, arts, and entertainment (particularly if from outside China) in favor of more "traditional" Chinese culture; and showing more hostility towards women's rights, LGBTQ rights, and their public visibility. Mao Zedong praised women for "holding up half the sky." But today they still occupy few influential political positions and none at the top level, the Politburo. Xi is encouraging women to have more children; they are pushing back and not complying because of the cost of child-rearing, housing, and the impact on women's professional work opportunities. The hashtag #metoo is now well known in China, and more women are speaking out about harassment.

—He is trying new economic and other approaches to development, for example, a new "dual circulation" system to focus on 1) the internal economy, domestic consumption, and national self-sufficiency in food, energy, important minerals, etc.; and 2) on external trade and economic relations to take advantage of what they have to offer. He worries about China's vulnerability to U.S. or other international sanctions and supply chain disruptions hurting China.

—He is working to re-invigorate state enterprises at the expense of private businesses. Recently, his operatives have been breaking the power of billionaires and large companies, and literally breaking up the latter into smaller entities, making clear who holds the real power. Again, Alibaba and Jack Ma are good examples. He has similarly reached into financial firms' operations, including foreign ones, to show who is in control. One must wonder if creativity and initiative will suffer, as they did under the old state-controlled economy, which Deng Xiaoping and his successors no longer believed served the country and began to dismantle.

—On the international front, he is pushing harder to enhance China's positive role by emphasizing its peaceful nature and attempting to mediate international disputes, e.g., Iran and Saudi Arabia. At the same time, he has unleashed his "Wolf Warrior" diplomats who have pursued a far more strident and even pugnacious tone vis-à-vis the United States, Australia, Canada, Latvia, the EU, and others who push back on China's actions. (Wolf Warrior diplomacy reminds me of Secretary Pompeo's promise to help American diplomats recover their "swagger"!)

—He is working to nudge the United States to the side of the world stage to open more space for China. He has decided we are a declining country that cannot stand up to China's growing influence. Building China's relationships, particularly economic, with Europe, and weakening Europe's relationships with us are important goals. He is attempting to build support for China with the influential BRICS countries: Brazil, Russia, India, China, and South Africa. He has been actively cultivating other countries' leaders, including in our "backyard," particularly in South America and with small island nations in the Pacific, most recently the Solomon Islands. It has been a wake-up call for the United States; at least, having woken up, we are now out of bed and getting dressed, but we face a determined Chinese effort to build its influence.

—He has declared that he and Vladimir Putin of Russia have an unlimited partnership. He is obviously worried but is still unrepentant that Russia has not successfully concluded its invasion of Ukraine. His rhetoric and actions hypocritically violate United Nations and other international organization commitments and norms. China's open support of Russia's invasion, rhetorically or otherwise, is costing it seriously in some courts of international public opinion. Many nations who condemn Russia's invasion fear a China that is no longer trustworthy in its international commitments. For Xi Jinping, building a relationship with Russia is a natural one: two autocratic countries with leaders less concerned about the distractions of democratic opposition; Russia has technology and energy resources of interest to China and in return can be an export market for Chinese products; Russia has international connections that can help China spread its own influence. Still, I would bet that Xi Jinping may be increasingly uncomfortable with a Putin who is not only failing in Ukraine so far, but facing perhaps serious internal pressures.

—From a national security perspective, Xi Jinping is challenged by the knowledge that China is directly surrounded by fourteen sovereign countries, many of which have had military and other conflicts with China over the years. Lying not far from China are other important countries he must pay attention to, such as Japan, Korea, Philippines, Australia, the states of central Asia, Southeast Asia, and even NATO. He has supported a vast expansion of China's military and has daringly claimed the South China Sea for China and heavily militarized it. He promised to halt further expansion in the South China Sea, but he did not. That's a poor way to win the trust of others. He pushes hard on Japan on ownership of the Diaoyu/Senkaku islands in the East China Sea. It's one way of keeping Japan on edge. He is boldly working to push the U.S. military outside of the "first island chain," namely, from Japan through Taiwan, the Philippines, and Southeast Asia.

—He declares that re-uniting Taiwan with the motherland is a "core" Chinese interest. We should believe him. He worries Taiwan might declare its independence and that the United States is encouraging it in that direction. China's military exercises around Taiwan aim to send warnings, but they also serve to stiffen Taiwan's resolve not to re-unite with the PRC. Might some PRC honey rather than vinegar be more attractive? Might Deng Xiaoping's "one country/two systems" constitutional provision have held perhaps a sliver of promise if China had continued seriously on its previous path of "reform and opening up" including in the political sphere? Or if it had not decisively ended Hong Kong's high degree of autonomy on July 1, 2020, with a new, chilling national security law?

—He has not worked or even traveled extensively outside of China, unlike other Chinese leaders and officials over the years. We can conclude that he does not have a very deep understanding from personal experience of other peoples and countries. When he travels, he is encased in a security and organizational bubble that allows little in the way of interacting with more than a handful of foreigners, virtually all foreign leaders. His two visits to Iowa were highly choreographed. So, he understands much of the world through the lenses of his growing-up years during the Cultural Revolution, his father's revolutionary CCP credentials, and his Tsinghua University experience. Interestingly, he sent his daughter, Xi Mingze, to Harvard University for an undergraduate degree. I would love to know what she learned and in turn, how much he learns listening to her experiences. She seems to be seldom, if ever, in the public limelight these days.

—He is challenged every day with increasing numbers of fundamental problems and trends facing his large and often fractious empire. I've called attention to them often: the monumental difficulty of governing 1.4 billion people successfully, particularly given vast regional cultural, linguistic, and historical differences combined with a history of fractious politics and warfare; maintaining high quality economic growth; sustaining very high levels of debt; fighting corruption; investing in food security given declining arable land; adjusting to impactful negative demographic challenges; finding good jobs to deal with high rates of young adult and youth unemployment; investing the vast sums needed to provide key medical, retirement, and social security systems for a rapidly aging population; reversing serious environmental damage; preparing for climate change threats from rising seas, drought, and melting glaciers.

Aiming to be the twenty-first century's great unifier of the country, Xi Jinping is most assuredly aware of the opening and warning words of the fourteenth century classical historical novel *The Romance of the Three Kingdoms: "The empire, long divided, must unite; long united must divide. Thus, ever has it been."*

Xi Jinping and China need a reasonably stable world order to keep their country united and to realize their "China Dream." They cannot afford a war or an armed conflict with the United States. The greatest danger will be an accidental and unintended confrontation that grows out of control. Then, to use a political science term, "all hell breaks loose" and we are all in mortal danger.

China's Perspective on the United States and What Worries Xi Jinping and the Chinese Leadership the Most?

Here are some of the current perspectives, worries, and fears, on the part of China's leadership in 2023. The United States needs to pay attention and take them into account in its foreign policy decision-making.

1. Once again, the United States is trying to "contain" China militarily and economically, as it did the USSR and earlier the People's Republic of China. Its policies are designed to weaken China so the United States can remain the number one power in the world.

2. While the United States is a declining world power, it still has the potential to damage China's interests. Militarily, the United States is building up forces in East Asia and encouraging Japan, Korea, Philippines, Australia, and others to increase their military capabilities aimed at China. The United States keeps high tariffs and otherwise limits imports

from China. It is waging economic war by targeting computer chips and other high technology items to harm China's development.

3. The United States and other countries are backing away from their long-standing commitment to a one-China policy and in doing so are encouraging Taiwan to declare independence. This is a redline and one reason China is building up its military capabilities. It worries that the United States might not be taking China's warnings seriously.

4. The United States slanders China repeatedly by making up lies about China's actions in Xinjiang and Tibet, and how China treats its own citizens. It is hypocritical. Look at its centuries of genocide against Native Americans and the enslavement of its Black population.

5. Is the United States as weak as we think it is?

6. While the United States looks weak and divided, it may have the ability to pull itself together in unexpected ways to counter and hurt China. It has done so at other times throughout its history.

7. China has many strengths; it also has ongoing challenges.

8. Is there any way the United States and Chinese political systems can genuinely co-exist, or will the United States continue to attempt destruction of our governance system based on Marxism-Leninism-Xi Jinping Thought, thus causing chaos throughout China?

9. How is there any possible way we can trust them?

United States-China Relations Historically and in 2023 from a United States Perspective

I *choose* to believe that there can ultimately be room for the constructive building of bridges if leaders on both sides of the Pacific step back from a looming abyss and again genuinely pursue some common ends. While peace, love, and kumbaya are a long way off, war and conflict can and must be avoided.

The United States for a long time has had conflicted views of China and the Chinese people. Early on in our history, the Yankee clipper ships led the way in building bridges of trade. They brought ginseng and ice to China and returned with a wide variety of Chinese products. As we built our railroads and cities, Chinese laborers were critically important—often taking on the most dangerous tasks such as handling the explosives to blast tunnels through the Sierra Nevada. Much of that early history was never recorded or was lost because there was little interest by American academics or others to preserve it. Stanford University has done an admirable job of collecting such history, including stories handed down through generations of Chinese families.

America's thanks to the Chinese workers was the Chinese Exclusion Act of 1882 banning immigration of Chinese laborers for ten years. There were exceptions for certain classes of people, including students, thus opening the way for Dwight L. Moody, founder of Northfield Mount Hermon School, to bring Chinese students to his newly established schools: Northfield Seminary for Young Ladies in 1879 and Mount Hermon School for Boys in 1881. He also recruited Native American students and students from Africa, including Pixley Seme, whom I wrote about earlier. The first Chinese boy to graduate was Chan Loon Teung in 1892. This was during a time when "elite" schools would not accept Black, Asian, Native American, or Jewish students.

Sadly, over the following decades, American views of China and Chinese people alternated from negative to positive to negative repeatedly. What's important here is that throughout the Cold War of the 1950s and 1960s, our views were generally negative, but Nixon's opening to China in 1972 led to five decades of closer relations and continuing support from a majority of Americans.

President Obama's second term of 2013–2017 coincided with President Xi Jinping's first term. As those years rolled by it became clear that Xi Jinping was increasingly in charge as general secretary and president. He signaled he would be a strong, perhaps even aggressive, defender of China's interests. He and Obama explored the idea first floated in the United States in 2015 of a G2 of the two countries, perhaps paralleling the G7. The idea was not further pursued. More recently, Xi Jinping talked about the Pacific being big enough for both countries. In his June 2023 meeting with Secretary Blinken, Xi referred to Planet Earth being big enough for both countries. He seems to be suggesting there will be room for both China and the United States on the world stage.

The election of President Trump in 2016 brought four years of tense relations between the two countries. What's important for this narrative is that politically, the Trump administration was determined to be seen as "tough on China." Such toughness in a variety of forms was increasingly seen as politically popular among some groups. High tariffs were imposed by the United States and controls placed on certain exports. China would not be cowed. Rhetoric became more heated and antagonistic on both sides.

President Biden came to office in 2021 determined to remain "tough on China," partly for political reasons, partly to preserve negotiating leverage. He has kept tariffs in place, but also has signaled his desire for more communication and meetings across the Pacific. China has held back, keeping up its heated rhetoric, including reference to being prepared for war. The differences across the board are large and if not managed well, will cause even greater, negative impacts in both countries and beyond.

Issues of Concern from a United States Perspective on China

What do many Americans worry about when considering our relations with China?

1. China's policies seem to have become increasingly unfriendly, unfair, and at times simply unacceptable. Trade and economic relations have become more difficult because of China's increasing restrictions on United States and other foreign businesses. American Chambers of Commerce in China have documented this decline in business confidence.

2. Chinese military maneuvers in the Taiwan Strait and South China Sea endanger U.S. military and other nations' transit. Their actions are unprofessional and could lead to unintentional death and destruction, as has happened before. The two militaries must meet to agree on deconfliction measures. China has transgressed international law by militarizing the South China Sea and harassing shipping of other countries.

3. China continues to make military and other threats toward Taiwan. There is increasing public sentiment in the United States for more support of Taiwan and against China's continuing hot rhetoric and military maneuvers. There is some sentiment for us to support Taiwan's independence. The president has suggested we might defend Taiwan if China invaded. The White House tried to walk that back.

My view is that we need to retain our successful diplomatic approaches of the last half century, which kept the peace and allowed Taiwan to develop democratic traditions, a strong economy, and productive involvement around the world. Taiwan needs to upgrade its defensive military capabilities. There is no sentiment in the United States for armed conflict or war between China and the United States, whether over Taiwan or other issues.

4. Levels of trust on both sides are so low that they make progress difficult in almost all areas. Both sides often seem to address issues only in zero-sum terms. We must stop using the word *competition* to describe our policy because it suggests only two outcomes: winning or losing. Instead, we should seek *collaboration* and *working together* toward mutually beneficial outcomes in critical areas such as illicit drugs and fentanyl killing our citizens. Or research projects to protect our cities from rising seas. Collaborative success could help to re-build a more productive relationship.

5. How can one trust that agreements with China will be adhered to? China for years has promised effective protection of intellectual property rights. It has not delivered. China's saying applies here: Much thunder, little rain. China strongly stands for non-interference in internal affairs of other countries and non-aggression toward the sovereignty of other countries as laid out in its obligations in the United Nations charter. China has clearly violated those obligations by supporting Russia's invasion of Ukraine. In Hong Kong, China made clear guarantees of a high degree of autonomy for fifty years and even enshrined them in its constitution. The watchword was Hong Kong people ruling Hong Kong. There is little left of true Hong Kong autonomy and of the important rights which made Hong Kong a world class business center, such as the independent rule of law, freedom of the press and expression, etc.

6. China's actions in the area of human rights are contrary to what Americans value and what China has committed to in United Nations and other international agreements.

7. China brazenly uses cyber hacking to steal information and undermine our government, business community, and society. It harasses, blackmails, and co-opts Chinese and Chinese Americans in our country to obtain cooperation.

8. Our two countries have fundamentally different histories, values, and ways of doing things. How do we discuss these openly and begin to find some common ground to build on?

What Would Richard Do?

If I were president, what would I do right away, now, recognizing the road ahead will continue to be rocky with many unknowns to react to along the way?

We must jumpstart some actions to cool the hot rhetoric and open bet-
ter channels of dialogue leading to a working together on collaborative
projects of direct benefit to both countries.

First, I would bring together leading United States political leaders and impress on them the following: our long-term safety and security are on the line. Unless we work together as Americans, with our allies, and with China, there is a serious possibility of conflict or disastrous competition in which no one will "win." We must take some risks to jumpstart our journey toward a more peaceful and less dangerous world. I would expect American leaders to support my following announcement and continue to work with me. Showing that the American people are working together will send a strong signal to China that we are deeply serious in putting the relationship on a new track and that we are united in doing so.

Second, I would announce this to President Xi Jinping and the Chinese people:

1. The United States and China must immediately reduce and eliminate the hot and negative rhetoric about each other. We must lower the temperature to a much cooler level. *Words matter!* We will immediately begin that change and look to China to join us.

2. Our administration will *cease using the word "competition"* to de-scribe our approach to the relationship. Competition implies winners and losers. It implies an end point. But there is no standard by which to judge how we compete and what would constitute "winning." It's a dangerous path.

3. Instead of "competition," we will use the word *"collaboration,"* which connotes "working together" toward common, mutually bene-ficial, outcomes. This will not be zero-sum work. It will be "win-win." The results will help each side see examples of how working together can provide positive, concrete outcomes for both. Doing so can build trust in the other's words, actions, and intentions.

It will take time to rebuild trust. We must begin to do so *now!*

4. I have teams standing by to travel to Beijing to start dialogues on specific urgent issues facing us.

5. The first issue is how to eliminate the deadly drugs and chemicals, particularly fentanyl, which addict and kill so many in our country and elsewhere. It is not in either of our country's interest to allow this killing to go on. As the negotiating group gets underway, we will invite Mexico

and Canada to join us in our work of smashing these evil gangs and businesses.

I am fully cognizant of the Americans who in the 1800s brought to China opium, which addicted and killed so many of your ancestors. *On behalf of the American people, I deeply regret and apologize for the crimes of those opium traders.*

To end the scourge of addiction, I will call on our Congress to pass my proposed legislation to provide programs to help all those who need it. Reducing demand for addictive drugs will complement our determination to eliminate the supply.

Please welcome our delegation, which is standing by and ready to work for positive and early results.

6. The second team standing by is an economic and trade team to discuss the lifting of United States tariffs on Chinese exports and Chinese restrictions on our exports. While there are many aspects to this issue, let's not be stymied by their complexity. Let's make some early decisions to get the ball rolling and show we can work together in ways not "zero-sum" but "win-win." The longer-term work of addressing issues will continue.

7. I have a team ready to travel to work on concrete recommendations on how to protect our great cities from the coming rise in sea levels. Shanghai, Hong Kong, Tianjin, San Francisco, New York, Miami, and many others need to take urgent and effective action.

8. Other teams are ready to travel or to welcome your teams to the United States. I propose they address urgent challenges such as public health and pandemic preparation; new forms of clean and green energy; medical science to find new ways to research and cure disease; and food security and research on new seeds and crops for the coming climate changes.

There are other areas of critical importance. The above "confidence-building measures" can achieve practical and useful results for our citizens and those of the rest of the world. These are all complex issues, but let's together begin *now* to create an atmosphere of *collaboration* that will bring short term practical and positive results and then, in the long term, make progress on other important issues.

As we make progress, we will invite other countries and international organizations to become partners with us.

Please accept my invitation for the sake of both our countries' citizens and the world. We can mutually work to realize China's Dream, America's Dream, and a Dream for Planet Earth.

End of proposed message to President Xi Jinping.

Footnote to the reader: The above will not come to fruition in this way in real life. What it is designed to do is emphasize the urgent need to cool hot rhetoric, substitute *"collaboration"* for *"competition,"* and create an urgency in supporting serious work solving real world challenges, thus leading to increased trust *over time*.

A Plea to Seize the Moment to Create a More Peaceful World for All Humankind

We face difficult issues around the world, requiring wise and effective leaders in the United States, China, and other countries ready to take risks for the sake of humankind.

As Americans, we face deeply dangerous divisions that will not be easy to overcome, particularly when too many political leaders run for office for the wrong reasons, namely their own personal or "tribal" ag-grandizement. Can we Americans find the way to reform our own house domestically, healing divisions and antagonisms to present a more uni-fied face to the world? Can we show that truly democratic and open systems of political governance continue to be viable in the twenty-first century? Can we pledge to set a far higher bar for the use of our military internationally? And what does that mean vis-à-vis Taiwan and China?

Those are all critical questions. If we don't bridge our political and social divisions, we will be on a declining path to become a mediocre world power. The most powerful face we can present to the world is that of a country united in purpose.

Will we build a better shining city on a hill? Will we brightly project the light of a democratic and humane society, potentially attractive to all, but be careful about not ignoring other countries' points of view? The world in its wonderful diversity is far too complex to attempt one-size-fits-all approaches.

I pray for the wisdom we so urgently need in the United States. I am not naive about the world and its many "bad actors." We must remain on guard and strong against those who do not wish us well.

I pray that we let go of the post–World War II belief that we are and must always remain the most powerful country in the world on all issues and therefore the unquestioned decision maker. Collaboration and working together domestically and externally can bring success. Our economy has many strong points. We must nurture it into the twenty-first century to bring along *all* Americans and treat *all* with equity and decency. The good news is that we have many opportunities to improve and get better.

China, too, must be restrained in thinking that its history should accord it the role of preeminent global actor. Yes, it should play an influential role in the world. At the same time, it needs to recognize it must often collaborate with others and even compromise in creating its role in the twenty-first century.

I pray that China's leadership will ultimately also bring wisdom and realism to its critically important relationship with the United States, a relationship impacting the entire planet.

Will we all, in our lifetimes, seize the right moment to alter course? I would argue that our only home, Planet Earth, our Pale Blue Dot as Carl Sagan called it, urgently demands that new course.

Chapter Ten

Life Continues Back in the Good Old U.S.A!

W ithin days after our SAS commencement in 2016, we bid farewell to friends and the school and boarded our trusty 747 for our return home and a wonderful family reunion in San Francisco.

We went first to Stanford University's commencement for the awarding of Eric's PhD in aerospace engineering. He had worked hard for his MA degree and then his Doctorate. He continued to work at NASA on the safe flying of autonomous aerial vehicles in the national airspace and now for Joby Aviation on its eVTOL air taxi, all the while supporting his growing family.

We also celebrated the awarding in May of Jonathan's Master of Business Administration degree from the University of Colorado. (We were still in Shanghai.) He too had thrown heart and soul into learning while running a business and supporting his family.

We observed that Kim and Susan should be honored as co-awardees of those degrees thanks to their steadfast support.

We enjoyed having time together with all the grandkids, sons, and daughters-in-law for a few days before flying to Denver and the Mountain West. Thus began our latest adventure to experience a brand-new part of the world and our country.

And then it was on to Golden, Colorado.

A Golden Life in Colorado, June 2016

Kim and Jonathan generously let us stay with them in their downstairs quarters. We picked up where we left off earlier in the year looking for the right house in the right neighborhood. It turned out to be more time-consuming and tension-filled than we ever expected. Supply was tight and prices were rising. Virtually no single-story homes were available.

What to do?

Then in mid-August, bingo! We were with our grandkids at a playground when I saw a new open house listing pop up. It was nearby in a good neighborhood, Mesa View Estates. We all went over. The kids checked out every room and proclaimed they loved it. It was large enough for all our accumulated possessions of decades; 5,200 square feet; play and sleeping room for all grandkids; a very open floor plan with high sloped ceilings; large recreation room with a bedroom, den, and kitchen; and a lovely den with built-in bookcases for Claire on the main level. It sits on the slopes of Green Mountain, on a cul-de-sac, with no one across the street from it and with views of the Rocky Mountains and Denver.

Could this be a long-term home for us? We negotiated hard and finally agreed on a price of $927,500. A bit high? Yes, but we were willing to stretch ourselves and get settled as soon as possible. Watching insane home inflation over the last six years, they say our home could now sell for much more. Now the market is softening, but we have no plans to go anywhere.

I nicknamed the house "Mountain View Manor"—the name of my grandparents' home at 1829 Orchard Road in Berlin, Connecticut. We do have a mountain view here.

Seven Years in Golden . . . and Counting

We have kept ourselves busy these last years. Much of our life has revolved around our grandchildren in Golden—Jackson, Clara, and Gillian—and the activities of our two families. It has been great having extended family nearby, with each helping the other out. And it has been particularly gratifying to see how much each child has grown. We like to think we've participated positively in their growth, whether through reading together, traveling together, playing games, or attending so many of their sports activities—baseball, soccer, or volleyball.

For the most part, the area has been congenial. It has grown rapidly in recent years, so traffic is often congested and road repairs haven't kept up. I have almost come to believe tire sellers are happy to see slow road improvements; the more potholes we land in, the more tires they sell. The schools in Jefferson County are on the whole excellent. Kim has involved herself in Mitchell Elementary—a fine neighborhood school—and learned how to get good teacher support for them.

We have been pleased to see that the Denver area has developed a healthy cultural and artistic life. Favorites are the Denver Art Museum, the Museum of Nature and Science, the Denver Zoo and Botanic Gardens, and Red Rocks. World class. Music is high quality.

Travel around the state has been fun. A favorite destination is Crested Butte, which is beautiful in summer and winter. Right now, Jonathan and Kim think that might be a good place to settle one of these years. Much more congenial than urban life.

I developed connections with Denver University's Korbel School of International Studies, including the Center for China–U.S. Cooperation run by Professor Suisheng Zhao. I attended numerous sessions and helped to organize others until the COVID-19 pandemic hit in early 2020. The intellectual stimulation was good.

I put together a well-received panel of four former U.S. consuls general to Hong Kong in November 2019: Kurt Tong, Steve Young, Richard Boucher, and myself. More than one hundred and twenty-five attended. We discussed Hong Kong's future given ongoing protests by so many Hong Kong people against increased Beijing intrusions. Half a year later China launched its new national security law for Hong Kong, signaling the end of the city's high degree of autonomy.

Travel afforded a good change of scene. Briefly, in 2017, I flew to Hong Kong to spend a few days helping celebrate the fiftieth anniversary of HKIS. New construction of the lower primary school was impressive. The serious questions relating to the future relationship with the LCMS were still not resolved. The visit was also a chance to catch up with other old friends such as Gage McAfee, Joy Okazaki, Art Kobler, Tom Gorman and others and have breakfast at our old haunt at the residence with Kurt Tong, consul general. The Dulls, Jim Handrich, and the Holtbergs also came to Hong Kong for the occasion.

Shortly after my return, Claire and I flew to New England to visit family and attend my fifty-fifth NMH reunion. There were still many friends on campus we had gotten to know over the years. Members of the class of 1962 had a good time trading memories and acknowledging the passing of more of our classmates. In 2018 I flew to Washington, DC, for the gathering for the hundredth birthday of Ambassador Ed Cronk, my mentor at my first Foreign Service assignment in Canberra. I was also able to spend time with some of our best friends, Richard Boucher and Carolyn Brehm, Parker and Anna Borg, David Passage, Jim and Sheila Mack, Lange Schermerhorn, Dick and Jeanie Teare, Jane Lincoln, Nancy Schneider, Clyde and Ginny Taylor. There remain so many more to see.

Family—An Update

Sadly, Claire's sister—Doris—passed away in Golden in March 2019 after several years of difficult rehabilitation after an operation resulted in paralysis. We helped Bob organize a memorial gathering in Denver and then one for the family and friends in Rhode Island in September 2019.

The number of grandchildren continued to grow, with the arrival of Philip Chester Mueller on November 24, 2016, and Marilyn Jean Mueller on April 14, 2019. Since we returned from Shanghai in 2016, we loved seeing how the kids continued to grow and mature. FaceTime has been a godsend to keep in touch with our San Francisco family.

For some time, Kim has been interested in lactation services, helping new mothers. It has been a long period of interning, with our helping with the kids. Her plan has been to start her own company. With COVID-19 and the need for personal distancing, those plans were put on hold.

Both Kim and Susan have taken the lead in supporting the family since the beginning of COVID-19, as Jonathan and Eric worked remotely. Both deserve enormous credit and our gratitude for keeping the kids safe and continuing to provide learning experiences as in-person schooling was problematic. What they each decide to do once the young people are a bit older and the COVID-19 pandemic recedes, we will wait to see. Each has serious professional experiences and skills that surely will find good applications.

Eric and Jonathan's support of their families—and parents—through this most difficult period was crucial as well. All these challenges of the pandemic, of keeping jobs and careers going, have been met with determination and goodwill.

Jonathan and his business partners have continued to grow his new company, Ascend Behavioral Partners, to support children on the autism spectrum and their families. It's remarkable to us that the company has grown rapidly, even during the pandemic. They also started a parallel revenue cycle management company, Element, supporting Ascend and other clients. Jonathan's interests more and more revolve around the medical field, networking, creating podcasts, and exploring more productive use of technology. He seems to be increasingly successful as an "influencer," as the saying goes today.

Eric, after almost two decades at NASA, decided to accept a position at Uber in their Uber Elevate program, namely, creating "flying taxis." One of his areas of expertise was the safe flying of UAVs (unmanned aerial vehicles) in the national airspace. That includes flying piloted vehicles over cities and in and out of crowded airports. A while later, Uber sold and merged its Elevate program into Joby Aviation's advanced plans for "flying taxis." Joby already had designed and built two electric six-rotor eVTOL (vertical take-off and landing) aircraft that would fly four passengers and pilot a considerable distance. Eric enjoys the private, entrepreneurial sector as a change of perspective from his time at NASA.

Claire says her favorite activities are those that include the grandchildren. They give her energy and stimulation and in turn she dotes on them. She admits to being an easy mark when one of them hopes for a new toy stuffed animal or an ice cream treat. Having one or more of them stay overnight with us is our "treat." We also frequently observe that the seven grandchildren are our "happy pills!"

We have stuck closely to home since early 2020, dodging the COVID-19 virus. We tested positive in December 2020, quarantined, and came through with fewer symptoms than many had. Claire seems to have lost her sense of taste and each of us may well have "long haul" symptoms including lower energy levels. We were both vaccinated and received booster shots twice once the new vaccines, thankfully, became available.

It is gut-wrenching to us to watch well over one million Americans die, to say nothing of the millions who survived but suffered and still suffer tremendously, and to say nothing of the millions more around the world. The fact that Trump and his administration downplayed the potency of the virus and for a long time denied the efficacy of the vaccine was irresponsible.

COVID-19 and "Make America Great Again" Strike America

I need to include in this narrative some observations about the pandemic, which has severely affected us and the country since 2020.

It is now 2023, three years since I first began to record my thoughts.

The pandemic caused by the COVID-19 virus has been devastating in the United States and around the world.

I think every day about my maternal grandfather, Carl Heinrich Maack, who died in 1918 in New York City of the so-called Spanish Flu virus. He was otherwise in good health and a successful businessman. The lives of his loved ones changed in an instant—a wrenching devastation of sudden, indelible absence. My grandmother, Oma, Christine Maack, and her three young children grieved. She then set about creating a new life for each of them. She persevered, as I wrote earlier in this memoir, and lived to see new hope and joy in her three children and six grandchildren.

How many millions around the United States and the world have similarly suffered such loss?

After being first identified in China in late 2019, COVID-19 exploded in March 2020 and kept most of us at home for well over a year. We created a family "bubble" starting on March 15 (our anniversary) and only saw Jonathan and family in person. We ordered food and other necessities for home delivery by drivers hired by Amazon, Target, and Whole Foods. There was panic buying of so many products as people stockpiled necessities, from masks to hand sanitizers to toilet paper to food. Zoom and Facetime allowed much of the nation to stay in touch and to work from home. If China had rung the alarm bells much earlier, sharing the information about the virus, and if the Trump administration had been more honest and proactive, the outcomes could have been different. The first version of the virus was bad enough. It then evolved into the more virulent "Delta" version and then into new versions of "Omicron," which are highly transmissible.

In December 2020 Claire and I, along with Jon and his family, all tested positive for the virus. Jackson, Clara, and Gillian had few symptoms, as was true of most children. We adults, who were otherwise healthy, recovered with light symptoms. Those who had so-called "underlying medical conditions" or who were not able to quarantine themselves paid the highest price.

Eric and family in San Francisco practiced strict quarantining and have not had any serious infections. They have struggled with the closing of San Francisco public schools for two years and with contradictory and confusing school board decisions. Here in Colorado, Jefferson County schools were more forward-looking and were able to get schools up and running again, with conditions of masking, etc. by the fall of 2020.

One of the most distressing outcomes beyond the death and illness is the loss of learning suffered by so many American children. Their schools closed and at-home learning was often not effective. The children and our society will pay a heavy price over the coming years.

The best news is that drug companies, particularly Pfizer and Moderna, were able to produce a new type of vaccine called mRNA which was approved for adult use in late 2020. Claire and I received our first and second Pfizer vaccine shots in January and February 2021; likewise, Jon, Kim, Eric, and Susan. A third shot (a "booster") was made available in late 2021 and another in 2022.

By 2021 the virus appeared to be receding. Many people began to go back to in-person gatherings with a degree of safety if vaccinated and wearing a mask. And then came Omicron and its new versions. We were less at risk because we chose to be vaccinated and wear good masks, known as N95s. But for others, the daily death toll was in the thousands. It has slowly come down. Overwhelmingly, those who now get COVID-19 are not vaccinated and will not wear masks. They are being encouraged by some political leaders, particularly Republican, to believe this is a political issue and not a medical one. Unfathomable.

The hospitals were full and overflowing for a long time, with medical staff stressed beyond reason and many leaving the profession. Other people who need non-COVID-19 medical treatment are not getting it.

There will be libraries full of research in the coming years reviewing in more detail the medical science, as well as the policy choices we made that have so deeply affected our society, economics, and politics. We will press China to volunteer more information about the origin of the disease. Wet market? Bats? Virus escape from the Wuhan Virology Institute? Not sharing more information has added to the distrust between our two countries, as has Trump's calling it the "kung flu." It is clear we will have no choice but to invest far more heavily in our public health systems and infrastructure to deal with future crises. Scientists warn that more deadly viruses causing pandemics are inevitable.

And What About Our Fractured Politics and Political System?

Speaking of politics, I will add here just a short description of long-standing divisions within our society aggravated by Donald Trump, president of the United States from 2017 to 2021. We face serious crises that affect our future as a fully democratic, constitutional government and society.

There can't be much doubt Trump will be remembered by historians as the worst president in our history. He is ignorant of how leadership and governance work in the United States. He is willfully uninformed, selfish to the extreme, and determined only to increase his own grip on power even if he lies, cheats, and steals. Some have made a case that he is seriously mentally challenged. Like a bulldozer, he breaks laws and tosses aside long-valued traditions, ethical and otherwise. He cares not a whit about anything or anyone other than himself.

We are gob-smacked that many Republican leaders have joined with him in his campaign of lies, pursuit of personal power, and deadly undermining of democratic values and traditions.

Trump's handling of the pandemic was well off the mark and made it far worse. For a long time, he wrongly claimed that the virus was not harmful and would disappear quickly. He called on his political supporters not to wear masks or get vaccinated because they restricted one's freedom. It was all for reasons of political power. White House staff regularly interfered with how the Center for Disease Control and the Federal Drug Administration addressed the pandemic.

Joe Biden won the Democratic nomination for president in July 2020 and was elected in November 2020. Eight million more Americans voted for Biden than Trump, but too many Americans still are believers in Trumpism. Trump continues to promote the "Big Lie," namely, that he in fact won and Biden lost. The Republican Party has become the Party of Trump and very few otherwise sensible Republicans will stand up to him.

Trump and his people organized a violent insurrection on January 6, 2021, invading the Capitol while electoral votes were being counted. They attempted to force members to falsely support Trump's re-election even though there is zero evidence of 2020 election fraud. Courts around the country threw out fifty-some petitions that claimed fraud.

The storming of the Capitol and the violence and death it caused should be a full wake-up call to all Americans. Our future and democracy are at stake. It is clear Trump is an autocrat and has sold too many people on the idea that only he can "Make America Great Again." His Republican supporters—including violence-prone Oath Keepers, Proud Boys, extreme "nationalists," racists, anti-Semites, anti-immigrants, and many who mistakenly think they can use his support to attack those on the "left" they dislike—are gaining power. States are passing laws to restrict voting rights and to give Republican-appointed election officials the power to overturn valid election results. The 2022 Congressional elections turned out to be less damaging to Democrats than most predicted. They retained control of the Senate and lost the House by the slimmest of margins. The political struggles are wrenching.

A specific danger is that through gerrymandering and election practices to keep many citizens from voting, a perpetual minority of voters will keep the majority from having a voice. Of course, that bodes ill for our society and grows the seeds of conflict, both violent and unlawful. Should we amend the Constitution to abolish the electoral college and tally the popular votes to determine the winner? Both Al Gore and Hilary Clinton garnered more popular votes but lost in the electoral college. I tend to think we should; and we should find other ways to protect minority voters but not give them endless rights to block progress. There are many parts of the Constitution that need updating for the twenty-first century, but being able to do so civilly and with reason seems out of reach right now.

We have learned more recently about the White House conspiracy to keep Trump in office by disrupting the January 6 Congressional vote to accept the state electoral college results. The House bipartisan "January 6 Committee" has done an outstanding job of investigating and then presenting publicly a coherent and riveting narrative of how Trump and his supporters have deliberately undermined the Constitution and used violence to advance their "cause."

With sadness, I acknowledge there is more racism, anti-Black, anti-minority, anti-Semitic, and anti-immigrant sentiment throughout our country than many of us had appreciated. Those roots go deep into our history. We must understand their origins and educate children and adults to how such attitudes came about.

The even bigger task is for *all of us to look to the future and build a healthier and more fair society.* Even while understanding the past, we need to *come together* on how we can—*with goodwill, reason, and compromise*—ultimately build the future society Americans deserve.

Critical questions revolve around why we are so divided as a nation. Why are so many willing to undermine our democratic practices, gerrymander districts, and keep Black people and others from voting? Why are some people so unhappy with changes in American society that they feel they must fight to "take back" their country. Is it because they are reacting against many of the social and other far-reaching changes of the last half-century which, in fact, so many Americans support? How many have been led to believe that a diverse society will lead to the marginalization of white people and western civilization? How many are interested first and foremost in power of all kinds and believe political office can be a path to gain it? Why will they not strive to put people first and treat all with dignity and equity?

There is also periodic reference to a coming "civil war." That seems impossible to me. Still, any resort to violence will only lead to more violence. Nor will the undermining of the work of our governments—federal, state, or local—solve our problems; it will only weaken the power of our leaders and government to help citizens in need and counter illegal activity. Bottom line, don't we need well-qualified people to staff functions of government we decide we want, such as honest and competent politicians, public health officials, diplomats, scientists, educators, military personnel, and so many more?

Ronald Reagan planted so many seeds of skepticism and contempt for government. His joke? "Hi, I'm from the government. I'm here to help." (Cue: Laughter!) Those seeds have sprouted and grown to become poisonous weeds, threatening our country.

In the meantime, there are periodic violent attacks against schools, law enforcement officers, and the public. We often find ourselves angry at the ease with which almost anyone can obtain a weapon and open fire. The scourge of gun violence is frightening. Mindless growth in access to guns, including the AR-15 assault rifle, has been devastating. The Supreme Court's rulings claiming the second amendment to the Constitution allows broad access to all types of weapons is against all common sense and twists the understanding of the amendment's meaning, which is specifically linked to having a "well-regulated" militia. Do we as citizens not have a right to safety?

The overturning in June 2022 of *Roe v. Wade* concerning women's health care and reproductive rights falls in the same category. Society deserves long-term stability and not one-sided actions of a Court representing the views of only a minority of Americans. One of the dangers given the reasoning of the Court is that there is now a possible basis to undo other settled cases such as gay marriage, LGBTQ rights, contraception, and other issues Americans broadly support. Fast forward to June 2023, the Supreme Court went even farther in taking down affirmative action, presidential authority to alter the student loan program, and upholding a religious/free speech right to discriminate against a gay person. Previously, it limited the authority of the EPA and other governmental bodies to regulate a variety of emissions.

Fortunately there are many good people working for solutions on these contemporary issues needing urgent attention. I believe the smarts and talents of our children and grandchildren will make a difference in dealing with huge challenges such as the already-arriving climate changes; dangers of cyber hacking and cyber bullying; technology allowing for the rapid spread of false information that undermines societies; providing medical care and food security for Americans and the world; driving corrupting money out of politics; imposing ethical guidelines on manipulating human genes and creating biological changes; controlling artificial intelligence and machine learning (witness ChatGPT, GPT-4, Bing) so they do not further upend our society and how we interact with each other; and, supremely important, how do we construct a public education system drawing in our "best and brightest" and providing the humane and solid education our young people need to solve all these challenges.

Improving Our Political Discourse

I will note that many people on varying sides of our political divides strike me as going too far in their rhetoric and tactics. Too many have not learned how to talk with people of differing viewpoints, often using accusatory and even in-your-face tactics rather than establishing ways of talking and listening to each other that could lead to better understanding and less divisiveness. Too often, people drive opponents into a corner and "whup 'em upside the head." Of course, everyone then digs in to defend themself rather than engage in healthy discussion. We need to demand the dropping of all phrases or descriptors that tend to demean or stereotype others. That includes so many of the words and phrases thrown around every day during this fraught election season.

We should insist leaders talk about their policies and what they will do when in office. We should drop all words which unhelpfully categorize and therefore lead to division, such as: liberal, conservative, neoliberal, socialist, far right, far left, progressive, nationalist, and many more? Those labels all reinforce "identity" as a primary means of categorizing others. People then feel they must link arms with their designated "tribe" to seek political power without having specifically said what policies or laws they would pursue if elected. Americans need to call them out for avoiding the hard discussions and decisions we desperately require.

For me, I remain a determined "middle-of-the roader" (there's another label!), firmly in the center of the political spectrum. One can, of course, define middle of the road differently depending on the issue. Still, I believe that's where so many Americans are, in their heart of hearts, not believing in radical or extreme change or action and ultimately putting people first. Not long ago I wrote an eight-page political manifesto for a new political party explaining my priorities: "The New American Party for All." It includes many of the ideas you've read in this book. Maybe I'll publish it and run for office!

Most importantly, I side with those who demand that our leaders put people at the center of public discourse and create policies that "Serve the People!" Chairman Mao would approve.

Words matter!

Now, in 2023, our politics continue at a white-hot pace. Trump has declared he is running for president again, even though he has already been indicted in various lawsuits and convicted in a defamation case. More indictments undoubtedly are on their way over highly classified documents and the January 6 conspiracy and insurrection at the Capitol. His political base seems to be holding together so far. His own rhetoric is increasingly harsh and incoherent. Interestingly, other Republicans have entered the race. Their decisions to do so indicate they believe Trump may be vulnerable and ultimately not electable. Ron DeSantis of Florida is relying on fighting the culture wars, using criticism of "woke" and "critical race theory" and trans-gender issues as cudgels. He calls for the banning of books and for parents to storm their school boards and vote-in "conservatives." He is not interested in genuine improvement in public education, something that should be among the top issues for *all* of us.

President Joe Biden has also declared his candidacy for re-election in 2024. The betting odds are that he can beat Trump. I believe he has done a good job as president in the face of all our enormous challenges. For two years he had a Democratic House and Senate that passed landmark legislation on infrastructure, green energy, climate change, pandemic aid, and public health. He has re-invigorated our alliances and partnerships around the world to both support Ukraine in opposing Russia's invasion and to deal with a changing global landscape. He could have chosen to step down at the age of eighty after one term and taken a victory lap. There are other up-and-coming Democrats who would have opened up the electoral process and potentially energized citizens.

Despite all the negative and potentially dangerous actions by Trump and others, I choose to believe our democracy will be tough enough ultimately to resist, longer-term.

An Upbeat Coda to Close This Memoir

We observe that many Americans remain hopeful about the future and remain generous toward others even while concerned about the challenges of these unique times. Crises around our country and the world do draw American attention and help. While television and the digital media often unhelpfully focus us every hour on one crisis after another, helping to heighten tensions in society, every day we encounter friendly people prepared to step up to help others.

Despite all the political turbulence, economic and pandemic disruption, inflation, and continued war in Ukraine threatening world stability, the Muellers and friends have been blessed in so many ways.

We thank God we have nice homes, in reasonably safe neighborhoods, access to decent medical care, and incomes to provide good food and other necessities. We also have dollars to help others by donating to food banks, community organizations, schools we believe in, as well as to political candidates we favor.

I will say unabashedly that we have all worked hard to get to this time in 2023. It has not always been easy. Others have helped us throughout our lives, and in turn we will continue to pay it forward.

We are determined to provide the very best education and growing up experiences possible for our grandchildren. They need to be smart and prepared for the coming changes caused by climate and societal challenges. We have confidence that Kim and Jonathan and Susan and Eric will continue to make a priority of working with them toward these goals.

We were able to bring off a hugely fun and successful Mueller family reunion here in Colorado for a week in July 2022. (Two previous attempts failed because of COVID-19.) We spent two nights at the Great Wolf Lodge, which has a vast indoor waterpark. That was fun. The seven grandchildren played and interacted wonderfully. Although the two families had not been together for two and a half years, the kids were not strangers to each other. The time together was also a chance for the adults to catch up and bond in all kinds of good ways.

We remain hopeful about the future and determined to actively do whatever we can to overcome current crises and make our country and the world better and safer for all.

As the old saying goes: "That's our story and we're sticking to it!"

Richard W. Mueller
Claire Mueller—Copilot

Appendix

Richard Walter Mueller Life Chronology Summary

1944 – December 1 — Born at Walter Reed Hospital, Washington, DC, compliments of the U.S. Army. Father is Walter Julius Mueller who served in World War II. Mother is Eleanor Maack Mueller. First home on South Capitol Street, Washington, DC.

1948 – February 2 — Sister Linda Christine Mueller was born in Columbia Hospital for Women in Washington, DC.

1950 – February — Dad had joined the Foreign Service after the war, and we were off to his assignment to Germany.

1950–1952 — Dad worked at HICOG (High Commission for Germany) in Frankfurt. We lived in Bad Homburg nearby. Attended a Department of Defense school, first and second grades.

1952 – Summer — Home leave in Silver Bay, Minnesota. YMCA on Lake George in New York remains one of my fond memories, a Maack family favorite. We visited several times.

1952–1954 — Bonn/Bad Godesberg. Bonn became the site of the American embassy. We lived in Plittersdorf, an American enclave of apartment buildings and shops along the Rhine River. Attended third and fourth grades.

1954 – Summer — Home leave in the United States.

1954–1956 — Berlin, Germany. Dad was director of the Berlin Document Center (BDC), a former Nazi storehouse of their records, personnel files, etc. His background in Germany and fluency in German were a perfect fit. Background checks on Nazi connections were performed on all German nominees for German government positions. Attended fifth and sixth grades at the Department of Defense school.

1956–1960 — Washington, DC, 6012 Welborn Drive, Woodacres, Bethesda, Maryland. Attended Longfellow School in Bethesda for seventh through tenth grades. My mother thought I would be challenged at an independent school.

1960–1962 — Attended Northfield Mount Hermon School in Massachusetts (at the time Mount Hermon School) for eleventh and twelfth grades.

1962–1966 — Attended the College of William and Mary in Williamsburg, Virginia. Graduated with a Bachelor of Arts major in economics and double minor in international relations and in German language and literature.

1966 – Spring — To my surprise, I passed the written exam for the Foreign Service in December 1965 and then oral exam in spring 1966.

1966 – August — Joined the U.S. Foreign Service, Department of State as a twenty-one-year-old Foreign Service officer (FSO), bottom rung of the bottom class, FSO-8. Paid $6238 per year (equivalent to about $50,000 today), but position looked pretty good to a new college graduate. Deferred plans to attend the University of Pennsylvania or the University of Virginia graduate program in international affairs (accepted at both schools). Long climb of the career ladder ahead. Many unexpected, unplanned, surprising, and wonderful turns on the road of life.

1966 – Fall — Foreign Service Institute (FSI). My father swore in my class of sixty new officers. He was still an active duty FSO serving as dean of the Center for Area and Country Studies at the FSI. Six weeks of A-100 Orientation Class for new FSOs. German language training to pass language proficiency requirement.

1967 – January — Off to my first assignment, U.S. Embassy Canberra, Australia. Loved stopping over in Hawaii, Tahiti (Bora Bora), and New Zealand.

Served in administrative, economic, and political sections of the embassy. Served as a control officer for visit of President Lyndon Johnson who visited for funeral of Australian Prime Minister Harold Holt who presumably drowned while swimming off Australia's coast. Spent a winter at the U.S. Consulate General Melbourne assisting with economic and commercial affairs. Two-and-a-half-week trip by car through outback.

1968 – June — Off to Washington for one year of full-time Vietnamese language and culture training en route to U.S. Embassy Saigon, Vietnam. Passed course.

1969 – July — Off to U.S. Embassy Saigon, political section. Political officer with countrywide focus on analysis and reporting on political activities of students and labor unions. Traveled regularly throughout the country and periodically in Southeast Asia (Thailand, Laos, Burma, Indonesia, Malaysia. Bali became favorite destination and culture).

1971 – June — Off to Washington to the Executive Secretariat, Operations Center (S/S-O). 24/7 operations supporting the secretary of state and Department of State, tracking worldwide events, and connecting the secretary to the world.

1972 – July — Off to work in next door office of Executive Secretariat, Office of the Secretary of State (S/S-S). Coordinating work of the State Department and staffing the secretary, including international travel with secretary.

1972 – October — Sister Linda Mueller and Bill Boudra married, Washington, DC.

1973 – January — Off to Vietnam for temporary duty in Kon Tum Province in the Central Highlands of Vietnam after peace agreement comes to Vietnam. Several FSOs with experience in Vietnam were chosen to return for six months to observe and report on implementation of the Paris Peace Accords and the ceasefire.

Chosen by a select committee to receive State Department's Director General's Award for Reporting, given to one FSO each year. Awarded for depth and quality of analysis and reporting on implementation of the Paris Peace Accords in Vietnam. Central Vietnam was in the forefront during 1973 for continued fighting and then serious attempts at creating peace initiatives (e.g., cessation of firing, creating lines of demarcation, exchange of prisoners, exchange of communications). Richard was fortunate to make connections quickly all around and report developments to the embassy and Department of State in Washington where there was intense interest. He had conversations with North Vietnamese cadres across a small creek to the west of the city. Kon Tum for a time appeared to be on track to show how local initiatives might keep the ceasefire and lead to a more peaceful situation. Sadly, as 1973 went on, Saigon, in particular, became nervous about possible loss of control and pulled back on initiatives and resumed fighting.

1973 – August — Off to Washington for S/S-S. Arrived the day Henry Kissinger announced for secretary of state. Served as head of small group to work with Kissinger and staff and facilitate the transition.

1973 – November — Returned from first around-the-world trip with Kissinger, just after Thanksgiving and met newest member of the secretary's office, Claire McCormick!

1974 – February — Traveled with Kissinger to Mexico, and five weeks in Middle East for Israeli-Syrian disengagement negotiations, April–May. Claire and Richard worked and traveled together for the Middle East trip.

1974 – June — Finished up in secretary's office. Six weeks experiencing America, driving across country and back. Claire met Richard in Denver; drove back together to Washington.

1974 – August — Off to Chinese language and culture training, FSI, Washington for first of two years of full-time study (Mandarin, of course).

1975 – March 15 — Wedding in our home, 2366 Great Falls Street, Falls Church, Virginia! Claire McCormick!

1975 – July — Off to Taichung, Taiwan for second year of Chinese language training.

1976 – June — Off to Beijing, China to serve as economic/commercial officer at the U.S, liaison office (USLO), a "pseudo" embassy of only about thirty-five staff. Formal diplomatic relations came only on January 1, 1979. Extensive travel in China.

1976 – August 10 — Jonathan Richard Mueller was born on U.S. Navy Base Yokosuka, Japan. Returned to Beijing in time for death of Mao Zedong on September 9 and beginning of reform and opening up promoted by Deng Xiaoping.

1978 – January — Six months refresher course in economics at FSI.

1978 – April 14 — Eric Richard Mueller was born at Sibley Hospital, Maryland.

1978 – July — Off to work as deputy director, Office of East–West Trade, Bureau of Economic and Business Affairs, Department of State. Focus on east–west trade and Jackson-Vanik amendment; negotiation of U.S.-China trade agreement; national security export controls. Travel to China, Japan, Paris, Budapest, Bucharest.

1981 – July — Off to work as deputy director for economic affairs, Office of Chinese Affairs, Bureau of East Asian Affairs, Department of State. U.S.-China relations took off with China's December 1978 Third Plenum decision on opening and reform, and in wake of establishment of U.S.-China diplomatic relations on January 1, 1979. Travel to China.

1983 – July — Off to U.S. Consulate General, Hong Kong as director, economic section for China and Hong Kong. Explosion of interest in doing business with China. Travel in China and Southeast Asia. Hong Kong remained premier China-watching post.

1986 – June — Off to Washington via Trans-Siberian train from Beijing through Mongolia to Moscow and Leningrad (six days), to work as director of S/S-S, Department of State, and as deputy executive secretary, for

George Shultz, secretary of state and after January 1989 for Secretary James Baker. Intensive responsibilities for making, coordinating, and executing U.S. national security policy.

1989 – July — Off to work down the hall as deputy assistant secretary, Bureau of Legislative Affairs, Department of State, for Secretary of State James Baker. Was the only career deputy assistant secretary in the bureau with focus on connecting political appointees to the Department and responsibility for intelligence issues and State Department appropriations/authorization issues. Much travel to Capitol Hill. Eye-opening experience in working with Congress.

Led negotiations with Capitol Hill for passage of Hong Kong Policy Act to allow the U.S. to maintain current relationships with Hong Kong after 1997 as part of China's "one country, two systems" constitutional structure giving Hong Kong a high degree of autonomy for fifty years. Otherwise, we would have had to treat Hong Kong the same as PRC. Passed 1992 unanimously in Senate and House and signed by president.

1992 – July — Off to FSI for a year of refresher Chinese language training (Mandarin, some Cantonese).

1993 – June–1996 – July — Off to Hong Kong to serve as U.S. consul general to Hong Kong. The position was chief of mission, ranking with ambassador and a four-star military officer. Consul general Hong Kong and consul general Jerusalem were the only consul generals who reported directly to the Department of State, not to an American ambassador (Beijing in my case). Hence the rank of ambassador. Consulate general with two hundred people, fifteen U.S. government agencies. Legally responsible for activities of all U.S. government agencies.

Focus was on preparations for 1997 handover to China. Hong Kong Policy Act of 1992 that I helped negotiate and pass in 1992 provides foundation and guidance on future U.S. relations with Hong Kong, designed to help Hong Kong maintain its high degree of autonomy and keep a stable U.S. relationship with China.

Met Bill Rhodes, Citibank, and NMH Chair, board of trustees. Later he convinced me to retire early after thirty-two-year career as FSO and take over as head of school of Northfield Mount Hermon.

1994 – June — Jonathan graduates from Langley High School, Great Falls, Virginia, and enrolls at the University of Virginia. Graduates in 1998.

1995 – December — I experience the high of a lifetime: being catapulted off aircraft carrier USS *Nimitz* in an F-14 Tomcat in the South China Sea. One hour of flight showing capability of F-14 including max 6.5 g-forces.

1996 – June — Eric graduates from HKIS. Enrolls Princeton University and graduates in 2000.

1996 – July — Off to work in Hong Kong as director, Asia Society Hong Kong Center. Nonprofit educational organization to build bridges between the United States and Asia.

1997 – July 1 — Hong Kong officially returns to Chinese sovereignty under China's constitutional structure of "one country, two systems" with a promised fifty years of "high degree of autonomy" vis-à-vis China. Attended official and unofficial United Kingdom and Hong Kong/PRC events.

Night of handover: Chinese chef on Convention Center balcony says to me and Nick Platt, "Old boss go. New boss come. Don't like new boss, I quit!"

What a pithy summation of how so many Hongkongers really felt.

1997 – Fall — Bill Rhodes visits. As chair of the board of trustees, asks me to be a candidate for NMH head of school, my alma mater, in Northfield, Massachusetts.

My response: "I'm a diplomat, not an educator."

Bill: "Don't worry, diplomacy will go a long way in the world of education." Was he ever right!

1997 – November — In Bali, Indonesia—serious discussion with Claire regarding NMH although it meant retiring at fifty-four, at least five-to-six years earlier than I would otherwise have had to retire. We decided to put my hat in the ring.

1998 – February — Visit NMH as candidate. Twenty-five meetings in two-and-a-half days tested my stamina. In New York City, board of trustees offers the position of head of school.

Claire and Richard: "Yes! We accept!"

1998 – July — Off to become NMH head of school. Much to say about our experiences over seven years and about the world of education. Diplomacy in fact went a long way in leading large school of 1,155 students, four hundred employees, and for educational reasons leading strategic planning, decision making, and preparations to move to one campus and downsize the school to 650 students. Needed to make school smaller for educational reasons of close-knit community with intense academic focus and student support. Controversial for some, crucial for most. Needed to call out the elephant in the room. Many say we "saved the school." Believe that's almost certainly right; too large and underfunded to survive all of succeeding financial/economic crises. It seems to thrive today.

2004 – July — Assumed role of president of NMH.

2004 – October — Mother passes away. Eleanor Maack Mueller. Buried in Woodlawn Cemetery, New York.

2005 – February — Visit HKIS as candidate for head of school. Previous service as trustee of HKIS and chair of the board, combined with State Department diplomatic and NMH educational experience carried the day.

Chair of the board of HKIS calls before Richard and Claire depart Hong Kong and offers position of head of school.

Richard and Claire: "Yes! We accept!"

2005 – July — Off again to Hong Kong to be head of school, HKIS. Jon and Eric both had attended HKIS. 1983–1986. Eric graduated in 1996.

2006 – October — Father passes away. Walter Julius Mueller. Ashes scattered Lake Tahoe and James River, Virginia.

2009 – October — Jonathan and Kimberly Soma were married, Reno, Nevada.

2010 – July — Off to Reno, Nevada to join Jonathan and Kim and to be there for birth of our first grandchild.

2010 – August 30 — Jackson Walter Mueller was born in Reno, Nevada to Jonathan and Kimberly Mueller.

2010 – October — Eric and Susan Philips were married, Grandview Park, San Francisco.

2012 – September 27 — Katherine Elizabeth Mueller born to Eric and Susan Mueller in San Francisco, California.

2012 – September — Jon and Kim move to Golden, Colorado.

2012 — Call from executive recruiter: "Would you consider one-year interim head of school of SAS?"

Claire and I: "Yes! We accept!"

2013 – March — Board of trustees of SAS offers one-year appointment as head of school.

Claire and I: "Yes! We accept!"

2013 – April 15 — Clara Elizabeth Mueller born to Jon and Kim in Boulder, Colorado.

2013 – July — Off to Shanghai, China, to be SAS head of school for one year.

2013 – Fall — Board: "Would you stay for three-year contract?"

Claire and I: "Yes! We accept!"

2015 – May 10 — Allison Edith Mueller born to Eric and Susan in San Francisco.

2015 – May 26 — Gillian Alma Lorraine Mueller born to Jon and Kim in Boulder, CO.

2016 – Spring — Jonathan awarded a Master of Business Administration from University of Colorado, Denver.

2016 – June — Off to Golden, Colorado to buy a house and be close to Jonathan, Kim, Jackson, Clara, and Gillian. Also closer to San Francisco and our other grandchildren.

2016 – June — First stop was San Francisco for awarding of Eric's PhD in aerospace engineering from Stanford University. Reunion with Eric's and Jon's families.

2016 – July — Accepted invitation to rejoin board of trustees of CAIS.

2016 – September — Close on our house, 15549 W. Maple Drive, Golden, Colorado. Our possessions of a lifetime more than fill up our five thousand square foot house.

2016 – November 24 — Philip Chester Mueller born to Eric and Susan in San Francisco.

2019 – April 14 — Marilyn Jean Mueller born to Eric and Susan in San Francisco, on the same birthday as her father, April 14.

2020 – March — Pandemic caused by the novel coronavirus (COVID-19) first identified in Wuhan, China essentially closes down the country. Millions die or are hospitalized. We hunker down in Golden, Colorado.

Guess we will be in Colorado for a while!

2020 – March 15 — Richard begins to write this memoir. We celebrate our Ides of March wedding anniversary—forty-five years!

2023 – July — Claire and Richard and family all have survived the COVID-19 pandemic, thanks to vaccines, N95 masks, and staying away from crowds and other gatherings. Our health is reasonably good at our grand, experienced age of seventy-eight. On the surface our country is back to looking normal, although many people are suffering from COVID-19 "long hauler" syndrome. Many workers are still working from home because it works well with family needs. And it avoids long commutes! The huge coming labor debate is whether to allow employees as much latitude as they would like to work from home

Stay tuned for a possible Volume Two once I re-energize from the effort that went into this Volume One!

Cited Works

Barth, Roland. *Improving Schools from Within: Teachers, Parents, and Principals Can Make the Difference*. San Francisco, CA: Jossey-Bass 1991.

Kissinger, Henry. *Years of Upheaval*. New York, NY: Simon & Schuster, 1982.

Made in the USA
Monee, IL
28 September 2023

43521281R00206